Broken Spirits ~ Lost Souls

More Endorsements...

"I have associated with educational psychologists for years and they have rarely known the very children they profess to know. Jane Ryan could teach circles around them, because she knows children, especially those with Reactive Attachment Disorder. As a chronicler of parents with unattached children, she has a wealth of information and the kind of book that every parent of a troubled child, every public school counselor and university teacher of children's psychology should possess. Without books such as Jane Ryan's, those who treat children will continue to provide verbal maps which are wildly divergent from the territories they think they are describing. I urge you—implore you—to give her book a good read." Donovan Welch, Ph.D., Professor, University of Nebraska at Kearney.

"Jane Ryan gives us hope for children with RAD and their families. As an adoptive mother of a child with severe attachment problems I have not always felt hopeful. There are many who might believe this book is written for families of children with RAD and professionals working with those children and families. That is not true. As Jane shows us, all of society is affected by individuals with attachment difficulties and the more we all know about it the better off we all will be." Wanda Freeman, CMSW, LMHP

"Open this book and one is immediately grabbed by behaviors we see exhibited in children all around us today. The feelings of love intertwined with utter helplessness and frustration these parents feel is real. It appalls me to think how many are fighting daily battles with attachment-disordered children and have no idea what they are dealing with or that they are NOT alone. What a lifeline this book is for those!" Carolyn Nelson, RN, BSN, psychiatric nurse.

"Jane tells her story and the stories of other families with children with RAD in her gentle, forthright manner. My eyes were opened and my heart saddened as I read *Broken Spirits ~ Lost Souls*. Such tragedies are these children with their fears of love and loss. The families that love them also experience tragedies as well as the society they live in. I urge anyone who is puzzled or worried about the violence of young people in our school systems to read *Broken Spirits ~ Lost Souls*. Jane's words will enlighten you." Merlene Paul, RN

"Jane Ryan's book shines a bright light into the murky and tragically misunderstood world of the Reactive Attachment Disorder. It is a sad, frightening and lonely place inhabited by an increasingly large proportion of families in the industrialized societies. Through Jane's eyes I have seen the terror and isolation, the social stigma experienced by families of individuals suffering from RAD. Her work has greatly heightened my awareness of the multiple and difficult ethical, social, psychological, and treatment issues presented by this disorder.

"In this highly readable, indeed enthralling, book Jane Ryan summarizes her own great experience with RAD and its victims. She makes understanding of and empathy with the sufferers easy. Her recommendations for treatment, and for societal management of this disorder, though stern by some standards, deserve to be taken very seriously by all concerned social and governmental bodies. She knows her subject well.

"Jane's book is a must for parents, as well as mental health, social service, and counseling professionals interested in family and child dysfunction. I believe it will be seen in future years as a landmark in the area of family relationship work, and as a guide to humane legislation in this area." Fred W. Llewellyn, M.D., Diplomate of the American Board of Psychiatry and Neurology, Inc., Certified by the American Society of Addiction Medicine, Inc.

Also by the Author

Motherhood at the Crossroads:

Meeting the Challenge of a Changing Role

Broken Spirits ~ Lost Souls

Loving Children with Attachment and Bonding Difficulties

Jane E. Ryan

Dear Barb,
Thank you
for your support
Jane Ryan
Oct 18, 2010

iUniverse Star
New York Lincoln Shanghai

Broken Spirits ~ Lost Souls
Loving Children with Attachment and Bonding Difficulties

iUniverse Star
an iUniverse, Inc. imprint

For information address:
iUniverse, Inc.
2021 Pine Lake Road, Suite 100
Lincoln, NE 68512
www.iuniverse.com

Do not diagnose this problem yourself. See specially trained professionals for an accurate diagnosis and treatment.

ISBN: 0-595-29717-X

Printed in the United States of America

To ALL my Children who are still the True Loves of my life.
And to the amazing families who willingly opened themselves to others for the sake of the children.

Acknowledgements

My special thanks to the following for their significant contribution to this work: Jim and Pam Rubovits, my Rhode Island College research advisors who said, "A little more research and you've got a book." In the early days Ann Taylor, M.D., Nancy Thompson, Foster Cline, M.D., Connell Watkins and Pat DeFeyter believed me, identified the problem, and then threw me a life preserver when no one else would or could.

My gratitude goes to Gail Trenberth who contacted the American and Canadian parents while Phillipa Morrall and the Adoption UK staff generously contacted the United Kingdom families in preparation for my visits. My gratitude goes to the other ATTACh professionals who have been encouraging over the years.

My dear, sweet, funny friends in Hawai'i prayed me into this project when I was full of fear and positive I couldn't do it: Katie Ishol, Kathy Lindstrom, Holly Turl, Jan McGrath, Lisa Dodson, Liz Aulsebrook, Lynne Smith, Carol Marsh, Lorraine Garnier, Suzanne Gilbert, Suzy Gavin and Pat Souza. The same was true of William Haning and Fred Llewellyn, my psychiatry guides, along with the fine staff of Hina Mauka. Alan Johnson and John Ishol graciously shared their computer skills. Leimamo Thompson and Melinda Garcia were wonderful secretaries and research assistants, while Robin Chun changed from laughter to tears during the first reading. Sharon Doughtie-Kramer spent hours transcribing miles of emotional tapes and Brandy Heckman, Ruth Viafara and Bev Major offered their valuable time and skills sorting them.

John Fremont offered early editorial suggestions, then Suzanne Inciong, Kathy Martin, and Brenda Lubrano left their marks by placing all those wonderful apostrophes and commas just where they belonged.

Stuart Long brought up the rear with final editorial suggestions, some of which I actually applied.

I'm grateful to the folks at 2 hospitals who tolerated my grandiose ramblings about writing this book—HSU, Castle Medical Center, Kailua, Hawai'i and MHT at BryanLGH Medical Center West, Lincoln, Nebraska—for their support even when they thought I might need a little evaluation of my own. Margaret Daily gave me directions while John Nason and the other CC cheerleaders offered their support based on blind faith. Marsha and Don Welch proved to be emotional anchors through this sometimes heart-wrenching process.

The forever love of JRL and PDL perpetually kept me going even on the darkest of days. My mother, Joyce Ryan, and sisters Trish and Julia Ryan were ever encouraging. Literary agent, Nancy Ellis, hung in there even when it didn't make sense. Finally, but never last, what a privilege it was working with such fine parents. You were wonderfully kind and generous to me during my travels to your homes and villages.

I am truly grateful to you all for your part in the completion in this labor of love. You all remain in my daily prayers. I wish you God's best, ocean breezes, and warm Aloha. Jane

CONTENTS

FOREWORD

As an adoptive mother, a researcher, a therapist, Jane Ryan has three unique perspectives to clarify a world of heartbreak and hope. It is the world of the attachment-disordered child. Such children exhibit the strange symptoms, unmanageable behaviors, and unloving responses that are so well detailed in this book.

Due to world conflict, ethnic uprooting, and the increase in displaced refugees, the number of severely disturbed infants is growing. Around the world these homeless and neglected children, sometimes warehoused in orphanages with poor care and high child-to-adult ratios, are then marketed to the world's prospective adoptive parents. The parents are told that the child "needs love." Often, the covert message is that "love will fix the child." Many of the increasing number of prospective parents have successfully raised birth children of their own so are confident of both their love and effective disciplinary techniques. As this book makes apparent, they are in for a shock when the child does not respond to either love or discipline.

Because human beings can't consciously recall their early years, there is the unconscious expectation that those years must not be all that important. But they are. For it is the nurturing given in infancy that leads all mammals, particularly humans, to respond in a manner that creates and maintains family, society, culture, and civilization. Elephants have much in common with humans: they are very intelligent and have relatively prolonged childhoods that require nurturing. Their social order is also similar, so when things go wrong in infancy, elephants show behaviors strikingly similar to those shown by disturbed humans:

In the October 2, 1994, Chicago Tribune (page 19) there was an interesting article. Someone or something was systematically killing beautiful white rhinos in the African Planesberg Game Reserve. The South African officials found the rhinos had gaping wounds shaped like elephant tusks in their backs. Surprising evidence showed young bull elephants were responsible for this unusual behavior. The only recorded incidents of elephants killing rhinos had occurred at water holes when mothers and young calves felt threatened. These young bull elephants were going on a rampage for no apparent reason. The officials came up with a possible explanation for this aberrant behavior: in the late 1970's Planesberg became a pioneer in the restocking of animals and baby elephants to other parks, those who would have otherwise been marked for slaughter. As part of the cull to keep animal populations manageable they were moved to Planesberg along with only two adult females to care for seventy or more junior elephants. Clive Walker, chairman of the Rhino and Elephant Foundation of Africa, believes the problem goes back to the childhood trauma suffered by these elephants and followed up by a lack of parental authority throughout their formative years.

As babies, these elephants watched their parents being slaughtered and then were trucked off to new and unfamiliar surroundings. The trauma of their childhood was expressed in adult rage. While males may express killing rages as a result of early life trauma, females often express their lack of trust in others, in less overtly violent ways, as demonstrated in the writing of my young female patient below:

"The intent of this writing is not to blame my parents or anyone else. It is an attempt to explain the hopelessness and frustration I experience. It is one of the hardest and most difficult tasks I have ever undertaken as I feel at a complete loss for words when attempting to convey the total sense of isolation and helplessness I feel. I am not sure I can communicate in words how I feel so much different than anyone else and, if everyone is truly as different from me as I perceive, I do not know how they can possibly understand how I feel.

"I felt my parents did not love me. I can recall being keenly aware of wanting affection and some kind of approval at a very early age. When the love that I craved was not forthcoming, I would tell myself, "They don't love me because I'm a monster. How could anyone love a monster. Monsters are bad."

When affection and nurturing care are withheld early in life, unloved infants are in danger of growing to become true monsters. To avoid such an outcome, human infants must develop three character traits during the first years of life, upon which civilization balances: basic trust, the foundation of conscience, and "cause and effect thinking" which is necessary to control internal impulses.

When Americans are murdered for no apparent reason, they are almost certainly victims of a crime committed by someone who has no conscience, has difficulty planning ahead, has poor impulse control, and is filled with rage. Some authors have warned that America is in danger of developing a new breed of "super-predators" due to an increase in numbers of uncared-for and neglected infants. Only time will tell if this is true. It is already known, however, that disturbed early childhoods played a role in the development of many well-known predators.

The most heartbreaking aspect of Reactive Attachment Disorder is that it has been well understood for such a very long time! Nearly sixty years ago John Bowlby and others described the problem and its cause. Now, over half a century later, our society does all it can to insure that young mothers, unable to maintain lasting relationships, even with an adult, are encouraged, indeed paid, per baby, to have larger families. The problem grows geometrically. Half a century later, John Bowlby's voice still hits the mark:

"Though such cases are sadly numerous, they are mercifully more open to treatment than the severe forms. On the immense task set by the treatment of the affection-less and delinquent character...Because of their almost complete inability to make relationships, the psychiatrist is robbed of his principal tool: he should be skilled in the management of patients who hate him; he has yet to learn methods of affecting patients who had no feelings for him at all. For instance, psychological treatment was given over a period of some six years to 80 girls in a small home for delinquent girls (ages 12-16). Half were successes and half failures. Response to treatment was related neither to intelligence nor to heredity. Its relationship to the girls early family experiences, however, was striking."[1]

The available evidence suggests that nothing but prolonged residence with an adult who has insight into the problem, skill in handling it, and unlimited time to devote to her charge is likely to be of much avail. There are answers. The answers, as suggested by Bowlby so many years ago, lie in prevention of the problem, for there will never be enough psychotherapists, adoptive parents, or jails to respond to the problem once it has developed.

Simply put, behavior follows money. That may seem callous, cynical, and simplistic, but, for better or for worse, it is true. Presently, our society pays young adults very well for having, then destroying children. The worse the parent, the more money there is available to them from government. The more children one has but can't afford, the better one is paid. Paying farmers for surplus crops, and surplus infants from young mothers has definitely worked. However, it is high time to reverse this trend and begin paying people for making responsible, rather than irresponsible decisions. I offer the following suggestions:

- No parent should be allowed to continually produce child after child only to ruin, abuse, and neglect these infants, then dump them on society for care.

---

[1] John Bowlby, *Child Care and the Growth of Love,* Penguin Books, Baltimore, 1953, 55.

- Youths "at risk" for pregnancy and becoming abusive are easily identified by most high school teachers. Such youths should be identified and counseled, instead of stressing how much help, free training, and how many special classes they will receive. It must be emphasized that having and rearing a child will be their responsibility and that rearing children is expensive. As parents, they could suffer many years of financial difficulty and the government will not or should not bail them out of financial trouble.
- Temporary chemical sterilization should be considered for all parents who have one or more children living at state expense. The chemical block would be removed when they have shown an ability to responsibly care for their child.
- We have produced many abused infants by paying all birth costs for young unmarried parents. Perhaps society should be saving the billions it costs to care for such children by simply paying young, unmarried adults very well not to have children.
- In-home care for young mothers must be mandated. In home "grand-parenting" programs for young mothers have proven long-term effectiveness. Women who test positive for alcohol and drugs during pregnancy should not be allowed to raise their children. Clearly, if one can't abstain from alcohol and drugs during a nine-month period, they will likely have trouble caring for the growth and development of another soul over the subsequent 17 years.
- Rather than attempting to place every disturbed child into adoptive homes that may be torn apart by their behavior, it would be well to consider building more group homes that could provide the structure needed to maintain the children and protect society, including locked facilities if necessary.
- Guardianship should be considered as a living-in-a-family option. Presently, if a family wants to work with and live with a disturbed

> child, the only permanent option is adoption. This, of course, locks them into being responsible to provide all the therapy and treatment the child may need as he or she goes through a rebellious and out-of-control adolescence. If not legally responsible, the parents will at least be at risk for the crimes the child may commit before the age of majority. Such parents have no respite; they are "stuck" with the child they adopted at ages 3 to 6. Although the disturbed behaviors the child projects is not of their doing, it is ultimately their responsibility. The "problems per pound" ratio remains roughly the same with children: a 10 problem per pound child weighing 50 pounds is but 500 units of trouble. A few years later, however, when the child weighs 130 pounds, and is now 1600 units of trouble and most parents simply can't cope. Ideally, there should be some way to return these children to an institution at state expense and the parents should be thanked for maintaining the child for all those years. Presently, it is far more likely that the parents will be castigated because the child is "still" trouble.

These measures may be considered severe, but the problem is severe. Some will argue that such suggestions defy basic human rights, but the children produced often move into a world without rights; many end up in jail or institutions. Those with whom they interact—often their victims—have both their quality of life and their rights violated.

Jane Ryan details the lives of *Broken Spirits ~ Lost Souls*, families in turmoil with young victims of early trauma. Perhaps after more than half a century of study, it is time to do something about the problem.

Foster W. Cline, M.D.

PROLOGUE

God help me, and even though I never wanted to be one of "those parents," my very first response, was to say, "My kid would never do something like that." I wanted to deny it and swear on a stack of Bibles, if that is what it took, to convince others of his innocence. But it was my kid who did it; it was almost always my child. He wore his deviousness like a knight's suit of armor—poised and ready to defend for truth and honor. And for the life of me I can't remember when he had either.

Quinn was unusual from the very first day I brought him home at four months old. He was my littlest baby and a pleasure to carry because of his diminutive stature. He hadn't been premature, just the product of two shorter than average parents. He had a cap of black curls, honey brown skin, and huge black, sparkling, commanding eyes. Quinn had been stuck in legal limbo for several months; he'd been released for adoption by his birth mother but had to wait for a final decision from the birth father. Just prior to his birth, the adoption laws had changed requiring a decision from both biological parents to keep their newborns or to relinquish them for adoption. The final choice needed to be made before the infants were available to be placed with a waiting family. So, during the required wait, my son was placed in a parochial "foundling home" and cared for by older, retired religious women. I was told he had been assigned a surrogate mother that served as his primary caretaker for the first four months of his life. Although I had concerns about the emotional effects of a prolonged wait on Quinn, I actually had no say in the process. I was just the excited, expectant mother waiting for the phone call telling me my third child was ready to come home.

His unusual behaviors? Oh, yes, I keep getting sidetracked with poignant memories of my baby. Although the strange behaviors of children and adolescents and the effects of those characteristics on their families is the focal point of this book, I'm having difficulty getting around to telling you just what happened during his early life. Several years ago I was diagnosed with Post-Traumatic Stress Disorder (PTSD), which I was told was the result of sometimes intolerable stress in the life I shared with my child. I'm not sure about that, but I find myself standing on the threshold of my isolated, secret life with a driving notion that I've been called to share my story. Although I remain fearful that I will be judged and, again, dismissed as just one more kook who fabricated a sad story, I take a deep breath, say a prayer, and begin anyway...

From the moment I saw him I was hooked. My first memory of Quinn was of his charm. With a look, he could "work" everyone he met. Even at four months he seemed amazingly old, somehow able to read people and to discern his own wants, then get others to do what he wanted without uttering a sound. Like myself, others were fascinated with the volumes he spoke with the snap of his magnificent eyes. But all was not peaceful and silent for long. On the first day, when I attempted to change his diaper, he shrieked uncontrollably, arched his back, kicked his legs, and seemed to try to throw himself off the changing table and onto his head. At first I thought I misunderstood his intent, but the message was reconfirmed each time I changed his diaper. I threw myself across him to protect my infant from harm. His shrieks grew louder and I could not console him. It seemed he did not want to be touched.

In all fairness to "Q," there was a short period of time when he seemed to settle into the family. For several months he appeared happy and contented from his perch on my left hip. As an adoptive mother, I could easily have been accused of overdoing for my children. During adolescence, my primary job was that of a babysitter. From fifteen to seventeen, I regularly cared for well over one hundred children and was considered to be the prize sitter on a small military base located in the far-off Newfoundland. My self-esteem was built on my ability to tend and keep children safe in their parents' absence. In addition, a professional caseworker had given me her "stamp of approval" and recognized my aptitude for being a good parent. By the time Quinn joined our family, I had two other children (who were 3 and 2) from the same agency during a time when placement of more than one child per family was unheard of. I was a stay-at-home mother who was determined to go to any length to keep my children happy. Besides, I did not want to disappoint the social worker. Then, one month after Quinn came home, I became pregnant. I carried my little one around with me for almost the entire pregnancy, my plan was to keep "Q" as close to me for as long as possible. I wanted to make up for any lapses in attention that might have occurred while he waited to join my family. But, a month before the birth, my pediatrician told me Quinn needed to get off my hip and practice living the life of a ground dweller. He was thirteen months old and did not take that quietly. He shrieked for five days, then he was off and running.

I am not going to give you a daily chronicle of my son's life, but I will share a list of his significant behaviors and his age when I first noticed them. The appearance of certain traits and the date they were noted were usually two different times. Quinn, by his very nature, was quiet and covert. For those of you who are aware of the roles played by children from dysfunctional homes, sadly, a description which well fit my family, he was my "lost child." Accordingly, he was amazingly sneaky, so we never really knew what he was thinking or doing. Most behaviors did not appear constantly at first, but crept slowly and steadily into his repertoire. Quinn's IQ tests, the results of which he could manipulate, indicated he was in the gifted range, yet he spoke only occasionally. There was one obvious exception to his reticence. When he wanted something or was "conning" someone, he was most accomplished verbally. His younger brother once described pubescent "Q" as someone who could steal a cow pie from the pasture, convince you it was from the sacred cow in India, and then you couldn't thank him enough for the once-in-a-lifetime opportunity of purchasing it for top dollar! My child was a skilled orator when necessary. These are the behaviors I recall and the approximate age they first came to my awareness. I still do not know if any of the behaviors below have disappeared.

Between four months until his second birthday, Quinn:

- refused to be controlled, threw tantrums when activities changed
- bit my neck or collar bone when held close to be consoled
- had screaming nightmares which woke him from a sound sleep
- would not follow directions and demonstrated no desire to please
- refused to stay in crib/bed and wandered the house at night.

During Quinn's second and third year he:

- made poor eye contact except when angry, lying, or wanted something
- methodically set his siblings up to hit him
- punched, kicked, hit other children
- bit siblings and drew blood
- set siblings up to take the blame for his actions
- stole, gorged, and hid food, stole from siblings and mother
- lied including "crazy lying"; ex. "I'm not doing ___" as we observed it
- hour-long temper tantrums, destruction of rooms rather than cooperate
- intentionally urinated in own and siblings' beds, on their clothing
- refused to follow teachers' instructions at preschool
- disrupted class—climbing on desks and bookshelves, kicking books to floor
- played in camp fires, had fascination with fire and gore
- broke own toys and blamed others, broke others' toys

- shrieked as if being beaten when corrected or told "no"
- whined and wailed when siblings physically touched him.

Beginning at his fourth birthday until the end of his sixth year, Quinn:

- ripped and poked holes in his own clothing
- set siblings up to fight with each other then "rescued" the loser
- threatened suicide
- threatened to kill peers "if you tell"
- threatened to kill mother (knives, fire) and siblings
- broke the family dog's back
- intentionally hurt self and not cry
- skipped school starting in kindergarten
- urinated on rugs and in corners of room and blamed family dog
- began running away
- set fires in and around house
- fainted when not getting own way
- tortured the family pets and killed the hamsters.

Between his seventh and eighth years my child demonstrated the following behaviors:

- vomited on dinner table (in home or restaurants) when corrected
- urinated into the family shampoo
- vomited on teammates if peers didn't do what he wanted
- stole lunches from peers at school
- smeared feces on walls of school bathrooms
- reported dying foster father to Social Services for abuse.

Quinn's behaviors became much more serious once he reached his ninth and tenth years:

- sexually molested younger children then threatened to kill them if they told

- broke into family friend's home
- began consuming alcohol
- tortured and burned small animals; threatened to burn siblings.

I am so sad as I write this list, a rap sheet of sorts—an unsuccessful attempt at an impassionate look at a child I have always loved. After multiple trips to counselors and therapists over his first 9 years, in which they had no idea what ailed him, Quinn was finally diagnosed with Reactive Attachment Disorder (RAD). In spite of our best plans and intentions I was told he never attached emotionally to anyone, a bond necessary to love and live well. That still breaks my heart, but my "heart problem" developed over time; his seemed congenital. I wanted Quinn to become attached to me, to anyone, and did everything in my power to make that happen. For years I'd visited professionals who knew nothing of what I was describing. I even held on to the hope I'd meet one who would believe what I was seeing and saying. I went to graduate school and earned a Master of Arts degree in counseling out of self-defense, thinking that if I became a therapist I would have enough skills as "Q's" mother to fix his problems. I was told to "just love him more" by well-meaning relatives. I felt guilty because in my pain I heard them say that the problem was me, that it happened because I didn't love him enough. My personal education has been long and I have finally learned that my emotional pain is nothing compared to the lifetime of no intimate relationships my son will experience. His loss is great, but our loss of him has been immense.

For the first several years of my children's lives I was ill prepared to deal with their incredible issues. I grew up in what I now lovingly call "la-la-land," in the fertile soil of my own imagination. I was the daughter of a career military man and moved frequently during my school years. The continual losses were so overwhelming that I retreated into a world of books and fantasies. I hid my feelings well, and did so with great regularity; consequently, never did I learn to talk about anything important like feelings or living concerns. So in my make-believe world I had a dozen wonderful children who had no problems, loved me madly, and never misbehaved or left me. Reality has always been a bitter pill for me to swallow.

When I was twelve, Dale Evan's book, *The Littlest Angel*, had a profound effect on my life. I learned she and Roy Rogers had an adopted family, and so decided that, too, was to be my path. Twenty years later I had a start on the family I'd always dreamed of: three adopted children followed by a biological one. My children were a variety of races and ethnic backgrounds, all incredibly intelligent and beautiful. I'd concluded that I was the luckiest and most blessed woman in the entire world. When the fourth was born I still wasn't sure my family was complete, the dream of having twelve children was very much alive in me. I'd been offered several children from local adoption agencies, but my husband did not share my fantasy, so refused to take them. I was very hurt and angry, but when he decided to leave the marriage I experienced unbelievable gratitude that we had not taken the additional youngsters. Then I was a single parent of children ages 6, 5, 3, and 2, and soon discovered I already had more than I could manage.

We struggled emotionally and financially for many years. My son's behaviors declined dramatically while my other children were being abused and confused by Quinn and his antics. I felt more alone and depressed than ever in my life. I became more secretive and anxious, increasingly more frightened for and of Quinn. Therapist after therapist was unable to see the truth of my child as he exuded charm and cooperation whenever observed. All in all it took eight frustrating years of searching for a professional who could accept or understand my experiences. After three days of discovering Quinn setting fires in my home, he was admitted to a midwestern psychiatric hospital for a long-needed evaluation. Upon admission the staff found it difficult to believe that such a sweet acting child could be as wild, unsocialized, and aggressive as

I'd described. But, perhaps to humor me, he was admitted under a "suicide watch." Little did they know, he was actually homicidal.

About two hours after admission my child brutally attacked another young patient, as he had done so many times to his siblings. My kid was slim, ten years old, and it took five adults—security and nurses—to put him into five-point leather restraints. Quinn remained in isolation and restrained for most of the first two weeks out of a need to protect him and the other children. The admitting nurse said, "Is that what you were talking about?" My secret finally pushed open the door, finally others witnessed the truth: my darling, smart, beautiful baby was also treacherous. He had no concern for others and would do anything to gain control over others in his drive to get his own way.

I have had a strong desire to write this book for about ten years, but have been hesitant to do so. As I remember the hopes and dreams of more innocent times, tears sting my eyes, overwhelmed with sadness for the pain we have all had to endure. My home, in spite of a deep desire and longing for it to be different, and prayers to a God I thought had forsaken me, was a modern day combat zone. However, this book is not about me; nor is it about Quinn, in particular. It is about children like mine and the families who love them. Our personal paths, Quinn's and mine, are revealed to you through the stories told by other parents. The family lives of those with attachment-disordered or severely disturbed children are profoundly alike. Some minute details vary, but the overall effect of these strong children on their loved ones is eerily the same. Through the stories of unusual families, you will learn about the impact a poorly known psychological malady has on families living with it, and hence, on society as a whole.

As I write this book, I find myself in tears from feelings long felt, but today that is okay. In spite of old fears, I no longer think I will evaporate into nothingness if I tell our story. There is a saying: "You're only as sick as the secrets you keep." I did not want to keep the realities of our lives secret; I told my spouse, my family members, and my friends some of the truth. Therapists told me I was awfully anxious and if I would just calm down we would be all right. My original family had no ability to comprehend what was happening, as it was too bizarre. My other children were very young and did their best to survive our personal, collective hell. Having never experienced the terrifying, dangerous behaviors of our child, my former husband was incapable of being supportive. (I need to say that those who did not understand, who did not believe, or who could not support us are not being blamed.) Above all else, I cry for my child. Reactive Attachment Disorder is a thief: it robbed my child of the love he needs and deserves, because he was unable to receive it. He was never able to develop a sense of caring, so cannot give back to the world in a positive way. I also grieve for the deep, unrelenting pain in his life, or for the lack of it; for missed opportunities; and for his inability to overcome his genes or his emotional makeup. A series of events before birth and during the early weeks of his life culminated in the resultant malady; he did not cause it. In the past I believed he was broken-hearted; now I understand that it is his spirit that was broken.

Living with someone with an attachment disorder is like standing too close, uncomfortably close, to someone you don't know. When you divert your eyes from direct visual contact, they remain right there in your path. When you look past their ear, your peripheral vision captures a clear view of their curious stare. Looking down at the ground provides you no relief. Instead, and as much as you may want to run from the forced closeness, you are confronted with yet another facet of the same person—the belly, or the tips of their shoes. Just like that imposing person there in your face, with an attachment-disordered individual, no matter how hard you try to divert your gaze all you get is another view of the same problem. I am now on the downside of over two decades of misunderstanding and of not grasping the depth of the problem. The mystery of attachment and bonding problems is coming into the light, the only place it can be solved.

Today I am grateful to the God of my misunderstanding. Intimate contact with this disorder has changed the course of my life. I had envisioned a somewhat dull, ordinary existence—marriage, raising a family into adulthood, worthwhile work, then retirement with my husband to travel until I became too old to safely leave home. Life as I imagined it would have "looked good" on the outside, clean and tidy, and lived on the surface as I'd begun my life, with few deep emotions. Instead, I have lived an amazing life forced into isolation by my shame and unbelievable sense of failure brought on by powerful thoughts that I had caused my child's problems. My solitary life has included continuous conflict punctuated by unexpected, overwhelming emotional and physical challenges. In place of calm and predictable I've experienced messy, overwhelming, and painful. I lost my child to institutions because by the age of twelve I was already unable to manage him at home. I also lost love, a marriage, a good reputation, and support because others did not believe me; then two homes because I had a choice—pay for his therapy or my mortgage. Suddenly, not being believed and regarded with disdain by my family and professionals forced my hand. I was finally pushed to consider my deepest beliefs and to develop a relationship with a higher power that could sustain me when earthly beings with human frailties failed me.

Consequently, because of such an unexpected lifetime, intertwined with this disorder, I am left with an enormous pool of empathy, understanding, sensitivity, and love for my children, none of which would have been true without the exact experiences we survived together. I have finally gained a sense of peace, self-respect, and hope that I am able to share with other families and those who share a kinship with me because of our mutual histories. It is by God's grace that I am gentle and kind rather than bitter and angry. Perhaps all the experiences in our lives are meant to enlighten, to guide, and to teach us what it is that we need to know. It is my confirmed belief that Quinn, who has had the most difficult time in life, has been my greatest teacher.

Letter to an Unbonded Son in Prison

We speak by phone, and you tell me
you are drawing women's faces.
I imagine you standing in a hall,
your rage now fetal in its cell.

Intimate across the distance,
you are articulate and quiet.
Otherwise lethal, you are
softened by your pencil's lead.

The irony is killing. As I listen,
all my scars blow open like old sores.
I curse your birth mother,
who, killing you in your core,

left you crying in your feces
and waltzed away the hours,
her aphrodisiac another lover's crib.
Son, I want to tell you this:

the wages of neglect are epidemic;
the wages of abuse will kill us all.
Now a cripple of the heart
and doomed to rage, your pencil

shades far subtler than your soul's,
immune to the love I gave you,
and still calloused to its toll.

Your Adopted Father

INTRODUCTION

I want to introduce you to children who express violence against their family members, who steal and lie, who threaten, and sometimes, kill. They are children filled with rage, a white-hot rage that cannot be put out by the soothing love of a family of their own. Most of the children cited in this book have been in foster care or are adopted. Not all adopted children have Attachment Disorder, but it is believed by some that all adopted and foster children have attachment issues, at least. Often children with attachment difficulties have experienced disrupted lives or trauma by very early ages. Unfortunately, youngsters who remain with their biological parents are not as immune to attachment problems as we would hope. Children living in their birth homes are also neglected or abused, perhaps more so in some cases. Adopted and foster families have agency officials observing and monitoring them closely. Without watchdog agencies involved, biological families are better able to maintain dirty, abusive secrets for longer.

At 2 my young friend Martina routinely rummaged through local dumpsters for food to sustain her frail body and her drug-addicted mother. Her mother's boyfriend had repeatedly raped her at gunpoint by 3. The message already hammered into her developing psyche: "I wouldn't have to go through this torture if my mother had cared for and protected me." Because of well-embedded beliefs and behaviors she appeared very old and "set in her ways" to some, and completely unsocialized to others. In the past, children with behaviors similar to Martina's would have been described as a "bad seed." Today we can begin to understand how the decision to stand alone, coupled with stubborn refusal to be dependent upon others, has been a necessary survival technique for some youngsters. Martina learned that her mother could not care for her so she became the parent at the extraordinary age of two. A neglected infant or toddler of ordinary character would have died, never able to summon the courage displayed by baby Martina. Such techniques can actually go mightily awry later in their young lives.

Reactive Attachment Disorder (RAD) has been described in the Diagnostic Statistical Manual—IV (DSM-IV), the bible of psychiatric clinicians. Authorities on the topic believe that significant breaks in the bonding or attachment process between mother and child, such as traumatic separations from their primary caretaker, early neglect or abuse, which occur within the first thirty-three months of life are ultimately most detrimental. The sensitive period includes the nine months in utero followed by the twenty-four months following birth. RAD is a complex syndrome manifested by distinctive behavioral characteristics, symptoms that are simultaneously fascinating and horrific. Living with children with full-blown attachment problems can be frightening. There are degrees of the illness, all of them mystifying and frustrating, at least. The long-term effects of untreated attachment problems can be horrifying to family members and to society at large. Out of their own internal hurt and terror youngsters become tough, invulnerable, and can be dangerous toward those who dare to love them. Their belief systems, often nailed into place before the development of language, become impenetrable. The goal of their behavior is to keep love and caring at bay in an effort to avoid further emotional pain. Attachment-disordered kids truly believe they do not need—or deserve—others in their life. First it is their families, especially the mothers, who feel their heat. Eventually, though, it is society that pays a tremendous price for continued ignorance.

Because the thinking of attachment affected children is so dramatically different from the norm, parenting skills used with normal children are generally considered to be an abysmal failure. Consequently, new methods and approaches must be utilized. *Broken Spirits ~ Lost*

Souls provides readers with an education. You will be privy to details of life with attachment compromised children as seen through the eyes of parents who love and want desperately to help them. The information presented will be illuminated through touching, personal interviews. Out of their love for the youngsters their families have struggled and sometimes suffered greatly in their efforts to keep their children with them. It is important to know that the names of the parents and children throughout this book have been changed to afford individuals full privacy and safety. In addition, my own children's true names are not used. It is my intent to educate, not to embarrass or expose my family, those who have suffered from this disorder, or any participants in this important project.

The material presented in this volume is the most up-to-date information available on these families today. I was very fortunate to have the help of American Gail Trenberth and Philippa Morrall of the U.K. in locating parents willing to cooperate with my research. Personal interviews with individuals and groups of parents of attachment disturbed youngsters followed written surveys distributed to those involved in parent support groups across the United States, Canada, and the United Kingdom. I interviewed experts in the fields of adoption, attachment/bonding, counseling, criminology, medicine, psychiatry, and psychology, as well as religious and spiritual leaders. An exploration was made of the most recent literature found in public and university libraries and that published by national and international parents' support groups.

This work provides you with a balanced look at a complicated disorder and its impact on families. I've attempted to approach such a difficult subject matter in a comprehensive yet simple manner for easy understanding as oversimplification would not do the topic justice. Scholars in the field often distinguish between Reactive Attachment Disorder and Attachment Disorders (AD). I, however, do not make such a distinction and thereby use the terms interchangeably. I do so because in my experience the differences between the two are insignificant. Also, they have similar causes, symptoms, and outcomes. I also do not differentiate between problems caused by neglect or those caused by medical problems. The disorder exists on a continuum, some children are more severely affected; thus, they demonstrate more symptoms than do others. Because of that, I do tend to use "RAD" to describe the most severe form of the disorder.

Broken Spirits ~ Lost Souls has been written for families with problem children. It is for those who wonder about the mental health or behaviors of their children and for those who are worried about what is going on with their youngsters. It will also help you identify children who are at risk for behavioral and emotional problems later in their life. Usually problem behaviors are first acted out in the family setting, but do not stop there. Eventually, negative acts spill out into classrooms and schools on their way to playing themselves out on society-at-large. Parents and family members with any of the following experiences would greatly benefit from reading this book. Those who:

- have children with major interruptions in first relationships during the first 2 years.
- are rearing adopted or foster children.
- have children who were victimized through neglect or trauma.
- have medical miracles, infants born early and who've lived longer than expected.
- have had premature, sickly newborns who've spent precious time in isolation.
- feel overburdened or anxious due to medical complications with their infants.
- have profound stress which took their attention away from children at home.
- have ill infants which caused significant separations from the primary caretaker.

- had a parent or spouse die and experienced an extended separation from the child.
- care for newborns and toddlers affected by drugs or alcohol.
- had a difficult pregnancy which caused the mother physical or emotional distress.
- had an unwanted pregnancy, perhaps the result of rape.
- had insufficient maternal maturity necessary to care for an infant.
- had a mother/caretaker whose own needs were not met in infancy.
- had a newborn with undetected physical illness, such as ear infections.

Broken Spirits ~ Lost Souls will enlighten you about a disorder I have grown to believe is largely preventable. You will:

- learn the causes, the symptoms, and the outcome with and without therapy.
- know what to look for in your child's behaviors.
- learn where to go for help or support if you think there is a problem.
- find out what to expect from your child, the professionals, and yourself.
- be given basic, effective parenting skills to use with challenging children.
- learn what we must do to remedy this dangerous predicament.

This work symbolizes a giant leap in understanding disturbed and disturbing children from their families' perspective. It will help move us toward solutions to solve a growing dilemma with kids who were previously doomed to institutions: hopeless, untreatable, and unrecognized until it was too late. This volume is written in the ordinary language of the today, as it is my hope that parents and grandparents of today's youth will be the first to read this book. Parents have a front row seat in their children's lives and the strength and power to force professionals to look harder and to dig deeper. Personal experiences with individuals in psychiatry, psychology, social work, counseling, and the ministry leaves me frightened for our future that such disturbed children are going unidentified and untreated. I have loved attachment disturbed children for thirty years and have been appalled at the lack of available information. I speak from the tears of my own experiences. There were times in which I felt I was the only one who knew of this disorder. *Broken Spirits ~ Lost Souls* is written out of love for my own children and out of a deep desire to support families and help children who still have a chance of becoming loving members of society.

Attending to the basic needs of ones' infant, toddler, or child must become our first priority. Two of the most important needs are guidance and limits to help youngsters learn to live with the concept of "no." When we fail to provide either for our children, no matter how noble our reasoning, we are being neglectful. Children coming out of neglect or abandonment—whether from the projects or gated communities—feel unloved, unsafe, unworthy, and hopeless. Martha G. Welch, M.D., a psychiatrist and attachment specialist from New York City, believes that the most severely attachment-disordered are individuals whose basic needs for nurturing are overlooked while they are being materially overindulged. During adolescence, peer groups become all-important to youngsters whose basic needs were ignored, perhaps due to what was called "benign neglect."

Many of our children have progressed into their adolescence with too much power. It has been difficult keeping an accurate count of the killings committed in the past year by adolescent males. Some of the most difficult youngsters are in control of their homes while simultaneously out of control in society. Boys whose threats of harm were not taken seriously have inflicted immeasurable pain and suffering on to their schoolmates. Individuals who threaten schools and neighbors are no longer from overcrowded inner cities, but have been the products of small towns and suburbia. Increasingly, upper-middle class teens from both transplanted and biological families, are involved in violent crimes and joining gangs. Gang membership, interestingly, provides children with rules, guidance, acceptance, and affiliation—all the outward signs of love that they crave.

We must take notice of these children because to remain ostrich-like with our heads in the sand could mean the deterioration of our communities due to divisiveness from within. The success of our society depends upon the strength of our very foundation, the unity, and health of our families. Our children are in jeopardy and their families are under enormous strain. Until we shore up our foundation, currently built upon shifting sands of emotional ailments, our society, as we know it, is in grave danger. To aid in your understanding of this difficult disorder I offer the following definitions:

Attachment—an emotional bond that involves affection, loyalty, and loving reciprocity between the involved caretaker and the infant.

Bonding—a uniting force or tie which occurs as the result of a complicated process in which the needs of the infant are provided for and satisfied by a primary caretaker.

Psyche—another term for the mind, one's spirit, or soul.

Psychopath—a person with an antisocial personality disorder who demonstrated aggressive, perverted, criminal, and/or amoral behaviors, believed to be the result of social, biological, genetic, and/or chemical influences or damage which occurred either in utero or within the first two to three years of life.

Broken-spirited children are everywhere. It has been a personal challenge to present this new information to you in a humane manner in hopes that this material aids your understanding of this emotion-filled topic. The children discussed here deserve our love and respect, as they did not ask for the difficulties they experience in their daily lives. Their native strength and ability to survive under circumstances that might have killed average children is awesome. These youngsters are not at all average individuals, nor could the parents of AD victims be considered "regular." The pages before you are filled with the thoughts and concerns of amazing human beings surviving extraordinary circumstances. During the personal interviews the love that each parent had for their child was tangible. It is my goal to convey the depth of their love and concern for children that they are rearing.

I am so very grateful to the families who participated in this project for without their help this book would be pointless. In July 1997, one year before my extended interviewing trip, I began researching the topic and surprisingly, began receiving phone calls and letters from parents of AD kids. The word had spread to the parents support groups and then one family to another. Many parents wanted to be included and I began receiving "Bless you" messages and written family histories. They told me about their fears, the isolation, and their feelings of being overwhelmed by children's significant needs. The common thread was that they'd been doing an enormous job—bigger than that of parenting normal kids—without any support. The idea that parenting attachment disturbed children is impossible without help from families, neighbors, child-centered agencies, and a mental health professional was confirmed. It was no wonder that most parents, while usually well balanced and previously successful, were much like boils ready to burst and spew. Desperation was a feeling known intimately by the parents who willingly participated; they shared their hearts and souls with me, elated that someone was finally listening. Hope spread like wildfire, along with their belief that soon, support and understanding, much like the cavalry of the Old West, was on its way.

Initially, however, many of them were downright suspicious of me. Because of their own experiences with unwilling, uninformed professionals the parents were, understandably, gun-shy. Similar to my past, most had years of heartbreak under their belts, their feelings heightened by misunderstanding and the need of others to lay blame. Most of the families interviewed for this book, part of an international project, are adoptive families, but some exceptions exist. Many children with attachment difficulties remain in their biological families. However, at this time adopters are easier to identify, are more informed on the subject, and consequently, more verbal. I told the organizers of my background as an adoptive mother experienced with attachment problems, as a counselor, and an author. I told them my goal was to present their stories to the world in a way that only someone who has lived with these children can.

Our current belief system leads us to think that, given enough information we can pinpoint a cause, blame the person responsible, and then, of course, fix it. Years ago my mother used to ask me if I was sure I wasn't imagining the problem. I assured her that I prayed daily for that to be the case. If the awful problems my children were having were the result of my overactive imagination the solution was simple: just fix me, "shrink" me, or whatever! I felt hopeless and was willing to do anything to have my children be normal. If someone had told me to put peach pits in my ears and hop around on my bad leg I would have gladly done so. I was so desperate to have my children be well I would have used anything, including voodoo, if it would have fixed me, and ultimately, them. Without exception, all of the parents I met felt the very same way.

The initial written surveys were distributed through parents support groups at home and abroad, and through therapists. I asked questions about their children's behaviors and about what it was like living with them. A few parents returned surveys unanswered because they didn't believe their children were affected. All of the parents who completed questionnaires had children already diagnosed as attachment compromised. I remain amazed at the numbers of identified families; in 1998 approximately three hundred families had been identified in the United Kingdom, by the organization now called Adoption UK. About one year later, most of the interviewees had completed written surveys, but some had not. By the time I crossed the United States, and Canada, arrived in the United Kingdom the numbers had swelled. In addition, some of the original participants had by then had their youngsters diagnosed by Greg Keck, Ph.D., when he visited their area. Then, many changed their minds about becoming involved in the study.

The personal stories presented here are one-sided and graphic in nature. *Broken Spirits ~ Lost Souls* is about attachment disorders from the perspective of the parents; consequently, they are fully subjective. Stories told by parents are presented later in this volume will inform you, frighten you, and provide you with a rare education which clearly demonstrates the problem. Most victims, even those who are now adults, have not yet shared their perceptions of growing up with this problem. At some point it would be revealing to talk to the children and say, "Just what was going on then?" "What was it that happened to you?" "How did you feel about those awful things that happened?" "What is it that you want us to know about you?" "What can we do to make it better?" and "What do you need now?" Sadly, so far we have been unable to go to the children and ask. Because memories of traumatic events in their early lives remain buried and unknown, it is impossible for them to know what, if anything, is the problem.

You will see for yourself that Attachment Disorders are not nearly as rare as we hope and pray. Any child born into crisis is vulnerable, for this disorder as the initial cause of such a horrendous problem occurs when the basic, life enhancing needs of the newborn and infant are left unmet. Therefore, any child from a family in significant conflict or a country experiencing civil unrest is at risk. Northern Ireland, Somalia, Afghanistan, Croatia, and Southeast Asia come to mind, but those countries certainly do not form a complete list. In many war-torn countries youngsters carry weapons and sacrifice their childhood for the good of the nation, while experiencing a life-threatening lack of the basics, including food, water, and nurturing.

You will be privy to the behaviors of disturbed children who are dangerous as early as just past the toddler stage. By their teens they have the ability to defy any authority and to seriously challenge socially accepted norms. At the very least, attachment-disordered children demonstrate the embryonic stages of a psychopathic personality. At most they are full-blown predatory psychopaths all consumed by their search for yet another victim. On your journey through *Broken Spirits ~ Lost Souls*, I pray you become enlightened while you honor the children and their families with your time and your developing understanding of the problems in their lives.

PART I—THE PROBLEM

CHAPTER ONE—
Laying the Foundation

There is a crack in the foundation that shores up our current family structure. Due to the presence of disturbances in their children, thousands of families are considered "special needs" and cannot handle the burden alone. The lack of success or the degree of imbalance in some of our special families are not personal failures! Instead, many of the problems are actually the result of serious flaws in our social systems. Because of inadequate resources parents often feel unsupported and are eventually unable to provide for the true needs of their offspring. Recently, I read about a Lincoln, Nebraska, foster family with several years of success in rearing troubled youths. A few nights earlier the nighttime caretaker, a man in his thirties, went upstairs to remind two sixteen-year-olds that it was time to quiet down for the night. The first adolescent assaulted the adult and was backed up by the second even larger youth. It was easy to surmise from the written public record of this particular family that they have needs greater than one individual could possibly provide. An assault on their caretaker by adolescents was a strong indication that their needs were far greater than most imagined.

We've continuously heard that parenting is "the most important job in the world." I fully believe that is true, but it is simultaneously the only job in the world which requires no experience, no training, or license. There are no limits to the hours that can be worked and no wages are provided. But if families are really the priority among the lawmakers, why are quality resources so scarce? Why can we not fully trust our politicians to follow through with plans that positively impact the quality of our family lives? When funds are cut on local or national levels, why does it come from the monies that had been established to improve the lives of our youngsters? Certainly our senators and representatives receive the pay raises they demand. Why can't our babies, our youth, and our parents receive the funds and financial backing that they so desperately need? The job of parenting is every bit as important as that of the lawmaker, and probably more.

During my life I have met an enormous number of parents. Some of them have possessed an amazing array of parenting skills; some have not. But, I have never met a guilt-ridden parent who was up to doing an adequate job of rearing their youngsters. When one feels bad about oneself as a parent or has a poor sense of self, then one's role as a parent becomes compromised. Without confidence in one's self or abilities, even the most minimal expectations in caretaking cannot be met. During the mature years of my life I have learned that being a "good" parent requires self-esteem and confidence in one's ability to meet the needs of your kids. You have to believe deep inside that you are smart enough, loving enough, and strong enough to provide for, and meet, the complex needs of your offspring. Harboring secret internal doubts will negatively color your decisions and approach to the most important job in the world—that of rearing the next generation.

We have become a nation of finger waggers and tongue clickers. When I listen to adults discussing the younger generation it is easy to hear the "tsk, tsk" in their voice or to see the "shame on you" gestures we may have grown up with. Blaming and shaming our youth and their parents have been common methods utilized in attempts to control the behaviors of others. Since the heyday of Freud we have believed that identifying the culprit and blaming the one we determined to be the cause of the problem somehow changed the situation. Perhaps that was an attempt to construct a sense of safety in a world that sometimes felt dangerous or out of control. Or, maybe it was a means of emotionally beating mothers into a state of submission. Although a noxious idea, using psychological or emotional means of making women behave have been employed throughout the ages. Today I still overhear conversations where someone is trying to determine the source of a problem. Together, the twins of blame and shame continue to undermine self-esteem and erode parenting confidence and skills. Not once have blame or shame enhanced or solved an already difficult situation. However, paradoxically, you will see how it is imperative for a youngster to develop a sense of shame because without its development the characteristics of empathy and conscience cannot exist. That sense of shame must come from within the individual rather than shame being foisted on them from the outside.

I believe most parents do an amazing job of loving and guiding their children. Even under incredible circumstances, such as in war zones or during periods of rapid social change most children and their parents still coming out shining. I love and respect parents as a highly diverse group and appreciate their differences, strengths, and weaknesses. I seem to understand, on a spiritual level, about their humanity perhaps because I have struggled so long with my own. After much emotional pain I finally learned that knowing the "why" of a problem does not change or solve the problem. I discovered that my adopted children intuitively mixed me up with their biological mothers. Under such circumstances that was understandable and expected, but the insight did not make them any easier to rear or make me feel any better. Although I may have gained an intellectual grasp of what was happening, the situation was not changed one iota.

Herein lies information about Attachment Disorder, and any discussion on attachment problems is bound to be an emotional one! It is a highly charged topic because it hits us where we live. We are deeply affected in our hearts by the children we love and fight to rear. Feelings of sadness and fear tug at our core, at who we are and what we stand for. In order to assimilate information presented in this volume you will need to examine any prejudices you may harbor and then determine if you're willing to add to your list of skills. What will be required of you is the deceivingly difficult task of changing your mind. Doing so is everyone's prerogative! Attempting to make changes with a closed mind, as I've tried on numerous occasions, makes taking on a new perspective an impossible task.

In my first book, *Motherhood at the Crossroads: Meeting the Challenge of a Changing Role*, Sue Villani and I identified a phenomenon we called the "Mother Crisis." A Mother Crisis is characterized and defined by a heightened sense of failure which results from unmet expectations or when the woman's "ideal mother" does not measure up to that of the "real mother." The data that led to our conclusions was collected during two national surveys of bright, educated mothers collected almost twenty years apart. At the beginning of the research I hypothesized that if women with apparently "normal" families and ample support–emotional, marital, financial–and child care, had emotional difficulties related to stress in their mothering role, what might be the experience of those without such resources or with special needs families?

Interestingly, mixed with the mothers' perceptions of failure were overwhelming feelings of shame due to believing they were guilty for the problems that occurred in the life of their offspring. Part of the blame-shame duo was foisted on them from the outside, but, all too often, their feelings were self-perpetuated. Of the mothers from the 1978 survey, 68% experienced a full-blown Mother Crisis. By comparison, however, the more informed and better-educated mothers of 1995 were not immune to the phenomenon either. Over half, 52%, reluctantly admitted that they continued to have difficulty with an overwhelming sense of failure and loss of self-esteem due to somewhat traditional roles taken on as part of their mothering "job." Less than ten percent of both samples remained noncommittal about their private, emotional responses to motherhood, so the final tally could have actually been higher. Most of the moms who experienced an emotional crisis found it to be unpredictably transient. However, even if the crisis was short lived, the long-term effects could be devastating on the delicate relationship between mother and child. The saddest part of the studies, which was not reflected in the statistics, was this: too many of the mothers were unable to realize their own magnificence as women and mothers because of their acute, and sometimes debilitating feelings of failure. It is those kinds of experiences and feelings of not being up to the task that our existing social systems fail to address. The last decade has ushered in revolutionary social changes instigated by unprecedented electronic advances. Not only are our youth bombarded with unfathomable amounts of information but they are inundated with overwhelming choices, as well. I'm not sure teenagers, in spite of all their bravado, are wired to live—or flourish—in continuous overload. Neither are their parents.

And just how does that information relate to families of children with attachment issues? First of all, it demonstrates the power of feelings involved in the parenting process. A person's internal experience or perception seems to determine one's level of success or their perceived success in the parenting journey. It is said that success breeds more success. And failure, or the belief that failure is at hand, will continue to set up a parent for more of the same. Parents who anticipate failure or an inability to succeed at a task, could easily give up. How many parents do you know who shrug their shoulders and avoid parental responsibilities while saying, "What's the point?" Or, "What's the use, the kid won't listen to me anyway?" Secondly, the mothers in the study were from families identified as "normal," whatever that actually means. Even if we could come to an agreement about an acceptable definition of "normal," we still would have a dilemma. Although they look super-normal, attachment disturbed youngsters are not usually considered "normal" even before their problems are identified. In fact, they are generally identified as emotionally, psychologically, or behaviorally disturbed in schools or in therapists' offices, some more than others. So, if mothers studied in *Motherhood at the Crossroads*, those living in "ideal" situations with all the necessary means of support and nearly unlimited resources had significant emotional crises, what can be expected for those with families who have youngsters with attachment difficulties?

Before a problem can be solved every facet must be examined as if being viewed under a microscope. We must look squarely at the face and depth of it to see the dilemma as it really is in all its ugliness and power. Hiding our eyes exacerbates any problem, especially problems within our families. We have wanted to believe that the schoolyard killings were isolated incidents, perhaps the result of some backwoods ethics. We hoped that teens Andrew Golden and Mitchell Johnson of Arkansas and Luke Woodham of Mississippi were anomalies—strange, one of a kind. We cried and prayed that we remain immune to such atrocities and that similar events never happened again. But then in the spring of 1998 fifteen-year-old Kip Kinkel from Thurston High School in Springfield, Oregon, went on his rampage killing his parents and two schoolmates. He was reported to be bright, funny, and perhaps somewhat troubled. Then in April of 1999, less than a year later, two gun-toting, bomb-making adolescents from the affluent suburbs of Littleton, Colorado shattered our sense of safety. They introduced a new brand of violence and one that could no longer be considered just another isolated incident. We could no longer wish it away; we could no longer ignore the planned massacre that caused the deaths of too many gifted youth.

Before the month following Littleton had passed, there was a proliferation of copycats. The police in Port Huron, Michigan arrested four handsome, articulate adolescent boys (two thirteen and two fourteen-year-olds) who had plans to outdo Littleton in magnitude and in lethality. Following the Colorado massacre my other job took me into our local emergency room. During the course of completing mental health assessments I met too many disturbed adolescent youths, children who assigned little value to human life. There was a frightening parade of kids from ages ten to seventeen who were brought to our trauma center out of renewed concern by parents, police, teachers, and family physicians.

Hasty referrals were made based on glaring warning signs that announced aberrant and disturbing thought patterns. All of the youngsters had concrete plans and had made homicidal threats toward other kids, teachers, parents, and/or siblings. Perhaps not all the youths were capable of such atrocities, or not all threats were serious, but which ones should be ignored? I've long believed it is imperative that we attend to all children who feel so desperate or alienated that they make violent threats against the lives of those around them. It is individuals with those kinds of problems that our existing social systems are setting up to fail. The political and economic systems, those held responsible for helping us provide for the needs of our families, are either non-existent, understaffed, or broken.

I do not know if any of the schoolyard killers have been diagnosed with Attachment Disorder. There are, however, striking commonalties between the schoolyard killers and children with attachment disorders. Articles written about the boys seemed to reveal common threads of early neglect or disruptions that permeated their stories. With or without a formal diagnosis of Attachment Disorder they demonstrate a level of broken-ness that terrifies society and will continue to cost lives if left untended. Sadly, the numbers of youngsters who are lonely, emotionally damaged, and disenfranchised are ever increasing. Our families and our children are in trouble because their basic nurturing needs were not met, weren't identified or were overlooked. Parents, too, experience an increasing sense of fear, loneliness, and hopelessness which ultimately leaves them with even fewer parenting options or enough emotional strength to do a good job. In the end the entire family and, eventually, societal safety will be the price to be exacted. To protect society we must, now, fully look at the problem! This is not a topic for the faint of heart. Our children are killing each other—a sure sign that our systems are failing. It is the right moment to take our heads out of the sand, to open our minds, and learn what we can from the sad and terrible occurrences around us.

Joey, an eleven-year-old, had been uncontrollable at school and had chased his teachers and peers with a knife while threatening to kill them. His goal was to become a member of the "Trenchcoat mafia" so he was brought to the Emergency Room for a mental health assessment. He was an adorable looking boy, black hair, honey brown skin, and beautiful black flashing eyes. He was cooperative and almost charming, unusual for someone of eleven, but maintained a far-off, dreamy look in his eyes. His biological father told me his son had been with the birth mother until three years before. Joey was extremely small for his age and appeared more like 7 or 8. The father said he had gained custody of the boy because he had been malnourished, and perhaps starved by his mother from early in life. The reported neglect appeared severe and included the lack of both food and emotional attention. The youngster was admitted to the children's unit for further evaluation. Several days later I observed him through the glass of a locked "quiet room" door. For hours, Joey had been screaming chilling insults and threats at the staff and was showing no signs of letting up. The sad youngster resembled a caged, wounded animal.

Martha Welch, M.D., a family psychiatrist from New York and author of *Holding Time* told me that both neglected and abused children are emotionally disturbed individuals with attachment issues, at the very least. Overindulged children and abused youngsters behave very much alike in the long run, but their thinking patterns are the only thing that distinguishes one from the other. A neglected/abused child wants-what-he-wants-when-he-wants-it because he never had "it" before. On the other hand, an overindulged child wants-what-he-wants-and-now! He feels entitled to "it" and believes "it" was a guaranteed birthright. The most damaged children, and ultimately most dangerous, according to Dr. Welch, are those who are overindulged materially while being simultaneously emotionally neglected. The "Here's $20 now go to the mall and get out of my hair!" would be a good example of such child-rearing practices. What came to my mind is a mental picture of Dylan

Klebold and Eric Harris, spending the weekend before the Columbine massacre in a well-supplied garage building bombs. Apparently their actions attracted only the attention of an adolescent living next door, but none of the parents were wise to their offspring's activities.

According to Keith Kuboyama, LSW, a Honolulu-based therapist with The Casey Family Program, there are significant differences between abused and neglected children, which become apparent during the therapeutic process. During attachment therapy youngsters who have been physically or sexually abused remain emotionally engaged, with their abuser, but in a negative way. It is typical within the abuser-abused relationship victimized children utilize people-pleasing behaviors and attempt to protect the abuser from the consequences of their actions. Neglected children, on the other hand, appear disengaged from the process. Because neglect, which means ignoring and not meeting their basic needs, negates a child's basic sense of value or any feelings of individual worth. With neglected individuals no relationship can develop with the victimizer. In fact, neglected individuals seem to show little reverence for human life at all. Their phony attempts at closeness eventually reveal a real lack of emotional depth with no recognizable connection to others. An obvious lack of conscience, guilt, or remorse for their own actions are red flags which warn therapists of trouble. The observations by both Welch and Kuboyama reinforced my belief that neglected children, rather than abused ones, are the most disturbed of all youngsters.

I believe there is such a thing as a "mothering instinct," but I don't think all women are born with the sense fully developed. Or perhaps they are not yet "tuned in" to it. Girls born to women who were never nurtured, loved, or had their needs as infants or youngsters met have been found to be at distinct disadvantages as mamas. It may be impossible for a mother to give her own infant something she never received or observed. Imagine the difficulty of a mother living in a war zone lacking the freedom or energy to lazily nurture her babies. Perhaps we are not actually talking about mothers of war, but it is easier to comprehend the effects of emotional poverty that accompanies such a situation. Babies born into poverty of any kind—emotional, psychological, chemical, financial, medical, or social—are disadvantaged and will require additional help and resources to make up for significant deficits.

When children's basic needs are not met, they become inwardly or openly rageful, which will eventually erupt on to family members, in classrooms, or out onto the streets. Children signal loudly when they are in trouble in a language that we may not yet be able to decipher. Gladly, however, attentive adults can learn to read them, much like we learned to understand the cries of our own newborns. In addition to offering you valuable support, I want to impart a true sense of hope, to tell you that there really is something we can do about a terrible problem that negatively impacts the life as we know it. While statistics and treatment options may be limited or discouraging, perhaps their lack will provide us with the motivation needed to take immediate and appropriate action. We are not powerless over the situation! As the result of both personal experiences and extensive research I've come to believe that most cases of attachment problems are preventable. I want to repeat that clearly—they are preventable! True, some of the suspected causes of attachment difficulties cannot yet be controlled, as our genetic contribution, for example. But we are not too late and there is still plenty we can do at the front end of our children's lives! We can learn to identify the basic, primary needs of babies, and hence, of our youth; then we can then learn to meet them. Nurturing others is the key we have sought for so long.

During her years as a social worker in Tennessee mental health facilities, Paula Pickle, LCSW, ACSW, CNC, and Executive Director of the former Attachment Center of Evergreen (ACE), Colorado, began forming opinions about children who'd been separated from their parents. Although the numbers have dramatically increased since those early years in her career. At that time 35 to 40% of their young clients were adopted and foster youngsters. What percentage, I asked, of their child and family staff had training with adoption and foster care issues, attachment, grief, or loss? "Zero," Pickle reported without hesitation, "and that's a problem. Children who are the most needy have staff who are the least trained to deal with those issues." From a professional perspective it was always confusing to her why there weren't mandates to deal with such issues. Pickle went on: "Why make parents spend years trying to access funds to help their kids while their behaviors become more and more ingrained, while the family gets more and more burned out, and feels more and more blamed?"

The social worker became very demonstrative when discussing possible alternatives. "Wouldn't it be better if we looked at prevention? If we looked at early intervention rather than wait till a child reaches the age of adolescence and then needs to go into the juvenile system? Economically," she said sadly, "it doesn't make any sense. Think about the wasted lives." Even though we are the richest nation in the world the professional doesn't know what it will take to get professionals and authorities to address this drastic issue. Pickle believes there are many societal forces which will dramatically increase the risks for our youngsters. Among her list of concerns were more cases of child abuse and neglect, widespread domestic violence and drug use, increased familial and national economic instability, daycare-reared children, and teen pregnancies. In addition, Pickle stated she's seen second and third generation attachment-disordered people attempting to raising their own attachment disturbed children. "You can't pass on what you don't have." She added, "Although we say we care about kids, I don't see that our society, our programs, or our policies are demonstrating that."

The Bonding Process

Now that we have an overview of some of the consequences of lack of nurturing, let's review the bonding process that is absolutely necessary for the mental and physical health of our wee ones. As early as the 1950's John Bowlby, an English physician, began studying the responses of institutionalized newborns and toddlers. He saw, all too frequently, what happened when the infants did not receive the touching and cuddling they required—they died. Today's youngsters, perhaps a little tougher than those of two generations ago with more scientific means of keeping them alive in the early stages of life, are still significantly affected by the lack of loving stimulation.

The following description is of the all-important bonding process that occurs during an infant's initial two years of life. For writing ease, and to balance out the places I have used 'he' this time I will refer to the newborn as a female. The description below is based on the teachings of Foster Cline, M.D., whom I hold in the highest esteem and consider the grandfather of attachment work with seriously disordered children:

Infants' primitive needs are those of hunger, warmth, dry diapers, socialization, and safety from injury and falls. The parent is alerted to the need by way of the infant's most dominant communication skill, that of crying. Neurological immaturity causes her to go rapidly from 0 to 60, so to speak, as they start with a whimper and quickly accelerate to a full rage response if immediate attention is not provided. During a rage reaction all bodily systems are stimulated to the max, including cardiopulmonary, circulatory, lachrymal, neurological, and digestive. Because of the heightened reactions, fists are clenched, muscles are tight, and her entire body becomes stiff with involvement. As she wails, her little chin quivers, too.

An infant's rage reaction is Mom's invitation to join the dance. At this point in the interaction it is imperative that appropriate attention be given. It is here that the skills of the mother become apparent and if not "instinctively" present, can be learned to help their newborn. Out of concern for her infant, Mom moves in closer to her young one to give love and attention. A parent has several tools available to demonstrate love and caring. It is at this point of the cycle that mother nurtures, she touches, smiles at, feeds, cuddles, soothes, croons to, and whatever else is necessary to console her distressed baby. It is important for Mama, or the primary caretaker, to be calm and purposeful in her responses to the newborn in hopes of eliciting a like reaction from her infant. With close physical contact using warm, direct eye contact, a soothing, gentle touch, rocking to increase labyrinthine (inner ear) stimulation, intimate smiles, and the use of sweet-sugary pet names, the mother models and invites her infant to reciprocate.

The goal of an effective caretaker during the intervention in a rage reaction is to provide relief to the overwhelmed infant. Gratifying the infant's discomforts is imperative. From the first maternal actions and interactions the infant grows in its ability to trust others. The child learns to trust and depend on her parents by learning that, over time, when she is uncomfortable and overwhelmed, her trustworthy caretakers will respond to her in appropriate and predictable ways. Specifically, they will do something to make her comfortable, full, dry, safe, and relaxed. The bonding cycle must be repeated thousands of times over the first year or two of the child's life in order to reach a positive conclusion. The newborn must discover over extended time that her caretakers are going to remain attentive and reliable. Then from success with the initial lessons, that of trusting primary caretakers, the child will grow to trust limits set by those individuals. She then, ultimately, gains trust of others and then of self.

When discussing the bonding process from a historical perspective, Terry Levy, Ph.D., formerly of the Evergreen Consultants in Human Behavior, Evergreen, Colorado stated, "If you understand attachment, you understand that millions of years of evolution goes into creating attachment. This is not just a psychological phenomena, this is a physiological and biological phenomena that is rooted in literally millions of years of evolution in our species and in other species for reasons of survival." Keeping newborns close to the caregiver, he went on, "creates in the caregiver a desire to love and nurture and protect the vulnerable offspring." In evolution, Levy continued, "there's good reason to connect and stay connected—for survival." If nothing gets in the way, attachment occurs naturally as a biologically rooted, instinctual, emotional, behavioral activity between the caregiver and an infant and toddler.

Levy went on to say that it is easy to describe and identify the necessary ingredients of the bonding process. All you have to do, he said, is to find a loving, together mom who has the ability to love and care for her infant and then watch her communicate with her infant. When the pair interacts the mother is happy and has a smile on her face. "She is not," as Levy said, "thinking, 'God, I wish I weren't here, I'd rather go and drink a beer.' She's at peace with herself 'cause she's so thrilled to have this little baby in her arms." When the mother makes eye contact the baby gazes back into her eyes. Mom smiles, baby smiles back. She holds the baby in her arms, firm enough for the infant to feel comfort, strength, and the safety without frightening or startling the little one. That is the beginnings of the process of attaching to another and characterizes the rudiments of reciprocity, back and forth interaction. Levy stated, "Mother comforts, loves and nurtures the baby," satisfying their primary need. Then, Levy added, "baby responds with pleasure, relaxation, joy" and gives the same back to the mother.

Through his significant research with institutionalized newborns, Bowlby grew to believe infants' primary needs, in addition to food, was touch. In fact, when newborns or infants were fed adequate amounts, but in a perfunctory manner, they would still fail to thrive. Specifically, their growth and development were stunted, which rapidly became life threatening due to a natural lack of any reserve. His final recommendations stressed the vital importance of using what we describe, today, as bonding behaviors of touch, eye contact, smiles, rocking, and cooing.

There is an important dance that goes on between a mother and her infant. In other words, both infant and mother must participate with each other. Bowlby stated in *Attachment and Loss: Volume 1*: "Attachment behavior has been defined as seeking and maintaining proximity to another individual." He also found that children experienced detrimental immunological changes one hour after separation from the biological mother. In order to cement the attachment between two, reciprocity must occur. In a reciprocal relationship, one gives and the other receives, each taking an active part in both giving and receiving. It is important to say that those same behaviors can occur, and are still vital, between a newborn and someone other than the biological mother. The reason I refer to mother, rather than a surrogate, is that now it is believed the entire process between mother and child begins before birth. Consequently, it is believed to be possible for both attachment and attachment difficulties to start during the pre-natal period.[1] It is now believed that the first thirty-three months of life, including the usual gestational period, are the most vital in establishing that all-important connection with other people. Dr. Welch, also founder of The Mothering Center in Greenwich, Connecticut, believes our current obstetrical practices interfere with the normal, intimate connection that has already begun between mother and her child before birth.

Due to the immaturity of a newborn, it has been assumed that its mother must lead their personal dance. Professionals now believe that newborns instinctively know their own mother and are able to identify her immediately. Records tell us of many individuals who, only moments old, initiate eye contact with their mom. When the mother is not readily available, they accomplish the communication by using their vision and auditory senses to follow the sound of her voice. She can be distinguished among all others by way of the infant's senses: sight, smell, taste, and sound. Bowlby believed the biological mother and baby are programmed for each other. Interestingly, the beginnings of the development of all the sensory skills occur in utero. Levy's conclusions are

---

1. John Bowlby, M.D., *Attachment and Loss: Volume 1,* Chatto & Windus, England, 1987, 194.

similar to those of Bowlby. They agree that significant interruptions or breaks in the bonding process lead to Attachment Disorder and kids who aren't able to reciprocate, are very selfish and only know how take.

In his book Attachment and Loss, Bowlby wrote: "Though there can be no doubt that a substitute mother can behave in a completely mothering way to a child, and that many do so, it may well be less easy for a substitute mother than for a natural mother to do so. For example, knowledge of what elicits mothering behaviour in other species suggests that hormonal levels following parturition and stimuli emanation from the newborn baby himself may be of great importance."[2]

Imagine yourself, for a moment, as a totally helpless individual. You know you need help and fully realize you do not have the skills or ability necessary to care for yourself. So, you hire assistance, two people who you need to be responsible. Georgia Sweetness always arrives on time, makes your meals, cleans your house, fluffs and primps you, and stays long enough to make sure you're safe, clean, and satisfied. Donetta Dimms comes late, is more interested in her social life or her own needs than in caring for yours. She sometimes does great work by making you an occasional gourmet meal or giving you a pedicure. Which one would you re-hire? Which one would you trust? Who would it be foolish of you to depend on? These questions are at the very heart of attachment problems.

It has always amazed me how astute newborns and infants are. I think they give their parents and caretakers ample chances to do right by them. According to Bowlby, if their needs are being ignored, infants redouble their efforts to get the needed attention. However, when met with the frustration or pain of isolation enough times, some wee ones eventually give up. Those individuals conclude, on some visceral level, that they are "on their own." Because of the seriousness of the bonding

2. John Bowlby, M.D., *Attachment and Loss; Volume 1,* Chatto & Windus, England, 1987, 306.

interruptions, the child has a choice, albeit an unconscious one: to live or to die. As far back as fifty years ago Bowlby described those who chose death, they just did not have the strength to go on. For some intrinsic reason, however, there are those who have the strength to choose life.

For those of you who are already parents, think of the time and energy required in attempting to meet the needs of your newborn or infant. I say attempting because, as you already know, life with all its surprises may interfere in your efforts. What happens if you are exhausted at the same time baby needs changing, again? Or what if you are trying to maintain wonderful eye contact, but can't because you've got the blues, your hormonal level is dropping dramatically, and you can't catch your breath or quit crying? How are you to meet their needs if the dog was just run over by a passing pickup? That's what I mean—life, just life. I believe that is why a Higher Source gives us thousands of chances to get it right. There are bound to be many attempts where our intentions are good but we just can't make the mark. I do not want to appear flippant or insincere. However, I am concerned that overanxious and overly responsible parents may be too worried to relax, to enjoy their new one, and do what may (or may not) come naturally. I also think that a missed chance to bond or attach can be absorbed into a child's psyche. The problem occurs when there are too many missed opportunities. Inadequate skills and a lack of interest in the infant, with all that entails, can cause lifelong attachment problems. When primary caretakers, mother or other, don't meet, or inconsistently meet, the needs of the infant, then the ability infants to consistently depend on her caretakers is compromised. Her ultimate ability to trust others may be damaged.

Those with incomparable fortitude to remain alive are the story, are the plot of *Broken Spirits ~ Lost Souls*. Although very much alive, they are tough, doggedly determined, independent, untrusting, and hard to love. Society may see them as charming, troubled, loners, "perfectly normal," or alienated. Such are the kids with attachment issues, at least, or with a full-blown Reactive Attachment Disorder, at worst.

CHAPTER TWO—
What is Attachment Disorder?

"Stevie had a skateboard. The woman across the street said she used to see him sitting on the front steps on the house, sucking his thumb. She said he seemed meek, perhaps 'immature' for his age." During the two-year period which preceded the murder the relationships between Stevie and his neighbors deteriorated significantly. One neighbor believed he was this same child who was committing petty thefts in the area, stealing milk, and the like. Another neighbor also reported, "Once Stevie threw a cupful of feces out of his upstairs window on to the side of his neighbor's house. Then, too, the boys would set little fires in the backyard." The local pub owner reported that the mother spent time at the pub at least part of each day until the birth of her youngest son. Stevie was memorable because, as the pub owner said, "He was a cheeky little bastard. He called my wife a 'slag'(a street term for a slut)."[1] One can only guess at what was happening in the lives of the members of Stevie's family. Or to Stevie. A woman who lived across the street remembered that on the previous Friday night Stevie was pounding loudly on his own front door yelling, hoping to be let in. No one responded to his pleas.

In the Los Angeles Times feature above the Charles T. Powers article boldly stated: "10-Year-Olds as Murderers: an Angry City Ponders the Horror." The subtitle screamed, "Britain: Death of child shocked the nation. But a look at the lives of the suspects suggests what happened in

1. Charles T. Powers, "10-years olds as Murderers: an Angry City Ponders the Horror", *The Los Angeles Times,* (Mar 2 1993): A4, Col. 1.

Liverpool could have happened anywhere." At 2 ½ years old Jamie Bulger met his end when other youngsters charmed him away from his mother at a local mall, walked him two miles away, tortured, and then killed him. Then little Jamie's body was left on the railroad tracks to be run over by an oncoming train. Powers stated, "There were two of them, actually, both 10, and Liverpool might well have lynched them, or stoned them to death, had it been given the chance, for their crime shocked the city and all of Britain." Upon closer examination of the life of one of the boys called "Stevie" came clues, hints to the reader about the quality of his short life. "He is one of seven children, all boys, ranging in age from 19 to about 9 months." They lived with their thirty-eight year old, divorced mother, who mostly lived on welfare.

The idea that a word as emotionally laden and ugly as murderer might be used to describe a European or an American child of today is beyond repugnant. That any of our little ones could ever be as sick or as calculating as the youngsters described above, terms normally saved for hardened criminals, is truly unimaginable. Such a concept, and worse yet—the reality—is indicative of a terrible problem deep within the core of our family structure. During a recent conversation, a friend stated she has looked into the eyes of young sexual predators and concluded that, in most cases, "No one was home." Missing was that indefinable connection which happens when two people are able to touch each other at a deep level or share heart-to-heart. Similarly, when you look deeply into the eyes of a child with Reactive Attachment Disorder you sense, or maybe feel, the absence of some vital quality. There is some necessary element that gives us our humanness and our ability to care for others, an ingredient that seems to be absent in the likes of the predators above.

Beryl Davis, Ph.D., of The Attachment Center in Atascadero, California stated that she believes that professionals working in the area of attachments need to clearly define Attachment Disorder. Currently, she said, it is possible to identify the symptoms but there is not yet a viable working definition of the malady. That, according to the experienced professional, hinders the educational process and ultimately interferes with providing an accurate diagnosis or appropriate treatment in a consistent and timely manner. Davis believes the window of opportunity for maximum outcomes is almost frighteningly narrow and without clear diagnostic criteria the already difficult job could be nearly impossible. In 2002 many professionals are still attempting to define and understand the disorder; often, it is not yet recognized.

According to the professionals at ACE, the pioneer of therapy programs for children with such problems, they believe that the brain of someone with attachment difficulties is significantly different from that of a "normal" child. Their extreme and extraordinary behaviors reflect the differences present in their thinking patterns. Anyone who thinks in an expected fashion would not respond or react to his/her surroundings in exactly the same way as do RAD kids. Pickle, of Evergreen, Colorado gave a clear explanation about the neurodevelopment of the brain in the ACE Autumn 1998 publication. It stated: "The connections (known as neural pathways) that are made depend upon the input the brain receives from the environment. The brain's task is to develop an internal process for receiving, interpreting, categorizing, storing and utilizing information. It is easy to understand how early abuse, neglect, abandonment, unrelieved pain, or other traumatic events can create pathways that have life long consequences for a child." A youngster whose neurological connections to the brain are intact would probably not go on a four to six hour rampage because they've been directed to get ready for school. Usual and predictable changes in a daily routine would probably not throw them into a destructive, out-of-control tizzy.

Although it has been identified in the literature as a severe disorder, RAD is still considered to be rare. However, I believe the statistics sited in the DSM-IV fall short. Attachment expert Martha Welch, agrees. She believes all adopted and all foster children have some level of attachment disturbance. No statistics are available venturing a guess at to the numbers of affected children who remain in their birth homes. Some literature estimates that perhaps eighty percent of mistreated infants have severe attachment difficulties. Sheila Fearnley, Co-Founder and Clinical Director of Keys Attachment Center in Leicestershire, England works with adult populations and told me she believes perhaps as many as half of all incarcerated adults display some form of mental/emotional illness due to attachment interruptions in childhood. More recent research has me convinced that the above estimates are out-of-date and significantly low.

Recently my daughter-in-law sent me an e-mail photo of a surgeon performing a life saving operation on a yet to-be-born fetus. The most amazing detail of the photograph was a minute area which showed the unborn child's underdeveloped hand tightly grasping the gloved finger of the surgeon. When I think about the strength of that infant's desire and the corresponding drive to affiliate with another human, I'm overwhelmed with awe and reduced to tears. Levy told me that after copious research we know a significant amount about infants before they are born. Modern tools and research approaches allow us to know volumes about developing babies. We do know, according to Levy, "that babies developing in the womb are quite responsive to their environment," as demonstrated by the wee one from the photo. They know about "sounds, stimulation, touch, conflict, violence. They're picking it all up biochemically through the bloodstream and nourishment of the mother." Anxiety, he reported, is biochemical and well as an emotional stimulus and, therefore, detectable by unborn babies. Physicians have also known for a long time that expectant mothers who are unsupported and isolated have more difficult pregnancies and deliveries. Levy shared that several years ago there was a Canadian study involving pregnant mothers who did not want their babies. Years later, he continued, their babies demonstrated more illness or pathology and more psychological and social problems than any other group of children, regardless of what was going on in their lives. What Levy believes the studies tell us is that attachment problems are "a family systemic phenomenon. It's not just between a caregiver and an offspring; it's between the relationship or the matrix of relationships in the lives of a family." It appears that a series of successful familial relationships in a mother's life can contribute to successful bonding and attachment with her child. A series of unsuccessful ones, however, can spell disaster.

We also know that Attachment Disorder is a relationship problem. Because of missing ingredients from their earliest existences, attachment disturbed children are unable to care sincerely and deeply about others or to live harmoniously with them. They are continuously hyper-alert, terrified of others, and unable to trust the promise of tomorrow or of their own personal safety. AD kids are prepared to do unto others before others get the chance to first do unto them. Perhaps the existence of a soul and all that entails remains debatable to some. However, my belief is that an Ultimate Power breathes a soul (life, spirit, or the like) into the life of a child upon conception. We, as the earthly gatekeepers, have unwittingly neglected our duties. It is the human intervention and the lack of appropriate human nurturing behaviors that causes irreparable damage to a fragile entity such as a developing fetus or newborn child.

It is understood among doctors and therapists that each developmental stage holds important work that must be completed, without which normal maturation cannot occur. Specifically, it is only when the issues are resolved and the skills are learned in the first stage of development that an infant can move on to the next stage of its development. When the infant is physically nourished, his/her body grows. But it is only with emotional and psychological nurturing that children acquire appropriate and adequate developmental growth. Janelle Petersen, RN, in *The Invisible Road: Parental Insights to Attachment Disorder* states, "...and lack of foundation results in no base for the establishment of a desire to explore their world and develop satisfaction in a sense of mastery." In the stories which follow you will repeatedly read about children who seemed to remain stuck in an earlier development stage—children of 10, for example, who have the behaviors of an infant stuck in a rage reaction. Without trust no infant or child will mature normally. They cannot; the work of the first stage of life has been left unfinished. The ultimate goals of the bonding process and the work of the first year are to develop an ability to trust others.[2]

The Symptoms

Not all attachment-disordered children exhibit all of the symptoms below, as behaviors appear in degrees, mild to severe, from those with the mildest attachment issues to youngsters with the most severe form of RAD. It is believed that the earlier the symptoms appear, the more severe the illness. The total numbers of symptoms out of the lot and the degree to which they exist are also important indicators of the overall severity of the problem. Reminder: unless you are a M.D. with experience in child psychiatry, you should not diagnose your own child. The reader must be cautioned that there are many children who are not just purely attachment disordered. RAD in and of itself is a complicated disorder, a combination of many symptoms or dysfunctional behaviors. Many youngsters have a complicated combination of attachment difficulties plus other psychological/psychiatric, neurological, and/or biological difficulties. Under any circumstances children with problems of this nature need to be thoroughly evaluated by professionals who have received specialized training, and whose practice focuses on attachment problems and attachment therapy. The following is the list of symptoms used in diagnosing Reactive Attachment Disorder:

Extreme control problems—Often these behaviors manifest themselves in covert, subtle, or sneaky ways. The child may appear, on the

---

2. Janelle Petersen, *The Invisible Road: Parental Insights to Attachment Disorder*, 2.

face of it, to be cooperating with rules or parents' instructions. The child will do anything—dawdling, crying, starting fights, playing sick, etc.—to get own way. The child will express affection, but only on his/her terms. Parents experience frustration, as their inner belief is that the child is intentionally sabotaging the activity. This is a continuous struggle and tends to take the enjoyment out of events.

Lacks ability to give and receive affection—Affected infants are not cuddly; backs arch or they become stiff when hugged or cuddled. Children seem to actively move away from human touch. As an older child he/she lacks ability to give reciprocal attention or affection. There is a phony flavor to affectionate gestures. Child appears stingy with time, belongings, or affection.

Superficially charming and emotionally phony—Uses both verbal and nonverbal cues to get his/her own way. Many are indiscriminately affectionate with strangers and use their cute and flirtatious manner to manipulate others. Can go so far as to lie outright to get the sympathy of strangers. They can rapidly turn into what I call, "all dimples and eyelashes"—full of bright smiles and batting eyes. Most children lack a genuine sincerity in their affectionate gestures. Their behavior and the emotional content are incongruent: while they are buttering you up they, simultaneously, leave you cold.

Crazy lying—Also called "primary process lying" which means lying in the face of the truth. Normal lying done by children is meant to protect or keep them out of trouble. Crazy lying is lying just for the sake or fun of it. There is no purpose to it; it defies truth as you have witnessed it. Primary process lying is a chronic problem and makes no sense to the parents. The children don't take responsibility for their dishonesty.

Stealing—This is usually a chronic and common problem and the children are generally sneaky and seldom actually get caught in the act. Rarely, if ever, do the youngsters actually own up to dishonest deeds. Money is common, as well as other personal items that hold no value except have special sentimental or emotional meaning, particularly to the mother and siblings.

Enuresis—Urinating in inappropriate places after age of toilet training. This is different than having "an accident" in the daytime or at night. In this case the child consciously urinates on floors, into beds (sometimes someone else's), on another's clothing, and the like. Many children can control the amount voided in an effort to avoid detection; however, the foul smell gives them away.

Encopresis—Defecating in inappropriate places once bowel training has been accomplished. Children who display this symptom usually leave "calling cards," the smearing of feces on walls and floors is common. Using feces as a weapon, as a way of getting revenge for real or imagined slights, is not unusual. The children do not take responsibility for this activity.

Eating abnormalities—It is common for RAD children to demonstrate a wide variety of eating difficulties. A list of common behaviors are: refusing to eat at mealtime; inability to chew or excessive drooling due to lack of swallowing; stealing and hoarding (hiding) food in their cheeks, in their rooms or other hiding places; gorging large amounts of food, possibly followed by vomiting.

Lack of eye contact—During important exchanges their eye contact is either fleeting or wandering. There are two notable exceptions: when the child is lying or wants something and attempting to manipulate, so their gaze is sure and steady; "The Look," known to parents of rageful

AD children, is a cold, dead-eyed stare that is both intimidating and frightening.

Extraordinary rage with poor impulse control—Those who demonstrate their rage overtly tend to have temper tantrums well beyond the second year of life so it is no secret that they are angry. Those whose anger has gone underground, who express their rage covertly, are no easier to live with, as their rage is expressed in hundreds of mean and sneaky ways. The children demonstrate a diminished capacity to think through behavioral choices before acting, many times causing them to automatically act in mean and hurtful ways. They tend to initiate and/or participate in risky and dangerous behaviors.

Destructive to self and others—The children make threats of potential harm to self and others, and many times actually carry them out. They seem to have none of the usual internal controls so will go to any length to control others or the situation. Those who intentionally hurt themselves are able to tolerate unusual amounts of pain. Many children sexually abuse siblings and others who they perceive as vulnerable.

Destruction of property—The children have a common history of breaking their own belongings and those of others as well, including tearing holes in new clothing and shoes. Damaging others' personal belongings seems to be a common way of getting revenge, as well. RAD children seem to derive pleasure and sometimes more energy from destructive behaviors.

Learning problems and developmental delays—Intellectual and emotional lags are prominent and vary in severity depending upon the trauma the child has survived. Although many RAD children test high on IQ scales, they are traditionally underachievers due to their acting out in school. Emotionally, many are 'stuck' at the age of the traumatic experience and lag behind those of his/her age peers. Sensory integration problems, involving balance, coordination, and tactile hypersensitivity or insensitivity are also being noticed.

Lacking cause-and-effect thinking—RAD children do not learn vicariously as they lack the ability to learn from their own mistakes. They seem to be "wired" differently; consequently, behavioral consequences usually effective for "normal" children are totally ineffectual with these children. Parents are unable to find a system using consequences that works for these children.

Lack conscience and remorse—The child displays an alarming absence of empathy, a trait necessary to engender restraint of negative behaviors displayed toward others. No remorse for harmful deeds is witnessed, and occasionally pleasure appears to be derived from hurtful acts committed toward others.

Poor peer relations, cruelty to to others and animals—Either the child has no friends or changes friends frequently. AD children are not well liked, probably due to their dishonest, mean, and "me first" approach to relationships. Their unpleasant behaviors are not reserved for those younger or smaller, but weaker individuals are especially vulnerable. Whatever friendships do exist tend to be superficial in nature. The children tend to be mean to people and animals and that, combined with their need to control others, leaves them unlikable to most children and animals.

Preoccupied with fire, death, blood, and gore—Many children are drawn to fires and may use excuses to get closer to a fire, light matches and the like. When fires are set they tend to be "controlled" and lit in and around the home. The message behind the fire setting: 'I will do this whenever or wherever I want.' They are also very interested in bloody, morbid, graphic movies, in road kill, and the like. Many attempt to engage parents in discussions of the minutest details about the dying process and death.

Incessant chatter and/or clingy—Constant verbalizations, asking persistent, nonsensical questions can be a way of manipulating others or maintaining control over the situation which forces the parent to give them undivided attention. The clinging is different than what is expected in a healthy child experiencing normal separation anxiety. RAD children can be demanding, needy, with in-your-face behaviors that are inappropriate for the age or developmental stage of the individual child. Often families grow to resent such behaviors as they prevent others from getting their needs met.

Abnormal speech patterns—As language skills can be delayed or lag behind age peers many children speak baby talk, in half sentences, or so softly they cannot be heard. There is one exception: when children are angry they can be heard and understood, as any previous language problems are suddenly absent.

Parents appear unusually angry and hostile—Mental illness in a child causes strong feelings in parents, with the more usual responses of sadness and worry. A RAD child is different due to the absence of the ability to trust others, but especially parents. Consequently, when a parent becomes the child's scapegoat he/she must protect him/herself from the child, provoking feelings of anger and fear.

Dr. Davis of Atascadero stated, "I think the defining factor on whether a child has Reactive Attachment Disorder is the level of anger of the parents. That is what these kids can do to their parents better than anybody." Davis said she raised two severely learning disabled kids and experienced much concern around their issues. But, the experienced mother said,

"We were going through it together and I was frustrated in pain for them. We were struggling, but it wasn't that deliberate pushing away" as seen in youngsters with attachment difficulties.

Causes of Attachment Difficulties

Fortunately, today there are more professionals than ever before who are considered experts in the field of Attachment Disorders. Until his retirement a few years ago, Dr. Foster Cline first worked with children at the Youth Behavior Program which evolved into ACE in Colorado. For well over thirty years Cline has remained a leader in the field and has braved skeptical attitudes of professionals and abundant negative public opinion. The diagnosis and treatment of such psychopathic-like children has always been highly controversial and, unfortunately, remains so. Hopefully, the situation is currently evolving, as now there are more professionals aware and available to the children.

The care of newborns and children can be normally overwhelming, but worse if complications arise. Some of the obstacles to bonding and attachment, which may contribute to the development to attachment difficulties, follow. Certainly some astute professionals are able to identify high-risk children but we do not yet know the exact combination needed to create disturbed children. Bowlby asserts that some children, in the absence of loving adults, attach to each other. During the interviews with parents from North America and the UK I learned many had adopted biological sibling groups. When more than one child of the group was diagnosed with RAD, it seemed the oldest, which the youngest often clung to, was usually the most seriously disturbed. Others, it seemed were born with a certain essence, perhaps spiritual in nature, that protected them from serious harm. Some kids who have spent part of their life in hell do grow to be loving, empathetic adults. I believe there is a powerful internal ingredient we cannot touch. Maybe, it is one of the still unexplained mysteries of life.

Early Parenting Interruptions or Separations

I would like to describe to you what I call the "Geranium Theory" of rooting, or attaching, in human terms. I do not wish to insult your intelligence, but this analogy (not originally mine) was enormously helpful to me in the past. Imagine a new geranium sprout in a small plastic pot. As the plant gets adequate sun and water, it grows and develops into a more mature plant. Under optimum conditions and exceptional growth repotting would eventually be required. When the geranium is removed from its pot, the health and development of the root system needs to be examined. Healthy plants should have a flourishing taproot with plenty of collateral circulation with multiple, small, minor roots; only then is it safe to carefully trim before repotting. If the geranium is transplanted too soon or has its roots trimmed prematurely, the plant will wither due to shock and eventually die.

Children and geraniums have something in common: their roots. If children remain in a home that nourishes their spirit and meets their physical and emotional needs they can flourish. But if the bonding process is interrupted prematurely, their root system will be disturbed. No one knows how many interruptions a child's spirit can tolerate before permanent damage occurs. Once a child has adequately attached to one loving caretaker, even someone unrelated by blood, he or she could then be successfully moved into another family, if such an event is necessary. This is a quite simplified version, but the basic ingredients are present. With that in mind, it might be easy to understand why the following incidents might cause further damage to an already compromised ability to trust safety or permanence.

Multiple foster placements—"breaking in" a new child, as I call it, is very exciting but can also cause enormous strain on the children and their new family. With serial placements, as soon as a child begins to feel a part of the family, it would be time to change homes again. Any child with any internal strength would eventually stop trying to settle into a new family because he knows it is only temporary and futile. Beverly

James, a therapist from Hawai'i, noticed another related problem in the 80's. Some foster parents eventually could not tolerate continually giving and giving to temporary foster children while getting nothing back, emotionally. And, sometimes the parents just gave up.

Failed adoptions—these can occur due to problems of the child or of other family members. Illnesses of other family members or divorces between parents can have devastating effects on all the members, but that is especially true of foster or adopted children.

Lack of parental support—increases the 'failure ratio' with kids. Pregnant women who have been rejected by family or society have an enormous burden to carry alone, that of remaining healthy and emotionally balanced during the pregnancy. Overwhelmed or ill parents are also not able to provide optimal parenting. With the increase in single parenting and decrease in extended families, high-risk children are more plentiful and more vulnerable.

Successful adoption after several foster temporary placements—a frequently transplanted child can become used to frequent moves, which can provide emotional distance from others, which they grow to prefer. Suddenly staying put with one family, coupled with the usual expectations of developing emotional ties, can be terrifying to a distrusting child.

National and International foster and adoption policies—below are two elementary examples of how foster and adoption policies can, unwittingly, lead to psychological breaks in a child's life:

Several years ago the foster system utilized by the State of Nebraska functioned as such: The Department of Human Services had identified certain families who cared for newborns well; some who were suited for infants or toddlers; and others who were especially adept with school-aged children. The State's ultimate goal was reunification of mothers and children so they intentionally interrupted the bonding process of children with the temporary foster parents. If an infant stayed in the foster system into or past pre-school, for example, he/she was moved to another foster home. Each move was for the satisfaction of the system and not designed to meet the bonding needs of the youngster. Consequently, every move rendered the child more harmed and eventually unreachable. Simultaneously, foster moms were distraught about severe behavioral and emotional problems they were seeing with their children. They didn't know the cause of such behaviors, and neither did agency social workers. Unfortunately, the State of Nebraska believed they were doing right by the children.

Sheila Fearnley stated, "Our practice here in Britain is if placement breaks down you put the child in a new family. So, consequently, you would have children as young as six or seven or ten or eleven with something like ten or fifteen placements. One 13-year-old boy I saw had fifty-seven moves and they were saying he's got an attachment problem. I was saying, 'Good, because that tells me he's healthy—he needs to have an attachment problem. He's moved so many times that attachments don't mean anything to him so he can't learn how to stay put.'"

Neglect and Abuse

Neglect—is severely detrimental to the child if it occurs during the first years of life. Evidence indicates neglect is ultimately more harmful than any other type of abuse. Neglect has a global effect on a child, that of negating their very existence. The long-term affects make a child believe that they and their needs are unimportant; they grow to believe they have no value at all.

Physical or sexual abuse—especially that which occurs within the first few years of life. No matter who the abuser, the child learns he/she cannot depend on parents for personal safety. A child believes it is mother's job to protect her young. Consequently, the child blames the mother figure for harm that befalls him/her.

It is important to state that not all children who suffer abuse experience overwhelming blows to their spirit. One notable exception was Anthony Godby Johnson. Tony was an unfortunate boy who grew up in

New York City, the only child of severely abusive parents. At 11 he had already had enough and was actively planning his own demise. Because of the depth of his despair, Tony fleetingly reached out for help and was caught by three loving adults. At fourteen Johnson wrote *A Rock and a Hard Place: Once Boy's Triumphant Story*, a book about his life. It is a true and touching account of a teenager's successful attempt to reclaim his life and the love he deserved. Sadly, Tony is no longer with us as he succumbed to AIDS at the age of 15, the result of repeated sexual assault by his parents' cohorts, but not until after winning his freedom from the deadly grasp of abuse.

Multiple caregivers—frequent moves during the first year or two of life spells automatic inconsistency in meeting the child's needs. Consistently good care, even consistently bad caretaking, does not have the same negative effects as does unpredictable, inconsistent care on the development of the individual.

After years of experience with adoptions, Lori Hunstad, a MSW, LCSW, from San Luis Obispo County, California noticed that children with the most difficult adjustments to family life were those who had been physically neglected and emotionally abused. According to Lori, kids who'd been removed from their homes on the heels of physical and/or sexual abused alone "seemed to function and fare fairly well." Hunstad added that most of the adjustments of abused children were smoother and more successful in tandem with good individual counseling. However, those with the most difficulty were those youngsters who experienced, "pervasive neglect with frequent moves; children left with numbers of relatives or friends." According to Ms. Hunstad, the situations where "mom goes out for a pack of cigarettes and comes back a week later" were ultimately the most damaging to the children.

Emotional Sources of Conflict

Prenatal influences—In *The Invisible Road*, Janelle Petersen wrote, "Denial of a pregnancy or rejection of the child even from the time in the womb are currently believed strong factors that result in Attachment Disorders." Maternal ambivalence toward the fetus or pregnancy can have overwhelming effects on the newborn. Immaturity of the mother, as can be found among young teens, is also a significant factor. Petersen went on to say, "Parents who have suffered frustration, verbal and physical assaults, acts of random aggression, embarrassment, and a sense of failure need strong support to overcome the problems they face."[3]

Prenatal trauma—attempts to abort a fetus prior to birth or a mother who is physically abused during pregnancy can be a source of trauma to the fetus. Due to the emotional and biochemical interconnections of mother and fetus, strong, overwhelming feelings in the mother are transmitted to the child growing in her womb, both loving feelings and those of ambivalence.

Mixed messages given by caretakers—also called approach/avoidance. Translated, they are messages that subtly tell children "come here—go away," or "I love you—I don't think I love you." Both are very confusing as youngsters are not able to interpret the true message and wonders, do they want me or love me or not? The question rarely gets answered in a positive way.

Poor parenting skills—especially within the first year to two of life. We tend to use parenting skills observed in our birth family, but not all were healthy or effective. One does not generally know one's own skills are defective until they are unsuccessful in producing the behaviors or outcomes we desire in our offspring.

Emotionally unavailable mother—it is possible for a mother person to be physically present for her child, but distracted and unable to identify or care for the emotional needs of her infant. This can include a

3. Janelle Petersen, RN, *The Invisible Road: Parental Insights to Attachment Disorder;* 3.

range of parental behaviors from frankly absent to perfunctory or mechanical parenting, which can be experienced as negligent or abusive by the growing child.

False Self-esteem—which is inflated or artificial, can be a set-up for future difficulties. The following example illuminates an important new finding:

Author Sharon Begley wrote in a July, 98 Newsweek article entitled, "You're OK, I'm Terrific: Self-Esteem Backfires," that when self-esteem is imposed on a child, given to them by a parent, for example, the desired effect—an internal sense of value—is not created. What it actually created in young ones was more shame, more anger, feelings that were ultimately acted out aggressively toward others. In that same article Brad Bushman, Ph.D., of Iowa State University agreed that when kids develop unrealistic opinions of themselves, a view rejected by others, the children could be potentially violent. According to psychologist Bushman's definition of narcissism, "High self-esteem that is unjustified and unstable..." can also be the cause of a dangerous outburst. He believes that the, that narcissists "are superstitious to criticism or slights because deep down they suspect that their feeling of superiority is built on quicksand." Bushman believes that is what happened in the case of Luke Woodham, the adolescent murderer from Pearl, Mississippi. Woodham killed his mother in cold blood as well as two students from this Gulf coast region. Woodham did not have a typical background of abuse common to other young murderers.[4]

Often parents believe they can instill a sense of self worth in their offspring by dressing them nicely or by just saying they are worthwhile. I've overheard counselors tell their clients that their self-esteem must come from those around them. If that is the case, what happens when those esteem-providers are too busy to shore up the child's flimsy

---

4. Sharon Begley, "You're OK, I'm Terrific: Self-Esteem Backfires", *Newsweek* (July 13, 1998): 69.

underpinnings? What if the winds carrying compliments change direction or find another mark? When a child is given a gift they feel is not deserved it must be destroyed. In addition, children who do not believe compliments also do not believe, or respect, the person giving the compliment. Children ultimately believe their own perception and decide the other is lying. Similarly, when an adult is given a compliment they feel is undeserved, they just don't accept it. (What, this old rag?) Think about the last Christmas that you gave your child too much. How did they act: loving and grateful or like a spoiled brat? Or were they quiet (and overwhelmed) while they played with the wrappings those beautiful things came in? Well-adjusted children can be loving and gracious at gift-getting time, as they believe deep inside they are worthy of nice things. On the other hand, if that place deep inside is empty or full of rage the child will be unable to fake a deserving exterior. True positive self-esteem comes from committing routine esteem enhancing acts, from living and doing the next right thing.

Medical, Chemical, and Neurological Influences

Severe, undetected or unrelieved pain—such as multiple untreated ear infections. Resolution of the bonding process requires that the infant receive consolation from the nurturing events involved in the bonding process. If a baby has an unidentified medical problem, one that causes unrelenting pain, the satisfaction phase can be compromised.

Hospitalizations during the first year—Many current medical treatments and techniques cause discomfort and pain. Many newborns that remain in intensive care units cannot be held or cuddled, as they require. Consequently, they do not receive the tactile or vestibular stimulation needed for their emotional health. In the old days mothers were not allowed to touch their ailing newborn, interrupting the life-giving process for both mother and child.

Hospitalization of the mother or primary caretaker—Many mothers experience post-partal depression sometimes requiring an untimely hospitalization. Mothers and their newborns belong together, and need to be together for the physical and emotional health of both. Separations of the bonding pair can cause permanent damage by an interruption of meeting the needs of infant and mom.

Prematurity and/or Neurological damage—birth trauma can be caused by a multitude of occurrences. Each assault, whether naturally, medically, or drug induced, can interfere with bonding and cause significant developmental or emotional delays in children. Many premature newborns spend countless hours in intensive care units unable to be touched or stimulated due to the inability of their immature nervous systems to handle the physical contact. It is difficult to imagine that such isolation, though it might make good medical sense, would not have long term negative influences on the emotional development of such a youngster.

Maternal drug and alcohol abuse—there is sufficient evidence to prove illicit drugs and other drugs of abuse, including and especially alcohol, cross the placental barrier and affect the unborn fetus. Some drugs cause cellular and organic damage in the developing embryo. Not all damage is as recognizable as Fetal Alcohol Syndrome (FAS) or Fetal Alcohol Effects (FAE). Fetuses, upon receiving its first drug, even in utero, may need to go through withdrawal at birth. The toll that such an ordeal causes a newborn is not yet fully known, but disturbances in the delicate neurochemical system, neuro pathways, and brain enzymes must occur. Developing fetuses and newborns are especially vulnerable to imbalances—chemical, fluid and electrolyte—some that could be permanent. After fifteen years of working with addicted adults I now believe pre-natal alcohol and drug exposure is a set-up for an addiction later in life. "Drug babies," those infants who are born demonstrating the signs and symptoms of drug withdrawal, have been on the rise over the past two decades. An inordinate number of the children who were involved (by proxy) in my international study were reportedly "drug babies," the offspring of mothers who abused crack cocaine, heroin, methamphetamine, and alcohol.

Welch, *Holding Time* author, told me that RAD children seem to have a continuous "...alarm reaction with constant adrenaline spurts..." as a result of early trauma. That, she said, "Sets off a stress hormone, which leads to a fight or flight response, overreaction and more misbehavior." Welch also stated the undoing of the youngsters hyperactive stress reaction is a major undertaking in a therapeutic setting.

Lack of vestibular stimulation—also known as labyrinthine stimulation, has to do with the movement of fluids in the inner ear, and can ultimately effect a person's balance. Many of the adoptive parents reported that their children were having sensory integration problems probably due to a lack of vestibular stimulation. That condition manifests itself in balance difficulties with frequent falling, clumsiness, and an aversion to human touch. The families reporting such findings had adopted older children who had languished for years in foreign orphanages. It seems they were typical cases of too little labyrinthine stimulation.

Sheila Fearnley, now a doctoral candidate is the mother of ten, four of whom are attachment disordered. Keys Consultancy Attachment Center was founded out of deep concern for her AD children and others like them. During our interview Fearnley stated, "I've changed from being straightforward and concerned only with developmental issues to now wanting to understand all the neurological issues. I'm beginning to see that some of the children have got some problems via their trauma. Therefore, their relationships are affected greatly as are their perceptions of the world. I believe there may be some neurological evidence that may help us understand these kids more."

Genetics and Heredity

I would like to take a few minutes to discuss the influence of genetics. After living with attachment disturbed children for so many years I have had a strong notion that genetics have played a large part in the lives I've watched unfold. I've had two experiences in my life that reminds me of the presence of hidden influences. I'd like to share those incidents with you:

Many years ago I was married to a man who demonstrated some unique characteristics. One day, on the way to a friend's home, my husband decided it was time to service the family car. As I waited in the passengers' seat of the car I observed his actions. While he used his right hand to wash the windshield his left rested on the hood of the car. The resting hand was poised in a position that I recognized as his "trademark" gesture, of sorts. Twenty years later I was, again, in the passenger seat, parked at a local gas station observing a man cleaning the windshield. Only this time it was not my husband, but our son who was servicing the auto. Dominic was using the squeegee with his right hand while his left remained at rest. I discovered that our biological son's hand position was identical to that of his father so many years before.

I'd made it my business to keep up with my children's tastes. I thought a good mother knew her kids' likes and dislikes, and what they thought was "cool." I am certain that Dominic would not have wanted to emulate his dad's hand gestures—if in fact he'd ever even noticed them. We divorced when Dominic was 2 so he hadn't spent each day with his dad. I don't believe his fathers' presence or absence had any influence on the resting position of our son's hands. So, I'd concluded my son's hand gestures were a sign of his genetic inheritance; that is the only explanation that makes sense. And if that is true—that there is a gene that can influence small insignificant bodily movements—what about the big things? What is the possibility of transmitting of personality traits via genetic codes? Couldn't temperament be inherited? Perhaps certain genes can predispose an individual to anxiety or even antisocial behaviors. I believe a small microscopic gene can, and does, influence the quality of a person's life in significant, and perhaps hidden ways. If I were a geneticist I might already know the answers to the questions above. However, I am not, so at this juncture I can only pose questions.

Matt H. is a successful physician's assistant living in San Luis Obispo with his wife, Catherine, and fourteen-year-old adopted son Bob. After seven years of abuse and neglect at the hands of his biological mother and California's Family and Social Services Department, Bob was placed with Catherine and Matt. Initially they were given very little information regarding Bob's past history. They had no idea what to expect of Bob's behaviors but have experienced the worst. He has lied to them, stolen from them, and threatened to hurt and kill them, typical behaviors of a child with an attachment disorder. Matt and Catherine lived with Bob for about six years, unsuccessfully going from therapist to therapist, before learning of this diagnosis. Eventually, they were informed that Bob's biological father was in prison and had been diagnosed with having an antisocial personality disorder of his own. The father's track record indicates the possibility of having psychopathic characteristics. Perhaps that apple didn't fall so far from that parental tree.

On the cover of their new book *Can This Child Be Saved?* Foster Cline and Cathy Helding stated: "Genetics plays a stronger role in certain types of behaviors than was once thought, and certainly a stronger role than most adoptive parents can feel easy about accepting. Denying this role is a mistake many families make and later regret."[5]

Types of Attachments

While working with families and their children with attachment difficulties, Psychiatrist Welch determined there are four basic types of attachments: secure, resistant, avoidant, and disorganized. Individuals

---

5. Foster W. Cline, M.D. and Cathy Helding, *Can This Child Be Saved?,* World Enterprises, LCC, City Desktop Productions, Inc., Franksville, WI, 1999, cover.

with secure attachments are able to experience the safety and joys offered in relationships and have the ability to trust. Children with a resistant type of attachment can be aggressive, have difficulty following rules, and actively fight any attempts to become emotionally close to others. Those who are avoidant tend to be withdrawn and maintain their emotional distance with others by remaining maddeningly passive. Disorganized attachments are characterized by behaviors and approaches utilized in an unpredictable combination of the first three. As with AD kids, it is apparent that autistic children are detached from people. Welch espouses the belief that autism is an attachment problem. It is also possible, Welch stated, that current behavioral problems such as conduct disorders, ADHD or ADD, either coexist with or are variations of attachment disorders.

The United Kingdom's Fearnley looks at the types a bit differently and stated, "There two types of attachments, indiscriminate and over-discriminate attachments. Indiscriminate are the kind of child that will be over-socialized, who will go to everyone and who don't seem to have any boundaries or stranger-fear. The over-discriminate type is when a child is very withdrawn, fearful of everyone. Not all RAD children are overtly destructive. Instead, some approach the world withdrawn, unable to communicate, with no ability or available skills to form relationships." The type of attachments can be determined by the behaviors demonstrated by each individual child.

Pickle, of ACE, discussed the growing numbers of children with Attachment Disorders. Pickle stated that she believes there's a dramatic rise in the frequency of this disturbing problem. "There's definitely an increase in child abuse in our country; I don't think it's just an increase in reporting." She is aware that the number of children who end up in an already overburdened foster care system is burgeoning, a system, the professional stated, which "is totally inadequate to meet the needs of these children." Pickle shared that in her estimation there are no mean-spirited persons among caseworkers, just individuals who have been overwhelmed by the sheer numbers of available children. Levy of Colorado, agreed. In his experience foster parents are overburdened, and, "They don't get appreciation. They don't get financial rewards; don't get sufficient training, or sufficient follow-through and follow-up support." In his opinion, it's a clear message of: "Here's the child—good luck!" In such a system, Levy went on to say, "if it doesn't create attachment disorders in the first place, it certainly can perpetuate attachment disorders."

Often children are placed in foster homes with openings rather than being placed where their needs can be met. According to Pickle, children are not given a choice about where they want to be. Instead, they are just expected to go where dictated by those in charge of their lives. Eventually, transitions become driven by a child's "What's in it for me?" attitude rather than by a desire to get close to the list of characters who pass through their lives. A pool or a trampoline or some other material possession becomes more important, or more predictable, and replaces a relationship with an unknown, perhaps frightening, someone. The social worker stated, "If you begin with attachment problems you don't see yourself as somebody who's worthy of love, who's worthwhile, who's loveable. You definitely don't see the world as a loving, caring place. I think every move reconfirms that belief." She also believes that each child who is removed from its family of origin must be considered a "special needs child." Pickle concluded, "We owe it to these children to offer them something better than what we've taken them from."

CHAPTER THREE—
A Problem for America, and Beyond

Americans report that they are repulsed by violence in their environment and yet are drawn, like moths, to its flame. In spite of our repugnance, or maybe because of it, violence has become a cinematic event. Perhaps it is much like a hole in a tooth that seems to demand exploration by the tongue. The past two decades have brought us a new genre of Hollywood fare presented in the form of high budget shoot-em-ups. We've been exposed to Rambo, The Terminator, and Agent 007, to name only a few. Many of the new films include pointless violence, with some movies violence seems to be the only point. There are a number of movies with sequels that include murder, mayhem, and humor. I'm thinking of some of those big money makers starring Arnold Scwartzenegger or Mel Gibson and Danny Glover. They are clever, fast paced and full of explosions and deaths, no doubt the source of multiple adrenaline rushes. On the small screen, for children too young for "R" rated movies at the theater, there are always animated cartoons. Saturday mornings are filled with ninjas and other warriors, wielding the most up-to-date weaponry. In the afternoons and during prime time viewing, over the past few years the likes of Jerry Springer gained extraordinary popularity with a devoted following. The program's dramatic increase in profit shares was not because he hosts the most provocative thinkers or scientists of our time, nor was it because he supported fine arts or presented creative alternatives to the problems of living. Springer gained notoriety due to his appeal to the basest elements of our nature. His show offers pure, uncut violence feeding the revenge fantasies of passive, or perhaps passive-aggressive, viewers.

Our individual and societal defense mechanisms have been strengthened and fortified over the past few decades. During the Vietnam War in the '60's, we were horrified by the images that were televised nightly via the six o'clock news into our safe, comfortable living rooms. Collectively, we breathed a sigh of relief grateful that Vietnam was so far away, a country many of us were unable to even locate on a map. Unless one was personally involved, or had a loved one in the fracas, that era became surreal to the average citizen. Then the 70's brought protests and riots to our own city streets. Haight-Ashbury, a neighborhood that evolved as a symbol of personal and community freedom, was ablaze. Its citizens tuned in and dropped out, legally and chemically. This time we knew the oppressors—and the underdogs—by name. Or at least we thought we did and that made the problems more real and much more personal.

The 1980's brought the United States some much-needed tranquility and a break from the rampant strife and conflict. During the "me" decade individuals devoted their energies to becoming, to actualizing, and to building their financial empires. Widespread peace was short-lived, however, when racial tensions erupted in Los Angeles in the early 1990's following the bloody beating of Rodney King by five white police officers. The evidence of continued and blatant racial inequality was never more apparent than during the King trial when all the officers were acquitted in spite of videotape that chronicled the entire incident. Los Angeles became a terrifying inferno of raw frustration and justifiable protests that pit family members and friends against one another. The question of who one could trust became the driving force in the lives of the disenfranchised. The answer was a thorn in the side of those so publicly abandoned. Perhaps the displayed collective rage was an omen of things to come.

The California situation was an ominous sign, much like an emergency flare discharged in warning that we, as a society, were in trouble. At that moment in history the rest of the country was so horrified we were unable to move in closer to see what was happening to our people on an individual basis. In reality, that was not the appropriate time for an examination of the issues. Los Angeles was on fire and it was a time to survive as best one could. There were neighborhoods full of folks who had been systematically and methodically hurt to the quick. The hearts and souls of those we failed to support were left weeping or scarred, perhaps permanently so.

Individuals who have been emotionally injured do not, like the lion of biblical times, limp off into their den to lick their wounds. Aggression is borne of the pain harbored in the nooks and crannies of one's psyche or spirit. Every slight, every insult, every unkind word leaves its mark on the delicate tissues of one's self esteem and then provides fodder for an oncoming, vengeful assault. Much like the intertwined winds and rain forming a twister, we know, soon, mother earth will be left scarred in its significant wake. And like all tornadoes, just where the outburst of power and rage will strike, is sadly unpredictable. Those who have been deeply wounded respond in a similar manner.

Children, as with adults, who live a lifetime swathed in conflict and chaos eventually project their resultant rage out on to the world. Examples of aggression committed by the hands of youngsters are dreadfully abundant. It is no longer enough to simply report that we have children killing other children. It is now imperative that we examine the issues affecting our children, and hence, society, on a deeper level. Abbreviated articles of murder and mayhem jar our personal comfort zones, but the effects last only for a few minutes. Newspapers devote sensational headlines to out-of-control children but then quickly move on to more recent happenings. Our news teams encapsulate shocking stories about a murderous child into perhaps three minutes of copy—we are presented with the highlights and no more. Who of us remembers the names of the youngsters in the past year that have been accused of murder? What do we know about them? And just why are so many of our little ones shooting to kill?

In an article which appeared in the February 24, 1993, Washington Post stated Jermaine Keith Merriweather, 15, was charged, along with four other youths, with setting a fatal fire and in the shooting of a cab driver. Prince George's Police Chief David Mitchell stated, "They met, conspired and agree to silence this witness. This is the most callous disregard for life that I have witnessed in 22 years as a police officer." According to author Jon Jeter, the police reported that the preparation for stopping a key witness was purposeful. In the firebombing of a Washington apartment building the five teenagers "plotted to kill, and then methodically assembled the apparatus to do it: gasoline, a beer bottle, napkins from a fast-food restaurant to use as a fuse."[1]

Even though we shake our heads and wonder what this world is coming to, we have become desensitized to violence. After thirty years of historical, social, and familial trauma we no longer feel the acute pain of our present time. Our mental and emotional defenses—which serve as protection to our tender underbellies—are intact; we deny, we minimize, and we diminish the importance of violent incidents that now occur with some regularity. We pretend, on some internal level, that unacceptable events are the result of someone's wild imagination that has been projected on to a media screen.

Interestingly enough, in some cases we, perhaps unwittingly, support brutality. Recently in Honolulu, Hawai'i there was a public event which was so violent in its nature and intent that the powers-that-be attempted to have it outlawed. Billed as an "ultimate boxing event," two men planned to face each other in a public boxing ring, ungloved and fully unprotected, for the purpose of beating each other senseless. Their goal was to win at all cost, no holds barred. Before the event many observers learned about the possibility of banning the event and complained bitterly to the reporters.

---

1. Jon Jeter, "A Callous Disregard for Life", *The Washington Post* (Feb. 24, 1993): Vol. 116, A1, Col. 1.

Vociferous fans were willing to go to any lengths necessary to preserve that event and others like it. At the event spectators were charged $50 or more to witness the "sport," as they called it. The fans were wild, obviously thrilled with the contest between the two men before them. It appeared adrenaline was the hormone that ruled the evening, and perhaps even their thought processes. Some of the fans appeared as aggressive as the participants and then categorized the bout as an evening of fun.

Something is wrong deep within our collective psyches. We suddenly find ourselves in need of guidance and unsure of how we are to proceed in living principled lives. Our innermost spirits are in an uproar, quieted only by extreme measures. More individuals are flocking to therapists, churches, and gurus than ever before. Alcoholism and drug abuse is rampant as both adults and children are turning to chemical solutions to solve internal problems. Drugs, those found in doctors' offices and on the streets, are used in an attempt to "numb out" and to help avoid inner feelings, those that gnaw at us and announce that something has gone gravely awry. Frustration and anger creep, silently at first, up and out of the depths of our core causing health and emotional problems. In an effort to relieve our own internal pent-up stress, we ultimately project on to the universe a level of violence that is equal to our own inner angst. Out of their own primordial wounds those individuals with broken spirits act out their rage on to the family and the world around them.

In their very public trial, the Menendez brothers, Lyle, 25, and Erik, 22, were accused of first-degree murder in the August 20, 1989 shotgun slayings of their parents, Jose Menendez, 45, a wealthy entertainment executive, and Kitty Menendez, 47. The brothers contended the murders were the outcome of years of physical, emotional, and sexual abuse they had received at the hand of their parents. In Alan Abrahamson's article (The LA Times, July 1993), "Menendez Called Self Sociopaths, Therapist Says," the author stated Van Nuys Superior Court Judge S. Weisberg determined that the label sociopath, which came up in a session with their therapist L. Jerome Oziel two months after the brothers killed their parents, "was so prejudicial it might endanger their right to a fair trial." Abrahamson also stated that in a hearing that excluded the jurors, Weisberg ruled that Oziel could testify that "the brothers viewed the killings as being planned and premeditated, not an act done in the heat of passion. Oziel also may testify, Weisberg ruled, that the brothers told him, 'We just get turned on by planning the murder. Once we plan it, nothing gets in the way. Once we start, nothing will stop us…And we can't change the plan because it's already formed perfectly.'"[2] Caryn James, in "Talking to the Menendezes," (New York Times, January 28, 1996) concluded, "Such a stunning lack of self-consciousness may not add much to our knowledge of the Menendez case, but it reveals more about these confessed killers than they seem to realize."[3]

Families of attachment-disordered children often experience them as "bad" kids with behaviors those parents easily described as "evil." However, this volume is not about kids who are bad, but about sick ones who do bad things. Because of early trauma they grow up with shattered spirits and lack the seed of warmth found in healthy, well-attended youngsters. Children with histories of serious illnesses as infants, left to lie in their own waste, or who languished in orphanages around the world are especially vulnerable to attachment difficulties or attachment disorder. As a reaction to such gruesome early starts, many young children appear to share common traits with the Menendez brothers, the young sociopaths sited above. Sometimes labeled "psychopaths" their pathology is characterized by a "mask of sanity," as it is called. They appear perfectly sane and emotionally stable but demonstrate no visible

---

2. Alan Abrahamson, "Menendezes Called Self Sociopaths, Therapist Says", The *Los Angeles Times* (July 13, 1993): Vol. 112, B1, Col. 2.

3. Caryn James, "Talking to the Menendezes", Critic's Choice/Television, *The New York Times* (Jan 28, 1996): Vol. 145, B16, Col. 3.

signs of either a conscience or remorse following hurtful acts. By comparison, healthy, attached (sometimes called "bonded") children have a deep, internal core of goodness no matter what nasty or nice behaviors they display. According to Dr. F. Cline, attachment affected are like onions: they are composed of several layers of truths and problems; each layer causes tears as it's exposed and eventually will reveal the absence of an inner core.

The parents I met while preparing for this book have children characterized as above. One eloquent mother described her angry, abusive child's out-of-the-home personality as "dazzling." Sadly enough, not one mother interviewed reported that their child demonstrated one iota of charm while at home with them when no outsiders were observing. Frequently, however, it was stated that their child's amazing abilities were utilized in an effort to manipulate the father. It was common for the charm to ooze, as if from every pore, during therapy sessions, and successfully so. Therapists were continually led astray and tricked by these baby con-artists, and continue to be though the professionals are loath to admit it. When a sunshine-and-sweetness approach failed to manage or control authority figures in the environment violence would erupt, but generally only in the privacy of the family home. Rarely, if ever, do these children lose control around anyone but members of his/her immediate family. In the 1940 book, "The Bad Seed," Rhoda, the darling little girl who plotted and murdered her classmate and the gardener, possessed the characteristics and abilities of a child with a severe attachment disorder. The 1997-1998 version of that same theme, as reported by loving parents across two continents who continue to struggle with their troubled children, indicates the illness seems to have survived, unchanged in nature but, sadly, more prevalent in numbers.

During our interview, Dr. Levy offered his view of the problems with attachment-disordered youngsters. He stated that because of the personality characteristics of children with Reactive Attachment Disorder most professionals are fooled by them and the children, therefore, go undiagnosed. Levy agrees that this is a tough situation from everyone's perspective. Once diagnosed, professionals ask how the disorder is treated. Behavior modification? "Doesn't work." Play therapy? "Doesn't seem to make a dent." Rational, cognitive talk therapy? "That's a laugh," stated the eminent psychologist, "these kids are street-wise, coercive, seductive, manipulative." In truth, he went on to say, "They are antisocial personalities in training, psychopathic personalities in training." Levy discussed the characteristics that distinguish both children with attachment disorders and adults with antisocial or psychopathic personality disorders, as it is called by some. Levy reiterated that they are impulsive, have little or no remorse or conscience, are hyperactive, angry and rage-filled, hold disdain for much of humanity and respect no one, especially authority, are filled with hate, lie and steal, don't trust and do not form personal or therapeutic alliances.

According to Dr. Levy and the guidelines for mental health professionals set forth in the DSM-IV, antisocial personality disorders are not to be diagnosed until an individual has at least reached young adulthood. I have a theory about why that might be so. Before a psychopath can be truly identified, one must have a clear and accurate track record, at least a ten-year history, detailing their relationships and life activities. The very nature of someone with antisocial or psychopathic characteristics is illusive. One of two patterns tends to emerge: they pop, unpredictably, in and out of the lives of those who know them; or they succeed in avoiding their company completely. Either way, there is usually not one individual who is able to accurately chronicle their past. Often police records are the most available method of tracking their whereabouts or affairs of a psychopath. "But we know," stated Levy, "that these children and young teenagers already have these characterological disturbances. They're not waiting until they're adults." The other thing these youngsters have that is missing in the lives of older versions is someone who has been keeping track of the individual's activities and movement through their early life. That attentive person is usually a frustrated mother, probably the only one who really knows the truth—most, but never all—about her child.

Bob is a clever fourteen-year-old from central California. During his early years with his biological mother he was severely neglected which necessitated his removal from her care by the State of California. Along with many other disturbing parenting techniques, as a wee infant Bob had been propped for hours in front of the television. His adoptive parents eventually learned that the TV had served as Bob's mother. In hopes of increasing his interaction with people rather than electronic equipment, they limited their son's time in front of the tube. When Bob started therapy with a Ph.D., the child went to work to gain the sympathy of the uninformed therapist. Eventually it worked so well that the psychologist began integrating television programs into their regular play-therapy sessions. Gradually, the professional added movies and then "R" rated films into their sessions. If they did not have time to finish viewing a movie during the session, the well-meaning Ph.D. sent it home with the boy to finish as "homework."

Throughout my studies of psychology, the one principle that left an indelible mark on my brain was this: All behaviors have meaning. In my experience such a concept has proven true and I've spent years working in the field of psychiatry applying that very principle. The behaviors demonstrated by our children give us hints about early events in their lives, and those snippets may be the only information we have. Overwhelming traumas and significant negative incidents occurred in the youngsters' lives usually before the formation of any language skills or before the formation of any conscious memories. Perhaps even before birth. Because of the timing of the neglect, even those with superior intelligence do not have the where-with-all to bring the events to their conscience mind or to verbalize their feelings about them. To date, too few have actually recovered from the ravages of early traumas or overcome the dark sides of their personalities to be helpful in this process. Because of ignorance or denial among the professional community, the chances for their identification and treatment are currently slim. Sadly, individuals left undiagnosed and untreated will never know what it is that ails them or what it is that drives them to do dangerous or bizarre things. In spite of their incomparable survival skills, they are unable to understand why they continuously challenge those who desperately try to guide them into a loving, caring adulthood.

In addition, there is a psychological construct known as "Cognitive Dissonance." According to general usage it exists in a state of conflict or during increased anxiety which results from inconsistencies between one's beliefs and one's actions. Cognitive dissonance can also occur when there is a discrepancy between one's perceptions of balance or harmony and the facts known to the individual. This is profoundly apparent in the lives of attachment-disordered children. Since memories of early trauma remain cognitively unavailable to the individuals, they then change the facts of their early lives in an effort to decrease the anxiety caused by the discrepancy. RAD youngsters are not aware of early trauma, but are aware of the fact that they do not fare well within their families. Most youngsters want to believe that their biological parents loved and nurtured them. Consequently, they frequently imagine they were removed from the birth parents by mistake and were then hatefully placed with mean, unloving adoptive/foster parents rather than accept that they had been injured or damaged by their biological parents. Altered perceptions or skewed interpretations of the truth foster angry and aggressive behaviors commonly directed at the replacement parents and families.

As four-year-olds, British twins Gerard and Mickey were bright, beautiful, and enormously charming. Shortly after their adoption and within their first week of play school, they successfully poisoned all of their schoolmates. The youngsters conned their schoolmates, entrapped them in the loo, and then fed them a potent disinfectant mixed with rust remover and bleach. The trusting nature of all the other children played into their willingness to drink of the poisonous potion.

According to their thought out plan, neither brother drank any of the mixture. All of the schoolmates required treatment for poison ingestion at a local Emergency Ward. When the dust settled, Gerard and Mickey were expelled for their dangerous antics, the first expulsion in a history of at least one-per-year throughout their school career.

A dangerous child, one threatening murder and mayhem, poses difficult problems to a society caught unaware. It makes parents, teachers, police, health care professionals, and our institutions wonder just how to handle children of this description. The two young Chicago boys who were recently involved in a murder were sent home following their arrest. No jail, no detention center or institution was prepared to handle criminals of such a tender age. Imagine what other harm a four-year-old can cause when he has already poisoned his play school classmates. Or a youngster of seven tender years preparing and planning to use a Molotov cocktail. Where do they go from there? What havoc will those same individuals cause as teenagers or adults? One can only imagine and shudder.

Most of the children you will read about in *Broken Spirits ~ Lost Souls* have those long-term dangerous histories psychiatrists look for while completing the diagnostic process. During an interview Dr. Beryl Davis of California discussed the comparison of individuals with Reactive Attachment Disorder with those classified as "psychopaths." According to Davis a psychopath is someone who has no conscience, is unable to feel empathy for anyone, who can hurt others without qualms, or simply has no connection to the feelings involved. They have no sense of reciprocity, of a normal give and take in a relationship. A psychopath acts out of their own inner needs and drives never taking into consideration the effects his behaviors would have on others. No one else exists as a living, feeling being in the mind of the psychopath, except when that person serves some function. They use people and are able to do that because they do not recognize the needs of others.

On the other hand, Davis stated a severely disturbed attachment-disordered child is by definition someone who is unable to feel or empathize with others and whose symptoms appeared before their 6th birthday. They aren't able to sense or recognize another person's feelings and their own feelings are so well encapsulated they have been unable to experience connections with others. A RAD child, she shared, "is in such pain and has such rage that there is often the need, the desire to make somebody hurt as much as they do." Typical thinking, according to the professional, is: "'I may be isolated, I may be cut off from the world, but somebody else will feel the pain. And I will have power and control over others!'" The psychologist went on to say that if she didn't know better it would be easy to believe that such children sit and plan every move they are going to make that will lead to the demise of their family. "Now I don't think these children do sit down and do that," she went on, "they just do it; that's who they are." Davis believes affected youngsters function much like the adult psychopaths, striking forcefully out at others out of their own emptiness and rage. She also worries that the incidence of attachment disorders will continue to increase dramatically because, as she stated, "We've lost our sense of family, our sense of connection within the family." She added, "I think we're going to be faced with an epidemic of these children who don't empathize, children such as the ones who went out and shot those other kids and teachers at the schools; those who don't connect with their fellow students as human beings. Our society is moving at too fast a pace. We're not slowing down enough to nurture; we're not slowing down enough to impart the sense of connectedness."

Daniel Andre Green, 18, is the accused murderer of James Raymond Jordan, father of the famous basketball player, Michael Jordan. The elder Jordan was killed while napping in his car on the side of the road in rural North Carolina. Green was apprehended due to his own unintelligent and egotistical behaviors: the teen drove his victim's automobile, used his cellular phone, then brazenly bragged to his friends about what he had done. According to law enforcement officials, although his juvenile records remained sealed, Green had been in serious trouble since he was very young. According to an August, 1993, New York Times article, "Green was paroled just two months ago after serving less than two years for assault with a deadly weapon with the intent to commit murder. Stone (Hubert Stone, Robeson County Sheriff) could not remember the details, but recalled that the deadly weapon was an ax." The sheriff said when Green was first arrested, "They (Green and Larry Martin Demery, Jr., also 18) were rude to us. They were very talkative and not upset."[4]

Attachment-disordered kids can be cute as buttons and charming beyond measure, but they can become their parents, and eventually society's, worst nightmare. The young afflicted characters are gifted with extraordinary skills of survival. They have an uncanny ability to identify vulnerable individuals who will eventually become the target of their pent-up rage and their inherent drive to be in control. When I visualize the youngsters in my mind's eye I see them as diminutive survivalists dressed in camouflage and armed. Actually that is identical to my view of the children who have recently caused countless schoolyard deaths. They are similar in that they seem driven to cause harm and will do anything to exert power over others. Although RAD children appear extraordinarily normal, even angelic by some standards, they do not fare well in the close relationships of family. Just what is that vital quality that seems to be so profoundly injured? After thirty years of loving attachment-disordered children I believe I have an answer. They seem to be missing that internal element known as the soul.

---

4. Robert McG. Thomas, Jr, "Suspects Have Spent Lives in Trouble", The *New York Times* (August 16. 1993): Vol. 142, C11, Col. 3.

The Soul—Some Ideas

Webster's Dictionary defines a soul as the following: "The animating and vital principle in the human being, credited with the faculties of thought, action, and emotion and often conceived as an immaterial entity."[5] Having "soul" during the 1960's was like wearing a badge of honor among members of the African-American community. My interpretation of 'soul' is that ability to have compassion and concern for your fellows or one who possesses the capacity to love. Even today, the old notion of being described as "a good soul" is a compliment.

During an interview Bonnie Grimmell, a social worker with Casey Family Programs in Hilo, Hawai'i shared some interesting observations about soul. When working with youngsters she has witnessed a pervasive emptiness that seems characteristic of those with attachment disturbances. She stated they seem to have an enormous void in their life, a hole in their spirits. Grimmell believes the goal of their demanding natures and behaviors is to fill that void, but that "nothing does it. I'm going to say this but it doesn't sound right…It's like there's some humanness that they don't have and they don't know enough to search for it. And we don't know enough of what to give them to fill that void."

Grimmell believes that a soul is that inner quality which makes us human. It's that hard-to-describe thing, according to the professional woman, that helps us make a "place for other people, find our place in the world and what we're here to do—our purpose." Grimmell believes attachment-disordered kids do not have that ability. Rather than chasing spiritual completion Grimmell thinks these particular children get stuck in the always difficult and often unsuccessful task of filling their internal holes. Her experiences with attachment affected youngsters have been profound and she reports she has seen these strong youngsters make

---

5. *Webster's Third New International Dictionary;* Merriam-Webster Inc., Springfield, MA, 1986, 2176.

amazing progress with appropriate treatment. In the long run, however, there is still something not quite 'normal,' maybe even something still slightly crippled in spite of the fix. She concluded, "There's something that's been crippled in relationships and in their spirit. I've seen that. I've seen where kids' spirits are just broken and devastated."

What does the presence of or the development of a soul have to do with children and criminality? And whatever does a soul, or perhaps the lack of one, have to do with the status of our society? In a recent interview, Revered Clarence Liu, former Chaplain of Hawai'i State Hospital, Kaneohe, Hawai'i, spoke with me about having a soul. He shared that this was a difficult topic because the soul is not an "it," something you can put your finger on like a nose or a knee. "It's not an object and can only be alluded to." However, the Reverend said his definition of a soul would include an ability to connect. He thought another name for soul was "connectedness." Liu felt it was easier to first describe some one without a soul. "That person looks like a classical psychopath: someone who has no connection with people; someone who can do anything to people out of his own interest and not have anything bother his conscience. Because that person does not feel, he's not connected and, therefore, he can kill or torture, or do whatever and he's not affected." Liu believes that having compassion and empathy, the ability to feel for and with others, are signs of the presence of a soul. "Soul is the ability of one to be integrated within themselves and, therefore, connected with other people, connected to the world, and ultimately, connected to God."

Reverend Liu believes that soulfulness can be sensed, intuitively, and easily. Because of the interconnectedness with others, someone with empathy and compassion has an intact conscience, feels remorse for wrongdoing, and demonstrates an ability "to touch, be touched by" others and life. Healthy individuals are not just pretending to be human, as do psychopaths, but truly are human in the fullest sense of the word. Dr. Robert Hare described the psychopathic personality in his

1993 book, *Without Conscience.* "Together," he wrote, "these pieces of the puzzle form an image of a self-centered, callous, and remorseless person profoundly lacking in empathy and the ability to form warm emotional relationships with others, a person who functions without the restraint of conscience. Missing in this picture are the very qualities that allow human beings to live in social harmony."[6]

As a practicing psychologist Davis has had time and experiences enough to draw some conclusions about the inner workings of RAD youngsters. She believes they are so enraged, so caught up in their inner fury, that part of their development has either been stunted or somehow missed. I asked about thoughts she'd had concerning the development of a soul, and Davis shared that she believes having a soul provides one with the ability to look out at the world and be able to feel and share the pain of others. A disturbed attachment leaves youngsters unable to share because they've never developed the ability to reciprocate, to give and to take love and caring within relationships. She went on to say that these children believe that if they don't take things first, they will lose everything and end up with nothing, including their life. "So it's absolute survival for them. They exist as isolated entities and they very much exist to survive." According to Davis, in order to do so, to survive, they have to fend off the world and everybody in it. They believe that getting close to others would cause their death. "If they don't keep people away," she concluded, "if they ever allow themselves to become vulnerable, I think they really do feel that they will die." In her opinion, that is the definition of what it is to lack a soul.

Going through the motions, pretending to care, or faking feelings for others—those are good descriptors of a child with an attachment disorder. When a person loves and behaves warmly toward others, they are

6. Robert Hare, *Without Conscience*, Pocket Books, Simon & Schuster, Inc., New York, 1993, 2.

experienced as "good" and perhaps spiritually as "God-like." I have a notion that when I connect with another person on an intuitive level, gut-to-gut, that the God in me is relating to the God in them. By Liu's definition that would constitute a true connection with another.

However, the parents I interviewed had not experienced or observed any deeply felt interchanges between their child and themselves. According to most parents their children remain distant, superficial, and calculating. According to Christian doctrine, evil is not only the lack of "God" within, but perhaps it is due to the internal presence of a "Satan." During the interviews when it came time to pick alias's for their children to maintain their privacy the parental responses were revealing. With some embarrassment and anxiety the parents referred to their children by names that were synonymous with Satan such as 'Damien" or the "she-devil." Contrary to their internal desires, they had actively experienced their children as evil on many occasions. One of the symptoms, a cold, dead, intimidating stare called "the look" by experienced folks, is equated to a devil's stare similar to one I saw portrayed on the popular television program "Touched by an Angel."

Tony Hicks used a 9-millimeter semiautomatic weapon at point-blank range in a surprise assault on Tariq Khamisa, a twenty-year-old college student who was simply delivering pizza. At fourteen, Hicks was the youngest person ever charged with murder in the State of California. "The thing that is incomprehensible about this case," Superior Court Judge Joan Weber said, "is how a boy at 14 years of age can have so much hate and anger inside and so little regard for human life that you took this young man's life over a lousy pizza." It seems as though the author thought clues to Hicks' current behaviors might be found in his past. Tony Perry, a Los Angeles Times staff writer, researched and on January 19, 1996, wrote the following: "A probation report said Hicks was beaten by his parents, who lived in South Central Los Angeles. His father served a stretch in prison. Hicks had moved to

San Diego to live with his grandfather but ran away just weeks before the fatal shooting."[7]

One youngster Grimmell, of Hawai'i worked with in spite of his naughtiness, demonstrated a strong, fiery spirit that the caring social worker admired. At some point in his treatment, though, she sensed a loss of that characteristic and began to grieve for him. Grimmell believed that at some point, and for some unknown reason, he "gave up hope for himself" in spite of the efforts of many dedicated professionals who tried to save him. Sadly for them all, the therapist reported, "At some point his spirit had just broken and I remember being so devastated by that because I wanted to know, 'How do you breathe life into this boy?'" That young man is now about twenty-two and the devoted professional believes his life holds more sadness and grief that she hoped for him. Grimmell stated that's "so sad because I know that with all of our training and education and resources we could give him every opportunity and none of that made a difference." None of their energy and hopes, the sensitive professional lamented, could instill a soul to replace a spirit that had been irreparably damaged. "I don't know how to breathe life back into these kids."

As you have read, it is only by knowing their history that we are able to recognize the psychopaths who pass through our lives. They usually avoid detection by moving quickly and stealthily through the lives of their victims. Most members of society do not want to spend significant time with these individuals. When a psychopath is nestled in the family cocoon, the threats to the family unit come from within. Assaults on family members are brutal and committed by darling babies who look sweet and charming to uninformed observers. In spite of the love for their child, each parent verbalized how difficult it was to live with their

---

7. Tony Perry, "Killer, Now 15, Sentenced to Prison", The *Los Angeles Times* (January 19, 1996): Vol. 145, A3.

child. AD youngsters are unequipped—unable—by their nature, to handle the demands of intimacy in a family. Even when, or if, they want to, they cannot trust, share, give, or accept love in a normal way; all the necessary skills required of a true family member. The typical conflict in this situation is as follows: the kid is doing everything in her/his power to blow their way out of the family while mom and dad are working diligently to keep the child in it. Sometimes, to meet this end, they unknowingly sacrifice their marriages, the other children, or their own health.

After what I've seen I don't think any special effort is needed to locate conscience-less people. I believe those who were emotionally neglected or traumatized as babies, and the grown-up, soul-damaged versions are more prevalent than we know. Once taught to recognize the signs and symptoms, (their true colors, so to speak) attachment disturbed, pre-psychopaths can be easily identified. Recently a handsome, charming twenty-year-old sat before me interviewing in the hope of admission to our drug rehab center. He reported this history: reared on a rural Pennsylvania farm, isolated and isolative; for entertainment he tortured, shot, and killed the plentiful kittens, puppies, and chicks. Scott said he "liked to watch the animals blow apart." Upon questioning the young man said he used to hate his mother, but had outgrown those feelings. When asked about the last incidence of torturing animals, he stated, "Well, I didn't torture it, but two weeks ago I just popped off the head of a dove. It wasn't torture because I did it fast." The young man smiled a chilling smile, and as he spoke demonstrated the manual technique used during the incident. His initial charm evaporated and was replaced with cold, glaring, argumentative anger when told his needs could not be met at this particular facility.

Although I did not spend an extended period with Scott I understood, intrinsically, that he is an older version of children discussed in this book. I was able to sense his lack of soul and my gut responded dramatically to Scott's demeanor and story. I experienced a full body response to him with visceral churning, goose bumps, and the hair standing up on the back of my neck. I've been trained by sick children and sensitive professionals to respect such responses as a means of self-preservation. In spite of a desire to have it be different, he appeared to be an extremely needy and potentially dangerous young man.

In Donald J. Sears' book, *To Kill Again: The Motivation and Development of a Serial Murderer*, he described the "homicidal triad." According to Sears in this phenomenon certain earmarks have been displayed by every serial murderer studied in the past century. The three symptoms include a history of fire setting, enuresis (urinating in inappropriate places), and the torturing of small animals. Most readers would recognize the names of Theodore Bundy or Jeffrey Dahmer. Ted Bundy has been connected with the brutal deaths of about forty coeds on a bloody path from Washington State to Florida. He was finally convicted for the deaths of four Florida State University coeds and after many escapes from prison was executed for his crimes in 1994. Jeffrey Dahmer was incarcerated for a series of grizzly murders in Milwaukee in which he entrapped, murdered, and dismembered many young males. It was reported Dahmer wanted maximum control over his victims and was even driven to kill them to accomplish that goal. Over the past fifteen years these two psychopathic serial murderers caused immeasurable pain in the lives of his victims and their families.[8]

It is important to know that not every child with an attachment problem is a potential Bundy or Dahmer. These individuals are at the extreme end on the severity continuum. However, it is also necessary to know that the Jeffrey Dahmers and Ted Bundys of the world *do not* just suddenly appear, fully-grown and lethal. It took years for such monsters to develop. Where were their parents and what were they doing? How

8. Donald J. Sears, *To Kill Again,* A Scholarly Resources Imprint, Wilmington, Delaware, 1991, 43.

many of their teachers or neighbors shook their heads or in their boots when they had to deal with them as youngsters? Was anyone paying attention to those two budding psychopaths? Of the adults in their lives, did anyone attempt to intervene? Sadly, how many folks had no idea what they were observing even if the signs had been present from early in their lives?

Frank Rich wrote "Loving Jeffrey Dahmer," a book review of *A Father's Story* by Jeffrey's father, Lionel Dahmer, which appeared in the March 17, 1994, The New York Times. In it Rich states, "What fascinates us about these psychopaths? Ms. Oates's (Joyce Carol Oates in The New York Times Review of Books) identified it as, "our uneasy sense that such persons are forms of ourselves, derailed and gone terribly wrong." According to Rich, Lionel Dahmer "tries to figure out what made his son practice necrophilia and cannibalism on some seventeen victims. This task isn't easy because Jeffrey Dahmer does not fit the classic serial-killer pattern. He grew up not in a foster home but in an actual home where he was loved, hugged and indulged despite his parents' divorce and his own alcoholism." Rich continued, "Mr. Dahmer judges himself a poor father because he prattled impersonally about the weather in letters to his son. He also suspects his own youthful shyness, fascination with bombs and fears of abandonment added up to a monstrous genetic inheritance." In the end, when all was said and done, Lionel Dahmer was just a father.[9]

At this writing I see living, frightening reminders of what *Broken Spirits ~ Lost Souls* is all about. On, August 11, 1998, Andrew Golden and Mitchell Johnson were sentenced to a psychiatric hospital for the murders of multiple schoolmates in their Arkansas schoolyard. Johnson will spend four years behind bars and Golden, six years for murdering other youngsters in cold blood. According to the report their sources

9. Frank Rich, "Loving Jeffrey Dahmer", *The New York Times* (Mar. 17, 1994): Vol. 143, A15.

said that the plan for the rampage had been hatched three months before the actual event.

On February 8, 1996, The New York Times ran a story, entitled, "It Takes a Village to Destroy a Child." In it author Alex Kotlowitz wrote, "In the early evening hours of Oct. 13, 1994, two boys, 10 and 11 years old, dangled and then dropped 5-year-old Eric Morse from the 14th floor of a Chicago public housing complex, because Eric wouldn't steal candy for them." Eventually the boys, both charged with murder, were the youngest inmates remanded to the Illinois prison system. Consequently, "they have come to symbolize the so-called super-predators, children accused of maiming or killing without a second thought." Both fathers of the youngsters were in prison; one mother has a track record of irresponsible behaviors; the other had a history of drug addiction, with all that entails. The truth as Kotlowitz saw it: "In the absence of loving, nurturing, discipline-minded adults, children become lost." According to the article, when one of the young murderers, James, was 9-years-old, he witnessed a gang-related murder and he was just 10 feet from the slain lad. At 11, James, "earned mediocre grades, mostly C's, and then in the third grade, when his father was arrested, his grades plunged. He couldn't sit still in class. He fought with other students." The story continued, "In fourth grade, the school ordered a psychological evaluation, which recommended only tutoring. That same year he flunked every subject, including gym and music. Nonetheless, the school promoted him."

The young man described above never received the attention that such experiences demand. Six months before the murders, "the police arrested James eight times on relatively minor charges from shoplifting to possession of ammunition, presumably bullets." Author Kotlowitz wrote, "James and his 10-year-old partner were not headed for trouble, they were well into it. Yet, no adult intervened." Kotlowitz provided an emotional conclusion: "These boys came from a neighborhood poor in spirit and resources. If we can't help rebuild their community, using schools as a foundation, we'll all end up running furiously down those stairs, hoping, praying, that we can catch one more child dropped by their families and by the institutions that presumably serve them. It will almost always be too late."[10]

On March 8, 1996, the Los Angeles Times printed some frightening statistics about raising crime rates among youth in our country. If we are wise, we will hear this report as a noisy trumpet warning of things to come. In an article entitled, "Number of Juvenile Murderers is Soaring" Ronald J. Ostrow stated, "Washington—The number of young murderers in the United States has tripled in the last decade, exceeding 26,000 in 1994, a U. S. Justice Department unit reported Thursday." It went on, "Over the same 1984-'95 period, the number of juvenile murderers using guns quadrupled, underscoring the part that availability of firearms appears to be playing a part in the mayhem." And, "An update of a study issued last September by the National Center for Juvenile Justice indicated that an earlier estimate that juvenile arrests for violent crime will more than double by the year 2010 may prove low."

"Demographics are expected to make the problem worse, with the number of teenagers 14 to 17 expected to increase by 14% by the year 2005, according to Fox (James Alan Fox, Dean of the College of Criminal Justice at Northeastern University). He said that the increase will be even larger 'among people of color—17% among black teen and 30% among Latino teens. Given the difficult conditions in which many of these youngsters grow up—with inferior schools and violence-torn neighborhoods—many more teenagers will be at risk in the years ahead.'"[11]

---

10. Alan Kotlowitz, "It Takes a Village to Destroy a Child", *The New York Times* (Feb. 8, 1996): Vol. 145, A21-25.

11. Ronald J. Ostrow, "Number of Juvenile Murderers Soaring", *Los Angeles Times* (March 8, 1996): Vol. 115, A18, Col. 1.

Sadly enough, the article pointed out that our youth are the victims of murder at an ever-increasing rate as well being the perpetrators of such violence. Mental health professionals report that children and adolescents are spending an ever-decreasing amount of time in the company of adults. Ostrow stated, "There are not people there to draw limits or be praiseworthy—to be positive or negative." I've witnessed this phenomenon daily within the context of my own involvement within mental health systems. Too frequently parents who are too tired or unskilled to care for their offspring bring the youngsters to the Emergency Department of our local hospital wanting their offspring to be admitted to the child or adolescent psychiatric units because the child didn't follow their directions or argued with them. The children in these situations appear forlorn and are often clinically depressed while actively entertaining suicide plans. The increasing numbers of parents, who abandon their parental responsibilities and their children in the process, leaving their youngsters unprepared to fend for themselves perpetually frightens me.

As an experienced professional Davis believes the priorities of many parents today are skewed and that they are more concerned with getting ahead in life than they are about what their youngsters really need. Parents, in her view, are more focused on careers, early planning for the best nursery schools and colleges, or getting the most goodies or material possessions. During an interview for *Motherhood at the Crossroads* a Texas mom told me she was feeling pressured to prepare her young son for an Ivy League college career. She relayed that she was driven by the hope that he would be a scientist so he could follow in her own rather large footsteps. At that moment the baby she was planning for was eighteen-months-old and already hitting and biting this mother when he came to her breast to suckle. "And those are the values," Davis stated clearly, "that take us away from our connectedness to each other and instead attach us to meaningless objects. We're not going to survive that." She sorrowfully concluded, "We have to make people aware of what RAD is, because it really is a cancer. It's eating the fabric or our society—we're losing our children. And what we're doing is breeding a nation of psychopaths, which is a pretty frightening idea."

The information presented in this chapter is graphic and terrifying. I must remind the reader that not all children with Reactive Attachment Disorder, or even those with milder forms, are destined to become murderers or to commit serious crimes. However, it must be stated that a preponderance of those who act out in violent ways against society exhibit signs of having experienced severe disturbances within the first relationships in their early lives. Upon close examination, most have demonstrated many of the dramatic symptoms of those who can be recognized today as having attachment disorders. Please read on for anecdotes that will make your understanding of this complicated disorder clearer and more concise.

PART II—THE PARENT'S PERSPECTIVE

Most of the children discussed in this book were neglected or traumatized early in their lives. I would like to think that this particular problem, so severe in nature, was limited only to American children, but sadly, that is not the case. While completing my research I was invited to meet with parents of attachment disturbed children from two continents. The project included parents found in well-distributed hubs from 31 American states; Alberta, British Columbia, and Ontario in Canada; as well as from England, Ireland, and Scotland. The children came from the following countries and presented alphabetically: Bulgaria, Cambodia, China, Costa Rica, Croatia, Guatemala, Korea, Philippines, Rumania, Russia, Sri Lanka, Thailand, and a variety of indigenous peoples from Canada, the U.S.A, and the United Kingdom.

The parents were predominantly professionals who received their children from seven countries around the world. There was a smattering of adoptions of family members, but most came to them through adoption agencies. The majority of the families, however, had several biological children who were older or already grown before the adopted or foster child entered their life. Overall, the mothers and fathers had positive experiences and success as parents before adopting their troubled child. The statistics below may help to describe this diverse group of families:

- Nearly two hundred families participated in the studies through written surveys and in-personal interviews, combined.
- There were a total of five hundred children: 185 biological and 315 adopted/foster.
- Of the adopted children approximately 43% were diagnosed with Reactive Attachment Disorder; 57% demonstrate significant attachment issues but had not yet been classified as having the full-blown disorder.

International Commonality

A phenomenon I repeatedly observed during the interviews with families of these disturbed children led me to several conclusions about attachment disorders. One of the most outstanding one was this: the national origin of the infant or child was insignificant, and the cultural or racial heritage of the birth mother, or the family into which the individual was placed, did not affect the symptoms displayed by a disturbed child. Historically, some mental illnesses seem to take on the unique flavor of the culture in which it exists. Schizophrenia, for example, looks different in various areas of the world; an Irish schizophrenic demonstrates traits or characteristics that are unlike those of an American with the same malady. However, that does not seem to be the case with children and attachment difficulties. Extremely controlling behaviors, the hallmark of RAD, were present even if the child was born in Russia, Costa Rica, America, or China, and reared by Scottish, Hawaiian, African-American, or Canadian parents. Specific controlling patterns might take on a personal flavor; i.e. in-your-face demands, exuberant charm, tantrums, excessive clinging, or a combination thereof. Ultimately, controlling behaviors are still controlling behaviors, no matter the accent or the language of the owner.

CHAPTER FOUR— The Families of The Broken Spirited

On the heels of significant and sometimes overwhelming disruptions, losses, early neglect or abuse, most of the youngsters discussed in this book ended up either in foster care or adoptive homes. In their search for ideal adoptive parents, social service agencies identified a list of preferable characteristics and personal attributes, acceptable standards that were to be met by applicants. Most requirements were based on the traits of parents that had been successful adopters in the past. Some of them described the couples' educational or income levels but many also included specific personality traits and/or religious practices. As agencies were overwhelmed with demands for physically healthy, blonde, blue-eyed babies, each agency became increasingly stringent regarding their wishes, and yet they still did not want for adequate numbers of applicants. Serious contenders for the dwindling number of children made it their business to meet or exceed the standards set by adoption and foster agencies.

On the other hand, it was not uncommon for 1970's parents with medical problems (other than fertility difficulties, a near requirement) or obesity to be rejected immediately, and so it became a waste of time and resources to even apply. Those determined unfit for consideration either gave up their search for children completely or turned to obtaining babies through what was known as the "gray" or "black markets." The health of mothers and infants, important issues with social service agencies and potential parents alike, became something of a crap shoot in the markets which involved "private" adoptions, infants obtained through individual attorneys or baby brokers. Regulation in the health and emotional care of the mothers and their wee ones, and honesty about their specific backgrounds, health, or living circumstances, became suspect, at best. At worst, reports were laden with blatant, bold-faced lies.

Historically, programs recruiting potential foster parents were usually not as strict because fostering a child and adopting one were viewed quite differently. Adoption was considered a permanent solution of what to do with a child who had no family or home; foster care was considered a stopgap measure to be utilized until a child could return to the fold of their biological family. In the 70's and 80's many loving and extraordinary foster parents were not allowed to adopt their foster child if he/she became available because of the established "rules." Such situations became heartbreaking for both the children and their loving foster families. Although reunification with biological relatives was the ideal, it was not always the healthiest option for the child. Many children became entrapped in a legal limbo while waiting for biological parents or grandparents to get their acts together, so to speak, and to be ready to begin parenting responsibly. Floating from home to home, never sure about one's future, caused significant interruptions in a child's ability to get close to others.

Many parents interviewed for this volume already had biological children before becoming interested in adding other children to their already established families. Seasoned and experienced parents understood some of the inherent problems of fostering and adoption, but many seriously underestimated the extent of those difficulties. Out of their desire to help children the majority of these particular parents did not want to believe their new family addition would have serious or unsolvable problems. Only in hindsight were they finally able to recognize the effects of increased disruptions or neglect in their child's life. Out of enormous hope and their share of ignorance, the parents sometimes applied emotional blinders or assigned simple reasoning and justifications as explanations for their children's disruptive and maladaptive behaviors. Only their tail-end insights helped them understand how their youngsters' particular backgrounds increased the chances of troubled behaviors.

In his March 1994, article entitled "Loving Jeffrey Dahmer," Frank Rich concluded that in the end Lionel Dahmer was just Jeffrey's father; nothing more, nothing less. He stated, "Mr. Dahmer's story is terrifying precisely because his blindness to his son's insanity was inseparable from his love for him." That experience is one that hundreds of parents I interviewed across the United States, in Canada, and throughout Britain could relate to without difficulty.[1]

Because of demands made by adoption agencies a generation or two ago, many adopters possessed the required characteristics, and, thus, as a group still have much in common. Levy shared what he thinks of as "good parents." Such individuals are emotionally mature and are parents by choice because of biology, through fostering, or resulting from the adoptive process. He believed the best parents mature in one of two ways. The majority was not severely damaged as children so they are in control of their emotions and they are not abusive. Others he's known were severely abused in childhood but recognized the problem and "worked it out," as Levy put it. The psychologist said some of the foster and adoptive parents he'd worked with had atrocious childhoods but worked through their feelings and became wonderful parents because of those experiences. "They've been there; they know what it's like." Good parents in Levy's estimation have an enormous capacity to love, can consistently set limits, and obtain the special therapy their children need followed by what he calls "corrective attachment parenting."

I was aided in my search for families of attachment affected youngsters to participate in an international study through a groundbreaking

---

[1] Frank Rich, "Loving Jeffrey Dahmer", *The New York Times* (March 17, 1994): Vol. 143, A23.

organization from the United Kingdom. Phillipa Morrall was the former National Coordinator of Adoption UK, originally known as Parent to Parent Information on Adoption Services or PPIAS. The organization was founded almost thirty years ago to help families interested in adoption or to provide those who had already adopted with information and support they needed. Mainly, Morrall said that they refer to themselves as a self-help group of adopters who help other adopters. As an organization they were looked upon with considerable skepticism when they began making discoveries about the bizarre behaviors of some adopted children. According to Morrall, some thought they were making excuses for their children's behaviors or for their own inadequacies as parents. "And that, of course, made us pretty mad because we all knew we weren't inadequate parents. Otherwise, why would we have been approved for adoption in the first place? In our experience not many inadequate people are approved to adopt; it's usually very exceptional people!" Consequently, "As a parent group, the professionals considered us cranky," she added. "Adoption, I must say, is still very much the last resort in professional eyes. It's not seen to be a viable option to many: they don't like children losing contact with their family, however damaging that family might be," the professional shared.

When discussing the adoptive parents she's worked with, Morrall stated, "I think commitment is the overriding sense of similarity in everybody. Their commitment is second to none! It's incredible that most of them have the most fantastic sense of humor." If a couple is looking for a child who will complete the picture of a "normal, whatever that might be" family, Morrall thinks they will be disappointed. But, "if you are a bit zany, that's great! I mean, maybe you have to put on a non-zany face to get through the adoption process, but keep your zany side available when this child comes along. It will make the experience more bearable." She also identified another quality that she considered nearly as important: a determination "to do the best for their kids." She concluded, "They can see where their children have needs and it's a long haul for many parents to get them recognized."

Why is it then, that parents who have been approved by "authorities," specialists in the care of family-less children, and who have had previous parenting successes, seem to fail so miserably when they adopt a child with disruption in their history? And what are the effects of attempting to incorporate new children into an already existing, integrated family? Details about couples' histories, their experiences with their children, and their expectations before the addition of a disturbed adopted or foster child follow:

Nancy R. of Overland Park, Kansas, and her husband John have been married 20 years now. At the time of the interview their biological children's ages were 17, 16, and 13, and their youngest child, an adopted girl, was ten. When asked to describe her life before adoption Nancy replied: "Very happy, very happy. We have been very blessed; we are a very religious family. John and I have a wonderful relationship and always have. I'm the talkative, outgoing, emotional, demonstrative one. John, who is an accountant, is very quiet, very stable, and just peaceful." The couple was married 2½ years before children came along. Nancy claims they've always had a wonderful relationship with their birth children. "Just excellent!" she exclaimed. They live on a farm in rural Kansas and she has had the freedom of being a stay-at-home mom, which Nancy loved. She was a room mother and very actively involved with all her progeny during school and summer activities. The busy mother described her brood as "full of hugs, full of kisses. We did a lot of stuff together as a family. A very happy home."

Nancy continued to say that when her youngest son was in preschool she had a hysterectomy and was unable to bear any more children. Although surgery was required for health reasons she was reluctant to undergo the procedure because she wanted more children. Nancy had always liked the idea of adoption as she thought it is a good thing to do.

John and Nancy talked about it for a while and according to the wife, "He was just as agreeable to the idea of adoption as I was." Their family and religious style includes family discussions of issues that affect them as a group. Consequently, they told their children to think about the possibility of adoption, suggested they pray on it, and that they would talk about it later. In the meantime, the Midwest couple took preparation classes to become adoptive or foster parents. At the end of the classes they had the usual "home study," necessary before a couple could receive approval for adoption or fostering. The duo was very enthusiastic about the possibilities of adoption so spent an inordinate amount of time discussing the topic among themselves and with their youngsters. They finally decided they wanted a little girl, of school age, so she would be close in age to their first three children. "We didn't want three kids and then one," Nancy reported, "we wanted four children. So we wanted one that would fit into the general scheme of things with our family and their ages. We wanted a child who would be younger, but fit in."

In order for the family to proceed with the adoption it was necessary to reach a unanimous decision. They voted anonymously by ballot. The rules, according to the mother: "If there was a "no" vote then adoption was out, because we were a team. This was going to be a five-way decision. Period. If there was one reluctant person then we weren't going to do it because we weren't going to mess up a good thing. But we had five exclamation marks. Let's do it! Oh, this is going to be great. How fun! Our hearts were just bursting!"

Mrs. R. said she kept calling their caseworker to ask, "Anyone yet?" The caseworker understood their excitement, laughed, and suggested Nancy settle down and wait. One day, just after John left to take their son to a church camp for the weekend, Nancy received the phone call from their caseworker. The excited mother was told there was a little girl available for them. "I was just delirious!" Nancy exclaimed. They knew little about her except that she was 5 and for some reason her birth mother had relinquished parental rights and the biological father had apparently never been part of the picture. At the time of the phone call the girl was in foster care and at their first visit she was "pretty wild, pretty hyper." The couple was told that the youngster had been abused, but Nancy admitted she thought she knew so much that she was sure the girl's problems would be overcome by their peaceful, rural, stable lifestyle. Nancy stated she was certain about many things: "We have not moved around a lot. My dad lives across the road. I have two sisters who live right there in the same town. I grew up in that town and we have a very stable life. I just knew that given six months that she would just settle right down and be part of our family, just as if she had been born to us."

Allyson, Nancy and John's sixteen-year-old daughter, shared that as children she and her biological siblings "always got along and it was a lot of fun." Their daughter shared thoughts about having a new little sister. She said she imagined, "someone I could take places, fix her hair and, you know, paint her fingernails. I was a cheerleader so I wanted her to sit down on the bench and yell with us. You know, have fun with her, have her stay in my room sometimes, like a slumber party, I guess." But after the arrival of the long awaited sibling Allyson sadly shared, "I think that we are kind of torn apart." According to the mature adolescent, the acting out behaviors of the littlest sister interrupted the previously cohesive family activities. Now, the adolescent reported whenever they try to do anything as a family one of the parents stays in the car with the youngest while the others completes the activity. Allyson said it happens that way "because she's always in trouble and we always get in fights because of her. It seems like Mom and Dad don't have as much time to spend with us, with the other three kids, because they're always taking her to the doctor or having to have talks with her. It's frustrating after a while."

On a more intimate level the young woman stated that her sister's behaviors embarrass her. Recently when one of Allyson's friends visited her home an argument between her parents and littlest erupted so her friend "got to hear all of that." In addition, Nancy's oldest daughter shared that she has observed her younger sister flirting and acting seductive toward her male friends. Nancy agreed that when Heather was about 10 she began flirting with her teenaged daughter's friends and boyfriend. "Or she would flirt with the friends of my son, he was junior high age and she was in kindergarten. She would wiggle and giggle and dance around wanting attention in not a good way." It appeared to Nancy and to her older children that Heather would try to get the adolescents to include her in their teen conversations. It also seemed like Heather wanted to be anybody but herself. "She either wanted to be a tiny little baby or a teenager." At the same time the little girl wanted to discuss adult topics, those way beyond her years—such as sex. Once she tried to engage her adult aunt into a discussion about the aunt's divorce. Nancy thought Heather wanted the aunt to confide in her as though she were a grown woman. Often Heather would sit with her grandfather and his lady friend when the precocious child would ask the older woman personal, intrusive questions about her physical relationship with her grandpa. According to the family members their newest member had a knack for making people feel uncomfortable. After many efforts to curb Heather's boundary-less intrusions and behaviors' her three older siblings quit reaching out to her. Nancy said her children would ask, "'When is she going to change?' and, 'Mom, why is she doing this?'" Allyson shyly shared, "I was so embarrassed all the time. I didn't like taking her anywhere." The big sister would tell her to stop a particular behavior, "Heather would say, 'Okay, I won't do it anymore,' but she wouldn't stop. That's real embarrassing," the adolescent added. Young Ms. R. concluded: "My brothers and I are closer because we don't get along with her."

Paula and Bob W. from Kearney, Nebraska shared some perceptions of themselves from their early years together. Paula spoke: "I think we were just a young couple with hopes and dreams of going on with life."

Bob had earned a degree in teaching but Paula hadn't yet completed her studies. Perhaps typical at that particular time in her life, Paula's main desire was to have and raise a family. She reported she and her husband had always gotten along well and that they felt very comfortable and natural together. Bob added his recollections of their early relationship: as a college requirement they actively participated in counseling with a professional who emphasized the need for well-developed communication skills. He believes their marriage got off to a good start with increased communications. Bob added, and Paula concurred, "That was one of the strengths of our marriage."

Paula shared that during the adoption process the agency delved thoroughly into their lives to determine if they would be fit parents. There was a list of requirements they had to satisfy: witnesses wrote reports testifying about their character; police fingerprinted them; they even wondered if the FBI was investigating them. The couple had physicals and obtained passports for their trip to Guatemala to pick up their child. They said they felt watched from all angles. Paula stated, "You're like in a fishbowl when you go through the adopting process. I personally thought that any baby, any child—didn't matter where they came from—if I could just love that child, then we would have a happy home." Bob and Paula's ideals worked successfully with their first two children, sons brought home at five days of age. Each previous adoption "was a really positive experience and a real blessing."

Like many of the parents involved in my international study, the idea to adopt and foster children came as the result of their strong sense of faith and a desire to help youngsters in need. Paula remembered a prayer she'd said a week before receiving their daughter: "God, I am so happy with these children that you've blessed me with. If you want me to have another one, you're going to have to drop the next one in my lap because I'm not going to go out and look for another." The very next week they received a phone call from the adoption agency telling them to get ready to receive their new daughter.

Sharon W., wife of David from central Wisconsin, talked about her own bumpy path to adoption. According to Sharon, husband David had been determined to adopt for a long time. After broaching the topic about every six months for several years, he finally convinced her that beginning a family through adoption would be something "very positive." Sharon said she'd concluded that since he wanted to adopt children so badly, she wasn't going to object and eventually participated in the endeavor. But, she stated candidly, "To be perfectly honest, I wasn't really in favor of adoption. So, unfortunately, it was a kind of one foot in and one foot out approach for me." The Wisconsin woman recalled that they'd initiated the required home study for adoption agency many times, but repeatedly stopped the process before its completion out of her natural reticence. Finally in May, having completed the study in August of the previous year, David traveled to Russia to get their new son, Yuri. For business reasons they were unable to travel together, so soon thereafter Sharon went to Russia to receive Svetlana, Yuri's full biological sibling.

Troy and Leslie W. from San Luis Obispo, California couldn't seem to share their experiences quickly enough. Leslie stated that professionally she is a Licensed Vocational Nurse with a Master's degree in Social Work, and six years of experience in adoptions at a local Social Services Adoptions Unit. "I saw all these little kids and fell in love." Troy shared that in addition to being a Registered Nurse he is also a Ph.D. neuropsychologist, with special training in behavior and diagnostic procedures. According to the couple they were married for three years before Leslie got pregnant with their first son and then she never conceived again. By the time Tray was 9, they considered fertility testing to see why they hadn't conceived again, but then decided against such extraordinary measures. Besides, the California mother saw adoption as an advantage because she didn't want to start all over again with a brand new baby.

They thought their lives were going well at that time and Leslie was just getting her social work career started. They'd talked about adoption periodically so were not surprised when the topic eventually resurfaced for a closer look. Leslie shared that as an adoption worker in the early 90's, "I had not read anything on attachment. I know it was there but I didn't read anything about it. I was telling people that kids might have attachment problems, but they'll attach. That's what we were telling families. That's what we knew; that's all we knew!" Troy also discussed his experiences: "I thought parenting was great; we had a great time." While Leslie was a student and Troy was doing his post-doctoral and research fellowship, their hours were flexible enough that they were both able to be home and spend time with their son. They reported the rearing of Tray was a wonderful experience for both of them. "He's not a perfect child, by any means, but it remained very satisfying and very enjoyable." Dad continued, "He's a smart kid, he's funny, and he has a lot of consuming interests. He's engaging and I enjoy his company. He's fun to be around." Mom added, Tray "was a very good baby. He was healthy, happy, inquisitive, and he adjusted well to everything. He went to college with me, basically. We were very proud that we didn't have to have him in child care." According to the mother Tray is still very inquisitive, very bright, and pleasant to be around. "Beyond the adolescent stuff he's a considerate boy," Leslie shared. He's "affectionate, he'll still give me a hug out in public and that always impresses me and he likes to do things with the family. He's not at the point where he can't stand to be around us yet."

Before the adoption they attempted to prepare Tray for the addition of a sibling with possible attachment issues. Since they did not know Sam, they kept the explanations and topics general but discussed such things as: "What would you do if this happened? What would you do if they wrecked all your toys? What would you do if they tried to be sexual with you?" and the like. After hearing about Sam they requested all the medical records for review. Following the first visit with him both parents had many serious concerns about his behaviors, as well as some considerable doubts about their potential union. Leslie stated her gut instinct told her not to adopt Sam and she even wondered silently what they were doing. She said sadly that she was not at all sure why they decided to adopt that particular child with so many apparent, in-your-face problems. However, she admitted that she was afraid that if they refused Sam that they wouldn't be able to ever adopt because they'd already refused another child.

Troy stated that in appearance, Sam looked like a small, young version of Woody Allen with a very cheerful, engaging way about him. In retrospect the father mused that his initial social skills were actually totally dysfunctional. His superficial cheerfulness and big grin tended to divert one's attention away from what was really happening. Troy stated that during their initial visit with the youngster, "There was level of motor activity and impulse control that was absolutely astonishing!" Sam tended to be totally oppositional, clearly evident from that first day, with obvious poor impulse control. By the end of the first day both adults were totally exhausted, but the child was still going full blast. Although both are nurses with advanced skills in behavioral sciences and psychology they stated, "We really didn't see the attention problems and the history of potential cognitive problems." They now see that as a major stumbling block. The knowledgeable father stated, "I think we just got sucked in by the big smiles and the almost giddy euphoria that he radiates. Besides, I'm a pediatric neuro-psychologist; I trained in a major medical center and should be able to fix behavioral problems. Or at least make it manageable." Leslie added that since she was familiar with adoptions and the difficulties involved, they'd get Sam hooked up with a therapist immediately. She vowed, "We'll do everything right."

The California couple had wanted a school aged child and, in spite of internal foreboding, brought Sam home when he was in the first grade.

They reported that the boy was in first grade for two weeks before the teacher moved Sam back to kindergarten because of aggressive behavior. Within the first weeks their child threw a desk and then pushed another kid out of pure defiance toward the teacher. On that day he was literally marched from his first grade classroom into the kindergarten class. "That was it!" Mother stated. Leslie went in to school and took articles on loss and grieving, and she told them putting Sam back into kindergarten wasn't necessarily the answer. Leslie said that was the beginning of her mission: not one of advocacy for Sam and for other kids like him, necessarily, but of educating the school. "It was a nightmare," Troy said sadly. "You'd go to the school and they'd just fling this child at you and say, 'Take him!'" Leslie shared, "I feel sorry for the parents who have one child like this and that is their only parenting experience. I knew we were not bad parents, but it (the situation) brought the worst out of me. I became a person I didn't know."

Troy stated that eventually Sam became "very hostile and aggressive toward family members. My mother is blind and he soiled himself and made a great deal of effort to climb up in her lap and to hug and snuggle. What he was doing was wiping fecal material all over her." Early in their relationship Sam struck and kicked Leslie's mother and "called her a fucker. I thought she's going to have a stroke or something. I know she wanted to draw off and let him have it," the daughter reported. Early in their parenting Tony and Leslie had agreed they would not use corporal punishment with their sons, but used time-outs instead. After watching his behaviors the parents came to believe that to Sam spanking and time-outs were the same thing, and neither was effective. The mother stated, "Corporal punishment isn't going to work with children who've been abused anyway." Leslie added that they were without family in their immediate area so her mother would occasionally visit and babysit so the couple could get out on dates, and the like. Sadly Leslie added, "I think we did that twice and then realized that we can't do that anymore—either she's going to hurt him or he's going to hurt her."

Laura R. of Scunthorpe, England shared during our interview that she and her husband had been married for twenty-five years. She didn't feel they'd had much time together before their daughter Joy was born two years into their marriage. But they had always wanted children and believed they had no outstanding problems in their lives, so were pleased with the birth of their daughter. The duo reported they'd very much enjoyed Joy, that she was an easy baby and a happy child who caused no difficulties. Laura had worked with children in residential care for a short time so felt she had clear knowledge of child care and the sort of children who were available for adoption and foster care. When they were ready they had intended to go into fostering, but not quite so early in their relationship. When Joy was 2½ they were approached by people from their church with a request. Six biological siblings, local youngsters, were suddenly being placed into foster care and out of their desire to help, Laura and her husband agreed to care for one of the boys. Although their initial commitment was brief and to be limited to three months the experience unexpectedly stretched to eight. Laura shared, "It was not a good experience for us. Looking back we felt we were too inexperienced and too young in our own relationship." The couple decided they would leave fostering for a time and perhaps resume at a later date.

Eventually the English couple felt ready and decided they wanted a long term foster child and one with the potential for adoption. And that is just what they did when Joy was 9. Laura continued, "When Ann first came to us she was sixteen-months-old and she came for a fortnight. I don't think we were told very much at all about her and her needs—only that she had had lots of moods and the relationship with her birth family wasn't stable." The couple was told the youngster was supposed to be a long-term placement, but after only two weeks in their home the agency insisted the toddler be returned immediately to her birth mother, as least temporarily. Apparently the biological mother was to be admitted to the hospital for unknown reasons. The following October the social worker called to say that the little girl was back in care and wondered if Laura and her husband would consider taking Ann back for the long term care. The mother recalled, "We jumped at the idea because to us she had always been a special child. We would have loved to have kept her the first time." Sadly, when their little Ann returned to them she appeared completely different than at her first placement with them. Mum said, suddenly, "She was a very unhappy looking child."

Later in her life, Laura and Peter's daughter became much more difficult to manage. According to the mother, as an adolescent, Ann was much more uncooperative when working with them and in doing her jobs around the house. Laura said Ann became verbally abusive towards her and even more so towards Peter. She said that was not so surprising as Ann had never wanted anything to do with Peter from the very start. The English mum said "that when instructed to help clean the evening dishes she would say things like, 'I'm not drying up, you fucking cow.' Or she'd write, 'You're a fucking bitch' on the bedroom wall or on notes saying 'Dad is a bastard' and 'Mom's a bastard witch,' and the like." She renounced them as her parents and screamed "I wish I wasn't adopted," particularly when the parents were outside in the street. The mother believed that was Ann's effort to embarrass them or at least make them look bad in front of others. Her teachers suggested that Ann get counseling when they caught her making abusive phone calls. Approximately two years before our interview Ann had telephoned an elderly couple nineteen times on one day saying she knew who they were, swore at them, said they were "child sex killers," and that she was going to get them. One of the neighbors told Laura that she was glad Ann was taken from the home. The neighbor had already been threatened physical injury with a knife by the out-of-control adolescent and was afraid the girl would do harm to the young mother as well.

Samantha and Sam M. of Santa Margarita, California talked openly, and proudly, about their family prior to adoption. They had three biological children and believed their family to be a great one! They wanted to share the love and enjoyment they'd experienced with their youngsters with other, unfortunate kids. Samantha's professional background was in child development and she thought of it as a career move for her to adopt abused or older children. She felt she and her family were ready for all that entailed. Sam said that he thought life as they were living it was reasonably normal, that they were a well functioning family. He shared that their children were all two years apart and believed they were emotionally close to each other. Sam and Samantha were anticipating their progeny leaving the nest within the next few years, leaving them with extra time and energy for more children. Plus that, Samantha wanted "...to do something good and positive. We enjoyed being parents." Samantha added, "We were a success; they are all successes." None of their youngsters had drug or alcohol problems and they enjoyed a good relationship with all of them. The couple thought of their growing children as independent beings who have been able to go out and find their own place in the world. According to the proud father, their oldest attended Chico State and was "a smoke jumper" which was a valuable and challenging career for him. Their daughter is developmentally delayed and was in special education. Nonetheless, they felt she was also successful within the context of her life; she resides in an independent living program and works in San Luis Obispo. Their youngest son attended a two-year fire academy. To these proud parents their offspring are the picture of success—they are all doing what they want and are living useful, productive lives.

The California couple began considering adoption when their youngest was fifteen. Initially they had wanted to adopt one child but were asked if they would take sisters Jackie and Cassie. The mother, shared, "We initially thought we'd like a seven to nine-year-old and just do something good, just bring him into the fold of this family. It was very naïve." Sam agreed about their naiveté and added that they believed an adopted child would, naturally, integrate smoothly into their family life. He said, "We just felt that whatever we were getting would just go right along with our family pattern as it had been." The pair participated in a vigorous six-week training program with Social Services in preparation for becoming adopters. Sam stated Social Services "didn't allude to the fact that there could be major problems." They had decided they couldn't handle youngsters with physical problems, but learned through the training process that some of the children might have emotional or intellectual issues due to their pasts. The couple was told they would be attempting to replace images, perhaps negative ones, of the child's birth parents. Samantha said they believed if they were forthright with the children, they'd reciprocate with honesty. "I have," the mother added, "a Bachelor's degree in child development; I felt it would be a piece of cake. I had no idea what I was in for! We were mature, we went in with our eyes open. We were told that the older child, Jackie, had emotional problems, but what we weren't told was that each of these little problems was equal to one great big disorder. You can't treat stealing as stealing, lying as lying, and tantrums as tantrums. It's part of Reactive Attachment Disorder that I had to discover that on my own."

Samantha reported that she observed her daughter Jackie, then 5, pounding the tiny paws of the kitten from next door. Eventually it was discovered that the kitty had three broken bones in his foot from the little girl's rough treatment. Although Jackie had functioned early in life as Cassie's surrogate mother, she was mean and punitive to her in many situations. Once, during the night she attempted to smother Cassie while the two-year-old lay sleeping in her bed. Fortunately one of their older sons came home, heard the commotion coming from their bedroom, and interrupted the attempt on Cassie's life. One day Jackie ran away from home because she was mad at Samantha for walking her to school that morning. Sam and Samantha's oldest son assisted in the search for the youngster and found her about four hours later. When located she flew into a rage and attacked her teenage brother "with a great big chunk of glass and a stick," Samantha relayed. The mother of several reported the grossest thing Jackie did, besides smother her little sister, was spit all over Cassie's bed. "Cassie always got accidentally hurt," the concerned mother said sadly. "Jackie accidentally slammed the door on her hand; she accidentally tripped her; she accidentally got her knee stuck in the door. She accidentally pushed her. Stuff like that; it was constant."

Tara and Bob W. of Edmonton, Alberta, Canada, described their life before adoption as "pretty normal, fairly easy." Brandon, their firstborn, was "very mellow and calm," so parenting him was easy according to Tara. Bob described their son as very respectful and easy to take places, as he seemed to understand and follow the rules. It was simple, according to a proud father; their child "made it easy to be parents." Tara had worked with special needs children in day care and as a kindergarten aide and shared that they started fostering because of her inner needs and desires. "I've always worked in child care," she said, "and I always felt like it was my calling to help children. I just wasn't being fulfilled" with one child. She didn't feel there was much she could do in day care on a day-to-day basis, so she believed fostering would be a good way to help another child through life.

The Canadian mother reported that early foster care experiences were a real eye opener for her. "I thought I'd seen behaviors before, but nothing like I'd seen once we got into fostering." They'd never dealt with youngsters with Fetal Alcohol Syndrome (FAS) and all the associated behaviors, an unexpected experience for them. Eventually, however, caring for children with such severe problems proved too difficult for them. Initially, the couple had requested older children, ones closer to son Brandon's age. However, according to Tara, after the unpleasant experiences with older children, Tara and Bob decided they'd rather work with babies "because they're a little bit easier and you have a little more input at a very early age." Or so they'd hoped.

Soon thereafter Bob and Tara became aware of a little eight-month-old girl who had been placed in a nearby institution called "Roseprest." Tara said the facility was known for the care of handicapped children so the couple found it strange that Cassi was housed there because she was not considered physically challenged. Plus that, other infants and toddlers were usually the first to be placed with families, so they again wondered why she was still available. It was under those circumstances that their daughter Cassi first came into their lives as a foster child, but one who soon became available for adoption. Bob candidly shared that the little girl arrived just after he'd lost his mother. His mother had unexpectedly died and was the last contact he'd had with family. Initially Bob said he was "reluctant to bring anyone else into the mix. I just wasn't prepared. I was not dealing well with the death," and all that entailed.

In spite of their concerns they were unexpectedly given a two-month time limit in which they had to decide to adopt Cassi or not. Under pressure from the adoption agency Tara and Bob decided to proceed with the adoption. Tara continued: "We love her, I mean she's a really sweet little girl. There's a side of her that we see that she's just a sweet, normal, happy little girl." But they have observed a part of their daughter's personality that does not strike them as usual or normal. For example, Cassi had never been unable to laugh in a genuine manner. In the past she'd laugh, reported the concerned mother, "but it's a phony, balcony (dramatic) laugh when everyone else is laughing." The couple shared that in the last year she'd grown significantly, both physically and somewhat emotionally. They recalled an incident when the entire family was relaxing in the parent's bed when Cassi got a case of the giggles. She apparently enjoyed it when Brandon wanted everyone to sleep in one bed. Reportedly, Cassi thought that was a hilarious situation but quickly became overstimulated. Ultimately, the girl couldn't handle the closeness with her family members so had to return to her own bed.

Tara stated, "That was the only time within two years that I'd heard that laugh before. And that makes it all worth while. She laughed—that was a genuine laugh. I've heard it since, but not very often."

The Canadian mother continued wistfully, "I still have my hopes. I still hope she grows up feeling loved and cared for and part of the family. Whether she will, I don't know, but we'll do everything we can and hope for the best and hope to God she doesn't get so severe like some attachment problems can get. That would really break my heart. I think there comes a point where you just have to let them go and that's got to be really hard. But we'll deal with that when it comes, I guess."

Susan R. of Overland Park, Kansas talked about their life and their ideas before adopting their family. She and husband David had been married 13 years with no birth children. Their decision to adopt a family, however, wasn't based on a need for an infant. "But rather," stated the mother of three, "we would just enjoy kids." Susan said they had been around kids for years, through friends and family. Since they enjoyed children, they'd borrow friends' youngsters to spend time with them or watch them over weekends and the like. So, they naturally believed they could just build a family and have similar kinds of experiences as when they'd cared for others' children. They thought it was a simple matter; others' kids would just live with them permanently, and day-to-day activities with borrowed youngsters would be similar to day-to-day activities with adopted ones. During the interview Susan described their early thinking as somewhat naive. She didn't think she and David had such extraordinary expectations of adopted children. However, the midwestern mother stated candidly, "Yes, there would be a few adaptations, a few changes in our scheduling. Eventually, if we just remained patient and steadfast with our original thoughts, we would eventually blend into a fairly workable, fairly comfortable situation, and be able to carry on and carry forward as a family unit."

Susan shared that she and David adopted two children, first a girl, then a boy from the Kansas Children's Service League. Their adoption experience did not progress or turn out they way Susan had anticipated. She went on to discuss experiences with their adolescent son, James. Because his behaviors escalated so rapidly and unpredictably, by age seventeen he'd already been charged with assault and battery. She was pleased to report that, so far, he had not yet pulled a knife or gun on anyone. However, the sensitive mother shared that she found her son's verbal threats to be the most frightening of all. She said he readily threatens to "Knock your fucking head off," "I'll burn your house down," and "I'll kill you." His threats to kill and burn her out were shocking to her. Susan believes his internal chaos and rage make him dislike himself horribly which perpetuate even more angry outbursts. Also, she said she thinks his yucky behaviors insure that no one else will like him either. Susan shared that the hardest and most frustrating thing about raising James has been his lack of cause and effect thinking. Sorrowfully, Ms. R. stated, "You just do the same thing over and over and over and over and it doesn't change anything that he then does in response." She went on to say she believe there must be a "loose connection in the brain and that's what it reminds me of—there's just a little short circuit there, it's just not hooked in. There are other times that he's fairly bright, but the processing is so different."

The Kansas mother approximated that one-third of James's teen years were lived at home and the remainder were spent in institutions because of his angry, dangerous behaviors. Throughout his adolescence the couple remained committed to reach out to their son, to visit, or call him frequently. Susan stated clear, "We felt that's our commitment to him." She said their efforts remained consistent even when to do so was inconvenient, or when friends or family questioned the feasibility of such action on their part. Susan and David were determined to remain in a relationship with their son for the long haul. There were heartbreaking times, Susan reported, when they'd driven across the state to see him but just before their arrival James had flown into a rage and was placed in a locked seclusion room for safety so they were unable to visit with him. Susan shared wistfully, "People would question why we would continue, but it was important to us to let James know we're here for him, no matter what. So we really have tried hard to connect, to keep connected with him as best as he will let us."

Kristin C. Rome, Indiana is home to the mother of an adopted girl and her younger biological brother, easily discussed her marriage before the children joined them. She and Terry were married in 1989 and received both children in 1994, after five years of a childless marriage. Before their family expanded, "Terry and I spent a lot of time indulging ourselves," Kristin shared. "If we wanted to do something, we'd make time to do it. If we wanted to buy something, we would buy it. It was a good lifestyle, one hard to complain about. But I was somewhat bored even though I was working part-time; I needed something else. I was always able to have or do anything I wanted but I was always somewhat lonely." The Midwestern woman reported that if they had a disagreement, which was rare, the issue would remain just between the two of them. She was pleased to state; "We'd work it out and move on. There was very little controversy."

Having children had always been a priority for Kristin and the driving force behind the plan to adopt a family. She reported she would periodically broach the topic with her husband but found out very clearly that such a plan was not part of Terry's agenda. She came to learn he never wanted kids and, consistent with that, had had a vasectomy prior to marriage. Because her drive for a family was so strong and her husband was thirteen years her senior, she was constantly faced with the dilemma: Should she pursue the topic in spite of her husband's desire to remain childless or give up her dream? For about two years the idea occasionally crossed her mind. The frequency of her thoughts progressed dramatically to the decision "that I wanted children and I was going to eventually become a mother whether he liked the idea or not." Fortunately for the couple, over the few years following their wedding Terry grew to accept Kristin's desires and had a change of heart. Finally her husband told her that if they wanted a family they needed to start the adoption process. They talked to the staff of their local Division of Family and Children Services and the process began.

The Indiana mother talked about two frightening incidents with her son, Ryan, where he'd become physically aggressive long after he'd been adopted. Kristin said that during the summer of '95 her son began to indiscriminately attack objects and people. To this day she believes he might have injured, or killed (as he'd threatened), a playmate he'd invited to their home if she and husband hadn't interceded. Ryan was 11 when he and his friend of 10 had had a nice day of fishing followed by more play. At the end of the day when they were preparing to sleep in Ryan's two-level bedroom, Ryan unexpectedly lost control. Kristin thought Ryan may have had a "flashback" and suddenly went into a rage and began screaming to get his friend out of his room, that he didn't want the boy there any longer. Ryan angrily headed toward the smaller boy to physically remove him from the house. The breathless mom stated, "When he rages it's like he's from hell; he is possessed! There's no way to talk to him or reason with him." To avoid injury to either child, Terry physically restrained their son. According to Kristin her husband had one arm around his neck and the other arm around Ryan's chest and arms. Ryan was butting Terry with his head with incredible force while Kristin was yelling and instructing Ryan to "Stop! Stop, you're hurting Terry!" But their son would not stop. The frightened couple moved their youngster to the floor and while Terry maintained his hold, Kristin wrapped her arms around Ryan using her entire body weight to restrain his legs. The mother reported he kicked and kicked for about thirty-five minutes until he was finally exhausted.

Kristin said that a week earlier, Ryan had attacked her as well. "I don't even know what it was over anymore," the bewildered mother shared.

"Something trivial, like take off your hat when you come in the house, or the TV remote. I think that is what it was." She said she knew he was about to go into a rage because of a particular look she'd seen in his eyes. In preparation she moved his boots and the glass topped table but before she was fully prepared, she said, "He jumped at me like a cat. He kicked my leg so hard that I had a bruise for a month, all the way down to the bone." Terry had to forcefully pull their son off Kristin. Even after the attacks the couple didn't consider that Ryan needed special care that a hospital could provide. However, soon afterward Ryan attacked another neighbor boy and they decided it was time to get the youngster treatment. After initial contact with the local psychiatric hospital it still took five days for the staff to decide if they were able to take him. The mother concluded, "So we lived with each other for five days waiting for him to explode again. The child was sheer terror for two years."

Kristin continued to talk about the changes in her relationship with Terry after the addition of the biological siblings, Michaela and Ryan. In the four years since their placement, Kristin said reluctantly, "Terry and I went from being a very affectionate, fun-loving couple to scared, frightened, worried about our standing in the community." She said because of the behaviors demonstrated by their children, they've become "angry" and "beaten down." The concerned wife said there had been times when they were able to have a good laugh or encourage and support each other to get though the stress. Unfortunately, Kristin shared, "Terry conveys two different sides or gives two messages. He loves the kids but he wants them to go away. He resents them. He sees them as an intrusion on his life. They're wrecking his life; they're making him old. He's very sarcastic and critical of them behind closed doors." The sad wife reported that over the past four years their marriage has turned, simply, into a child-raising partnership. They don't travel anymore, nor do they go out on dates. Their conversations "consist primarily of griping about the kids." Kristin told me that she has been treated for depression and that she thinks her husband ought to be, as well. She knows it's not her place to diagnose him, but she said, "He's angry His anger goes in cycles of about every two weeks. He's despondent." Their arguments have increased in the past year, and they "have begun shouting at each other just the past month." A very sad, quiet Kristin stated: "I really think that if we don't do something, such as marriage counseling, or take a real good look at what these kids have done to destroy our marriage. It would not surprise me if we would separate for a while or get a divorce. A great deal of it would be attributed to the kids."

Chuck and Jane D. live on a central Nebraska farm. Chuck is a veterinarian with a busy practice and Jane is an at-home mother to their seven children. The couple reported that they had about eighteen months together before children were born to their union. When asked to describe their marriage before offspring, Jane commented, "The first year of marriage was, well I would consider it wonderful. It was just him and I and we really didn't have a lot of friends at the time so we just did a lot of things together." Chuck chimed in, "I thought it was real good. I graduated from medical school and had taken a job in Illinois and we were very comfortable there." Jane continued with her explanation, "We had three children in the first five years of marriage, but our children were fun to be around. They were all at home, and I was a stay-at-home mom. Our business was out of our home so I was with the children all the time and we did a lot of things together: planted gardens during summer, walked a lot or bicycled. We had three lovely children. I had no problems with them."

At some point, however, the Nebraska couple thought about adoption and that it would be nice to help other children. Chuck and Jane are religious people and considered their home a loving one with enough love to share with more unfortunate youngsters. Jane continued, "We thought we were financially well off enough to adopt one or two children and incorporate them into our home. You know, we felt stable enough, I guess." Before they were ready to adopt the duo started praying for guidance. With regards to more children, Jane said they wanted to, "just kind of incorporate them into our own family, make them part of ours, and we would just raise them as ours and go on. We prayed about it for about two years." The sensitive mother said most of their children thought adoption was a good idea and were excited about the possibility of a larger family. Their oldest child, Howard, however, was obviously non-committal about the idea but the parents decided their son's lack of enthusiasm was related to his quiet disposition. Later, however, Howard shared that he had not wanted more children in the family, and that he had never been for the idea at all.

Chuck shared in the telling of their family story. The couple had been married for fourteen years and their three children were teenagers and "over halfway grown." About that time Jane and Chuck were told about a sibling strip, a group of four biologically related children whose wish was to remain together as a family and not be separated. The thought of having a second daughter was okay with the father, but Chuck admitted that he wasn't very enthusiastic about such a large group. His excitement diminished as time passed. He and Jane discussed potential problems at length but felt their connection to the children was God driven and that they had been led to help this particular family. Since they had an agricultural background and lived in the country, the loving pair felt that they could offer the kids more opportunities than would be available in a city situation, more fresh air, and more activities. Financially they were equipped to handle the kids' necessities—food, clothing and the like. The couple felt they could give them enough individual love and attention so they could survive within the group. "That was our hope anyway," Jane added.

Together Jane and Chuck recalled the information they were given about the sibling group prior to their arrival. Jane shared, "What I can remember learning is mainly that they were just a wonderful set of four children that were in a bad situation. They were from Costa Rica, originally, but spent two years in North Platte, NE, being adopted by that family. We were told that the family was not providing for the children very well." The social workers from the Department of Social Services felt that the problems that were occurring were the couples' problem and had nothing to do with the children or their behaviors. There were, however, some details that the agency staff would not discuss about the case. As far as the anxious couple knew, they were just four wonderful children who found themselves in a bind. Jane clipped out an article that appeared in their church bulletin describing how wonderful and perfect the youngsters were. They were quick to say that they did not expect four perfect children, but that was what they had read about them. Soon the youngsters came, three more boys and a girl, to live with their family. Once they got to their new home, the social workers continued to say they felt that any existing problems had to do with their first American family but never attributed problems to the children themselves or to difficulties in their early beginnings.

When the new family joined the existing one, their ages were as follows: Berry, 7; Dotty, 9; Kevin, almost 11; and Darin, 12. The ages of Jane and Chuck's biological children were Derk, 12; Karla, 13; and Howard, was 15. Consequently, there were two teenagers with five more waiting at the doorstep and all seven children were eight years apart, from the oldest to the youngest. At the time of our interview all seven had entered adolescence and not one of them managed to retain their perfect and problem-free façade.

Jane continued and almost became breathless when discussing the relationships between her children. She admitted, sadly, that she believed there was instant friction between Howard, the oldest of the biological strip, and Darin, the oldest of the adopted sibling group. "Both wanted to rule," Jane said. Howard was the oldest and biggest child but Darin was not about to give up his position as the self-imposed leader of the adopted portion of the family. According to the exhausted parents, Howard soon asserted himself and seemed to take over as head of the children. Unbeknownst to them, however, Darin secretly retained his position and wielded powerful covert influence. If Darin's biological siblings didn't obey him, even when Howard had established the rules, or perhaps, especially when Howard established the rules, Darin would take matters into his own hands. The parents didn't realize that the boys were physically abusing each other, but mostly, though, it was Darin dishing out the beatings. Jane added, "They were very manipulative, they would get one another in trouble. Basically, it was the oldest child getting the other three in trouble because he was the oldest. He Rules! It took us a while to figure that out." They encountered some sexual acting-out later, victimization between the siblings and children from outside the family. Chuck and Jane felt that during the first couple of years nothing got out of hand but believe it "easily could have if we'd been totally asleep at the job as parents. And the constant bickering between each other, the gripes about everything. Nothing was satisfactory."

The Nebraska couple said eventually there were sibling rivalries, literally, between every child for one reason or another. Jane shared that they had noticed all the children would go through what she considered "a honeymoon stage" followed by some wild, outrageously stupid stunt. One of those events was during a visit from their minister and his wife. They'd had a nice meal together one afternoon. They'd eaten about 2:30 and fairly quickly so hadn't spent much time at the table, and when they were finished the kids went outside to play on the trampoline. By the time the adults went outside they were confronted with thick, black, billowing smoke rolling across the skies. It was summertime and there was a burning ban in effect because it was very dry posing increased danger for grass fires. The experienced couple knew the fires weren't caused by spontaneous combustion and that whichever kids were out-of-sight were the ones to look for first as they were probably the culprits. They apprehended two boys behind the house where Kevin was showing

Derk how to start fires in the tall, dry grass, and then how to stomp them out, which had been unsuccessful.

Jane and Chuck shared that around Thanksgiving of that same year, Kevin talked someone into taking him to town to buy a high powered BB gun. On their way back home he shot out a window of a passing vehicle and the glass shattered, showering two babies buckled in the backseat of the car. Kevin seemed especially adept at gaining their attention, even in the most negative of ways, and lived from disaster to disaster, according to Jane. He also seemed especially good at getting away with things "because he was the one everybody liked." In Kevin's wake the youngest two, Dotty and Berry, felt they weren't getting enough attention and so they intentionally caused some chaos in the house. Jane said, frustrated, "I mean, we're talking major stuff that goes on in the home." The couple said the children seem to go in cycles; while one was raising a ruckus and getting attention, the others tended to be quiet. Then it was another child's turn to do something to get noticed. The parents said there seemed to be some one-ups-man-ship going on and a desire to outdo the other kids with their antics. Jane sighed, "We just go in these cycles and when one is really acting loving, then I know I'm supposed to be watching the next one because something is going to happen."

Rose, wife of Jack L. of California shared that eventually, following an impressive honeymoon period, their daughter Hope lost control in front of the couple and their biological siblings so, finally, others had a clear view of the true nature of Rose and Jack's daughter. "She would end up pissing everybody in the family off so bad that our other children turned into little gang members, convicts ready to kill this child." The couple reported that once Hope whipped her siblings into a frenzy, so to speak, she would suddenly regain her composure and return to her well-worn angelic pose. Hope would then, according to Rose, "calmly sit on the furniture, fold her little hands, and get this grin on her face. In my opinion I think she is lucky she still draws breath today." The couple said they were always fearful that one of their other children would snap and end up hurting her out of their own frustration with her behaviors. The experienced mother said she thought the most detrimental thing about living with RAD kids is the creative ways they use to try to disturb the relationships within the family. She believes Hope has, "worked overtime to sever the ties that have bound us together all these years. It has been real scary."

Martha G. of Kansas City, Missouri is a married mother of eight children: three biological, four adopted, with one foster child currently in her temporary care while awaiting the birth mothers' release from incarceration. Regarding her motivation to adopt: "I'm the oldest of thirteen children so having a large family never seemed overwhelming. It just seemed like something that we were supposed to do. I'm a nurse at a children's hospital and seeing all the children there who need homes, I felt like it was something my husband and I could do—bring in some kids who needed places to be and a good home. And we felt relatively confident that we were good parents and had the resources."

Martha believes all of her adopted children have attachment issues, at least, if not full-blown RAD. She shared that she explains the problems of attachment to her older, biological children as part of her parenting and preparation process. "I try to explain a little bit about attachment to them; they understand that they don't like it. They don't like what this behavior might be and what this means. It scares them when they've heard some of the stories about other kids who are extremely violent and dangerous. We have some friends who have a little boy in residential treatment; they've seen him be pretty extreme. That kind of scares them like that's something that their brothers might be able to do."

Sunny and Reggie M. of San Luis Obispo talked about the relationship between their adopted children, Joshua and Jennifer. Sunny stated that Joshua was about 10 when his sister joined him already 3 ½ years old. "He wanted to get a brother, and well, here comes this little spitfire girl who already had a mouth on her and she was very independent. You know, my way, my way! They have always had this not nice relationship because they're both very strong-willed." Against all reason Sunny continues to hope that they will eventually like or love each other. However, the mother shared, "It's a hard call because they're so busy being at each other." In retrospect Sunny thinks that Jennifer's behaviors toward her eventually set the brother and sister up for more conflict. Jennifer brought chaos and violence into the home, something that did not exist between the couple or with Joshua. Sunny said, "She's a neat kid, such a neat kid, but there's just that other side of her that's so in a rage and so resentful." As soon as Jennifer joined the family, Joshua's "life was over" as he knew it, and he was not able to accept their new bouncing, cursing bundle.

Kate H., the mother of two children from Northants, England talked about living experiences with her thirteen-year-old adopted son, J.D. During an incident when he lost his hair-trigger temper, he threw a snooker ball at his eleven-year-old sister. "Fortunately," reported the amazing mother, "Stella's reflexes are very well tuned and she dodged. The ball went past her ear and smashed a very large patio window." Her son showed no remorse for his actions or made any apologies. According to Kate her boy's view of the incident was that it was Stella's fault for irritating him, her fault that he threw the ball at her, the girl's fault that she ducked, and that the ball was loose and able "to break the patio window rather than Stella's skull." During another incident her son punched his sister full in the face because he was angry—everyone had had fun at a family outing except him. After she was hit Stella jumped out of the car and had to be collected by her father. The girl refused to reenter the automobile while J.D. was there. Their young daughter "was completely hysterical" and terrified of her brother. From then on Stella refused to be left alone with J.D. Instead she shadowed her parents through the house and into the garden to remain safe. The son's response to his sister was to call her names and continuous refusal to take responsibility for his actions. Kate concluded: "The other child is living just as much of a traumatic existence as your attachment disturbed child. What child of 10 deserves to be brought up being called 'a tart' or 'a cow'?"

Mattie W. of central Nebraska is the mother of six children, two adopted boys and four biological girls. After frequent aggressive behaviors by the youngest son, their older son decided that he did not want to be Scot's brother. By that time the younger brother had earned a poor reputation and was considered to be "a rotten kid and nobody liked him," Mattie relayed. In an effort to decrease the stress caused by the youngest, Mattie's husband Dan started taking Scot with him on errands. In his attempt to give the other suffering family members a break, "the squeaky wheel" got the lion's share of time alone with Dad. Eventually, the other five children began to feel neglected and depressed; it seemed to them that the way to get attention was to cause pain and havoc within the family. During the interview Mattie sadly reported that, in spite of the fact that all the siblings are now adults, they still resent Scot for taking their parents from them prematurely. Today Mattie and Dan believe not telling the other children about how bad things were with Scot backfired and ultimately hurt them all the more. Their previously successful communication systems were completely dismantled and the older children's unhappiness increased.

Connie R. a single mother from Lompoc, California verbalized concerns about all three of her daughters. Through the hospitalizations and surgeries necessary for her youngest, Alexis, the stressed mother realized that her two older daughters were paying a price. She finally said, "I'm burning out here. I had my two other kids, so I said this isn't fair to them. The girls are more and more troubled; they're acting out more at school. They're not getting enough of me." Connie's single state caught up with her and she became burdened by the all the responsibilities she had trying to meet the needs of three growing daughters. She shared, "My God, what I found out is that Alexis was threatening my other girls. They are all so different. My girls were terrified of Alexis, just as frightened of her behavior as I was."

Beverly James, MA, a twenty-three year veteran and therapist of some renown from Hawai'i has worked with traumatized children for over two decades and had some interesting ideas about the potential parents of such disturbed kids. She would like them to know, in very real terms and before taking a child, what it could be like living with an AD youngster. However, she added, "Every adoptive parent I have ever worked with got glassy-eyed because they have some mantra going that 'I can love this child to death; I can love, love, love this child to health.' And they believe it, God help them, they believe it." Ironically, she said, that is exactly what is needed for kids such as these, someone who can make that kind of commitment. In her estimation parents who fearfully "tiptoe" into an adoptive or foster situation won't be able to handle the demands of the enormous task before them.

I'm encouraged that you have stayed to read every page. Your actions honor the parents who have lived through hell and then poured out their hearts. I hope you absorb all you can from families who are living proof that this disorder can be survived.

CHAPTER FIVE—From the Honeymoon to Reality

Throughout the interviewing process I was enthralled by the degree of commonality experienced by families whose places of origin were as diverse as their ethnic and racial heritages. Once I had heard enough stories about the children's initial behaviors and the early relationships between foster and adoptable children and their potential parents I had to ask some important questions. For instance: In their efforts to get kids placed, do the orphanages or adoption agencies tutor the children in acceptable behaviors before initial visits? Is it possible that the professionals withhold medical and psychological information about the children, as it seems? Is information about the youngsters' personal histories intentionally withheld in an effort to enhance the children's chances at placement? Initial behaviors employed by the children, amazingly similar ones used by kids from Hawai'i to the smallest British hamlet, seem to captivate anxious adults while overwhelming their internal warning system that problems may exist. Now that you are familiar with the signs of attachment problems, you will be able to detect the presence of difficulties from the very start—something most of the parents I met were unprepared, and unable, to do.

For those of you who have never fostered or adopted a child you need to know that the entire process is a profoundly emotional one. Without exception the folks I met were filled with hope and excitement about the adventure being presented to them in the form of a new child! They told me how their hearts felt they would burst with love and pride when they considered the possibilities available to them with the addition of a new, special member to their families. It might also be helpful for those who have never heard of a 'honeymoon' period to describe what one looks like. It is a time when youngsters, those new to the environment, look lovely, follow rules and directions, and behave like well-adjusted adults. In general, there is minimal or no limit testing going on and new parents are lulled into a false sense of security and begin to think, 'We've got this adjustment licked!' That, of course, usually occurs just before all hell breaks loose. However, Beverly James, from Hawai'i, thinks the term 'honeymoon period' is too simplistic and frivolous to be useful. She believes that when children move into new environments, as with foster or adopted kids, they are "numbed out" perhaps as a means of surviving yet another emotional upheaval. James thinks it's not unusual to have otherwise alert children be under-responsive around strangers. We know, she added, that foster kids "fall down and bleed and have cuts and they won't feel the pain. That's not spooky, we do that with hypnosis all the time." However, in several months—or for as long as they can remain superficial—they eventually start being real. Interestingly enough, James shared, that is known as intimacy. "It's negative intimacy, but nonetheless, it's more real than the 'hearts and flowers stuff'" to which AD youngsters are unable to relate.

Impression Managers

Now you may be able to imagine the confusion and desperation some families felt when the early, apparently wonderful start faded rapidly and was replaced by young strangers whose behaviors no longer made sense. You are about to meet children who are expert "impression managers," youngsters already capable of managing others opinions of them. Most attachment compromised youngsters seem to have an inborn sense of how, and who, to "work" so their needs will be met. Such behaviors ensure their continued survival without having to become entrapped by human emotions or enmeshed in situations that require reciprocity. As you are learning, young ones who have had difficulties with bonding cannot tolerate emotional closeness. Such requirements represent the antithesis of their internal theme—the need to remain alone if they are to make it through life. RAD kids already demonstrate amazing skills at manipulating and positively influencing the opinions of even the most cynical. The behaviors employed by the children from first visits seem to successfully captivate, and consequently assure, their placement in potential homes.

However, new parents are not the only ones left in the dark. Cute, freckled, diminutive survivalists are capable of hiding their most negative behaviors from professionals, as well. Over the years I have developed many beliefs about adoption and foster care agencies that are staffed by loving social workers and counselors, by those described as "helpers." Many professionals in the field seem to maintain high levels of hope for their clients, no matter how chronic the disease process appears. In general, they are certain that what they are doing—placing children—is right and good for each family and for society as a whole. Simultaneously, they tend to be overly busy human, fallible professionals, often under-staffed and under-funded who sometimes miss important things.

In the meantime, attachment-disordered youngsters view professionals with the same level of disdain as they hold for actual and potential parents. No matter how things look, or how they might appear, lack of trust remains the true underlying issue and one that will not be bridged because professionals or other adults are acting in the best interest of the child. Even when they are "all eyelashes and dimples," they are still—or yet—managing others' opinions of who they are and what they are really like. Angelic, that's often the guise they pick, angels with halos! They can be darling and funny and energetic and affectionate and smart and incredibly beautiful, characteristics that all parents want their children to possess. We continue to believe that beautiful, smart, charming children, even when neglected or left unattended and near death, will grow up to be bright, social, problem-free, and successful adults. What is the rest of that fantasy? Ah, of course, they will also love us madly and would never dream of breaking the rules or refusing to take care of us in our old age!

To this day available and needy children are still marketed and presented by adoption agencies to potential families through a variety of means. I still cannot look at what I call a "Wish Book" filled with photos of adorable children in need of homes without a visceral, internal maternal response. Unfortunately, it often appeared that their true histories and natures were either minimized or ignored. I've come to believe that an agency's fear is that new parents would reject a particular toddler or young child if they knew the details of the youngster's past or if they had a clear idea about the long term ramifications of that history. What results is an interesting dance between injured children, frightened professionals, and potential parents who are left in the dark. The injured youngsters present a phony peek into heaven; the professionals pretend they are telling the whole truth; and anxious parents, out of ignorance, miss internal cues and "red flags" that might be silently trumpeting a warning—truly an ominous start to one of the most important relationships in existence!

Upon placement, the initial honeymoon phase may last for weeks, but with others, for only moments. And when the child's honeymoon is over, then what? Hints or full-bodied collisions present a discouraging picture that may be in total contrast to first impressions. In the paragraphs ahead parents tell about their youngsters' real behaviors, those which replaced the ones seen in the early days of their relationship. Sometimes the truth about the traumas, which have had significant effects on their babies' behaviors, came to light. The realities of the situation are shared as well as some unanticipated effects on siblings and other family members. Often the children's histories had to be surmised, indications given with maladaptive behaviors which showed up after the angel-like act was finished. Ignored or minimized traumatic experiences eventually outshout active behaviors and quiet lies. Upon looking closer, you will clearly the see the common signs and symptoms of attachment disorders, those obliterated by the heat of first moments. The parents' discoveries of the abuse and neglect their youngsters endured without support and in the silence of their aloneness. The early manifestations of problems follows:

Kristin C. of rural Indiana discussed the first visit she and her husband Terry had with their adopted children. Michaela and Ryan were placed with the Indiana couple on the heels of situations that proved to be traumatic to the young pair. "It was easy to see that even though they were only nine and ten they were doing their best to be on very good behavior. They were tense; they smiled in a very tense way. They had practice with meeting adults who wanted to take them home; they knew how to nod their head when you would say something silly. We were nervous too. They did a beautiful job of hiding any problems they had at that time. What we saw during that first visit was definitely not indicative of what we were going to see within a month of getting them to our house. Michaela was the perfect daughter: she liked to cook; she liked to clean. She was sweet, she was adorable, and I remember thinking 'How could anyone ever be dissatisfied with this child because she is so perfect?' Ryan was hyper, he was running knocking into things; he was tearing up, dismantling, destroying. Neither of them would come to us for any reassurance, for any advice. They had their own mother-son pattern fully in place between them. They didn't need either of us."

The adoption agency had shared some basic information so Kristin knew a bit about the biological parents: the mother had some type of mental illness; their father was an alcoholic and reportedly used drugs; and they were both heavy smokers. The couple concluded the children had been nutritionally neglected as their teeth were "basically rotted." Their daughter and son were two of four children born one year apart to the same mother. Prior to her placement with Kristin, Michaela spent four years in foster placement following her removal from their mother's care. When six, Ryan was admitted to a psychiatric hospital due to feelings of hopelessness and anger problems. He had been admitted from foster care and hospitalized for a month before their birth mother abandoned him. According to reports the biological mother eventually permanently abandoned all four children, and then just disappeared.

Kristin continued to share about the history of behaviors of her adopted children. "Michaela is very distant, aloof," Kristin stated. "Whenever you try and get close to her she becomes extremely distant." The adoptive mother said that in his grief following abandonment Ryan changed radically and then was diagnosed with a number of psychiatric illnesses. Following Ryan's discharge from the hospital the pair stayed together but were moved around from a pre-adoptive home to foster home which cared for fourteen children at one time. Kristin shared with distaste, "They took turns using the beds in twelve hour shifts because of lack of space." Eventually they were moved to yet another foster situation with a family who had recently lost an eight-year-old daughter in an automobile accident. According to the angry adoptive mother, "The Division of Family and Children placed my kids in that home knowing full well that it was a double dose of grief for everyone. In that home they were severely emotionally abused." That placement was followed by more chaos and the pattern continued.

"I knew that Michaela had been the mother figure [to Ryan] for years," Kristin stated with resolve, "and that I would have to deal with that. I knew that she internalized everything whereas Ryan attacked everything." The children lived in the same town as their extended family and former foster families. Their children's increased anxiety levels and acting-out behaviors followed visits with their former caretakers. Kristin said she knew about their school performances and grades: "Michaela's were really good and Ryan's poor." Michaela's greatest skill, the new parents discovered, was to mastermind situations that would upset or cause chaos within the family. According to the mother, her daughter had an uncanny ability to draw people to her, some from school and others from the counseling center. The mother felt that their name had been "dragged through the mud" by her daughter and that people in their community believed Kristin and Terry were somehow mistreating or abusing Michaela.

Troy and Leslie W. of San Luis Obispo reported that their adopted son Sam had suffered through multiple abuses in his young life. According to limited reports he'd been exposed prenatally to alcohol and possibly methamphetamine. The first known assault on him occurred at three or four days of age when his birth mother drowned him with liquid baby vitamin supplements. After resuscitation by medical professionals Sam experienced frequent bouts of apnea and had to be put on a home monitor for a time. Because of problems in the relationship between his biological parents, the boy was passed around during infancy and during his early years accrued seven or eight placements by the age of five. According to their informational sources Sam was moved from his biological mom's care, to birth dad, on to foster care, and then was returned to the birth father. Well after Sam's placement with them Troy and Leslie were told by the child's biological grandmother that there were a number of men revolving through the mother's household who used Sam as their "punching bag." The youngster's records indicated that both his legs had been broken by age two; that he had been the victim of sexual abuse; and at one time had been beaten unconscious by his birth father.

At the time of Sam's placement the adoptive parents were unaware of his extensive history. Later, however, they learned that Headstart records contained copies of occupational and physical therapy evaluations, the results of his victimization. After leaving his biological father's home, and prior to the placement with Leslie and Troy, Sam lived with a family for eighteen months while believing the placement was permanent. In fact, his name had been changed in anticipation of that adoption. Shortly before the legal adoption the parents walked in on Sam during playtime while he was lying on top of their daughter. They reacted vehemently, accused him of molestation and immediately had him removed from their home. The couple firmly declined the option of counseling, so, at six years old, the little boy was banished from the home he thought would be his last.

The frustrated mother said the goals for Sam at school were identical to those at home—he needed to follow the rules. He had not developed an ability to utilize "cause and effect thinking" nor did he possess any ability to reciprocate, as do well-nurtured youngsters. "He never tried to please anybody; he didn't get that," reported Leslie. He wasn't doing well in school but repeating a grade was not a large concern to them. They did wonder what would happen to Sam if he could not learn to care for others or learn from his mistakes. When the couple first got him, at six-years-old, he didn't know his colors and couldn't write his name. Because of his rough start he was unable to accomplish basic skills most first graders are expected to do. His mother commented, "He just did not seem able to put two and two together. I didn't realize at the time that two and two was irrelevant to him." It was determined, due to Sam's emotional immaturity, he should be moved back to kindergarten and that an Individual Education Plan (IEP) should be developed to help him. The couple thought Sam should be at the meeting since the meeting was about him, so they took him. By that time Leslie suspected Sam had attachment and bonding problems, so she read every bit of information she could get on the topic. She'd learned how indiscriminately affectionate they are to strangers, and true to form, Sam physically cuddled up to the principal. The distressed mother removed her son from the lap of the principal, who objected, saying it was okay for Sam to sit on him. Troy and Leslie explained that it was not okay and it was symptomatic of the problem behaviors children like Sam had.

Troy described Sam's pattern: "Even if it was something that he wanted to do, he would act out in some fashion so that he couldn't go. It was almost orgasmic [for their son] in the sense that when the consequence was delivered, there was such a sense of relief on his part. It was such a nightmare, he had to keep a certain level of chaos in the family in order to be comfortable." Troy said eventually they became prisoners in their own household, and it hadn't taken long to occur. They'd always been family oriented so their vacations were spent in the company of extended family. As a couple they felt their dates with each other were less often than was good for most marriages, but most of their social activities were family affairs, which they both enjoyed. Because of Sam's behaviors they weren't able to continue the visits as they had in the past, nor could their family visit them in their home. Baby-sitters refused to stay with the child more than once, and he couldn't be taken to social events.

To the bewildered couple it seemed as if Sam became punishing, particularly to Leslie, especially when some of the confusion would subside. The mother reported that life with Sam "was chaos and struggle from the moment he got up in the morning 'til he went to bed at night. It was unbelievable!" Leslie added that at first he would threaten her by saying "I'd like to kill you" or "I wish you were dead." The threats progressed to "When I get big. I'm going to come back and kill you." Perhaps because of his size and age the mom didn't take Sam's statements so seriously. But eventually he developed a specific plan: "He was going to get up in the night and get a knife and come in and kill me." Troy said Sam announced his plan in a very calm, matter-of-fact manner and added that he knew where the knives were kept, all in preparation for following through with his plan. Leslie was the only one whose life was threatened. Equally frightening, Sam had the habit of getting up and wandering around during the night. One night Sam had an accident in his bed. When he awakened, he got up and tried to clean the feces off himself, and then went outside to dispose of his pajamas in the trash. He then came back into the house, put on a clean pair of pajamas, and then went back to bed. The sleeping parents never even knew he was out of bed.

Although Troy is a psychologist, he found his son's combination of behaviors simultaneously fascinating and distressing. The father stated, "His stuff was psychological, a constant series of carefully selected behaviors designed to cause distress in other people. So it would be spill, drip, drool, smear, disobey, argue, very subtle ways of demonstrating that I'm going to get even you with you." The mother shared that Sam remains hypervigilent and uses unseen antenna to read people. Troy considers such talent "a gift." Agreeably, Troy is the family peacemaker, "so the game was to get dad all atwitter." Sam could simultaneously make the toilets overflow, the dog bark, and litter the floor with cereal. "It's remarkable," Troy shared "how he could really size up the situation. In other settings with other family members he would plan out what it was that would get them. I think of him as a budding psychopath." Leslie chimed in; "We tried to instill that conscience. It struck me funny that with Tray (their first child) we were successful. Thank God we were successful parents with him." The teachers would ask Leslie and Troy to review the rules with the child. The parents said he could parrot back the rules "verbatim" but was still unsuccessful in modifying his behavior. Leslie shared, "The rules do not apply to Sam. They apply to everybody else around him and he will be the first to point it out that somebody else is breaking the rule. But they do not pertain to him and that has been the way, consistently." The father stated sadly, "He can use the rules, manipulate them to his own end. And everything is run through his own filter. Sometimes it's very hard to figure out why he's doing something. But it's clearly motivated behavior, he's doing it for a reason."

Sharon W., wife to David, from Mequon, Wisconsin, stated that after about six months of living with them, their son Yuri has considered his new mother to be the enemy. She said the small boy has made it perfectly clear that he does not want her interfering in what he thinks of as "papa's time." Sharon reported the manipulative behaviors, although used extensively by the sister Svetlana and her little brother, it was actually first utilized by Yuri when the tyke would stick out his tongue or do whatever needed to maneuver time with his father and get rid of her. Initially Yuri and his biological sister, Svetlana, were unable to sit down or remain still for any significant period of time. It seemed to the inexperienced couple that the pair were "just running around constantly." Sharon said she now believes that their increased activity level was due to overstimulation, but she's not really sure of the cause. "It wasn't as if you could sit and hold them and try to establish some relationship by touch. It was simply impossible," the sad mother replied. The parents feel like they're just skimming the surface with their children and aren't able to get beyond the superficial, and charming façade they present. Sharon believes that the youngsters have survived by pleasing adults, mostly adults who are strangers. Two weeks after Svetlana joined them the family went to a hockey game. Prior to the game Svetlana had made it clear she wanted no contact with Sharon whatsoever. Suddenly, when they were around people they knew, those unfamiliar to the children, "she was hanging all over me, kissing me and just gazing at me. It was fake; it was all for show. It kind of gave you the creepy crawlies," the Wisconsin mother said with a sigh. Even though Yuri is eleven, he still searches, and finds, people who will let him sit on their lap. Recently the mom found out that her son sits on his teachers' laps during assemblies while the other children sit on the floor. "I'd say that is a danger signal," Sharon said. She wondered aloud, "Am I ever going to truly penetrate or reach this kid?"

Lindsey V. of Bucks, Britain, is the married mother of one daughter. Not all attachment disturbed children are overly active or aggressive. During a discussion of the 'honeymoon phase' Lindsey told me that before placement their daughter had talked incessantly and demonstrated many active attention seeking behaviors. However, the frustrated mother stated, "when she first came to us, she changed completely. We didn't have a honeymoon period. She changed completely almost overnight to become this, what appeared to me, to be this withdrawn child who didn't speak, who didn't give anything, who would sit for hours and hours doing nothing. Just staring into space. And that's what she does basically most of the time now." There had been periods that Lindsey described as roller coaster like, times when she was talkative, "lovely company, absolutely delightful." But then, for no apparent reason, her outgoing personality would disappear and was replaced by a quiet, withdrawn youngster. "And then," her mother said, "she'll go to bed and wake up and be the same withdrawn child who sits for hours, for weeks on end and does nothing but stare into space." That is how she acted since coming to live with Lindsey and husband Dave. Lindsey reported she'd spent valuable time trying to decide what motivated her child. In the end, she concluded that the amount of effort didn't matter, she couldn't help the girl climb out of her shell. Sadly, the mother shared, "She was determined to sit and do nothing. That's what she does most of the time."

Samantha and Sam M. from Santa Margarita, California, shared their daughters' histories. The father told me that initially he and his wife decided to adopt a little girl, Cassie, into their family. At that time they had no indication that there was a second girl, the older sister. At 2 ½ Cassie had already been through one placement following her removal from the care of her birth mother, who was incarcerated due to drug abuse and theft charges. Sam and Samantha visited the toddler only once before the placement and had not been told of any existing physical or emotional problems. The parents reported Cassie was beautiful and innocent and they "immediately fell in love with her." Samantha stated one week after their initial visit that Cassie was suddenly, "dropped off at five o'clock in the evening by the foster mom. I was appalled that Social Services would allow such a traumatic change for a 2-year-old, but that is what happened." Eight years later, Cassie has never again seen her former foster parents.

Eventually Samantha and Sam were told about Cassie's five-year-old sister, Jackie. Although the little girl had already had nine placements, for unknown reasons, the couple reported no internal warnings were noticed. The loving pair said they still believe, "She just needs stability; she just needs a home. She just needs love." After time with their daughter, they understand that Jackie's early life was riddled with physical, emotional, and sexual abuse. Reportedly, the mother and her boyfriend were on heroin so were unable to care for the child. While Jackie was in the care of her birth mother, it was not uncommon for a meal to consist of a bag of potato chips while forced to sit in the corner of the room. Because Jackie was the older of the two, and the daughter of a woman incapable of mothering, eventually she became 'the mother' to her little sister, Cassie. Samantha said sadly, "She had a big load to bear early." By the time Jackie joined the Santa Margarita family, her body was totally scarred from bug bites. Her new mother reported the dirt under Jackie's arms was so thick it took six months to clean because the skin had grown over the dirt. Head lice had left sores all over her head. Sam and Samantha were still angry that Social Services allowed the series of tragedies to happen to Jackie. In an effort to give their child the care she so desperately needed, they used ample amounts of lice shampoo and antibacterial soap. The mom, overcome with emotion, stated, "You think you're going to scrub this kid clean and give her some clean clothes and life will be good. It isn't. A bar of soap is not big enough—you cannot wash away years of neglect."

The California mother said that the baby, Cassie, immediately became part of the family; however, that was not the case with Jackie. Samantha said she felt different about their older daughter "right off. She was selfish. There was no two-way street of a relationship; it was her way or no way." Two months after Jackie's arrival the family decided to take a trip to Mexico as a means of bonding with their new daughters.

Social Services sent them with their blessings. It was during that trip that they observed some disturbing signs of things to come. The well-meaning couple bought Jackie a silver bracelet as a 'welcome to the family' gift, but she totally destroyed it. They were amazed at how much strength was required to bend and twist the silver item. When the deed was completed the youngster just grinned and held it up for her parents to behold. In addition, the 5 year-old ate more than required by a child her age. She did not quit until she vomited. Sam and Samantha did not yet realize that such was the beginning of some very serious behaviors. The astonished new mom shared, "She was sneaky; she could walk across a room full of people and steal something right in front of your face and you'd never know it. She was hypervigilent and I wasn't."

Samantha slowly learned that she, too, needed to be ever alert so she could keep a close watch on her daughter. "Then," said the experienced mother, "I saw some alarming things. She knew what you were doing every minute, every second. She didn't sleep, she lay there. She could hear better than any child. You could be whispering in the corner and she knew what you were talking about." Sam joined in, "She didn't sleep at night. She would be up in the middle of the night play-acting. I'd get up to go the rest room and hear her jump back in bed. She was dancing on the bed and jumping at three in the morning." Samantha said she believed Jackie didn't like her from the start of their relationship. The little girl wouldn't talk to her new mother or look her in the eye. When anyone else was present "she was superficially charming to the max: the hugs, the kisses, the 'I love you's,' the sitting on your lap. To this moment she still does that. I mean it's just incredible, and ten minutes before she'd been just sitting there stone cold, mean looking and not responding."

Mattie W. of Kearney, Nebraska talked about the history of her son, Scot, not yet three at the time of placement. Until his adoption Scot had spent varying times with his biological mother, in hospitals, and in foster care. Mrs. W. reported, "It was just a really traumatic, rough two years" for her son, the youngest child of her six. At Scot's birth his mother was about 16, not married; her own aunt had raised her. Apparently, the young mother wanted to keep Scot but had no idea how to rear him, and had no mothering skills or role models available to her. Mattie and husband Dan were told he'd been hospitalized a few times, with the last being the most severe, for malnutrition. Following that hospital stay the infant was temporarily placed in foster care. Ms. W. stated that her home state actively promotes returning children to their biological families. Consequently, at about eighteen-months-old that's what happened to Scot. It was reported that following his return to the young mother she left him lying in his crib unattended for two days without food while she "went out."

The experienced Nebraska mom believed there must have also been an incident that involved water, but she never learned what had actually happened. The sensitive mother stated, "When we got him he would scream in absolute terror when I put him in the bathtub, even with an inch of water. I have no idea what that was all about." Mattie and Dan were told the birth mother would tie the toddler in his high chair, offer him food, but then yank it away before the youngster could eat. Scot became very frustrated and angry when the mother treated him in that manner which seemed the precursor of serious eating problems. In addition, the toddler hadn't been fed the right kind of food so didn't know how to chew when he joined the Nebraska family. Scot's new family would watch him stuff food into his mouth, then force himself to swallow it whole. "He would eat until there was nothing left to eat." Mattie continued, "I think because he was denied food he was just going to eat everything he could get his little hands on. Consequently he would throw up a lot because he didn't chew." At mealtime the family offered chewing lessons in which the family members masticated in unison hoping to teach Scot how to use his teeth to break up his food.

When Scot first came to be with Dan and Mattie, the child already had some unusual behaviors. "He had one toy; it was a stuffed cow, and he was very possessive of that. If anybody else would touch it or pick it up, he would grab it and say, 'Me, me!'" He seemed to understand everything but spoke only a few words at a time. He was already potty trained and appeared very coordinated, more so than any of my other kids as far as throwing a ball or pedaling a tricycle. "He slept on his back," she continued, "and was stiff as a board. There was absolutely no way you could move him—he was just rigid. I don't know how in the world he ever got rested. He didn't like to be held or cuddled or kissed right from the start. We thought having five other kids, hey, we can overcome this, but it just never happened." According to the mother Scot didn't cry much and seemed to have an amazing tolerance to pain. But he also had what Mattie described as a "trigger temper," he became very angry, very quickly. In addition, the young boy began running away unusually early. He was constantly destructive and broke anything he got his hands on, especially if it belonged to his new mother. Scot also destroyed his own items: chewed on the corners of collars; pulled the elastic out of socks; pulled the cuffs off shirts or pajamas; and poked holes in clothing. He also ripped the casings off the pillowcases and sheets. By about kindergarten or first grade he damaged items by putting them on light bulbs until they got hot enough to burn and he pulled wallpaper off the walls. Mattie said while overcome with tears, "There were no consequences for him—nothing mattered. There was no punishment that made a difference."

Joyce K. of Nipomo, California discussed the current situation with her five-year-old son. The experienced mom talked about Mike's behaviors on their first visit together. "The first day that we went in to meet him, he ran up and hugged us. He'd never seen us in his life before, ran to the door and hugged us. Right away I went, 'Ohhh!' That's very abnormal for a two-and-a-half-year-old child to do something like that, to be very friendly and very outgoing. If he had used cars to sell, he could have sold a lot of them." Joyce continued to say that Mike, "knew very instinctively who to go to get something. In a room of people he could tell who to go to and get what he needed. Very manipulative, I mean for the age, and always very charming. I've never seen a child that age, that perceptive." She explained her son; "It's just that the way he manipulated used to be more outwardly apparent. But now he'll find better ways to get what he needs or get something out of people. I mean, he learned what didn't work very quickly." And then added, "He just gets better at it all the time. He gets slicker all the time; it's just a better sales pitch the next time around."

Joyce and her husband had not yet been told about his history although the youngster had been with them for two years. "A lot of his records," she shared, "are still sealed so he actually hasn't been adopted yet. We're considering it still because of the things he exhibits we've been really holding off on the adoption part with him. We're backing off with that, we're just kind of waiting and seeing. There is some pressure to adopt him because of course DSS has a quota every year for adoptions now. So, there is some pressure to adopt him, but that's their problem. Our thing with Mike is doing the best we can for Mike…and for us."

Laura R. of Scunthorpe, England said about her adopted daughter: "We will never know her real history; we can only guess what happened." Ann was removed from the home of Mr. and Mrs. R. from the ages of sixteen to twenty months while she was supposedly being reunited with her biological mother. However, they were told that during that particular period of time their daughter, in addition to many other caretakers, had been in the custody of a man who had been married to her mother at the time of Ann's birth. The stepfather had a repugnant reputation in their community as a sexual abuser. Years later an adult woman disclosed to Ms. R. that that same man had sexually abused her. Laura stated sadly that she believes it was quite possible that he had sexually abused Ann while in his care. "Looking back at her abnormal behavior towards the bathroom," the confused mother continued, "my feeling is that she probably was abused in the bathroom." Laura said her daughter was extremely frightened of bathing, of having her hair washed, or having her clothing changed. "She absolutely screamed! To wash her hair you had to do like you do a new baby, to rub the towel tightly round and hold her in the sink to wash her hair and she'd be screaming all the time." In addition, the toddler "was very greedy for food. She would take it off the table and she would eat far more that was normal for a child of sixteen months," her mother reported. "She would do things like go into the dustbin; she would pick up any food that was around on the floor. And if we were out in the street she would want to pick up the chewing gum and eat it." While in nursery school little Ann would eat two dinners; she couldn't seem to get enough, but then she would be sick and vomit. The day after Ann joined Laura and Peter they went out to eat and they said she just sat on the chair and didn't relate to or look at anybody. The new parents were told that Ann had spent a lot of time on her cot (bed), probably somewhat isolated from others. But not long after when the tyke went to a shop with her mother she made eye contact and chatted away with people she didn't know at all, the mother stated, somewhat stunned. Her behaviors, especially in comparison with her older sister Joy, were "always strange," shared her mum. "She used her ability to put on this gorgeous smile—I can see through it, and that's why everybody else thought she was wonderful."

Following visits with her birth mother Ann's behaviors deteriorated. During the visits the biological mother sat with her back to Ann and did not deliver promised birthday presents. Laura stated, "She just had so much anger directed towards us. Ann came up and grabbed me around the neck and pulled tight. If I hadn't been stronger than her, she would have really got me with that." Laura recounted other hurtful behaviors committed by her daughter: doors slammed in her face; kicks under the table that she'd deny; items thrown from their table; drawing pins (large straight pins used in sewing) secretly placed in the food at mealtime, to name several. Ms. R. continued, "As far as actually living with the child, these are very demanding children. You can't ever fully relax. You have to stay aware of where they are and what they are doing. If they are upstairs, which bedroom are they in? What have they damaged while they've been up there? What have they taken? It's difficult to get out or to get away because these aren't the types of children old friends will want to have for the week." Their neighbors became aware of early difficulties with Ann because with the close proximity they could hear the constant ruckus.

After failed attempts at therapy for Ann and the family, they tried family discussions with negotiations around necessary house duties. Laura said she would negotiate her day off, a time she didn't have to do any work at all. But then when it came her turn to do the chores, she wouldn't do anything. The mother said there would always be a battle or she would be relieved of her responsibilities rather than argue about everything. "She just wouldn't do it," the sad mother stated. "Not long before she left, if it was her turn to wash up, she'd wait until you weren't looking and then she'd spit all over everything. You had no alternative to rewash the stuff; grinding type of behavior which is very wearing." Eventually Ann's behaviors became too much for Laura and Peter to handle, and she was removed from their home and placed in care.

Sarah D. of Shawnee, Kansas, mother to son David, stated that within the first few days of life his biological mother abandoned him at the hospital. Consequently, he was immediately placed in foster care where he spent the next ten months. After extraordinary efforts to reintegrate him into the chaotic birth family, the infant was reunited with his birth mother by the fall of his first year. By the following spring his biological parents filed for divorce and by July their divorce was final.

Apparently David was then moved to the birth father's home where he remained for approximately the next three years. During those following years, according to the adoptive mother, "About every despicable thing that could happen to a person happened to this boy. Despite how many hundreds of reports and papers, nothing happened to him; nothing safe happened to him until he was 3 ½. That's the part I can't live with," she said choking back sobs, "I can't believe that much was allowed to happen. I know we say we're doing things to protect all parties involved. But, you know, the birth dad doesn't need to be protected. He's a monster!"

Soon after David was placed with Sarah and her husband, Rex, the youngster was admitted to a psychiatric institution, against their deepest desires, but out of necessity to keep David, and those around him, safe. While he underwent three months treatment for his emotional problems, she pursued the social worker to uncover an accurate history. In her stubbornness and determination Sarah believed if she knew something of David's history, it would offer clues as how to properly treat her child. The desperate mother phoned the social worker, again and again, to insist that she be allowed to read David's records. Finally the social worker relented and made the records available to the frustrated mother.

Sarah went to a municipal building in Kansas City where she was taken to a little room which contained a small desk full of official looking records, five or six accordion folders, each about ten inches thick. When asked where her child's records were among the reams of papers, the agency representative stated they all belonged to David. Tearfully the sensitive mother stated, "I had never seen that much paperwork. When we moved him into our house there was only one of those folders and it wasn't even full. I remember saying 'Were did all this other paperwork come from?' She said it had always been there. I just wanted to grab her and say 'It was not!'" The mother told David's worker she was not leaving until she'd read and made notes on everything. The young woman sat down and started reading but part way through Sarah knew she wasn't going to be able to finish. "I had to quit," she said overcome with sadness, "because I would just start crying. I mean, I went through a box of Kleenex!" At one point she left the office and went to the bathroom and thought she was going to vomit. "But all I could do" the overwhelmed mother stated, "was just lie there in the bathroom in this gross, nasty city building. This is just so gross: I'm on the floor, on my knees, just laying my face on the toilet seat, and I'm thinking this is how desperate we are. I'm a sane, middle class woman lying on the floor of a filthy bathroom. The bathroom had not been cleaned, I don't know who used it last, and what they've done there. But all I know is I am literally on the floor sobbing on this toilet seat. And at that point I thought everybody has given up on this child." Out of her grief over David's most recent hospitalization she added, "Even us."

Connie R. from Lompoc, California is a single mother of three biological daughters. Her youngest, Alexis, had an experience which changed her life completely. At eighteen months the toddler drank a caustic poison which had been left in a Texas motel room they'd rented while on vacation. Her immediate injuries were so severe that the wee one had to be airlifted to a nearby hospital for life-saving surgery. Alexis' esophagus was destroyed and had to be replaced with a portion of her colon. Before the accident and the terrors of the recovery process Connie said that her daughter had been outgoing, loving, and affectionate. "She was a real bubbly little kid," she added. In the long run her daughter has experienced a lifetime of medical problems and multiple surgeries. The tearful mother stated: "Her entire life was disrupted. She was different from the time she had the surgeries, even when she was in the hospital. I remember looking at her and she just was vacant. She just wasn't there anymore." During those years parents were not encouraged or allowed to remain with their children in the hospital setting so Connie and Alexis were forced apart.

The traumatized mother shared that the daughter she knew no longer existed. She was no longer "effervescent and outgoing and engaging. She was not present to what was going on in an interactive way. She didn't make the proper type of eye contact; there just weren't the correct kinds of involvement or interactions or reactions to things." Almost immediately Alexis became isolative and full of rage. Her mother shared that she began to have temper tantrums, like never before, which did not end until about her eleventh year. The little girl became increasingly violent, so much so that Connie became fearful for her classmates' safety in school. Then, because of her long term specialized medical and new psychiatric needs, Alexis continued to spend much of her adolescent years in hospitals and away from her mother and sisters.

Louie F., from Finedon, England, is the mother of a severely disturbed adopted boy. During a group interview she shared the following experience: "We didn't have a honeymoon. The first time Adrian came here to live he threw everything out of his room and down the stairs. And I'm talking about drawers, bedside cabinet, bedside lamp, books, clothes, toys, clock, everything. And that was a real attack on us because we had made his room so special for this boy. He'd been visiting the last three or four weeks and he'd been excited about coming to this room that we had lovingly prepared and decorated and planned for him. He was four years and ten months when he came and he destroyed that room the first night he was here." The sad mother stated that his behavior over his time with them had actually changed very little. Louie said that the periods between outbursts varied, "But always, you never know when that anger is going to erupt again."

Susan and David R. of Overland Park, Kansas, shared that when their children were placed with them Ann was eight, and James was almost five. They both had the same birth mother but different fathers; their birth mother had married three times and had a child from each union.

Another brother, one older than Ann, was taken by his birth father because the man realized that the mother was incapable of parenting that boy named Philip. Ann remembered a bit about him and that Philip's father would not allow the younger two siblings to be involved in his family unit. Even as an adult Susan's daughter did not understand just why she wasn't allowed to be involved with her older brother and his family. Ann had been the product of the second marriage, which apparently had not lasted long. According to scarce reports it had been James's biological father, their mother's third husband, who had been physically abusive and sexually inappropriate with Ann. The Midwestern couple was told their youngsters were available for adoption because Ann had been sexually abused. Their son was removed from the home on Ann's shirttail but the professionals thought James had somehow been spared the rough treatment. Later, however, the social workers became more honest with Susan and David, and then opened the youngsters' files to them. Eventually it became apparent that, indeed, their son had been abused, but even more damaging, and also had been the victim of frank neglect. During the interview Susan stated, "I do think James was probably abused—emotionally and possibly even sexually—because of some of the horrendous behaviors that we see. James has incredible anger, incredible rage." The mother continued, sadly, "I just can't believe that a child who hasn't had some pretty intense abuse could be that angry." Her belief is that her son suffered neglect by being left, unattended, in his crib for days and hours on end without getting his basic needs met. Once James was described as a "purple baby," an infant who cries and cries out of their inborn need to affiliate with no one to respond to the cries; no one to touch them or care for them. The experienced mother believes that it is possible that the rage felt and demonstrated by her son could have come out of the time that he was left, wanting, in his crib.

Full of emotion, Susan reported that James acted up almost from the start. His teachers in daycare reported troublesome aggressiveness and physical attacks on other kids as well as on some of the adult caretakers. It became so bad that people from the school charged James with assault and battery. Susan and David forgave their new son and attributed his acting-out to new life changes, all the adjustments involved in becoming a child adopted into their family. The mother said, sadly, "I think we were so naïve; we didn't know what we were really seeing for many years. That was unfortunate for all of us." They discovered early in their placement that they had to constantly monitor both James and Ann. The Midwestern couple kept a high level of vigilance and constant supervision because the children proved they couldn't be trusted. Since early teens James demonstrated a fascination with fire; consequently, he set many fires not far from their home. Susan said she believed the fire setting occurred off and on throughout his life spent in their home.

During his teens David and Susan's son spent only two years at home with his family. According to his mother James eventually became institutionalized and more comfortable in psychiatric facilities than at home with them. The first time he was taken out of the home was when he was about ten years old. The boy had run away from school and when the police picked him up James became threatening toward them. When the police officer questioned James about his plans, the youngster told him he was going to get Dad's gun, kill his Mom and Dad, and then burn the house down. The officer told the parents that in spite of extensive experience with children he was most frightened by their son. Apparently James clearly stated what he planned to do; he knew where the gun and gas containers were kept and knew what he needed to do to make good the threats. The police officer himself felt uncomfortable and told the frightened parents that he would not let their son return home without proper follow-up care. Initially James was sent to a local group home, which didn't work because, as Susan said, "They didn't know what to do with him; they had no clue how to handle him. He was then admitted to an inpatient psychiatric facility" for about a week and a half. According to Susan they had no idea how to treat James either because they didn't actually know what was wrong with him. After some time "they threw up their hands" and then sent him on to a state institution where the youngster spent almost two years. Eventually James returned home at the request of Mr. and Ms. R. The couple felt the institution had done nothing except contain him for the length of the hospitalization.

The couple told me they'd never pressed charges against their son but shared they had enlisted the aid of the police in recent months. Reluctantly Susan said, "We were concerned about him but with his past history we felt a real obligation to let the community know that he was out there roaming around somewhere." The experienced mother said the toughest thing about rearing James was that just when she felt like things were going well, then the situation would rapidly fall apart. "I want things predictable," she said. "I like predictable and with this boy nothing is predictable." The frustrated mom used to think if they'd had a horrible morning and if she put him on the bus kicking and screaming, then a horrible day at school was nearly guaranteed. But that was not the case with her son. On other days when his day started well, happy and cooperative, Susan would get a call from his teachers five minutes after he got off the bus telling her he was already out-of-control. Susan said there was never any correlation between the start of the day and what would happen next. "You never could predict one thing or the other," Ms. R. said with a sigh.

Nancy R. of rural Kansas talked about their daughter Heather's first days with her family. "She was extremely loud and just ran around, just ran and ran and ran and she didn't sleep." The experienced mother spoke in a rhythm perhaps as rapid as one that might have matched her daughter's initial activity level. "She just ran everywhere, she never walked. She didn't sit still. She didn't sleep. She never quit talking. She couldn't sit quietly in a car, just wild like that. Just like a spring that is twisted so tight. Just very, very wired." Nancy stated she and her husband

John had only two to three visits during the month-long get acquainted period. Once the meetings started the adoption agency began putting pressure on the family because of living conditions they'd determined were dangerous for the child. The social worker told them they had to quickly decide what they wanted to do. "Do you want her or not?" they were asked. The mother of three stated, "We had to really hurry. We didn't have a long time to decide. She was the right age (five-years-old), she was a little girl, and my heart was just bursting with mother love!"

According to instructions from the adoption workers the visits and Heather's placement with them remained clandestine. Nancy said that when they had visits they had to meet in secret places and the youngster never knew where she was. Nancy had been told there was a man, the child's abuser, who was trying to get physical custody of the little girl and the agency was working to avoid that situation. The youngster had experienced both sexual and emotional abuse, reported the mother, and "had seen a lot of physical abuse from the abuser toward her biological mother. She was dirty, she was hungry, and she had been very neglected. She had been fondled quite a bit; she had seen way too much." Because of that, and due to the small community where Heather was living, Social Services wanted her placement to occur with a family from another area as well as when the abuser was out of town. Nancy continued, "The day that we picked her up to take her home, we met at a restaurant, at a secret place, and they had a trash bag with a half a dozen pieces of clothing that were tossed in the back of our Suburban. She climbed in; we climbed in." The social worker told Nancy and John, in a somewhat offhand manner, that they would have to change their new daughter's name to maintain her privacy and so the abuser would be unable to locate her. Nancy said that on the way home that day they talked about the necessary name change. It was decided that the older children would choose one name and that she and James would each choose another. The confused girl got to choose her new name from the three picked by her new family, but didn't have to decide that day. "And after a few days she chose the name Heather," shared Nancy.

The Kansan mother of four told me that after six months Heather continued to be "just as hyper as she had been." The exhausted mother said that nighttime was still difficult for Heather and the rest of the family, too. The youngster spent much of the night awake and active. There was no sign the family could see to indicate that Heather was sleeping at night. She would be awake and prowl almost cat-like through the house. The little girl would steal food from the kitchen and then hoard it in her room. Nancy said if Heather was caught during her nightly activity she would make up some wild reason: she thought she heard her name called; she needed a drink or to go to the bathroom. The child was quick to fabricate reasons or what might be acceptable answers. The family became frustrated with Heather because she accepted no blame for anything that she did wrong. In the meantime, she reacted to John as though he were the abuser, so remained distant from her father. Nancy said that out of the girls emotional reactions she remained constantly glued to, which continues even today. The weary mother shared, "When she is with me she is very manipulative and cruel. I've often likened the situation to a little stray dog—you reach out to pet a little stray dog that looks sweet and is wagging its tail at you. It needs a home and it looks hungry; you reach out your hand to pat this little dog and it bites you. You reach out, and you reach out, and you reach out, and every time it bites. Eventually you quit reaching out."

Jane D., a central Nebraska mother to seven children in almost as many years talked about the behaviors of her newly adopted children, a biological sibling strip of three boys and one girl. When Chuck and Jane first met the girl she ran up to the car and said, 'You're my new mom!' Dotty threw her arms around Jane's neck. Jane's reaction was understandable, "I mean," she said, "she was just wonderful! I just had never met anybody who was so accepting and loving. Her eyes were just big and excited and I just could not believe that these children had been taken out of the home; that someone had not accepted them." The couple said it was an overwhelming greeting and that the first two weeks were wonderful and full of good will and friendly behaviors. The dumbfounded mother reported that after the first two weeks, Dotty became more reserved and began to withdraw. However, when the girl ran into the room, she'd throw herself at her mother for a bear hug, and the new mother would invariably get hurt because Dotty would either step on her toes or "accidentally" slap Jane's face rather than wrapping her arms around her neck. The mother told me with sadness in her voice, "There was always some type of pain involved in hugging her, and it's always an accident!"

According to the exhausted parents, the children, subtly, slowly, and one at a time, started saying "I'm not going to do what you ask. You're not my real mom." Chuck and Jane found that surprising especially after such an auspicious start at forming a new family group. However, "I thought this is an adjusting period of time, we just need to get over this hump," Jane maintained. The couple shared the parental approach of: "You need to learn to do what I say. I'm the mom, I am in charge here and you will have to do as I say. I won't ask you to do anything I won't do, but you need to do everything I ask." One of the children told his teacher that he would not do his homework just because the teacher expected it of him. "He just flat-out refused," as the dumbfounded mother put it. But when the stay-at-home mother went to parent-teacher conferences the teacher said their son was a most charming boy and that she just loved him. According to the same teacher it was their daughter who was having the difficulties, something the attentive parents had not known. They said it was all very confusing and hard to decide what was really happening.

Jane and Chuck discussed the little amount of history they knew about their children from Central America. Jane said about two summers before the children had found out that their birth mother was a streetwalker. The couple, thinking their children had enough to deal with, had hidden the little bit of paper work they had from the four siblings. But Kevin found the papers that described their mother and that they probably all had different biological fathers. Up until then the youngsters believed the older two had one father, and the younger two another. According to the sensitive mother the new information, "hit them like a ton of bricks that their mother was on the street." Other than that bit of information the couple knows little about their children's backgrounds or medical histories. The couple has been forced to make guesses or to surmise what happened to their transplanted youngsters in their early lives based on their demonstrated behaviors.

Jeannette N. from Hawai'i sadly shared some experiences she'd had with her attachment-disordered foster daughter. Annalee was an adolescent when she first arrived at Jeannette's home and was cooperative but "honeymooned" for about one month. However, the foster mother confided, "The longer she was there, the more aggressive and violent she got." Ms. N. said that the nocturnal uresis wasn't unusual for the girl, that Annalee wet the bed almost nightly but would then ignore the accident and pretend as if it had never happened. Her mother believed the adolescent did not want to take responsibility for her behaviors so would hide the bedclothes and eventually cause every thing around her to smell of urine. An even more unpleasant situation occurred when Annalee stood in front of Jeannette and defecated in her pants while staring her mother in the eye. That behavior occurred several times during the three years she lived with the Hawaiian mother.

Because of her obstreperous behaviors Annalee did not do well in school either. The busy foster mom told me the girl's social worker or the police would be called to school several days each week to quell an uproar she'd instigated. According to the experienced mother it was not uncommon for the principal or Annalee's teacher to call and say that she was having severe problems. The adolescent girl would get upset over seemingly trivial situations and then would not be able to keep herself from escalating and becoming totally out-of-control. Annalee was a physically large, strong girl who would not let anyone touch her and reacted vehemently when anyone came close to her. In addition, during the fracas she'd refuse to go to classes so the police would be called to help defuse the situation. However, in spite of their best efforts, her mother shared, Annalee would become aggressive, defiant, and violent toward the staff and other students in school. Once, in a fit of rage, she assaulted her teacher and beat her with a heavy chain. Sorrowfully, Jeannette shared, "Nobody could contain her. She'd just throw the kids all over the schoolyard. She'd be screaming and yelling, cursing, carrying on—just belligerent." According Ms. N. it was rare for Annalee to be able to remain under good control for a full day. It was more usual for something or some situation to send the girl into a wild, unpredictable, emotional reaction.

Perhaps out of feelings that originated during infancy, Jeannette's foster daughter was self-abusive. Ms. N. said Annalee would scratch or cut herself on her arms and hands with any sharp items she could find. In addition to her problems at school the girl was reportedly dangerous and threatening toward family members at home, as well. "She would just lose it," Jeannette said sadly, "and get knives and stand over me and threaten to hurt me. She threw things at me. She threatened to burn down the house many times." At the end of her stay in the home, Annalee and her sister Lynette would get into physical altercations at home. The frightened mother would get between the girls to try to stop the violence. During one incident Lynette went into another room in an effort to diffuse the situation, but Annalee followed her and by the time Jeannette caught up with them had Lynette on the floor, hitting her. The mother replied, "I took hold of Annalee's ponytail with one hand and just picked her up and held her. She was shocked; that's the first time I had ever touched her in that way." Finally, the mother came to believe she could no longer safely manage or care for her foster daughter at home. Following Annalee's departure Jeanette was left to clean up the messes the adolescent left behind, including scrubbing feces off all her bedroom walls.

Martha and Joe L. from Grande Prairie, Alberta, Canada talked about the behaviors of their son, Kurt, with much pent-up emotion. At age 7 his mother said he was "dimpled, blonde-haired, green-eyed, just insanely cute." The parents of a slightly older girl were so excited about the addition to their family. "When he first moved in, I really wanted to love him." Martha shared tenderly. The couple told me that initially he went through what his mother called the "perfect child syndrome." To her that meant that the boy always looked good—his affection seemed phony to her—but nonetheless, he looked great, especially to those outside their home. Kurt was more demonstrative and cooperative with Joe than with her and, seemingly, from their first moments together he ignored her or engineered the situation so Martha was left out. "He was polite, he was nice, and he would hug me in front of Joe." the new mom shared. He'd say, "I love you, Mummy. He never called me Mummy. It was just fake."

For an unknown reason Kurt seemed unable to tolerate the physical closeness of others. On one occasion, however, Martha recalled, "When he first came he wouldn't let me touch him; wouldn't let me get close to him. He got a really bad sliver and it was festering and it hurt. He waited till it was quite bad before he told me." Martha wanted to help, to remove the splinter and suggested it to the frightened youngster. To reassure him, she explained what she would do to carefully remove it. The experienced mom did not want to force the issue, as she was afraid such an approach would ultimately backfire. Finally, after three hours of considering his options, Kurt decided to let his new mother minister to him. Martha disclosed, "I did the whole mother thing, every time he asked me to stop, I stopped. It had to be him giving me his hand, which eventually happened. I really wanted to mother him and I think that was the only time he let me."

Although Joe and Martha had been told that Kurt had witnessed his birth mother's suicide and that he had been the one to call 911, no one had mentioned anything to them about sexual abuse. Eventually he did let his mother touch him, but then he tended to sexualize the experience. In the place of the warm mother/son affection Martha envisioned Kurt translated physical closeness into sexual messages, apparently unable to accept it as simple nurturing. In spite of the constant rejection from her son Martha stubbornly continued to try to break through Kurt's resistance to her. Feeling unprepared for such behavior, Martha was shocked when her son acted out in sexually inappropriate ways. She reluctantly shared about bedtimes when she tucked her children into bed Kurt would "bite my breasts or he'd kiss my breasts or rub his genitals against my leg." She recalled that when Kurt first came to them he didn't know how to wash himself well. She sadly described the following incident: "I tried to wash his hair in the bathtub; I tried to be really matter-of-fact. I'd put lots of bubbles in the tub to make him feel more comfortable." When it was time to rinse Kurt's hair he'd lie down in the tub and then bring his feet up by his ears, and lift his legs up over his body. Martha described his behavior: "His heels were up by his ears and he'd thrust his ass up in the air. When I bent over the tub to rinse his hair out he'd thrust his bum up into my face." In spite of her internal frustration, the mother remained calm but told Kurt how uncomfortable that made her feel. The experience was so unpleasant for her that Martha decided that she wasn't going to wash his hair for him anymore, that he'd have to do it for himself.

When she set limits on inappropriate behaviors he would tearfully say, "I'm sorry. I'm sorry. I'm sorry. You don't want me. I'm a bad, bad boy." Martha went on to explain, "His behaviors were such that you couldn't ignore them. He called me 'a cunt,' 'a fucking bitch,' followed by, 'You don't like me, you're just a bitch—you're just like every other fucking woman.'" Martha felt that Kurt was continually challenging her to discipline him or at least engage in a battle. In other incidents in the home, "He would rip his pants open and expose his genitals to my daughter. He'd drop something on my daughter's lap and then before she could even react to picking it up, he would dive for it and grab her crotch in the process. He looked at my daughter one day when she was petting the dog and said, 'Oh, you just want to hump the dog.' He turned every good, normal thing into something sexual for my daughter and I. It was just awful." Fortunately, the bewildered parents were able to recognize their son's behaviors as the red flags waved by children who have been sexually abused. He had been with them for only three months by the time they took him to therapy for the first time.

There were also other behaviors that had the Canadian couple concerned. Martha shared that once while she was driving Kurt in the backseat he had his feet up on the back of the passenger side, he "was kicking the seat. He was screaming and swearing and calling me 'a fucking bitch.' He was so mad he couldn't even breathe." With some difficulty Martha remained as calm as possible and decided to go to see her husband at work to get some support. Once out of the car she held on to Kurt's arm to prevent him from running away. The mother continued, "So I'm hanging on to this body, the wet noodle, and we walk into the store. He's just seething—I'm numb, I'm just numb! He sees Joe, sticks out his bottom lip and said, 'I made a bad choice.' I've never seen anybody who could be so mad one minute they couldn't breathe and then the next minute, stated calmly 'I made a bad choice.'"

At home Kurt "peed all over the house right off the bat," his mother recalled. "He was peeing in the bed, in his bedroom, peeing on the walls, peeing on the laundry, peeing on my pillow. Kurt tried to pee on my head when we were at the beach. He didn't pee on the carpet; he peed along the baseboard. It just reeked in his room, just reeked! I'm in there trying to feel where it is wet and he's laughing at me, sitting on the bed watching. He laughed and said 'The carpet's not wet; the carpet's not wet anywhere!'"

Kurt, according to his mother and father, tended to be loud and demanding. Martha said it didn't matter whether he was being called for supper or she was giving him his allowance. Any request for interaction would elicit the same response: "He'd slam his little body up into the wall and let it slide down and crash his butt into the floor. He used to work himself up to a big tantrum. Do you know how some people use self-talk to calm themselves down? He would use self-talk to talk himself into a big fit and end up screaming at me and yelling that I didn't love him. He would often confuse me with his birth mom and claim that I had done things that she had done to him. And I knew it wasn't about me, but it still was hard to take." During the course of therapy Kurt revealed he "had dreams of stabbing me and then taking great relish in telling me about them. I'd wake up and have him standing beside my bed and kind of dazed out." Martha went on to describe her visceral response to her son, "It's like you're being shell-shocked. It's like something hits you in the chest and then you don't have an opportunity to respond to that, and you're hit again."

Paula and Bob W. of Kearney, Nebraska, talked to me about their first impressions during the initial meeting with their daughter in a Central American orphanage. Bob stated, "She didn't like me; all the kids in the orphanage didn't like me. They were afraid of men." Or so it seemed to the soft-spoken man. Paula remembered that Susie was dressed in red pants and a red and white T-shirt top. She had on shoes that appeared too big for her with laces that were tied in a knot around behind her ankles. The little girl was hiding behind the leg of one of the workers, peeking at them perhaps to see who they were. Bob and Paula believe having the experience of visiting the orphanage was valuable for both of them. During the adoption process they had compiled and then sent their new little girl a scrapbook with pictures of themselves and their family so she would know who they were. The couple thought the workers had instructed Susie to give them a hug. Initially the little girl didn't have physical contact with them, but she eventually hugged Paula and then ran back to hide behind the worker. When the new parents toured the orphanage, they were taken into the crib-lined room reserved for the babies. When Paula picked up and cuddled some of the babies, Susie came immediately and clung tightly to her side. The mother stated, "I thought, 'She doesn't even know me but she would grab on to me like she was almost jealous, even then, that I was giving anyone else any attention.'"

As they left the orphanage for the final time, their new daughter, upon instructions from a worker, ran through the facility waving goodbye to everyone. The couple noticed that in spite of the excitement of the moment, and although she had been there for a significant period of time, Susie never approached or hugged anyone. Paula revealed that, "She really did come as a newborn baby. Nothing that she had on her was hers to keep. I asked her to take a shower so she took the shower with cold water. I'd try and get the water warmed up and she'd turn the hot water off and take a cold shower." As hard as she tried, Paula was unsuccessful in providing her new daughter with the comfort of a warm shower. What the mother was about to learn, through one of many experiences, was that she would be unable to provide basic comforts or please Susie.

Bob shared that he'd expected their daughter to be full of fears during her first days with them or to cry and scream as she left the orphanage with adults who were strangers to her. But to their surprise the little girl handled the trip to the United States with unexpected calm. Bob said, "When we got to the plane I thought we're going to have real problems with her, but it was great. We landed in Dallas and Des Moines and in Omaha—she was ready to just keep flying all day long." The trip consisted of many flights which "didn't bother her a bit." Paula shared that, "The first night we spent in Kearney I got to sleep with Susie 'cause I didn't want her to sleep alone upstairs in the house. And that was the first time that I could see a separation of how our family used to be." In the past when they visited their grandmother's home, due to space considerations they would need to sleep upstairs. But before they settled in for the night the family would snuggle together, chat, and enjoy the event. However, due to Susie's profound fear of men, the midwestern couple decided that Bob and her two new brothers would not be allowed upstairs with her. "So," Paula lamented, "it was my responsibility. It was a start of a separation of what the family used to be like."

Allen and Ann N. of Indianapolis, Indiana received their son Anthony from foster care when he was nearly two years old. The new mother said that all they were told about Anthony's problems was that he drooled excessively. "We noticed right away that the drool just poured out of his mouth; his shirt was soaked." Ann shared. Anthony wore bibs, which became bigger and bigger as their child grew larger, because of the excessive saliva. The toddler had been receiving therapy at a local hospital for the problem. Early in the placement, during a family activity they were sitting on the bedroom floor of Anthony's older sister. "Instead of enjoying the event, he began screeching." Allen said with bewilderment in his voice. "We take a lot of pictures—you could see the terror on his face. You'd think that there was a murderer in the room. That was the whole thing; the whole thing was trust." Or actually, the lack of it was their reality. Allen added, "He was afraid of everything."

The Indiana couple continued to tell me about behaviors that were both obvious and problematic from early in Anthony's life with them. In spite of his age the youngster was not talking. The pair said he didn't even try to talk or to mimic sounds as most baby's do. However, he made grunting, guttural noises and then expected others to respond immediately and to give him whatever he wanted. The little boy demonstrated signs of significant eating problems, as well. When the youngster joined their family, he ate only applesauce and similar soft foods that would slide down his throat without having to be chewed. The toddler didn't seem to know how to chew so at the therapist's suggestion they were to put peanut butter on the roof of his mouth and offer spaghetti to him. In an effort to help her youngest child, Ann said, "I brought him home and tried the peanut butter and he wouldn't open his mouth!" Sadly, Anthony also demonstrated unusual sleep patterns. Ann stated that on one occasion, one typical of her son, "I tried to lay him down and he was just stiff as a board. Those eyes, which became characteristic in all our family pictures, were huge! He would not go to sleep, he would squirm, he wanted to sit up and he didn't want to look at me. We just barely touched; you could see he was not about to go to sleep or to relax or lie comfortably in my arms." Soon they became aware that their new little one hated to have his diapers changed and hated the bathtub for reasons the sensitive parents were unable to determine. Ann, bewildered, reported that all the activities above left their little one screeching. "It wasn't really crying; it was just mad screaming."

Ann and Allen shared that activities, which their first three children loved, did not seem at all interesting to Anthony. During family outings their youngest began shrieking, which continuously confounded the parents because they could not determine the source of his discomfort. Filled with emotions, Allen talked about experiences with their son: "We'd love to go on walks; he hated to walk. He wanted to crawl; even over two-years-old he hated to walk. We would go on walks in the evening and we'd drag him kicking and screaming the whole way. We thought the more we did it the better it would be." The couple was accustomed to using that time with their first three children to teach about nature and to make it fun. The sad father stated, "We ended up pretty much not doing it or leaving him home because it was just a horrible ordeal. Everything that used to be fun with the other kids got to be horrible because he wasn't going to do it." During the hot Indianapolis summers their primary family activity was swimming at the local pool.

Allen continued, "He hated it; he hated the water. I thought he'd just get used to it, so I'd take him in and he'd scratch me and scream until the lifeguard said 'What are you doing to that kid?' I was so embarrassed I just ended up letting him sit out."

Allen shared that it seemed to take this youngster "forever to be potty trained. He wouldn't poop for days. He would wait and wait until he had to go to the bathroom and then he'd stop up the toilet." That situation occurred repeatedly. At the same time the youngster had difficulty with enuresis as well. "He used to urinate in his bedroom and the whole house smelled like urine," the mother added. "I can remember," Ann related, "going on vacation, he must have been seven or eight, and on the way back from Chicago he peed all over the back seat of our brand new van. He didn't say a word to anybody and just sat there in it." At thirteen, when Anthony went to the Attachment Center at Evergreen for therapy, he was still wetting the bed.

A flood of memories washed over Ann and Allen, remnants from their life with Anthony. They said that in spite of all his upsetting behaviors they believed that, at least initially, Anthony honeymooned and got along well with the other children, but never wanted the kids to touch him at all. By about three-years-old he began to get aggressive, including biting and hitting his siblings and other kids as well. The parents sadly relayed that he'd take their belongings and destroy them in some way. "Every toy in his room was pulled apart." Allen went on to say. "There would be holes in his wall where he kicked in the wall. Oh, yes, he'd rip his clothes, every pair of socks, his shoes. He tore up everything!" Once he'd started school, Ann knew when the phone rang it was the principal instructing her to come and get Anthony because he had, again, disrupted the class. His teacher told Ann that her son's behaviors were most interesting to watch. The experienced mom divulged, "She said he can go from table to table and know just the person to say the right thing to get the whole group stirred up. She said that's what he does daily—goes from one person to the next causing problems in the whole classroom. So the principal would come and take him out of the classroom until I could get there." Those skills became their youngest child's modus operendi. Ann continued, "It just seemed like, eventually, he really did get to know each one of our buttons and know the precise words to say to get us going." According to the couple no one was spared his attention; he aggravated the kids at school, his siblings, almost anyone around him. The parents shared that when he got older, their son lied and stole anything that belonged to his siblings so the other kids couldn't keep anything of value in their rooms. In addition, Ann relayed that at one time he manipulated her parents into paying for good grades in school. After a time of using the system her parents had prescribed, Anthony billed the unsuspecting grandparents for unearned A's and B's. In fact, his grades were actually D's and F's. Eventually Anthony's language started getting him into trouble as he became disrespectful and verbally abusive to them and to his teachers. Ann clarified that their son never showed a softer, sensitive side. The mother said sadly that her son never caught on to usual family loving, "He was never vulnerable. He always made you pay for making him afraid," as their son saw it. Anthony's destructive behaviors continued well into his teen years and throughout the time spent in military school.

Jane K., Wauwatosa, Wisconsin, speaks about Tina, a pretty little 7 year-old: "When she first came into our family we didn't know very much and at first she was pretty miserable. She is very controlling: if you sit the salt shaker here, she moves it there. She was always very tired and it wasn't just the tantrums. It was probably because she was trying to control everything. I put her in daycare 2 to 3 days a week and that was not a good thing. Daycare was not structured enough so we had a lot of tantrums with a lot of kicking and screaming when she came home. Oh, yes, we had stealing and we had lying. Anytime we'd go anywhere I'd come back and she'd have a whole handful of my earrings under her pillow. She'd steal things and hide them, like my husband's contact case. I just found that a few weeks ago; she probably hid that two years ago. I couldn't leave anything on the dresser because she would take it. She would do the typical lying: no, I didn't eat that and you could see crumbs on her face. I got so I started patting [her] pockets before we left the store. She got mad at me a couple of weeks ago and took my glasses and hid them under the bed. I looked everywhere and couldn't find them. She returned them to me the next day. With Tina there has been a lot of indiscriminate affection; she would go with anybody, stay with them all day and not be bothered."

Lobaida H. from Lakewood, Colorado is a foster mother of some renown. She reported to me that over the past many years she has helped rear or worked with approximately138 to140 attachment-disordered children. In general, she said by the time these children get to her they are not attached or bonded emotionally to anything or anyone. "They have no feelings at all, are pretty empty and real hollow-eyed with no remorse for what they do." At the time of our interview John was thirteen had been in her home for only three months. "John is like the Unibomber; he reminds me of Ted Kaczinski," Lobaida stated. "He is hollow, he's empty, and does not care about anything or anyone. He started stealing his mom and sisters' underwear and masturbating in them. He was stealing things and money from the family home. He was threatening to kill his mother and siblings. He frequently gets expelled from school. He pokes the students in front of him, pulls hair, teases them, and calls them names. And if things aren't going his way he'll shove them against the locker and threaten to kill them." The amazing foster mom shared that John is very smart and carries an "A" or "B" average in his schoolwork. Although the adolescent tests very high on IQ tests, he doesn't demonstrate any common sense. In addition, John has discovered that a bizarre behavior sometimes gets him attention. For example, Lobaida said at McDonalds he'll wolf his food down within 45 seconds. "He'll shove it down then he'll stick his fingers in his mouth and try to pick the food out, or he'll pick his nose right in front of everybody. Or he'll open up the catsup and suck on the packages; then he's got catsup dripping all over his face." According to the mother the boy constantly brings negative attention to himself. He will cheat at cards or Monopoly, as it's very important to him to win and will go to any length to make that happen. She stated, "He'll always want to play with a smaller child so he can control them; then he will hurt them."

Lobaida also shared about another of her foster children, Drake, age 14, who had been with her for two years. Almost out of breath, the mother told me of his history: "He was setting fires in the neighborhood and sexually abusing neighbor children. He also started having sex with his cousins, with his brother and with his sister before he was 12. He would masturbate in public; he was sexually conscious at all times." Lobaida had to remain alert to Drake's behaviors for the safety of the other children in her home. She had younger children who weren't so capable of defending themselves against someone with such predatory sexual behaviors, so she invested in a camera. At the time of my visit the experienced foster mother had cameras in the bedrooms and in the hallway and used a VCR to tape activities in the bedrooms. She also placed alarms on the doors so she could remain alert to the children's comings and goings. Lobaida stated, "He stole my under-wear and was masturbating in it. That experience makes you feel filthy and horrible—violated. He went to the library and came back with all kinds of satanic books, books about the occult. He hurt his brother, his sister, and his mother. He himself has been violated so much that he is out to get even."

Tara and Bob W. from Edmonton, Alberta talked about their daughter, who joined them at eight months old, placed in their home from an institution. When asked what she looked like to them when she came home, the sad mother replied, "Dead. Cold. It was awful. Her eyes were blank; that's why I say dead; her eyes were blank. There was never a smile; there was never a laugh." The father added, "She had a constant frown. Her skin was leathery." They were told she had had seizures, but later found out her medical problems could have been related to a drug withdrawal. They also reported that Cassi was severely overweight; consequently, she had significantly limited motor skills and had not yet learned to crawl. Tara shared that Cassi hadn't experienced any solid foods, and took all her nourishment by bottle. In spite of that fact, it was suspected she had a milk allergy, which the parents believe to still be true to this day. They said a most amazing experience is to watch Cassi drink from a bottle. "It would be gone in half a second; there was no enjoyment in her feeding. I've never seen a baby drink that fast." When the enthusiastic couple tried to cuddle their little one, "she would scream blue murder and was stiff as a board." The exception was when they put her down and left her alone. The mom said that when they leave her alone in her crib she "is fine." According to Tara, "She was quite happy with that—no smile or anything, but there was no screaming."

"So who knows what happened to her?" the concerned mom mused. The couple hated that she had started her life in an institution rather than in the bosom of a loving family. Because Tara had worked in daycare settings, she knew how little time was available to tend to the significant needs of each child. They also suspected that Cassi experienced neglect on the most basic level because daily activities seemed to terrify her and caused her to "scream blue murder," as the mother put it. As time passed, introducing food to her was a most difficult process. Instead of eating like they'd hoped, Cassi would sit "in the high chair and just bang her head." Mom stated, "She used to pinch herself, scratch herself, bite herself. When she'd fall, she'd never cry." Bob talked about her behaviors that indicated the presence of anger in her, "You watch her eyes when she'd go into rages; they'd just glaze over. She's not there; she's gone. You can see it in her eyes that she's not focused on anything; she's just gone." Previous experiences with older RAD children convinced them that they would be unable to handle another with attachment difficulties. Nor did they want to. However, they soon changed their minds. "When Cassi came, yes, these were very bizarre behaviors but we figured because she's so young we could handle it," Tara stated with honey in her voice. After time with them and quality cuddling, some of their baby's initial behaviors seemed to subside. But, "There was no real bond there because if one of us would leave or some stranger would come in, there was no difference, no making strange."

Once the visits between Cassi and her biological mother started, the little girl's behaviors became bizarre again Tara reported that when she returned from those meetings, Cassi "would just start banging her head on the cupboards again and we couldn't hold her. We couldn't snuggle with her anymore; she went right back to stiff as a board and screaming blue murder." The Canadian couple attempted to figure out what was wrong with their child but was alone in their endeavor. "When you meet Cassi she's sweet as pie," the mother cooed. "She's lovable; she's very cute; she's very fun to be around, and a real show. We're trying to tell people something's not right here and even our good friends are saying, 'You're just overreacting.' There's just not something normal here." The family has two cats and they teach the kids how to properly care for the animals. When their daughter is left with the pets "suddenly the cat's meowing and Cassi's got the cat hanging up by the tail." Bob stated that with Cassi "if it's quiet she's doing something she shouldn't be doing; if it's quiet, you have to go check." Recently the father said he thought he heard something—or maybe nothing—and knew it was time to check the little girl. Their cat had been sleeping in its bed, but Bob said, "Cassi had it with two hands wrapped around its neck and was holding it up in the air by its head. The cat was limp with paws in front, not scratching, not doing anything. The cat was just hanging there."

Tara shared, "Cassi's pretty young so we're still learning about attachment disorder. I'm still hoping to God that she's okay." The couple told me in many ways that they maintain a high level of hope that she joined them early enough and that their love and attention will be enough to undo a troublesome start in her life. They pray Cassi does not become as dysfunctional or as disruptive as the other children with the disorder can get. Bob and Tara reported that occasionally their daughter acts out in characteristic ways that is a "reality check" for them. The hopeful mother stated, "She's still got some severe issues to deal with, and they're not going to go away as easy as I'd like." The loving father concluded, "You hold your breath and you hope nothing else is coming."

Martha G. of the Kansas City, Missouri, area talked to me about two of her adopted, attachment affected children. They were exposed to drugs in utero "and nobody knows what that's going to mean coming up in their development." Baby Alex joined Martha and her husband when he was three months old. His birth mother had used drugs and alcohol heavily while pregnant with Alex. When their little boy was born, the medical staff believed he was blind and deaf because the newborn had no startle reflex or no emotional affect. Martha said, "you could snap your fingers in his face and he just wouldn't even move." However, with the increased attention, love, and nutrition Alex is right on target, developmentally. Her adopted sons "come from very deprived, very violent backgrounds," but now both six-year-olds, Alex and Derrick, have almost caught up academically, can read and nearly have mastered their numbers.

However, according to the generous, loving mother, Alex continues to have difficulties. "He can't sit still and, behaviorally, he's a problem. He is probably hyperactive; we've not had him diagnosed yet. He's very strong and impulsive." Martha went on to say that he seems to be inherently drawn to aggressive behaviors. When he gets a table knife in his hands, he starts hitting it on the table. Even though he's repeatedly told not to, he continuously hits the table and tries to leave marks. When he's unloading the dishwasher, Alex goes "for the knives first; he and his brother go at it with each other, like a sword fight." Because of the beliefs of the parents, the children do not watch much television. The books they read are also monitored and they do not let them have weapon-like toys in the home. In spite of all the professional couple's efforts, their sons were still drawn to violent activities. Martha believes, based on his current propensities, that Alex will eventually become "a bully. He likes to get attention by just butting his head against people. He breaks about every toy he has and he doesn't care." The alarmed mother stated that approximately two weeks before the interview she interrupted Alex and Derrick out in their yard. The boys "had cornered one of our dogs and were hitting it with a baseball bat." She anticipates that both her sons will continue on their path of destruction without ever expressing any regard for other person's rights or property. Martha shared that her son Alex "doesn't really know his strength so he can hurt them pretty badly and that does not seem to bother him."

Along with early developmental issues, this mother of six stated that Alex seems to demonstrate some sensory integration problems—he tends to fall down or trip easily. His increased coordination difficulties make him fall or bump into other people. During a therapeutic "holding session" with his mother, Alex told Martha that he did not believe that he would be her son forever. He fully believed he was in their family temporarily but would eventually be moving on to live with another family. The unbonded youngster had never been with any other family since joining Martha but still had not gained the notion or concept that he was a permanent member of the family. He was very certain that he would not remain with his family for long. But, brother Derrick, on the other hand, "acts like he knows something's going on," Martha shared. "He's fearful of the dark; fearful of any change at all." The little boy has developed the normal concepts of what's happening today and then tomorrow. Derrick's teachers had him bring a toothbrush to school in preparation for a visit from a dental hygienist and a talk about teeth. The youngster was convinced he had to bring his overnight bag, his pajamas, and his clothes—he packed everything—because of the request for his toothbrush. Derrick was terrified because he thought he was being taken away from the family he was beginning to love and trust.

Robert and Sue J. of Gravesend, England are the parents of an adopted boy and girl. Their little boy joined their family when he was three and a half years old with a terrible history. The parents cautiously told me he'd been a "failure to thrive" infant who had been severely neglected and abused. The toddler had had skin ulcers and eruptions because his birth mother had injected him with salt. According to the medical records she had injected salt into his joints, his hands and feet, and his anus. Consequently, he'd had a colostomy because of the interference with his normal rectal activity. Within the first eighteen months of life the tiny boy had been hospitalized twenty-seven times including visits for blood transfusions. In spite of the level of sickness of his birth mother it took the authorities six or seven months before they removed him from her care and placed the youngster in a safe foster home. And still, according to Sue and Robert, social services spent ample effort in trying to rehabilitate the birth family rather than removing the victimized child. Although their son had never received any therapy, they were told that the boy had some form of an eating disorder. The biological mother had been anorexic so the authorities thought that perhaps he had inherited similar eating problems. Sue said her son didn't eat and that the food she offered him was pureed or watered down as he didn't know how to chew. The shy mother believes his start has had a bearing on his overall development. By this interview the youngster had been with the family for four years. Robert stated, "He's put on half a stone of weight in those four years."

Unfortunately, the couple had not been told any of the toddler's history before his placement in their home. They first saw him through a patio door and heard him being told that the strangers were his "new mom and dad." Robert said they saw "this poor little child come running down the pathway saying, 'Mommy, Daddy.'" Ten days of visits followed their introduction before the couple needed to make their final decision about the adoption. The concerned father said, "It was like the child was programmed to be nice to them; to be a good little boy because he wanted a mom and dad." When asked about the child's behaviors during their initial visits, Sue stated, "Very superficial now looking back on it. Very loving, over affectionate, over demonstrative."

After a honeymoon period of about six or seven days, the tantrums began. Sue stated, "I mean they were quite hard to bear. They would go on and on; sometime it would be four or five times a day. He would manage to keep it going for sometimes up to an hour at a time." During the rages their son would fall to the floor, kick the floor with his feet, scream at the top of his lungs and go rigid, "stiff as a board," according to the amazed mother. The little boy also had many strange behaviors that they did not understand, and he did not follow directions well at all. Stealing and soiling himself showed up early. The couple reported that along with his unusual eating patterns there were times when he pulled tufts out of the carpet and ate them as well. Sadly, their little one became destructive, including self-mutilating, very early: he scratched himself, broke toys, tore or ripped wall paper, carpet, his clothing, and almost anything within his reach. Currently the worried couple said he has "a real thing for sharp instruments, like needles, pins, carpet tacks, and things like that." They have also found him standing, sort of spread eagle, on the sill of a window approximately thirty feet above the ground. In addition to their son's unusual and sometimes dangerous behaviors, their daughter has begun demonstrating similar behaviors. Robert and Sue verbalized significant concerns about how they will be able to protect their children, perhaps even from themselves.

"I agree with President Clinton and the emphasis on adoption," stated Paula Pickle of ACE. The professional has some concerns, however, which she was willing to share. She stated that currently so many adoptions occur where the parents have not been adequately informed about their children's backgrounds and histories. "I think you need to allow adults to make adult decisions about how they're going to spend the rest of their lives." This seasoned professional believes parents need to be given full knowledge of the problems and the support of honest placement workers. "Then," she said, "you've got a partnership where you can actually make a difference in the life of a child." According to Pickle, adoption workers are fearful that if they tell parents the entire truth no one will want to adopt those youngsters who most need homes. She shared that it takes an entire team of aware adults and a society willing to shoulder some of the fiscal responsibilities to successfully rear attachment affected children. Pickle concluded, "I think that as a nation we need to help families be successful to raise these very special needs children. That means putting some resources aside for the families and for the children so that adoptive families can fulfill their commitments. Unless we do those things, full disclosure and financial support, I see this presidential initiative on adoption failing miserably."

CHAPTER SIX—
The Mothers' Experiences

During a recent interview Dr. Welch stated she believes all foster and adopted children have some form of attachment difficulties. Since Bowlby's work over the past sixty years, it was discovered that detrimental immunological changes occur after only one hour of separation of an infant from its biological mother. The specialist stated emphatically that the biological mother and her baby are programmed for each other. The duo is made for each other—chemically, emotionally, biologically, and neurologically—in every possible way. According to Welch current birthing practices, even under optimal conditions, are disturbing to such vulnerable creatures as the newborn. Then, under even more difficult circumstances and no matter why an infant cannot remain with its mother, the adoption/fostering process causes further interruptions in the bonding process. She shared that babies undisturbed in utero or during the birth process "are born knowing what to do if they aren't interfered with, and they also know how to engage the mother. You can get intense eye contact from a baby." She continued, "What do you see in adoption? You see all this disturbed behavior that drives parents nuts. And the best of normal parents can't behave normally to that disturbed child."

American, Canadian and British mothers I met during the interviewing process were very verbal and filled with emotions about their experiences with their children. Initially, the women were hesitant to share their histories involving their beloved 'chosen' children. As you shall read, virtually all the mothers share a common history: they have been blamed for the behaviors exhibited by their children. Due to the children's covert behaviors, husbands and extended family members, among others, were excluded from the realities of the true interactions between mother and child. Because they were not privy to the truth of the illness in action, the moms continued to be misunderstood. Tragically, even when they shared their fears or the often terrifying experiences, the mothers were not believed. Armed with a high level of empathy and my own personal experiences, I was able to dissolve the mothers' reticence to talk about their own powerful, emotionally laden experiences.

Dr. Levy talked about the relationship of mothers with their attachment affected youngsters. As you are learning, such disturbed children are profoundly oppositional with parents, caregivers, and authority figures. But, he stated emphatically, "mostly their rage is directed towards the mother figure in the family." The psychologist reported that the origin of such reactions is based in historical roots. "The maternal figure," he shared, "the mother, is most significant in the early stages of development in terms of bonding and attachment." Fathers are very important in his estimation, and certainly infants and children can and do attach to fathers. He also believes fathers are influential and help determine how well the mother-baby bond develops. Levy continued, "So these children act out their anger mostly towards mother figures because their pain, their emotional pain, their grief, their loss, and their rage is about the loss of a deep, enduring, safe connection with mother." Another reason he thinks moms are the targets is because in our society the mother is still the primary caretaker; she still sets the limits and is the disciplinarian while dad is off at work. "And so, they're going to act out against the person who sets limits, who says no, who creates structure, who disciplines." Traditionally, he emphasized, that person is the mom. Even if a male abused the child, Levy said, it's still the mother who is held responsible by the child. When the children become very frightened or when hurt, they become rageful at the mother who failed to protect them. "Remember," the seasoned professional stated, "biologically, as well as psychologically that maternal figure's supposed to love and protect. That's instinctual; that's built into the system."

Pickle, added that she believes the success or failure of her children can determine a mother's sense of self. She's not sure that is how it should be, she said, but that's how things seem to be. The mother-child connection, their bond, is such an integral part of a mother, and its lack "does a great damage to one's self-esteem." Pickle knows about attachment disorders from two profound perspectives. She is a licensed clinical social worker, but first, she was and remains a mother. Early in her career she and her husband became therapeutic foster parents out of their concern for what was happening to young children given up by their families. After special training they received two biological siblings, a boy of seven, and his sister, four-and-a-half. The couple was told that the children needed love and security, but Paula knew from her mental health background that was no doubt a simplified version of the truth. She said she had no idea about the total extent of their needs until she lived with the youngsters for a while. However, she was tested early in their relationship. "I can remember the second day they were in my home," Pickle candidly shared, "being up at four o'clock in the morning reading my strong-willed child book and vowing that my 4 year-old was not going to get the best of me."

In spite of her professional preparation, Pickle talked about the tremendous stress placed on her family because of the behaviors of her new children. Her daughter was described as an "in-your-face-aggressive-taunting sort of child" who kicked things, among the list of many destructive behaviors. The beautiful child left holes in the walls of the family home, demolished her bedroom furniture, defecated and urinated all over the house, then wildly and intentionally physically charged windows in an effort to hurt herself. Her "wild child," as she called her, also physically attacked her, played with knives, and generally, ran amuck. Their son tended to be more passive-aggressive so his destructive behaviors were less obvious and done on the sly. The loving mom told me about the despair they experienced as the result of trying to find answers and going from "one professional to another trying to find somebody who had a clue what was going on" and who could provide them with ideas about what could be done. The problems eventually became so pronounced that the social worker and her husband made a pact to never leave only one parent alone in the company of both children out of fear for their own safety. She said that one result was that their marriage became much stronger, "out of necessity," and in spite of the inordinate stress on them. Pickle has written a book, *Life in the Trenches: Survival Tactics for Parents* and a handbook entitled "Basic Training" based on her own experiences.

The mothers' experiences that follow demonstrate how the symptoms of Reactive Attachment Disorder are manifested in their daily lives of their loved youngsters. The following personal anecdotes are glimpses into the lives of women and children who live in nearly continuous strife.

Catherine H. wife to Matt of San Luis Obispo, California talked about her experiences with their only child, Bob, who was placed with them at seven. The mother told me the youngster was very demanding from the outset of their life together. Nothing ever seemed "enough" and even after a nice day of family activities, he would still continue to demand more fun, more special activities. Catherine and Matt felt like they were treating him well and provided him with many activities young boys usually enjoy. After playing together at the video arcade, they'd stop at McDonald's for supper, because they knew he loved movies would often rent one on the way home. However, Bob would "continue to ask for more and more and more" as his mom put it. He wanted to do everything his eyes took in; when he saw the bowling alley, he pressed to do that as well. When the parents would said "no," he would fly into a rage, run into the house, slam the door, and throw temper tantrums that could last as long as an hour and a half. The parents educated themselves on how to handle their angry child including the use of behavior modification techniques. However, Catherine reported, nothing worked with Bob. Matt added his observation; "He's twice as gifted as we are at dealing with conflict, causing it and managing it to his advantage. And it does not take a toll on him; he thrives on it." Mom shared that "it leaves us exhausted." Both parents now suffer with migraines, which they'd never had before their son joined their family. Catherine said there have been stressful times at the dinner table when she couldn't swallow her food. She said her food would become unpalatable because she became "so nervous just having Bob across the dinner table from me."

In spite of the difficulties they'd been having in the midst of Bob's pre-teens, Catherine and Matt heard about two other children, a four and a five-year-old who became available for adoption. Initially the couple decided to foster the children while they were making a decision about adoption. Matt said, "We were sick; we had no idea how sick." Bob was nine at the time and reacted with severe jealousy over the attention given to the younger children. In an effort to instigate their removal from the home, Bob began hurting them. The parents observed that he would frighten them by growling at them and then escalated to twisting their arms. Catherine said, "We found a metal meat pounder in the front yard and on the kitchen counter another day." But the day they saw him in the front yard threatening the children with the meat pounder, they had had enough. Matt called a family emergency and then called Social Services and told them to take the youngsters out of the their home because they were at risk of being physically harmed by Bob. Sadly, the two children were removed from their home within a day. Catherine said quietly, "I was just so heartbroken." Both parents tearfully shared their story in measured tones; Matt wrung his hand, his knuckles white. According to the husband both children had begun to emotionally attach, but especially to his spouse. According to the loving husband, Catherine continued to mourn their loss for nearly three years and she still keeps a picture of the girl with her.

When he was fourteen, Bob took a cantaloupe and drew a man's face on it, then he wrote Matt's name on it, and stuffed an ice pick into the face on the melon. "That was a gruesome picture. He then set it outside the bathroom and when Matt came out this cantaloupe greeted him. It was sick." Catherine stated. In an effort to take the power and the fear out of such a macabre event, they put the cantaloupe on the kitchen counter and left it there for several days, minus the ice pick. That same night Bob took darts and stabbed them through the pictures of the family on his wall. Catherine added sadly, "It frightened me for how this was going to pan out in his life."

Paula W. and husband Bob of Kearney, Nebraska discussed the behaviors of their daughter upon her arrival to their home. Paula said from the first moment with Susie in their family she "never had a waking moment alone. As soon as I was up, she was on the edge of my bed." To the experienced mother it appeared the youngster did not know what else to do. Susie didn't seem to know how to entertain herself and she couldn't read. When Paula did things with or for her sons, it was always done with Susie right by her side. It felt to the mother as if she could never get away from her, like a forced, uncomfortable intimacy. At that time her husband Bob had many professional commitments so Paula felt like she was virtually alone with her new, "extremely clingy" daughter. During the first week home Susie, ten and just brought from Guatemala, was scheduled to begin working with a tutor, but the child stubbornly resisted being taken for English lessons. Mother said, "She wasn't screaming, she was just going to show me that she wasn't going to go. I tried to hold her up and point her in the direction [of the car]. She just melted down like butter and then she'd just roll from one side to the other and so I got down to try to stop her. Then pretty soon we were both rolling back and forth on the floor. And I thought, 'Boy, am I stupid.' You know, I always say our relationship never got any farther than that, not that we laid and wrestled on the floor anymore. But our relationship was never any more than a bunch of wrestling—emotionally, mentally—it was just wrestling time."

Prior to Susie's arrival Paula had been a teacher's aide in their son's classrooms, and after the girl joined the family Paula assisted with her daughter's class as well. However, after a while the head teacher told her she could no longer assist in that classroom. Paula was banned from any classroom her daughter attended because, as the teacher told her, "I made Susie too nervous." The mother was sad and disappointed, but mostly was in disbelief. "I didn't think I was making her nervous. Now I think it was just a manipulation" on their daughter's part. At the expense of appearing paranoid Paula thought her daughters' m.o. was to determine which activities her new mother enjoyed and then sabotage them. Eventually both Paula and Bob grew to believe that idea because Susie did not, or could not, seem to enjoy anything and appeared driven to wreck the fun that was experienced by the rest of the family. In addition, Bob stated, "Susie was always intensely lying but I don't think that she ever knew when she was lying. I think she always thought that her lies were the truth. It's such a bizarre way of thinking." They grew to understand that is was their daughter's way of attempting to design reality and to align that reality with her perception of the world.

Paula reported that she remembered the week before her daughter ran away for the first time. In an effort to bond with her only daughter she would go into her room to play with her and to tuck her into bed at night. On one particular night the lights were out and Paula was sitting intimately on the side of the girl's bed. Although Susie was frequently angry with her, on that night she didn't seem mad and appeared very calm. Susie said, according to her mother, "'I pray every night you'll die in a car accident.' Paula said, 'Oh, you do?' and she said, 'Yeah, I do.'" The mom responded to her daughter out of her religious belief system and was meant to calm them both. That approach did not change Susie's mind, nor did it remove the chill that went through Paula's body. In another incident her husband Bob took Susie out for a driving lesson. On their return and as they were pulling into the driveway Paula was waiting for them in front of the garage. Bob instructed Susie to apply the brake but instead she hit the accelerator; both parents believe that was a deliberate effort to injure her mother. Paula later told her friend, "I will not be in the vehicle alone with her because she is out to destroy me." Paula's friend told her she was being "ridiculous." That same friend felt pity for Susie so took her out to teach her to drive, but before the lesson was over, Susie had totally destroyed the friend's car. Paula stated that her longtime friend "thought I was all wrong, that I didn't know what I was talking about."

Amelia B. from Atascadero, California described their son's behaviors as constantly demanding from the time he came to them at eight years old. He needed Mom's time and attention continuously. "Mom! Mom! Mom! Mom! Mom! All the time," Amelia emphasized. He also displayed oppositional behaviors and constantly disagreed with what was said to him. The mother stated, "It's kind of like the Chinese water torture system; by the end of two weeks the slightest thing just set me off. I had no idea that I could be as ugly as I can get after a two-week vacation and 24 hours a day with D.J. He can turn me into somebody that is not very nice." Amelia shamefully shared that she felt like a screaming, shrieking shrew, a part of her personality she'd never known existed. She found the entire situation more stressful than the experienced mother could have ever imagined. "I think he is so self centered," she said, "and so intent on being in control of every situation that he overlooks being nice."

Amelia said D.J. was such an angry, sad child, and it seemed like nothing made him happy. Soon after his arrival "he was into everything." The mother said he would experiment with the cleaning chemicals they kept in the bathroom. She said, "He was mixing things together to see what they'd make." They had to remove all the chemicals from the bathroom in an effort maintain a safe home. At night he had difficulty sleeping so during the dark, quiet hours of the night he "experimented" and burned out all the light plugs in his bedroom. Amelia and her husband Joe found it necessary to get up frequently during the night to monitor his behaviors. From the age of nine it became apparent that D.J. was already in trouble. Amelia stated emotionally, "I was exhausted; we couldn't let him alone for a minute. We had to supervise him constantly." The couple employed the aid of her sister for occasional respite care. Amelia said that once while at the aunt's house he made a Molotov cocktail out of an old tin can and a bottle that he'd found in the garage. He was attempting to put the gasoline in it when he got caught. The frightened mom said, "I think he was just doing the thrilling thing; he knew how to do it and he was going to show off." That was their wake-up call, heralding that they needed more help for their son than they could provide at home. They called child services to report the incident, and he was quickly picked up and taken to a group home for safe keeping.

Elizabeth E., from Ormskirk, England is the mother of Eliza who was adopted at the age of 10 months. The adopters shared that a frightening trait about their daughter was her inability "to actually express emotion. She never cried; also, she could never hug. My son and I used to get hold of her tightly just to make her hug." But, according to the mother Eliza never responded in a reciprocal manner. After Eliza had spent her young lifetime with Elizabeth and her husband Howard, many of their friends began talking to them about feelings the young girl stirred in them. Elizabeth shared, "Many of our friends tell us, now that she is older, that they hated her coming to their house because of fear. They could never define precisely what she did, but there was a constant worry and fear. Our friends and relatives were always extremely wary of her, not from what we said about her, but because her very presence in a situation emanated a sort of tension. She generated tension wherever she was."

Dina B. from Providence, Rhode Island shared that when Monte came to her at twelve weeks from a New England foundling home, "He didn't eat well—he didn't want food. Eventually I discovered that he ate pretty well if he could feed himself. He would take his bottle reasonably well. So I actually resorted to putting a great big X in the top of a bottle and feeding him his cereal, even vegetables and meat, through that bottle." When Dina attempted to feed him with a spoon or to hold his bottle, he forcefully pushed everything away. Even at the tender age of three months he seemed to have a clear idea about what he would accept and what he would not. She stated that her first observation of him was that he was "very much a stranger." With her other babies by the age of three months she felt she already knew them. However, Dina shared, "here was a little being who was obviously formed, more than a brand new infant, who I didn't know yet. I was very, very eager to know and love this child." The first difficulty she noted was that he was exceedingly difficult to comfort. By the time Monte arrived she'd already had one baby and thought she had learned how fussy babies act. The intelligent mother felt she could determine when quiet walking or more feeding, a diaper change, a bath or bed was needed. But those usual approaches did not work with Monte. He cried at times the experienced mother could not anticipate. She said after routine activities he often "would scream for three-quarters of an hour." There was a sleeping problem, which the eager mother could not comprehend at all. He screamed when everything should have been okay, according to the mother. She shared, "For the first time in my mothering I felt that I had to work not to hurt my baby with a slap or something because it was so unbelievably frustrating." Once in an effort to appease him and to keep him safe, she took him outside on a beautiful summer's day and sat him in the grass. Monte was probably about six months old, physically advanced, and sat alone very well. Dina then went in the house, shut all the windows and doors, "and went to the farthest part of the house till I could gain control of myself. He had just been screaming and crying and being difficult for such a long time."

Tara W., wife of Bob from central Alberta, Canada reported that two months after Cassi came into their care, her eating problems became extremely pronounced. Tara stated, "She'll eat all day if you let her; it is constant." Like the parents of other children with food and eating difficulties, their interpretation of the situation is similar. Tara and her husband believed it was "probably a sign that she didn't have food for a very long time." They grew to understand that when an infant had its' early nutrition withheld, the child reacts by overeating or hoarding food in an effort to prevent further starvation. Tara shared that after their foster daughter's arrival to their home, meetings were established between Cassi and her birth mother in an effort to reunify the pair. After the visits with her biological mother, the little girl, Tara stated, "started banging her head on the cupboards again. She started banging her head on the table very, very hard. And we couldn't hold her anymore; we couldn't snuggle with her anymore." Gradually they began making progress and received some reciprocal affection from Cassi. Unfortunately, following her meetings with the biological mother, Cassi "went right back to stiff-as-a-board and screaming blue murder." Tara stated that it appeared that her daughter needed to repeatedly relearn how to trust and how to let down her emotional guard, a feat that has been laborious and anticipated to be a lifetime activity.

Ann C. of Olathe, Kansas sadly shared that when her son Timothy was three he attempted to kill her other foster child, Samuel, a boy who was two years younger. The first attempt occurred during a visit from their social worker. The adults were sitting in the kitchen discussing the children while Timothy and Samuel were playing in the living room.

The mom stated that there were no unusual noises coming from the other room, an intuitive thought that alerted her. She said her immediate thought was that she needed to interrupt what she was doing and go check on the boys. Ann said when she rounded the corner into the living room she found Timothy was holding Samuel down on the floor, and "had a coat over Samuel's head and was strangling him." When she sharply called his name, "He looked up and the look on his face let me know he knew what he was doing. He knew it was wrong." Ann said that was her first real "wake up call," the one that clearly spelled out to her that the son she loved was in serious trouble.

Ann said that up until our visit Timothy had made three attempts on Samuel's life. When Samuel was two, they moved into a house with a pool and since he was too young to have fear, walked straight into the pool. Ann dropped everything in her arms and jumped in after him. Timothy stood on the edge of the pool watching with a look of curiosity. His mother shared, "He was just staring; he wanted to know what was going to happen. And it was like he was watching a movie," untouched by the horror of the situation. Ann's impression of her older son: "He had no feelings whatsoever and he didn't care." that Samuel was in trouble. Soon after that incident Timothy took a baseball bat and when Ann was not looking he swung the bat as hard as he could, hit Samuel in the head, and knocked him out. The mother said she finally understood clearly that "Timothy had a violence problem." She said she would never forget the following incident: they had just moved into their new house, her husband was up on a ladder painting, and the boys were marching through the house playing. The little ones were marching and singing; Sam was in the front with Timothy behind him. Samuel sang, "Hi ho, hi ho, it's off to work we go." Tim was singing, "Hi ho, hi ho, it's off to kill people I go." The concerned mother stated, "It was just an intrinsic part of his being to hurt and kill." Ann shared that later, "We had the children baptized in the Catholic Church. At a particular point in the baptism ritual the priest asks them questions and they have to respond. The priest asked, 'Do you reject Satan?' Timothy said, 'No.'"

The Kansas mother of 11 year-old Timothy worries that her son is already exhibiting extremely inappropriate sexual behaviors and has for about a year. She reported that last year at a baseball game he went over to a woman who was a stranger to him, sat down on her blanket, and scooted his body next to her so that they were touching. He then put his arm round her shoulder. Ann shared that his behavior, in spite of his being only eleven, appeared sexually provocative. The sensitive mother was left in a quandary as to how to handle such a situation. Later, a neighbor woman of about 50, told Ann that Timothy invited himself into her home to ask if she wanted a backrub. Before the neighbor responded, the youth started rubbing her shoulders. The woman tearfully reported to Ann that the child had rubbed his body up against hers and that he had an erection at the time. There was another incident with yet another woman. That time Timothy approached a mature woman from the back while she was sitting on a chair. Ann said he put his arms around her neck, crossed his arms over her chest, put his hands on her breasts and then squeezed. His mother sadly reported that he is also starting to make aggressive sexual moves on the "little girls in the neighborhood and on his female cousins."

Ann tearfully shared her son's most recent incident of dangerousness: "His rages were very impulsive, you can't always see them coming. He had been told to stop something and he didn't like it." As was usual for Timothy, when he was told "No" he became defiant and verbally abusive. Because of those behaviors his mother was disciplining him. She said she had to take him up to his room because he would not go willingly, and sometimes she had to restrain him to keep him and others safe. Ann added, "Tim's getting real big for age 11; he weighs about 130 pounds and is very, very strong so I can't restrain him well." As they were going up to the stairs, her nine-year-old was sitting on the stairs. Apparently shook by the incident, she "watched Timothy go up a couple of stairs, stop, turn around, pick up his foot and stomp as hard as he could on Samuel's neck. He could have snapped his neck." His mother reasoned that incident occurred for no other reason than he hadn't gotten his own way at that moment. Later that same summer Timothy "Picked up a fireplace poker, turned on me and told me he was going to kill me with it. He didn't attack me with it, but next time he might. I certainly fear that he's serious." By that time Ann had learned that physical labor helped Tim because the activity occasionally calmed him down. One day as he was mopping the kitchen floor, she heard him say, I wish God would let me kill my mom when she's sleeping. The frightened mother said her first thought was, "Four years into therapy and we've gotten nowhere."

"I'm divorced from Timothy's adopted father," Ann shared sadly, "and I can look back and say Timothy had much to do with it. He disrupted our whole household. We were always focused on a trauma surrounding him and how to fix it, and Brian didn't like coming home to that environment. I wasn't paying attention to him. I was paying attention to how I was going to help this child."

Helen S., a British mother of a 17-year-old girl who was placed in her home at 3½ years old after several years of neglect from Manchester, England, described her teenage daughter Carla when she was a little girl: "She constantly wanted your attention, absolutely, all the time. I mean really, really all the time. She's obviously had a tremendous rejection; she needs more than I'm giving her. I felt like however much I tried to do; it wasn't enough." Helen felt like somehow her daughter capitalized on her rough start. The child followed her around the house continuously. "There had to be conversation all the time, and when she'd run out of conversation she would come up with nonsense conversation. She'd ask you what time it is, and then she'd ask you again and again a minute later. She would do that for hours on end." The mother said Carla did anything she could think of to keep a conversation going and it felt like she was being forced to listen to her. Helen said the girl's incessant chatter "would go on from five o'clock in the morning when she was getting out of bed and still be doing it when she was falling asleep at night."

Helen described her daughter's emotional behaviors as if presenting a false front, "very insincere, like a sort of automatic doll. She always spoke in a monotone voice, as though she was leaving something out. Very unnatural, really." Her mother experienced Carla "as if she was acting a part." Reportedly, the girl was totally attracted to strangers and was especially interested in anyone she'd just met. Helen said her daughter would introduce a stranger as her best friend. Even from the time she was a little girl, she apparently felt closer to those whose name she barely knew and would approach people on the bus and ask to sit on their knee. The mother stated, "Because she was so pretty, so charming, and so attractive in every way, people played up to that." Today, at seventeen, her daughter still prefers virtual strangers to her family members and, according to Helen, "thinks it's appropriate to behave with that person as though she's known them for ten years."

Mattie W. of Kearney, Nebraska talked about her sixth child and second adopted son, Scot: "The birth mother wanted to keep him for of a 'playing house' kind of relationship. His mother had no role models or any parenting skills." Scot was hospitalized multiple times in his early years for many serious health problems, the last time for malnutrition. That nutritional problem was the most severe and the one that finally prompted his placement in foster care. Mattie said eventually he was returned to the care of his biological mother even though she still hadn't developed adequate parenting skills. Reportedly, his birth mother severely neglected and abused Scot. Apparently, among other events, she tied him in the high chair, would offer him food but would remove it before he had a chance to eat. Those maternal behaviors caused the infant enormous frustration and kept him perpetually hungry. Scot was also left unattended in his crib for 1½ days with no food or care while she went about her life. Consequently, when Scot was adopted at three years old he had pronounced eating problems. He would either wolf his food by swallowing it whole and unchewed, or just let it slide down his throat, as he had not yet learned to chew.

Mattie said that all through Scot's time in their home there were the problems. The other five children fully experienced their youngest sibling, as his behaviors were not kept from them. But, Mattie confided, "Dan was not seeing the behaviors I was seeing. These kids are so manipulative; they play one parent off against the other. When he was home with me he was abusive and would not do anything I asked him to do. When Dan came home, [Scot] would be just sweet and sit by him and want to be read to—he'd want Dan's attention. So this was causing a problem in our house." Eventually the other kids decided they did not want to be around when Scot was present. Mealtime, Mattie told me, was a disaster. The other children would leave the table and go to their rooms, to avoid him. Mattie said her youngest son "was delighted; this is exactly what he wanted. He had the living room and the TV to himself."

The central Nebraska mom added, "He was very charming and very nice with strangers or with company. When I would relate to my friends some of the things that happened at home, they'd give you this look." You know the one Mattie told me, the one that says, "Yeah, right, that sweet little kid? I can't believe you'd think he would do a thing like that. This must be you; you must be causing the problem." After repeated experiences with his sneaky charm and with disbelieving others, Mattie stated she thought, 'I'm losing my mind.' Mattie emotionally divulged that when Scot was eleven she finally said to her husband, Dan, "'One of us has to go; it's either Scot or me. I just can't do this any more.' By that time he had thrown a clawfoot hammer at me and had hit me with a pipe. It was getting worse. When he abused me he was either in a rage or he was really calm. He would look at me with 'the look.' It's the most frightening look I have ever seen or ever hope to see. He would say, 'I'm going to kill you' and I knew he meant it. I got to the place where I was afraid to stay alone with him." She eventually begged her husband not to leave her alone with their son. "And then finally I said I can't do this. You've got to do something."

Sharon W., wife to David of the Franklin area of Wisconsin, is the adopter of two Russian children, Svetlana and Yuri, biological siblings. They were to have received both children at the same time, but that did not happen due to a snafu in the paperwork. Consequently, Sharon said, "David went to Russia by himself to get Yuri and I went by myself to get Svetlana." After collecting the children in that particular manner, they discovered some long-term consequences they had not expected. Sharon said their children apparently developed ties with the first parent they met. According to the mother whichever parent "rescues" the child from the orphanage was considered the hero; the other is "the enemy." Sharon went on, "When Yuri arrived home, I was considered the enemy for a long period of time, and he did not want me taking up his papa's time. He'd stick his tongue out at me and generally see if he could get rid of me. He was eight when he came; he was and still is a very self centered and manipulative little boy. It took about six months to get through to him that he was not going to split us up."

Sharon went on to say the transition with their children was difficult because of their behaviors and their language differences. The new mom shared that they were fortunate and located a young woman from Ukraine who worked with them and their children the first summer they were home. They ultimately were able to communicate some things to Yuri and Svetlana through the Ukrainian tutor. They would meet about every other week to have serious discussions with both children. Sharon said she thinks the whole concept of adopting older kids and being unable to communicate with them for about six months because of the language barrier was something no one prepares you for. The parents said they knew about 10 words of Russian and the children knew no English which was very frustrating when a child is trying to share something with you. Yuri was "a non-stop, motor mouth, constantly talking in Russian. After about three weeks it occurred to him that nobody understood a word he was saying. He got very silent for about two weeks."

Pat F. of Elkton, Maryland talked about her son Craig, now in his mid-twenties, part of her family since he was six months old. Today, unfortunately, she said, "I don't believe a word he says—Craig still does primary process lying. You know, lying for absolutely no reason." According to his mother he continues to make up stories about the jobs he holds, or doesn't have, and about incidents in his life that never actually occurred. Initially, "He makes them sound so believable," but when she follows up on the incidents, she is constantly reminded of her son's inability to be honest.

The worried Maryland mother shared an experience that occurred after Craig, then a teen, had been removed from the house. Pat and her family live out in the country with no neighbors nearby so, somewhat dubiously, they got a gun that was kept continuously under lock and key for self-defense. One night her husband was out of town and she heard the sound of someone breaking in. Pat went to investigate and discovered "my son tiptoeing around to see whether I'd pull the gun and try to shoot him." Later there was a break-in and someone stole two credit cards, ransacked her daughter's underwear drawers, stole a hidden jar of loose change from that dresser, and the gun. To this day Pat believes it was Craig who was the culprit. At that time their son did not have a key to the house because they had changed the locks to protect themselves from him. The burglar left the computer, TV's, and the VCR's. Ms. F. claimed they are not wealthy but had many valuable items that could have been removed from that house but weren't. "Our total loss was $10 plus that gun." Pat stated she surely did not like being burglarized, and especially by her own son. Part of her, she shared, "was in a panic as to what's he going to do with that gun." To date the registered handgun had not surfaced. They've had many moments of panic because the police have called asking about the weapon. "It's living a life in fear" because of their son's behaviors. They removed him from their will when Craig was thirteen. "He did try to talk me into suicide; he also tried the same with his younger sister. He would make threats." Initially their wills said that everything goes to their spouse, but if both parents die their two daughters would be their benefactors. They made the change clear to their son. "I don't think most people have to tell a kid they have been disinherited, so don't kill us for the money."

Gretchen W. of mountainous Conifer, Colorado shared about the history and behaviors of her disturbed daughter, Susan. By 13 she needed different foster care because her behaviors were so unacceptable at home. Historically, she would have periods when she would follow directions and be somewhat pleasant to be around. Her mom referred to that as the "up part of her cycle." During those periods the professionals did not seem to grasp that there was also a "down part." About three months later Susan went into the worst part of her cycle, according to her mother, and attacked the current foster mom with a curling iron. She left the mother shaken and also left holes in the wall. Gretchen shared, "She's much larger and getting much more violent. She's not so self-abusive; she's going not only after children but after adults too." Apparently Susan's language was especially nasty by then and the members in the family were having difficulty living with the foul language. According to her adoptive mother, "Her perception of reality was totally out of whack. She could be screaming in your face and you could very calmly suggest she take ten minutes to calm down and think about it. And her perceptions of that picture were that you were screaming at her. Her whole perception of reality was very distorted."

Gretchen stated, "The relationship we had was dysfunctional. It was not healthy; she was turning me into her victim, for years, her victim. The therapists all sounded the same. For the first few months they'd start out concentrating on me—I must be this terrible person because I have this terribly screwed up kid. By the time they would finally understand it was Susan who had the problem, they'd try the same stuff. They would instruct Susan to yell at me and tell me how mad she is." Eventually Gretchen tired of being yelled at as Susan always unloaded her anger on to her adopted mother. In reality, the tired mom believed it was the birth mother that really deserved the teen's anger, but the girl was unable to communicate directly with the woman. Consequently, Gretchen caught the rage meant for the first mother, a fact that seemed to be missed by the professionals.

Reluctantly, Gretchen shared that after the death of Brad, another special needs adopted child, she felt completely burned out. She felt she had nothing left to give her daughter Susan. However, she divulged, "I didn't want to throw Susan back into the system with nobody being there to advocate for her and look out for her." By that time Gretchen had taken her daughter to 40 therapists for assessments and for appropriate, effective therapy. She reported they were "all the same and start out with 'Well, gosh, what have you done?'" Gretchen felt indicted, as it seemed they were looking to pin the blame on her. "They don't understand attachment disorders and they don't understand Susan." The overwhelmed mother shared, "I'm sure they were frustrated. At her worst she's a monster; at her best she can be fairly compliant. But you never know how long those little spells are going to last before she falls back down into the 'down part' of her cycle. So what the therapist in these treatment facilities would see is Susan going from her very, very worst to her very, very best, and they would say, 'We fixed her.'" In her conversations with the staff Gretchen would say, "'Isn't that wonderful; it's time for her to go home. I understand your viewpoint and I see your perspective. Now, try to see mine. You're looking at one year of Susan's life. I've looked at Susan over ten years of her life and have seen her go from her very best to her very worst to her very best to her very worst to her very best.' But they didn't want to hear that. They wanted to believe that they fixed her and it was time to send her home. And so this time I'm not buying it; I don't have the energy. I don't have the strength to go through this again. Susan has wasted her childhood going in and out of hospitals, in and out of residential facilities. This has got to end. This is not good for her; it's not good for me. I can't do it again." Brad, because of his perpetual sweetness, was the "absolute joy of my life" and his death was the most devastating loss Gretchen had ever experienced. She believes the experience changed her enormously and after his death she didn't have the same energy or the same drive to keep fighting her daughter's fights. Those battles were both for and with Susan.

By the time Susan reached ten, Gretchen "owed $38,000 to the Attachment Center alone. I'm still paying that off right now, and that didn't include all the testing centers and the hospital. All together it had to be probably a little over $200,000." Due to the lack of financial resources Gretchen was forced to look to other agencies for help. She finally involved her county Social Services but they didn't have the funds to voluntarily place Susan in a hospital either. Eventually, Social Services had to legally take custody of Susan, which required a court hearing. The overwhelmed mother did not have to relinquish custody and didn't. What did happen was the State of Colorado took temporary custody of the girl by filing a "Dependency and Neglect Petition" against Gretchen. Under the circumstances it was considered a "no-fault" petition due to Susan's out-of-control behaviors. It was also determined that due to her special needs no one could care for her in a home; she needed care in an institutional setting. The sensitive, caring mother said the unfortunate part of the approach they were forced to take is that the "Dependence and Neglect" charge is a permanent part of her own personal legal records.

The Colorado mom emotionally revealed that at some unseen point she had finally had it. She said, "I'm just done with this. This kid has screamed at me for ten years. I don't know what I have done to ruin her life; she screams this at me constantly. I've spent a lot of money, a lot of time, and a lot of energy trying to fix her. And it's not there; it's not working." Gretchen decided that at the end that as a good mother she would help her daughter get, "at least to a point where she can have some happiness in her life. So I figured this time we need to get her settled somewhere. I can still be her mom, but she doesn't have to live with me. Let's get her somewhere where she can finish growing up and have some joy in her life. This has been ten years of just misery." At this writing Susan was fourteen years old and safely living in a residential treatment facility. Her weary, sad mother reports she's not doing well and believes it is going to be a continuous, ongoing battle for her daughter.

Rose L. from the San Luis Obispo area of California described their relationship with their adopted daughter, Hope. Mom tearfully shared that from the start, "She wanted to eat me alive, emotionally." Their little girl was engagingly charming, maybe more so than usual for being only two years old. Rose remembered the night that she heard a "horrible scream" at 2:30 in the morning. She immediately woke up and found little Hope standing right next to her bed. The mom asked her if she was all right and the toddler answered, "I'm okay. I just wanted to know where you were." According to the mature mother that was at the beginning of their relationship and thereafter she was unable to have a conversation without Hope being there, with the child doing everything in her power to interrupt it. Rose disclosed, "I couldn't have a friend come over and do anything because Hope had to be the center of attention. She would charm people and piss me off is what she would do."

The California mother said that her daughter Hope, "Eventually it got to where she wanted dad to be mad at mom. At three it seemed she was the little genius trying to pit everybody against me. She was successful to a certain degree; I lost the respect of some of my children and my husband for a time. She would be this manic child during the day. Then daddy would come home from work and the kids come home from school and she would be little Shirley Temple." Rose was telling her family about the terrible day she had had, but was not believed because Hope was so successful at obliterating the truth. Rose would say, "I hate this kid. What's going on here?" Eventually the situation developed into a downward spinning cycle where Rose was left feeling that Hope was trying to destroy the family. In reality, Hope "was successfully creating doubt in people's minds about me."

Rose stated their troubled son, Bradley, remained with her family for only four years. Shortly after joining the family, he began showing signs of sexual behaviors toward other children in the home. He had tried to inappropriately touch Hope, but the girl rightly would not tolerate it and told her mother. "We thought we had nipped it in the bud," the mother shared. About four years after Bradley's arrival Rose left home for a weekend to attend her grandmother's funeral. While she was gone, Bradley sneaked around the house at six in the morning and viciously sexually attacked his sisters, Hope and Jordan. According to the mother, the youth "Inserted a missile into their vaginas and rectums and hurt them pretty bad. The detective who interviewed him said this child scared the hell out of him and gave him the creeps." The detective reportedly asked Bradley why he had put his hand over their mouths and the adolescent replied that he didn't want to hear their screams.

The overwhelmed mother told me living with her attachment-disordered children has dramatically changed her. The mother said that since she was not prepared for how cunning, dramatic, or manipulative their behaviors would be she was easily fooled, something Rose did not like. She concluded, "I was real angry and bitter towards everybody for a few years. I think I was just trying to get up to the top and stay afloat."

Sheila F. of Leicester, England and the mother of ten talked about what her twin sons were like just after bringing them home at three years old. Gerard and Mickey were home for six weeks when Sheila started noticing they wandered around the house at all hours of the night. Then, also, they would hide their dirty clothes in the house so

Sheila would not be able to find them for long periods of time. They cut up their curtains and they hacked up their clothing. Both boys would sneak into the parents' bedroom and defecate, an act they would only do in their parents' bed. Sheila continued, "They would wee anywhere. They would take doors off but would leave them hanging so when you opened the door you hit your head," because the doors would fall off the hinges. At about age four-and-a-half they were already terrors in school, the beginnings of school problems that caused their removal from schools nearly every year. At one point the incredulous mother shared they kicked the headmaster and other youngsters and locked the children and teacher in the classrooms. Their mother also shared that, "I couldn't take them to church because they would dismantle the pews. They have a fascination with dismantling things."

Lobaida H., the successful therapeutic foster mom to over 100 children in her career, from Lakewood, Colorado, talked about John, a 13-year-old recent addition to her ample family. The mother shared that he is not doing well in spite of plenty of pre-planning. There had been a staff meeting with the mother and school officials before the adolescent was placed with Lobaida. Ms. H. enjoys a wonderful reputation of long standing and John was accepted because of the positive history with this particular foster mom. The frustrated mom shared, "This is my ministry with the children. They said because of my ministry they would work with me to see if we could get him turned around." The youth attends the small school and the mother insists John knows the rules and regulations. The ground rules, she told me, had been made clear to him before he started attending that particular institution. He was conditionally accepted and has remained there on a temporary status. According to their agreement any time he does anything wrong, breaks the rules or acts out, they send him home. Together the mother and the school administration decided that to help John there would have to be "zero tolerance" for his negative antics, inappropriate behaviors, or for playing dumb and pretending he doesn't know the rules. "Most of the time he's home because he continues to push buttons on people."

Ann N., wife of Allen from Indianapolis, Indiana, when discussing disciplining Anthony stated she had never disciplined him with spankings, nor had she with her first two, Nicole and Michael, either. "But it got to the point with Anthony I didn't know what else to do. At first I smacked his hands, that didn't do any good, then he'd turn around and do it again. I ended up spanking him and I'd feel terrible. I remember one time I bruised my hand smacking his little bottom. That really got my attention. So, then I think I got a wooden spoon; the whole time it's feeling horrible inside me." She didn't want to let him do the things he was doing but did not know what to do to successfully stop the hurtful behaviors. "What do you do," she asked, "after the third time he's thrown rocks at the neighbor kids?" The first consequence would be to take him into the house and have him stay inside all day. But as soon as he went outside, he'd get another rock and, again, throw it at the kids. Ann said she continuously wondered what else she could do to get through to her son. "I remember times when I felt like an abusive mom. I thought Stop! Stop! Stop! Because I could almost spank him until who knows what." And yet, nothing deterred Anthony. "I was so mad at him for disobeying and for just being so mean, for being everything that we tried to teach him not to be."

The sensitive mom reported that Anthony was twelve when he went to Colorado to the Attachment Center at Evergreen for a two-week intensive therapy program for his attachment difficulties. "When he came home he was awful, horrible, the worst," although she had been with him for the entire session. Ann proudly reported that she became more assertive as the result of the therapy with her son. "It kind of empowered me," she said, "to take control and to say 'I can't take this. I am going to take care of myself,' which was a new idea to me." It had never dawned on her that a mother could take such a stand and it invigorated her to use the new skills. "You don't want to do things my way?" She'd say to her youngster. Then, "I've got someplace to take you" when he didn't cooperate. There were respite care homes arranged for their use when Anthony did not follow their instructions. Ann felt using the new therapeutic approaches increased the stress and tension that already existed between she and her husband, Allen. When she talked about using the therapeutic techniques Ann stated, "He could not stand me doing this stuff (using the new therapeutic techniques)." In spite of intensive treatment his behaviors continued to deteriorate. Because of his unsafe actions, Anthony was eventually placed in a military school. The adolescent was being considered for return to the Indiana couple's home. When discussing his possible return, Ann stated, "It is real scary to me. I have this feeling that I've been trampled on and used and abused by him so much that it's going to be real hard for me to trust him. And I know that's what he's supposed to be trying to do, to be developing trust with me."

Martha L. of rural Alberta, Canada shared her feelings about her eight-year-old son Kurt: "I thought I was going insane. I couldn't believe how angry I was. I never experienced the kind of anger I felt" as a result of Kurt's behaviors. She said she was amazed but she had never experienced such intense anger even toward her husband. The unexpected situations she was thrust into with her son left her unprepared and contributed to her reactions. She'd go to kiss him goodnight and he would sexualize it by "kissing my breasts or biting them or rubbing his genitals against me." Martha said she found that bewildering and confusing and added, "That was really hard to take." Her expectation of adoption was that she would take a loving, nurturing approach. Unfortunately, to her surprise she found that he continuously rejected her motherly care, but added, "And then, when it appears that he possibly was going to accept me in a loving nurturing way, he would somehow turn it sexual." Martha seemed to suffer continual shocks; none of which she felt prepared for. She went on to say: "Do you know anybody who fought in Viet Nam? That would be like a typical day with Kurt. Actually what I'd do is send him outside because mostly I couldn't stand being with him." Both parents found it difficult to be at the dinner table with Kurt because of his table manners. "He would eat, burp, and fart at the table then cause problems with his sister." Joe and Martha believed he would cause havoc in an effort to be sent to his room, a means of avoiding routine chores. The mother said, "The better I got at letting him face the consequences for his own actions, the worse his behavior became."

Due to other behaviors displayed by Kurt, Martha and husband Joe considered locking his door at night to maintain their safety. Canadian Social Services prohibit such actions by the parents, so instead, they put a lock on their daughter's and their own doors to insure their safety at night. They also put an alarm on Kurt's door so the family knew when he came out of his room at night. However, that arrangement was frightening because it gave him free access to the rest of the house during nighttime hours. The child had a history of arson prior to his placement with Martha and Joe and they feared he might return to those behaviors when given the run of the house. They were terrified they all might be burned out of their home or killed. After all, Martha and her spouse decided they needed to leave their door open so they could hear what was going on at night.

Martha talked about an incident that occurred when she and her children spent a holiday with her mother who lived in southern British Columbia. Because of his busy work schedule, her husband Joe was unable to stay with them during the vacation. Martha reported that Kurt hated her mother and that she "was the only other woman he was real in front of, right off the bat." During the holiday Kurt acted as though he were miserable in his grandmother's company and demonstrated that by soiling his pants in front of her. One day they decided to go for a walk, on a day that Kurt seemed particularly mad at her. In fact, Martha believed he'd been angry with her throughout the week and thought a walk would be good for him. In the rural area walkers used a sidewalk which ran along the side of a busy major highway. As the trucks whizzed passed Kurt waited until an opportune moment and then pushed Martha off the sidewalk and into the path of an oncoming tractor-trailer. Martha and Joe had been told that Kurt had witnessed the suicide of his biological mother, and the youngster had been the one to call the authorities. His adoptive mother said that after pushing her, "He made some comment about me committing suicide and he was laughing. He thought that was funny and it didn't bother him one bit. He had dreams about stabbing me and then told the doctor, the psychiatrist, and me about them."

In addition to living with the symptoms displayed by their children, those common to attachment difficulties, the mothers shared profound experiences perhaps caused by more stress than readily met the eye. Because responses exhibited by women from halfway around the globe shared amazing similarities I have collected their stories and placed them together in this chapter. It seemed to me, one or two mothers having similar experiences made a quiet statement. However, when many unrelated women shared startlingly similar stories, I began to listen in a new way. I was reminded that my role with the families of such disturbed children was that of student. As you have read, many women experienced increased difficulties in their marriages with the addition of an attachment disturbed child. Many mothers, upon discussion, believed the marital discord was the result of a set-up maneuvered by the AD kids in their attempts to divide the parents and control the family. Anecdotes that follow are typical examples:

Pat F., Craig's mother from Elkton, Maryland shared that when he got older if she prevented him from doing something, her husband tended to defend him. Bob would ask me why I made Craig cry. "Why didn't I simply let him go to the bathroom when he wanted to?" he would say. Craig had a history of being sexually inappropriate with his teenage sisters that the father did not believe. Pat attempted to explain the inappropriateness of Craig's choices to her husband. The youth became an expert at "splitting" the parents, so Pat and her husband developed disagreements about their son. The babysitter, thinking she was helping or protecting the child and the husband, would give two reports after watching the children. The sitter would tell the mother the truth, but leave important details out of the father's version and then swear the sisters to secrecy. The babysitter told Craig's sisters that since their father worked hard as an ER physician that they should not bother him with the stories about what had really happened The young woman unwittingly added to the triangulated communications already present in the home. It fueled the disagreements between the parents and the differences in perceptions were dramatically widened. So when Pat tried to discuss serious behaviors with her husband—that Craig had hit his sisters with a pipe he carried—she was, again, not believed.

Finally Pat, tired of communication problems and the resultant discord, announced to her husband that she was leaving for a few days. "You watch them," she instructed. "You don't get a sitter. You don't play the computer; you don't read or work. You watch them." She moved out and went to stay in a little cabin for three or four days with her husband's agreement. On the first night, Pat had been gone perhaps eight hours and was about 100 miles from home when her husband called in a panic. He said, "You have to get back here, things are terrible! It's awful and I can't stand it! There's an emergency! Get back here!" Pat didn't know what happened but went back immediately. Her husband was a computer hobbyist and had kept a record of Craig's behaviors. When the wife arrived home, he showed her the list. It included: "threatened and pushed the girls; shoved his sisters into the walls; when he wanted to go where father or sisters were standing he'd knock them down. He had threatened Michelle by holding a lighter in her face and threatened to burn her." Pat looked at the list and said, "'What's the problem? You said there was something terrible happening here, something that had never happened before. This is that way he behaves.' That was normal in our house."

"There's one major problem for the parent of a RAD kid;" Pat shared, "it tends to isolate you from other people. It just got too hectic trying to pull him off of people's kids." She said she believed others had misguided perceptions that she was overprotective or neurotic when she was, in fact, attempting to protect their children from the aggression of her own youngster. "On the other hand, people get rather upset when your child hits their child with a baseball bat." Pat believes that a painful part of the problem is society's negative reactions to the overwhelmed parents of attachment-disordered children.

Ms. F. nervously disclosed: "I feel bad about myself as a mother." In retrospect this mother of three believes she should have left the family home when Craig was a little boy. She now thinks, "One of us should have taken the girls and one of us should have taken Craig. It's not because my husband and I couldn't get along." She said she wishes she had separated her daughters from their disturbed sibling for their own safety. Daily, she continues to carry the burden of guilt for not protecting them from the emotional and sexual abuse heaped on by Craig throughout his life with them. Pat reported that both girls live as far from home as possible and believes they have difficulty in relationships with men because of their terrifying brother. She still believes that doing all she could to keep Craig home was harmful to her daughters, especially to the youngest, adopted sibling. "I'm left with guilt about being a bad parent," Pat said tearfully.

The Maryland mom concluded, "We were living in a state of panic. It was just that Craig could not be here." Pat told me she could not trust her son at all, that she could not take her eyes off him out of fear of what he would do, especially to her girls. The daughters, at her insistence, locked their doors to keep him away from them and to remain safe. Pat said, "If one of the girls was taking a shower Craig would go in, try to knock her down and play 'Psycho.'" As the result of his dangerous behaviors he was eventually sent to a military school. Pat said the transfer to a school with a disciplined approach was not so much "for Craig's sake. I'm past the point of trying to protect my son. I was trying to protect my daughters; I didn't think they deserved this. I just wanted him out of the house as much as possible for their sake."

Because Attachment Disorder is a "mother issue," moms continue to be the target of hurt and rageful children. Unfortunately, the women also become the focus of scorn by husbands, family and friends, teachers and therapists alike. More than one mother told me that if enough people tell you you're worthless or bad, pretty soon those charges become believable. Responsible and often overly responsible women become foster and adoptive mothers. With expectations sometimes too high and left in the dark by the agencies, emotional crashes are inevitable. Blame gets heaped on mother; then she automatically takes on the guilt for the child's failure to attach. The anecdotes below demonstrate the problems very clearly.

Sarah P. of Arvada, Colorado, has been therapeutic foster parent to thirty-five boys over the past several years. The experienced mother said that she has witnessed "lots of anger at mom. This was interesting to us. Even though in our home my husband Jack is the primary caretaker, much of the anger is directed at me." Sarah described the following typical situation, which would happen more often at the end of her workday or in the summertime. This particular situation involved Sam, a RAD teenager in their care: "I went out to run an errand of some kind and when I came back Sam was sitting (a usual therapeutic consequence used with attachment-disordered kids). I came in and said, 'Hi, Sam, I see you're sitting. Bummer.' His response was 'Fuck you, Mom!' I said, 'What are you mad at me about, Sam?' His reply, 'Dad made me do push-ups.'" Sarah now believes that most children harbor great anger towards mothers because they felt that their own mom didn't protect them as infants and toddlers. "I thought, coming into this," Sarah mused, "that it was a primary caretaker thing, but it now seems to be a gender thing."

Catherine H. of central California shared that son, Bob, would make things at school, art projects and the like, typical of grade school children. "But," Catherine lamented, "he would always give them to the neighbors on the way home. He would not bring anything home to give Mom. He did not give us any Christmas gifts, Mother's Day, Father's Day—absolutely no acknowledgement on the day. He wanted to put zero effort in making us feel good about being parents." Catherine added that Bob was constantly hyper-vigilant, persistently on the lookout for who knows what. She said he always kept weapons—knives, a BB gun, a bow and arrows–beside him in his bedroom. Some of them were apparently hidden, but others were left out in plain sight. The anxious mother said their experiences with therapists were not positive. A common occurrence was when the therapist "would take about 20 minutes to talk to me, and he would put more guilt on us for what we weren't doing or we weren't understanding Bob enough." Catherine said that usually it was thought that Bob just needed more adjustment time to settle into their home. The most recent therapist instructed Catherine "to serve him more specialty foods to make him feel really special and, you know, make up for the love his mother didn't give him. I felt really just out of wind, out of energy to carry on every day."

Mattie W. of Nebraska sorrowfully reported that by the second or third grade their son Scot was always in trouble, and was "always hurting somebody." The local elementary school staff attempted to assist using several behavioral modification programs, but none of the special techniques designed and instituted to help the youngster were successful. The boy's behaviors were frankly destructive at school, yet the school counselor eventually told Mattie that she was "the problem." If enough people tell you that your child is fine and that you are the source of the problem, Mattie reported that, "you get to thinking, well, maybe I am. And then the guilt sets in and you're thinking, 'What am I doing with this sixth kid that I didn't do with the other five to make him like this?'"

Tearfully, Mattie stated, "I started to hate this kid so much because he was causing such upheaval in our family and tearing our family apart. I thought this is not a normal feeling for a mother to have for a child. Why do I feel like this? I must be crazy; I must really be losing it. And as time went on I even had thoughts of suicide." Mattie had never before experienced depression and certainly had never entertained ideas of ending her life. That frightened her even more and added to the questions she was already asking herself. She wondered in secret if she was the sort of person who could kill herself. She also worried about why she would have such feelings. At one point she thought she should leave the family and thought, "They'll be better off without me. Scot is the one that hates me, he doesn't hate anybody else in the family." Fortunately, she did not act on the decision to flee and found out later that Scot cared as little for everyone as he did his mother. "But," Mattie said, "those were the struggles I went through."

Amelia B. from California talked about her attitudes toward adoption and life with attachment-disordered kids: "I would say don't adopt—don't do it. I'm pretty wise with children and these guys have me stumped. I've worked with handicapped kids for years. I would say don't adopt. If somebody offered me a long-term kid right now I would have to say no." Amelia, a mature woman, told me that having RAD kids has instilled her with enormous fears about the condition of the family. She now believes children with the same illness as her adopted son D.J. causes devastation to families. D.J., who is biologically her grand-nephew, was removed from his birth home at six years old because of neglect. Two weeks later he was placed with Amelia and her husband, Joe. She told me they had no inkling that there was anything emotionally wrong with him as no one had heard of Reactive Attachment Disorder. Consequently, she revealed, "I spent the first year and a half blaming myself, thinking that I was a lousy mother. I had no idea there was anything wrong with him. I thought it was all my fault. I blamed myself and other people blamed me because they felt I wasn't either strict enough or, in other circumstances, I was too strict. The kid was just a spoiled brat out in public. He would make scenes and beg for strangers' sympathy, grandstanding to make me look like an idiot. After about a year and a half I was at my wit's end."

Martha L. from Alberta confided that soon after Kurt joined her family, she started doubting herself and it had to do with the first time she spanked him. Although she had another young child, it was the first time she'd used spanking as a consequence. Martha divulged, "My hand felt like it was on fire. I couldn't breathe. I plunked myself down against the wall and I cried. But what was more upsetting was not that he needed a spanking; it was more that I wanted to hurt him. And I had never experienced that feeling in my life ever before." This usually generous mother shared that she had wanted Kurt. She had gone out of her way to bring this child "into my home to love and nurture and raise. You know," she said, "become the child's mother. And suddenly I wanted to hurt this kid and it just shocked me. And it hurt me about myself. Not only did I feel guilty about my behavior and my anger toward Kurt, but also I feel guilty that I put Sanya, our daughter, in a position of danger, time and time again, for two years. I shouldn't have done that."

Sharon W. of Wisconsin confided that she'd come to the conclusion that there are so many things that can happen to the children. Kids, she thinks, which have been separated from their birth mom between one day old and three years old are at extreme risk. Then, she stated, in order to get through to them "You're really fighting quite a battle here and I don't think anyone prepares you for that." Sharon is an active reader on the topic of attachment disorders, especially since becoming a mother to her disturbed children. She shared that, due to the lack of preparation to care for youngsters with overwhelming emotional problems, she didn't read enough before their arrival. The new mother has grown to believe the most difficult stage for her is when she must consciously remind herself of the reasons for their behaviors. "I find myself," she divulged, "losing it and really I need to keep in mind what's behind it all. I'm having trouble doing that." She believes that in the middle of all the fracas that her children need structure in their lives. However, Sharon said, "My husband doesn't like to have much structure and he will openly disagree, so there's a bit of conflict going on. We're still at that stage I think we should have passed about a year ago."

The Wisconsin mother has occasionally tried yelling and spanking as a means of disciplining them, to no avail, except that she ends up feeling guilty. Sharon had decided, before the children, that if she had kids she would never spank them. Sharon reported that her parents spanked her as a youngster and raised their voice to her as well. The results, she confided, "made me worse and belligerent; it created anger and resentment." Through her readings she has developed some ideas of better approaches to discipline. She feels she should be putting those new ideas into practice but despite her desires that's taking longer than she hoped. Perhaps due to the language barrier and their start in a Russian orphanage, she found it extremely hard to reach them, other than by holding them, for the first six months.

In spite of pure motives that led them to foster and adopt children, the women paid a price for their sometime altruistic decisions. The mothers below share about the high emotional and financial costs involved in attempting to rear attachment disturbed youngsters.

Paula W. of Nebraska, shared that the addition of Susie to the family caused enormous emotional upheaval and personal angst for her. "I think" she said, "that I was trying to put my family together and it wasn't being put together. We were five individuals in the same home but we weren't a family. We were just five individuals functioning as little individuals. I was trying to help Stephen. I was trying to help Aaron. I was trying to help Susie." Eventually Paula realized that under the circumstances no one could have a healthy relationship. She found herself pretending to be happy and believed the remainder of her family was doing the same "I was just someone who'd just be going through the motions. You go through the dishes, the laundry, the whatever, and I couldn't help any of them, emotionally, any more. Susie had me—I don't know if she had me—I allowed her to have me emotionally distraught."

Paula said she remembered crying continually and couldn't even hold the tears back when their caseworker visited. Tearfully, she confided, "I had no one else to talk to that would understand; I thought she would understand. And all she understood was that they'd picked the wrong parents for this child. I didn't know how to deal with Susie; I didn't know how to love her." Six weeks after Susie's placement the caseworker was removed from the case, but not before she "...wrote a letter to Guatemala saying that they had placed Susie in the wrong home. And I think that I would have been at peace to have her move on at that time. But Bob really wanted to try and so that's when we decided to keep her a little bit longer." Their daughter, however, ended up staying with them for seven more years. In the meantime, "Even our counselor said nobody would have ever guessed that we were having problems. You couldn't let the mask down because you couldn't face reality; you didn't know what to do with it. What would I do with the reality if I would say life is always upside down? I couldn't face that. So I had to live in a pretense and always say that I'm happy when I'm not."

Martha L. of Alberta said recently she's had a disturbing experience when she looked at some "before and after Kurt" pictures. Kurt was diagnosed with a severe attachment disorder about one year after he joined the family. Martha hesitantly shared that during the year that led up to the RAD diagnosis, "I went from a size 10, with my hair combed, to size 16. I couldn't shower when the kids were home because I couldn't leave them alone. I looked like hell. I was no longer brushing my hair everyday. I no longer showered everyday. Some days I didn't even get out of my pajamas. My life has been forever changed from the experience of this child." She said when her husband Joe came home at night, she'd be in tears. By eight o'clock she'd have their son in bed, and would already be sobbing. "I didn't know how to cope. I was a mess; I'd never been like that. At one point the social worker came to visit, and I was thinking about trading Kurt in. I was thinking about giving him back and getting a different kid."

Mattie W. reported Scot spent most of his adolescent years in institutions due to his dangerousness. Scot is currently in his mid-twenties until recently was incarcerated in a maximum-security prison while paying for his crimes against society. This veteran Mom said she dreaded his release. Although she thinks it doesn't make intellectual sense, she continues to harbor fears about her own personal safety around him. During his adolescence, Scot repeatedly threatened to kill her, and she believes he was, and is still, capable of causing her grave harm. "We loved Scot from the day we picked him up. You can be so angry with him and you can think he's such a rotten kid. But you still love him and I probably always will. We would do anything we can for him and that's what we felt we did with Scot. We spent our life savings and some of my grandmother's life savings trying to get help for him. When nothing works, when love doesn't work, and caring doesn't work—it leaves such a hole in your soul."

All the mothers told me about arriving at a point in their life with their beloved child where they had to make a grave decision. Some planned suicide, others planned their escape from the family. All of them, at one time or another, considered removing their child from their home for the sake of the remaining family members. When mother reached the end of her rope, one door closed tightly leaving the need to open another and to pass through with the resolve that something must change. The women's stories below are clear examples of reaching that significant moment.

Sue J. of Gravesend, England, is the mother of two attachment affected youngsters. The stressed woman talked a bit about their attempts to find help for their family. She and her husband had been trying to identify a professional who could assist or find respite care for the children. Sue said she was offered respite care for both children—four hours for each, on alternate weekends. The mother said she was glad for the option, but did not think it would be adequate time for her to rest or get recharged. Disturbing enough, the couple was unable to locate any sort of help during frequent emergencies they experienced with their children. During our interview she talked half to me and partially to her empathetic husband. Tearfully, she said recently, "Well, I just broke down and cried, didn't I? I just really had enough. I didn't know what to do and I said to Robert, 'You know I can't go on like this. Something's got to give somewhere.' I mean, it's that close. It was close to us saying that that's it; we're giving up."

Marcey D. from San Luis Obispo sited several disturbing experiences that led up to the final decision to overturn Alli's adoption. Once the family began needing respite care, the depth of Alli's attachment to them—or the lack of it—became clear. Marcey shared that when they came back for their daughter, they realized she hadn't missed them at all. That opened the mother's eyes to the realization that "whatever we were doing wasn't making any difference to her. I mean we were going nowhere, paddling very, very, very, very hard. It was killing us." Marcey did not like the notion that she had to control and isolate her daughter, for everyone's safety, because the divisions reduced the quality of their life. Marcey and husband Dan believed the quality of life with her was eroding and that the other children felt the stress as well: Jeff stayed in his room much of the time and Bill left home. The sad mother stated: "She doesn't have a conscience, she just doesn't. It's just not there. And I think for the longest time I was so angry with her because I thought 'Here she is, so smart, this child is so smart. Why can't she see all these things I'm teaching because it's going to make her life good? Why can't she get them? I think she can get them, she just doesn't want to, doggone it!' Sadly, Marcey stated she's come to believe that Alli cannot make proper choices and that she may never be able to think beyond the present moment and her current needs.

Ms. D. stated that she's no longer angry with her because she's accepted that Alli's incapable of controlling herself enough to do things that are good for her. On the other hand, Marcey stated she couldn't accept that she hurts other people and appears to enjoy it. Living with the destructive behaviors "erodes everything good about your home; I felt like that's what it did to me. I love her—I know I could survive with her, but the cost was just too high." Marcey stated that before their adoption experience she felt strong and capable. She said she'd never had to fight for her life before and that is what the challenge with Alli turned out to be. Tearfully the mother stated, "It has left me a little neurotic. It's left me a little fearful and worrisome and weak, weakened in many ways. Vulnerable, God, so vulnerable that a small child who you adore and you want to love and you're so committed to can just destroy it all and pull the rug out from under you. And they're not even responsible because of who they are. That's left me shaken."

Hong B., from Bechenham, England, the mother of two adopted preteen daughters admitted that she has mixed emotions about her daughters. In the Chinese way, mothers are strict disciplinarians. "I learned things from my mother that I apply to the girls; it's inevitable. We believe that although you give them love and affection, what you do is discipline them for their own sakes, not for our sakes." In spite of, or perhaps because of her strong beliefs, Hong finds herself feeling conflicted in her parenting role. Surprisingly, she finds that her daughters do not respond to her guidance as she had as a child. Their violence, one toward the other, was foreign and unacceptable to her. But try as she might, Hong was unable to rid them of such ferocity. The frightened mother claimed she would not have a violent child in her home, but got little or no support from the adoption workers. The behaviors were dismissed as "normal children's behaviors."

Eventually Hong began to feel duped by the adoption agency. She felt she couldn't cope with the situation or bring herself to choose only one child and reject the other. Hong was told that "If I say that I'm not going to adopt Girly, Dolly will also be removed. That would be tragic." The mother said that she just wanted her daughters to grow up happy. "If I have two years and I'm still not making Girly happy, then I'm not doing my job very well, am I?" The diminutive mother tearfully shared, "I was going mad; I became so depressed. I stayed in my house for six months and I lost a stone, about forty pounds." Her frightened husband John frequently found Hong sitting perfectly still, overwhelmed, and staring off into space. "I had been full of hopes," the sad mother stated, "I wanted to give a home to nice kids and if this was the way it was going to be I couldn't carry on like this."

Martha L. of Canada, said they finally decided that Kurt could no longer live with them. The parents were finally able to identify two continuous problems they could not live with: the sexually acting-out toward Martha and daughter Sanya and his habit of urinating in inappropriate places. Joe tensely shared that on the final day in their home, Kurt "took Martha's coat, brought it into the bathroom, peed all over it, brought it out and handed it to her. That was it. He left that night." Kurt had lived as their son for well over a year.

Kate H. is an English mother of two children. J.D. is the older of the two and is attachment disordered. During a discussion about her son's daily behaviors she shared this experience: His verbal aggression had been increasing, but she said he'd never threatened her physically since an incident long before. "He raised his hand to me once," she said, "and I grabbed him by the throat, with my knees knocking, my heart thumping, and pulled him close to me. I said, 'I was brought up in an area of Liverpool where a child of five would eat you alive for breakfast, J.D., and spit your pips out. Don't ever raise your hand to me again because you may not have a hand to raise when you look at it again.' I was shaking; I burst into tears afterwards. I went out into another room and my husband had just got hold of me. I was terrified. But to some extent it's worked, because he's never, ever raised his hand to me." She's not so sure her bravado will work forever, because he is becoming bigger and more aggressive. Kate verbalized concerns that her approach might not have been the proper path to a threatening child, but for the time being, it had worked. She concluded, "I keep him off balance because he doesn't really know what I'm capable of. There's always that question mark, 'What will she do if I hit her?'"

Martha Welch, M.D., stated that even though we do not want it to be so, disturbed behaviors among adopted youngsters "is a given." The new mom "does not have the biological setup for bonding to the adopted baby." The sooner a child is placed with a non-biological mother, the more successful the attaching. Bonding success is particularly improved, Welch told me, if the new pair is placed in a situation where they are in continuous physical contact for several days following placement.

However, Welch believes if you give a mother a four-year-old with a history of neglect, the chances of good bonding are minimal. However, do not be disheartened. The psychiatrist stated, "I believe there are a lot of ways to effect an attachment in adoption, if we would just pay attention" and take immediate and appropriate action.

When the experiences occur before the development of language, or at a precognitive stage of development, only educated guesses can piece together their true past. Attachment-Disordered individuals are like jigsaw puzzles or, on a higher level, a grand mosaic design. Each piece, each tile has a meaning all its own and are scattered out much farther than across a tabletop. The clues are spread out, in disarray, across the expanse of their lifetime. It's no wonder, particularly among "healers" and "fixers," that it was the mothers of such disturbed individuals who had the most difficulty living with their broken spirited children. Interestingly enough, I have noticed a fact that was repeatedly thrust into my field of attention: no matter the cultural or ethnic beginnings of the child or the parent, the stories all have a similar flavor. So, too, is the case with the fathers. Although their experiences are significantly different from those of their wives, the fathers of RAD kids can also easily relate to each other.

CHAPTER SEVEN—
The Fathers' Stories

The fathers I had the honor of interviewing were, simply put, awesome! Because of my own unfortunate experiences and personal biases, I felt joyfully blindsided by men who were as committed to the welfare of their troubled children and to the overall health of their families as any I've had the pleasure of meeting. Every individual was unabashedly in love with his wife, as reported by both the men and the spouses, and fully involved and interested in rearing his family. As a group, they were bright, articulate, spiritual or religious, and had been full partners in the initial decision to adopt a child. Another characteristic they had in common with their spouses was an internal vision of how an adopted youngster would fit into their already beloved family.

Often, and in spite of their involvement in family matters, fathers were usually the last to see what was going awry within the family after the addition of a disturbed child. As you have read, mothers tend to be the first target of unbonded individuals. Siblings are usually next in line for the abusive behaviors metered out by AD kids. And Dad? Ah, Dad is usually spared direct violent tactics but is generally the unwitting victim of advanced manipulations. Once the disturbances became apparent to the father, conflicts within the constellation had already woven themselves into the fabric of the family. By then the tentacles of illness were a significant threat to each member and the family as a unit.

In *Holding Time*, Welch stated that it took her five years in private practice for her to figure out what was different between appropriately treated youngsters who developed reciprocity and bonded and those who did not emotionally attach to others. "If the father did not support the mother adequately," she stated, "attachment couldn't be done with these severely disturbed children." Fortunately for the women and the children involved in my study, these fathers were ultimately very capable of adequately supporting their wives. First, however, they had their own metamorphoses to complete before they were able to make significant differences in the lives of their families.

I pray that in your reading you are able to appreciate the courage it took to become as open and honest as the fathers in the following stories demonstrate:

Bob W. of Kearney, Nebraska stated that his mind was made up long before the addition of their third child. He believed strongly that a persistent and loving family would take care of, or totally eliminate, any problems experienced by a transplanted child. He and his wife had already adopted two boys who were happy and well adjusted, so they were certain his theory was correct. Naturally, Bob believed the approach they were practicing with their sons would be successful with a daughter as well. The father sheepishly indicated that in some ways he and his wife Paula thought of themselves as invincible and all-powerful. He stated, "If anybody can make it work, we can." Later, during the unanticipated difficulties, Bob learned that his "I'm-going-to-make-this-thing-work-no-matter-what" attitude caused him to be blind to some of the warning signs Susie emitted almost immediately. Although he felt somewhat intimidated by the politics of foreign adoptions, his ensuing fear seemed to make him all the more stubborn in his resolve to succeed with his beautiful ten-year-old daughter.

Bob shared that as soon as Susie was introduced into the family a curious thing happened: within the first two to three days everyone began taking sides. Their oldest son, Stephan, at 12 was two years older than Susie, and "did not like her right out of the gate," as he put it. But Aaron, slightly younger than his new sister, enjoyed the idea of having a bigger family. With hard won hindsight, Bob believed his oldest child was mature enough to recognize some of Susie's problems and could see what was happening. Somehow Stephan was able to see how Susie manipulated and lied to Paula. Problems occurred immediately when Stephan stepped forward to protect his mother, a stance that was not popular with the other family members. In spite of the changing allegiances Bob continued to encourage the family to "buck up," to put their heads down, and plow through the collecting storm. Initially, the involved man believed Susie was an innocent who was being victimized by their sons. Consequently, he did what he thought was right—he became the protector and champion of his little girl. Today, Bob believes that his "bulldozer mentality," as he called it, interfered with his ability to appreciate the dramatic familial changes and see the entire situation clearly. His wife Paula, he shared, was very frustrated with Susie's behaviors and the new family configuration. There was suddenly an unwelcome schism in the family and his wife longed for the relationships they'd once had. In his confusion with the new situation, Bob felt guilty for pushing the adoption in the first place. He also thought he was being blamed for the changes, so he stubbornly clung to the belief they could still resolve the issues and work through the grief. Eventually, after much emotional soul searching, Bob had to admit that they could not redo the emotional connections that had come unraveled.

Perhaps because of his unyielding resolve, the family hung on to Susie in spite of her continuous chaotic, destructive behaviors. The couple did not take their adoption commitment lightly; they renewed their decision to keep her in the family and to help her however they could. By Susie's eighth grade year their home life was crumbling. It was then that their daughter's antics became public and could no longer be confined within the walls of their own private hell. The sad father said she was excellent at making the rest of the family look foolish, or even criminal, while she was very accomplished at portraying the part of an innocent victim. "So to the outsider," Bob said, "she still looked like a pretty sweet girl." Once her negative, sometimes dangerous, behaviors spilled out into the school and on to their small community, she began amassing a legal record for the many incidents she initiated. Eventually, law enforcement and the courts became involved in their family matters. Bob shared that going to court because of the charges against Susie was very humbling because they'd always been considered to be somewhat of a model family in the community. In spite of the legal assistance Bob and Paula could see their daughter's behaviors spiraling downward, increasingly out of control. As stubborn as he was, the devoted family man was not able to see the extent of the deterioration within the family until his youngest son, who'd always liked and supported Susie, could no longer stand to be around her. The sad father stated, "Both boys got to the point where they didn't even want to be at home anymore. That hurt." However, he shared, the most hurtful and devastating thing was his own lack of understanding about what was happening to their daughter. Bob said they had no clue why Susie was so unhappy or why the entire family was in such turmoil. They had invested a lot of their lives, emotion, and money into her and felt they were getting "trashed for it. It really hurt."

The stubborn family man shared that he developed a new mind set out of his need to survive the constant turmoil and finally realized that he had to take care of *all* the family members. Finally, he realized they were being blowing apart from the inside. Throughout their experiences Bob said Paula repeatedly asked him if she was crazy; but he just believed that Paula just needed to be stronger when dealing with Susie's problems. Paula told her husband that she felt Susie was out to get her, but Bob truly believed Paula was imagining it. Eventually, he witnessed Susie telling his wife she was a rotten mother and calling her "evil and saying all sorts of things about Paula that weren't true." The Midwestern father said their daughter would say such things about him too, but with much less frequency or fervor. He finally could see for himself and understood that Susie's rage really was directed at his wife. Bob was then able to develop a clear view of Susie, and he could see that she really was out to hurt his wife.

Because the professional couple had protected their privacy so well, many neighbors and friends remained unaware of the severity of their problems. Bob described themselves as a "closet attachment-disordered family." They didn't want anybody knowing what was happening within the family because they didn't understand the problem either. The determined father finally decided he needed to save the rest of his family if he could, which necessitated making some tough decisions. The new resolve fueled a decision to limit Susie's influence, and perhaps her future, in their home. According to Bob, the final decision needed to be made in the best interest for the rest of the family. By then Susie was seventeen and Bob was in complete agreement with his spouse and the family that their girl needed to be removed from their home. And so, Susie was placed in a group home setting which has allowed the family to begin their healing process.

Ian F. is a professional social worker from "someplace in England," as he reported, and married to his soul mate, Louie. For the interview the couple met with several friends yet remained comfortable while sharing his experiences as the father of an attachment disturbed son. Because of his professional role, Ian thought he would have been more realistic than most about his expectations of an adopted child with a complicated history. But he wasn't. He believed deeply that since he was aware of reality, and if he could hang in there two or three years, the child could be turned around, perhaps almost made new. Ian's internal theme seemed to be, "And you just keep on going." He added, "Call it arrogance, call it denial, call it what you like. Probably both and more, but I thought that somehow we would turn the corner and we could do it. And, well…we didn't." Their son was with them from November '87 until March '94 when he had to be relinquished because, try as they might, they were no longer able to safely sustain him in their home.

Ian continued, "I would say the three weeks immediately after his departure were the worst three weeks of my whole life. I was totally traumatized and all my commitments, all my beliefs about who I was and what I did fell apart, really. And it's taken a long time too. I'm not going to get over that, but kind of manage it." Ian went on to say that he had been given a very clear picture of his son's history; that he had been a product of the care system; and that he'd been removed from his parents due to severe neglect. The father continued to believe that his understanding of his son's past would overcome all and that the source of the problem was intellectual in nature. "But," he shared, "because of that draw as a parent, that in some cases, even though you've got the information, you actually push it away. You almost deny the awfulness of the background, and only later does it catch up with you. We knew the fundamentals about Adrian's background, but I don't know that I took that on in its entirety. It's only when I lived with him I saw how it impacted us and how Adrian behaved, I think, that one really made the connection." Ian shared that he is now wiser, but sadder, following his parenting experience.

Corky Y. is a Protestant minister from a small town in central Nebraska. He and his wife Ann were married seven years before they adopted their first two children, both boys. Similar to other families I'd interviewed, they had enjoyed their boys and felt they were having success in guiding them through life. Eventually they were asked to foster an eight-year-old girl, whom they joyfully added to their family. All of Corky and Ann's decisions to adopt came out of their strong religious and spiritual beliefs. So although their foster daughter had already demonstrated a strong propensity to act out both sexually and aggressively toward their sons, they decided to go through with the adoption anyway. Corky believed that the problems, if there were any of any significance, would go away with a good home and under their loving guidance. The minister shared that he was ultimately dumbfounded to learn what really was going on in their home. Corky said he had no idea of all her negative behaviors that occurred when he was gone from the home. He said, with apparent embarrassment, "Ann's the one that understood what was happening, and I thought she was blowing it all out of proportion." He emotionally admitted with reluctance that because of their differing perceptions, he was continually upset with Ann. In hindsight he believes he did see some of the daughter's acting out, but didn't realize they were maladaptive or didn't understand the significance of those behaviors. "I observed them," he said, "but I didn't *get* them." Although Corky and Ann normally got along well they began arguing when discussions about their daughter were broached. Their older son was very upset over the increased tension and the younger boy began hiding in his room because their fighting disturbed him. When sharing about his current relationship with his daughter, Corky stated, "Oh, she manipulated me very well. I'm still not sure I see all of it, even today. She can still wrap me around her finger faster than I'd like to admit."

Troy W., the Ph.D. living in San Luis Obispo talked about his experiences with 9-year-old Sam. As the result of early neglect and deprivation, he was fully unsocialized when first placed with their family. The little boy was so wild that they could not even take him to the grocery store. Troy said that in order to be able to take him along to shop they first took him just to the parking lot. On the second trip they carried him up to the door. Then on the next trip, they took him just inside the super market door. Eventually, practically an inch at a time, Sam could go with Troy and Leslie to purchase the family's groceries. Troy said once they took Sam to a sports shoe store in a little mall in San Maria. They managed to get him only about ten feet inside the door before the youngster began wildly grabbing shoes and items. They had to leave immediately because Sam was unable to control his own behaviors in the shops.

Breakfast time, according to the father, was a continuous trial. It was a mealtime where they first discovered just how stubborn and unsocialized Sam was. For example, at the morning meal, Sam would choose his cereal from a few choices but then just sit motionless at the table with his prepared meal in front of him. When Leslie encouraged him to eat, the silent, resistant struggle began. Another behavior that confounded Troy was his son's refusal or inability (Troy and Leslie did not know which was the case) to chew his food. When he did decide to eat instead of chewing in the usual manner, the youngster would take huge bites of food and try to force himself to swallow it whole. Troy frequently observed Sam eating in what looked like slow motion while the food would run out of his mouth and down his cheeks and chin. The milk from Sam's cereal eventually ended up on the front of his clothing.

They also learned that Sam was an inordinate procrastinator and would not follow the directions given him. It was either Sam's way, or no way at all. The child would get stalled and his tasks would go unfinished. When the youngster was supposed to be preparing for school he would dawdle getting dressed and end up being late because of it. While brushing his teeth, for instance, he would get distracted and end up smearing his eyeglasses with toothpaste. Many of their young son's behaviors did not make sense to the parents, both experts in the mental health field. It appeared to Troy and Leslie that their son moved from one mess to another, all of his own making.

Troy said that the job of being Sam's parents required both adults to remain at home. The couple couldn't leave the house because what they had "was like a tag team thing, both of us kind of spelling each other in order to get him ready for school and out the door. Leslie would start to get wigged out because he would be trying to irritate her so I would step in and then he would work me for a while. Then she would step in so we just kind of tag teamed it back and forth to get him ready. Then we get Sam out the door and he walks to the bus stop in these little baby steps—to intentionally miss the bus. Or he gets to the bus stop then runs back and forth in front of the traffic, throwing stones at the bus. He got thrown off the bus several times. If you're going to masturbate on the bus, you always sit right next to the principal's daughter. This is a small town and that was effective beyond our wildest dreams for getting him thrown off the bus."

Troy, a psychologist and his social worker wife, Leslie, reported that Sam's biological mother tried to kill him twice within the first month of life. The adoptive mother said that he was hyper-vigilant with remarkable emotional antenna used to read other people. Father stated, "It's a gift. He can read your facial expressions, your gestures. It's almost like he has some kind of radar; he can size up your weaknesses, what bothers you, whatever. He can read people very quickly and if he chooses to can provoke them or manipulate them in some fashion. Others either think he's the most wonderful child or they'll be shocked at what he's done."

Troy was eager to talk about his observations of Sam and his attachment difficulties. "I believe the reason for his behaviors is survival. It seemed like I saw glimpses of him letting go of his need for control; it seemed like there were genuine moments of vulnerability with him." The psychologist said he saw Sam's behaviors cycle as has been described in the work of Dr. Foster Cline. "He would go underground and give you a glimpse of hope, only to resurface even worse, weeks, months, whatever, later. It's a matter of survival—he thought he might die if he trusted us. He would keep things in such a constant state of chaos for him to survive. He could not stand normalcy. Whether it was because he didn't know it in his brain. Whatever the reason, he just couldn't do it." Before Sam was removed from the family and taken to an institution his older brother was heard to ask Sam why he couldn't just be a regular kid.

During his life with them Sam spent significant periods of time in hospitals and psychiatric institutions. Consequently, home visits with him were mostly during the holidays. The parents consciously opted to keep communications with their son superficial as neither partner had the energy to engage in power struggles, which would certainly ensue. Their child continued to initiate frequent battles so they chose not to make any demands on him so their interactions have remained intentionally casual. The father said he was sad about visits from the 11 year-old because their activities were not at all like their usual lives. Sam continuously sabotaged any fun, so the couple decided they couldn't go out with him or do the things that were usual in the course of their daily lives. Visits felt very artificial and strained according to the California couple. Sam talked about coming home to live with the family but the parents doubted the sincerity of his words. They've maintained Sam's room for him but when talking about the feelings around Sam's return to the family, Troy stated, "I'm terrified—beyond terrified; it would be voluntarily choosing chaos. As he matures physically, what I anticipate is a lot of my having to physically restrain him. I see he's charming and involved with girls; girls love him and he's going to be involved in sexual behavior. And he's going to be involved in drugs; he's going to be involved in semi-gang or antisocial behaviors. I'll be dealing with police, law enforcement, irate parents of pregnant girls, and drugs. That will be absolute chaos! I won't be able to make a living; I won't be able to be a husband and father. I mean that's what life *was* like and I don't know at this point if I could choose to go back to that." Troy told me that during a conversation with the director of the facility caring for Sam, he'd said, "'You guys did everything right; you were just understaffed.'"

Troy emphatically said that the experience of having a child with a full-blown Attachment Disorder has dramatically changed his life. The sensitive father said, living with a RAD kid, "is almost like we are living with a cartoon, kind of one dimensional. I mean he's so into cartoons, it's almost like that's how the world is with him. When he comes home it's like a cartoon, no real feeling of depth. We don't make any more demands on him than cartoon people would and he seems to be fine. It is like a cartoon because in cartoons the anvil drops on somebody but it doesn't bother them. Well, he can hit back or whack somebody and it doesn't bother them, it doesn't bother him. It is kind of a 'Beavis and Butthead' world. But it's not."

Robert J., of Gravesend, England, is the father of two adopted youngsters. During our interview he openly talked about his concerns for and feelings about his life with two difficult children. The frustrated dad shared, "I mean I look back to my own childhood and I can't remember ever being smacked, scolded, or whatever. But I can remember if my mom said, 'Well go upstairs and get changed, I went upstairs and got changed. I didn't make a big fuss about it and then I was outside playing with all my friends. And all of a sudden it was, 'Oh, Robert, come in for your tea, and I'd go in for my tea. Try doing that with these two and you've got no chance. You literally have to be more Victorian, more strict."

When asked what he would tell other couples contemplating fostering or adoption Robert became very definite. He stated, "I'd just say forget it. Whether it be a nice straightforward one-day-old baby that's had no problems and you foresee no problems, I'd still say forget it. Because what we've got I wouldn't wish on anybody." Robert and his wife agreed that the situation was worse when one realized it was young children who had been affecting them in such profound ways. Robert candidly replied, "If it had been an abusive adult, I would probably be serving time. It's as simple as that. They've gotten me to a point where had they been adult, and I'm not violent, but I would have retaliated in some way. I would have hurt that person. That is as bad as it got. A couple of times I've had to walk away for the fear of what I may do. And I've just walked and I'm literally shaking inside."

Although Robert was referring to a situation with his daughter, his feelings included their son when he made the following statement: "I mean I personally would have then, at that moment in time, sent her back; given her back. I know it's probably the wrong thing to do or wrong thing to think of, but we adopted them to give them a start in life. I mean, you can only take so much whether it be from a child, whether it be from another adult, until you then think to yourself, 'I've had enough! That's it! No more!' And I would have gladly sent her back so that Sue and myself could have got on with our lives. As far as I'm concerned, I married Sue and that's it—we're together for the rest of our lives. Anything or anybody tries to come between that, then up go my defenses."

Sam M. is a mature father from Santa Margarita, California, who with his wife Samantha adopted two biological siblings, Jackie and Cassie. According to Sam, Cassie seems to have settled into their family, but Jackie has not been able to accomplish the same feat. Before the sisters joined the couple, at 4, Jackie served as Cassie's mother, a relationship which was disturbed when the girls joined Sam and Samantha's family. Sam said he works out of the home, so is not around Jackie and her behaviors on a daily basis, but when he comes home from work Samantha has taken all she can for the day so "unloads" on him. Sam said he tries to be empathetic and supportive, but there comes a point where he doesn't want to hear about Jackie's misbehaviors anymore. Samantha interjected that when Sam has had his fill, he "calls me a raving bitch." The husband emphatically stated he has not wanted to be called at work about the situation because there was nothing he could do about the child's problems or his wife's frustration. Sam's own relationship with Samantha had been so focused on the chaos in their home that their conversations have been limited to problems with their children. "It's really putting some stressors in our life," the concerned father stated.

Cassie, the younger girl, has had many calamities befall her, mostly instigated by her older sister. Following an incident Cassie would get appropriate care and sympathy from the parents, acts which seemed to stir up Jackie's jealousies and concerns about getting less love and affection than her sister. He said their worry over Jackie's negative behaviors toward her little sister have squelched any ideas of going out to socialize with others; consequently, they had stopped seeing their friends altogether. And on a sad note, Sam said they have ended up feeling like their daughter's jailer, an experience that is unacceptable to both partners. Because of their inability to maintain safety for both sisters, the couple decided to "set aside," to undo Jackie's adoption. Sam believes he will be able to move on with his life-after-Jackie without difficulty. He commented with emotion that crept up unchecked from deep inside, "It's really unfortunate, but I'm not going to look back and think about it at all. What's done is done. We tried; we gave it 300 percent. We're moving on; we've got other people to worry about. She was a great kid—she was physically active, she could do things, she was coordinated. She's the kind of little girl that you could have played baseball, done all kinds of stuff, with. She should have been a great kid; we love her for what she *could* (italics are mine) have been. It's really unfortunate. I'm optimistic that once it's done we'll take this big deep breath and we'll move on. That's the kind of people we are. Our family will survive." Sam passionately continued, "I guess I'm most angry at her birth mother more than anything in the world. Just how could anybody do that? We could go through all the history about how she was treated when she was a baby, but won't. How could anybody do that to his or her own flesh and blood? And that's what I'm most angry about!"

Bob W., husband of Tara from Alberta, Canada, talked about his life with their a three-year-old daughter Cassi, Bob sounded overwhelmed when he talked about the extraordinary attention his daughter needed, and demanded. He said that whenever he does anything, chores around the house or talking on the phone, she continuously interrupts each activity. The little girl does that by leaving the immediate area and getting into an activity for which she's been scolded in the past. "She really does require a lot of attention," the amazed father stated, "an extreme amount of attention. You can't do anything without having her there" under foot. Bob said he expected children to need attention, but found Cassi required one hundred percent at all times, a fact that he found endlessly stressful.

Over the past year or so Bob and Tara attended a support group for families of attachment-disordered children to help them maintain, according to them, "some balance and a little sanity." Bob said he listened attentively to the stories shared by the other parents and silently prayed those scenarios would not be repeated in his family. But, all along, he shared, there has been a small voice telling him that maybe Cassi is like children other parents describe. Bob stated wistfully, "Maybe the hopes that you had and the dreams that you have, you're going to have to let go of and just accept that maybe things won't be quite what you had in mind for the child and for yourself. And it's scary." Bob added that at the same time one must look at what is happening now. He thinks that the progress achieved and the interest taken by Canadians in the area of attachment problems is far behind that of the United States. According to Bob, Canada has recently become aware of attachment disorders so believes he and his support group are somewhat pioneers in the field. The Canadian dad mused that if this were ten years down the road many techniques would already be available to help them deal with their child. He feels there will need to be more pioneering and forging of trails before arriving at a solution. "I do have some reservations about what the future holds, and we may have bit off more than we can chew."

Duane C. of Waverly, Ohio shared his experiences with his now full-grown daughter. One thing he'd noticed about Catherine as a youngster was that she would stand on the sideline and watch other kids activities. Most times, however, she did not actively participate in activities with her peers, perhaps due to her behavioral and emotional problems. The

Midwestern father said his daughter was an accomplished liar as well. He said Catherine had an advanced ability to compulsively lie about anything and then successfully convince others that she was telling the truth. Duane remembered her inordinate ability to control others and to change the plans and activities of the family. Her obstinance would purposefully delay the family or interrupt their activities. Consequently, during her teen years she stopped attending family events because by then the family members had learned to not wait for her or to give her the power to sabotage their fun. He said the hardest thing about parenting a child with RAD was the unpredictability of the child's reactions and not ever knowing what was going to happen next. In high school she wouldn't get a job as was expected of her, nor would she apply herself in her studies. Duane said there was a possibility she was a brilliant child, but "we didn't expect her to get all A's, but we did expect her to work at school and try to do the best that she was capable of." It wasn't the grades that were so important to him and his spouse, but the effort. According to her father, Catherine is now the mother of a five-year-old who is nearly ready to begin school. Recently Catherine told Duane and his wife that she was proud of the fact she hadn't taught her daughter anything about numbers or letters in preparation for school.

When I asked Duane what he would like to see be different about adoption practices, his answer was thoughtful. Duane wished he and his wife would have had more information about their daughter's history, including details about what had happened to her before the placement. He thought more information about attachment disorders would have been helpful and would have given them some inkling about the path ahead of them. Perhaps, he mused, that would have prepared them for the unpredictability of RAD kids. Then they might have known how to respond to their child and her bizarre behaviors.

Discord continued to remain part of his relationship with his spouse due to, he stated, the unpredictable family dynamics. He believes his wife still has the ability to escalate their daughter's explosive, irrational behaviors and because of it can make situations more difficult than they had to be. But he realizes that, even though he wanted her to, Catherine wouldn't cooperate with her mother either. Now that their daughter is grown, he does not expect to see her again. Sadly, he said his wife continued to resent him for not supporting her the last time they saw their daughter. He is able to recognize that his wife has a mind of her own and tends not to take his suggestions. Their typical quandary, according to Duane, occurs when Rena uses her own approach to their daughter, which inevitably ends in conflict. Duane concluded, "Then I'm in the doghouse because I didn't support her and don't defend her." His answer to the problem was to terminate the relationship with Catherine to avoid being accused of being unsupportive of his wife. He has become painfully aware that their daughter has always created strife between them. He guessed that his wife finally realized that he was not a perfect person and wasn't always going to defend her, especially in situations where he believed she created the problem. He recently concluded, "I think if I do anything, it's going to be to avoid contact with Catherine so that there is no more conflict with Rena and I don't have to be on the defensive." He was sad that, because of the situation, he's been forced to choose between his spouse and his daughter.

Chuck D., husband to Jane, is a busy father to seven adolescents. The first three were born to them and the next four are biological siblings who were adopted from Costa Rica. At one time all seven adolescents were living on a farm in rural Nebraska. They'd had their adopted children for about eighteen months before the incidents described by Chuck occurred. "It was one of those days where regardless of what you said, each child was at each other's throat, and it started out in the very early morning, I mean even before breakfast. They were just at each other constantly and like Jane said, she'd had it by noon just breaking up little skirmishes here and there. And so I had given them a couple of jobs outside, hoped to get them out, get some fresh air. It was a nice day in late summer. The social worker told us that when you have them about two years all hell's going to break loose. That was her quote, 'All hell will break loose.' We kept thinking what does she mean by this? She never really divulged any information. And up to this point we'd gotten through these minor skirmishes but we didn't know what we were in for. And this was the first day of the rest of our lives, so to speak." Chuck's wife added that they had adopted all four children, but in some ways it felt there had been pressure put on them by the adoption agency to do so. They were difficult enough during their "honeymoon" period as foster children, but the couple believed that once they were adopted, they lost control as parents and that the fighting and bickering increased dramatically.

"And the problems definitely multiplied in every child, the adopted children I'm speaking of, very specifically." the father continued. "But that day I'd sent them out to work and do their jobs in separate areas. Somehow they found each other and I had broken up a fistfight twice. And the third time I finally just took the oldest child and we went completely to the opposite end of the farm and found a new job to do. He was blatantly defiant of what I was having him do. This was always their complaint, that they were our 'slaves,' that we had adopted them to be our slaves. The amount of chores we had around our farm was minimal. Most kids would have loved to have been on our place 'cause there was not that much work. I mean everything was on automatic water, they didn't have to carry anything. We were digging out a water trough so that the overflow would drain out of the corral instead of in the corral. A five minute job, shovel, a little dirt, that's all that was happening. At that point he lost his control and I lost my control. I disciplined him at that point—we're talking about spanking. I mean we're talking about a fourteen-year-old child that needed to be spanked and he got it. And it was less than a week later that Social Services and law enforcement gave us a call on child abuse charges. Something we ought to mention about this particular child is that he came to the United States with

Hepatitis B and with contagious chicken pox. But this child bruised extremely easy, all you'd have to do was touch him and his body was sensitive in the nature that he showed a bruise. So a spanking was going to show some bruises. That's all that was necessary for Social Services. It didn't make a difference who did it; I was to blame because I spanked this child. And, of course, those things entail lawyers and courts and time in jail. The sad father continued, "I have never done anything like this before. I had barely had a traffic ticket, and was held with good esteem within my church and socially in the community. I was a professional person and I had a thriving veterinary practice."

The situation was as devastating to Chuck as it was to his wife. While Chuck was jailed for a few days, Jane remained at home with all the children. That led to more problems because Jane was "as fed up with" the aggressive behaviors as Chuck had been. Suddenly, within just a few days Jane was trying to handle seven teenagers alone, unassisted. Chuck was released from jail on his own recognizance but at the suggestion of his attorney remained out of the home following the incidents to give everyone a cooling down period. Chuck and Jane agreed it would be an appropriate and positive step in attempting to rectify an extremely emotional situation. One of their hopes was that others in their community would become more aware of what was happening within their family. Chuck thought a few people had some idea of what he and Jane had to deal with on a daily basis, "But we had limited resources. We had met with very few professionals that understood the situation that we were going through. Or even the magnitude of having four kids this way."

Jane shared that during Chuck's jail time and the court hearing two of the children reacted "really funny" to the situation. The youngest son was just beside himself; he was crying and screaming and telling the police they couldn't take his dad away regardless of what they thought he had done. The boy also told the officials that his father had not bruised his brother, as they believed. According to the parents the things their adolescent son said did not make sense until after the trial. Then the youngest and the second oldest son went to the mother with the truth. The night before they had beaten Darin, the youngster Chuck had been accused of physically abusing. According to the brothers all the boys were downstairs in their room located at the opposite end of the house, so far from the parents that they couldn't hear the fracas. Apparently the oldest boy beat up the youngest and two other brothers helped in an attempt to settle the general conflicts among themselves. Instead of ending the altercation they continued to beat on Darin in an effort to get him to leave their youngest brother alone. The adolescents left their brother covered in bruises on his back, down his arms, around his neck, and then remained silent about the incident. Chuck had willingly admitted to two swats on the boy's buttocks. The authorities had been unable to determine the source of all the body bruises, thus charged Chuck with physical abuse. The two middle boys went to the police to report they had beat Darin up that night. They were fully aware they had caused the bruises but didn't tell anyone because they were afraid they too would go to jail. Chuck and Jane's sons were so ashamed they had let their father take the blame for something they had done. They've never yet had the courage to tell Chuck directly what happened.

Chuck shared that during the court proceedings their oldest adopted child was removed permanently from their home. The adolescent was placed in foster care and the parents decided quickly that that was the best situation for all involved. That was when they learned how abusive Darin had been to his biological siblings and how threatening he had been toward all the other children in the family. His absence reduced the group of their "ringleader" and diminished much of the aggression within the family. The Midwestern father reported that essentially they had cut all ties with their oldest adopted son. Social Services reported to them that the boy was acting like a model child while in their care. The fact that Darin was in the same small town and continued in the same public school system made the situation uncomfortable for the other children. But, according to the parents, in spite of his constant presence the other three kids began to blossom during a short-lived period of calm. Later, however, the children collectively reported Jane for throwing scalding water on them, in spite of the fact no burn marks were found on any of the youngsters. Their adopted daughter recently started attacking Jane or hurting herself and blaming it on her mother. She injured her own arm with scissors, then went to school and told her friends, the counselor, and the school nurse that her mother stabbed her with a steak knife. According to Chuck the children all knew how to get an immediate response from Social Services and the police. The second son, sixteen and the one with the sweetest reputation had been dealing drugs out of their home for the previous year. The couple caught him with drugs in their home and made several, unsuccessful attempts to help their son. According to Chuck, "That's what he wants to be—he's a drug dealer. He has found himself a wannabe gang member, has tattooed his body and his brother's body. He has already gotten two girls pregnant."

"These kids have no conscience," the veterinarian stated when discussing their attachment-disordered children. "They have no inner feelings. They've only bonded to themselves; they do have those allegiances. Loyalty is a good word, but that's as far as it goes. I mean they're out to get whatever they can get for themselves; it makes it real difficult. I contend we still love these children and hope for the best. But we don't like these children very well." The father sadly concluded, "What I want everybody to know, not just people that are thinking about adopting children, but counselors too, is that until you have one of these kids, you don't understand the magnitude of their capabilities. This is a real situation—these children are in desperate need of help. It's a situation that is a "no-win" for the adoptive parents. Their disease is mental and developmental and there is no recourse; there is no healing. There is a simple compensation in life and until they learn to compensate, they're going to go through some terrible struggles. Most of these things are very evil; I think many times they're satanistic in response. The things that we've seen in our home are satanistic-like actions. And as hard as we try to bring Christianity and good wholesomeness to them, they refuse it. What happens for the parents here is that you set out to do the very best you can, to love these children, to bring them up, to make them responsible, effective members of society. By the time you get into the middle they start acting out, these teenagers, and you find that you're the one that has lost your friends. Your close friends don't want to be around you any longer; we've even lost our friends at church. We've lost our pastoral staff; we have no support there. We find ourselves that we are evil, we are mean, and we are abusing people. That is not us at all; we're completely demoralized. Whatever integrity you had, whatever social status you had—you're just lost in society."

Konrad C. of Central England discussed his experience with his nineteen-year-old son who had been with him and his wife since the boy was very young. He admitted that when a casual onlooker observed his family, it would appear as if the family was "perfectly normal and problem free." Konrad shared that ninety percent of the time the son was not acting out in an aggressive manner "But," the father shared, "it's this constant feeling of treading on eggshells and there's been an occasional incident of some money problems. It took me three hours of interrogation by me to find out who took it, but I had my suspicions." Eventually his son took responsibility for the incident, but not before concerted effort and anxiety on his parent's part. The father admitted he and his spouse have been using what is popularly know as "reverse psychology" with their son in the realm of his school marks. It appears that the adolescent has decided to get at his parents by achieving the lowest grades possible. In the past such behavior would have caused the concerned parents enormous grief and worry and would have kept them hooked into attempting to fix the boy's problem. Konrad reported that he and his wife had done some emotional work and their youngster's tricks no longer affected them in the same way. The father believes their son's failure in school was his way of attempting to control them, of maintaining power over them. Gladly, the man reported, "But that's died a bit now because we demonstrated that we really don't mind whether he fails or not. And in fact we encouraged him to get the lowest results possible because we want this behavior to show up in the school, you see. So we've actually positively worked at this and on approaching teaching strategies and learning styles now which are alien to the school." He reports that the headmaster is now making an effort to work with their son, using techniques that are new, and somewhat foreign, to the professional. "I'm quite mischievous really! I have a lot of fun with this and I'm getting quite a kick out of it, to be quite honest."

Allen N. of Indianapolis, contrary to some parents, had no difficulty recalling examples of unacceptable behaviors enacted by their disturbed child. Allen sounded somewhat pressured when he sadly shared some of their son's shocking behaviors. He said, "I remember calling home one night when was out of town. When Ann finally came to the phone she was out of breath. I jokingly said 'Have you been running up and down the steps?' 'No' Ann emphatically said, 'I just had to wrestle Anthony to the ground to keep him from hurting Michael.'" By that time Michael, the older brother, started defending himself against Anthony who was becoming increasingly aggressive with age. Adolescent Michael felt challenged by Anthony so, "'they were gonna go to the backyard and have it out. Anthony said, 'I'm gonna take a knife and I'm gonna cut you up.' We were missing two knives—I never did find them.'" Frightened by the antics, Allen summed it up, "It was almost like he was out-of-control or at least to the point that he'd started doing so much stuff he couldn't stop."

The gentle father continued to identify problems demonstrated by their son. Allen stated, "He's had a thing for candy. He'll steal, kill, and rob—anything for candy! We would find piles of candy wrappers behind his bed and his dresser. He would never admit it." According to his parents Anthony would lie and steal, get caught, and then deny that he had done anything. The father continued, "I was standing there watching him. He'd say, 'You're a liar, you didn't see me do that.'" After the youngster learned about the 'Tooth Fairy,' he hatched a plan. "He sat upstairs in his bed and pulled a tooth out—not a loose tooth. I came up there, there was blood all over everything, but the tooth was under the pillow. He wanted the 'Tooth Fairy' to come so he could get some money to buy some candy."

Dan D. is a probation officer from San Luis Obispo, California, who believes he deals daily with children similar to his most disturbed daughter. He and his wife Marcey are the biological parents of two sons, and the adoptive parents to two biological sisters, Terry and Alli, who were 4 and 5 years-old at placement. Dan felt he had extra empathy with their daughters because of his own disrupted, disjointed childhood. Because of problems within his birth family Dan had been moved frequently but finally ended up in the care of his grandparents at the age of seven. The professional man felt he had missed out on usual advantages of children by not being close to his own siblings. Consequently, adoption was less of a charitable act to him and more of a means of "fulfilling the thing that I'd never had; that closeness of having brothers and sisters in the same household." The idea of adopting children brought him joy and concerns of increased responsibilities as well. The couple built an addition on to their home to make adequate room for two more children. Because of his own background Dan and Marcey were certain their new youngsters would have plenty of "baggage" of their own. Finding a harmonious balance between total focus on and ignoring their problems became an important issue during the planning stages.

It seemed sudden to the San Luis Obispo couple that the siblings became available for placement, as they did. They knew the little girls had experienced significant changes in living arrangements but believed they had not been physically or sexually abused. Apparently there was some possibility of neglect reported but Dan and Marcey had no idea about the effects neglect could have on youngsters. After several visits, and within three weeks, the couple was pressured into taking both girls. Although Marcey had done much research on the effects of abandonment on adopted children, neither was wise enough to know what signs were indicators of potential problems in the future. It appeared to the experienced couple that although Alli was the younger of the two, she was more aggressive than the older sibling. Dan stated, "Alli showed more of her ability to manipulate the situation or the person, thing, animal, whatever it was. And when it wasn't going her way it amazed me how intelligent she was in her ability to change her manipulation within a fraction of a second."

It wasn't apparent to the couple at first, but eventually it became clear that it was their biological children who were the ones really suffering. Initially Dan and Marcey spent so much time helping their daughters get settled into the family that they were unable to see that their boys were beginning to suffer from neglect of their own. Dan stated, "I kind of felt that there was so much focus on the two girls that the boys were missing out on what they'd had before. Luckily, at first it wasn't too hard, and the boys took a back seat. But after a while they didn't want to take a back seat anymore." The young girls began aggravating the more benevolent older brothers. The girls made attempts to get the adolescents to physically hurt them, behaviors that had never been part of their family life before. Eventually their sons developed coping skills of their own and significantly reduced their time at home or in activities with their parents and sisters. "And so Alli was playing family members against each other." Dan and Marcey found that to be extremely difficult and confusing for them, as they didn't feel prepared to handle the situation.

Dan continued to share about behaviors he and his wife noticed. According to the involved father his youngest girl could switch personalities, depending on what it was she wanted. She would initially "be the Barbie doll"—cute, sweet, with big, winning smiles. If that didn't work she would become instantly aggressive. Once during a visit from Marcey's mother Alli was sweet and socially amenable as long as grandmother paid undivided attention to her. But as soon as the grandmother talked to her sister Terry, the younger girl hauled off and hit the older woman's knee. The mother-in-law was unsure what had happened and was not expecting such behavior to be displayed toward her. "I watched the whole thing," Dan stated. "Alli went from this little devil face at my mother-in-law until my mother-in-law looked down at her. Then she had this big old smile on her face and she just picked up talking where she left off." According to the couple their child demanded constant attention and would go to any lengths to ensure it.

After three years with the family the California couple decided they could not longer maintain Alli within their family. The father of four felt the situation was more stressful for Marcey. "I mean it did affect me; don't get me wrong." Dan believed his personal childhood experiences prepared him more for the problems that came with the adoption of their daughters. With his background he felt it was easier for him to ignore some of the acting out and to not react to it. "It was more personal and more emotional for Marcey. But I think there's a different bond between mother and daughter than there is between father and daughter." Dan said his own lack of childhood made it easier for him to disassociate from Alli's behaviors and to not take them personally. "When you see a child, even when all these things have gone wrong, or the horrible upbringing that this child has experienced, and all the things that have gone wrong in the family it's very easy, I think, to allow the emotions to say, I'm going to help this child. But in the process of allowing that decision, it may ruin your life."

However, all was not lost for Dan and his family. The father believed that he became stronger as the result of the experiences with Alli. "I think I've become a better person because of it. I think it was more the trials and tribulations that you had to go through to stay strong and keep the nucleus of the family together. You either had to pull together and create more of a bond or a greater bond, or we would have just all fallen apart. We've been through the worst and we're still here."

John B., father of two adopted girls from Bechenham, England, shared his concerns and feelings for his family. John was adopted himself as a youngster and told me that he's sure his personal experiences influenced his feelings toward his own daughters. "I remember seeing the video of the girls and even then I had an attachment to Girly, which has proved to be the case right now. I am very attached to both, but Girly and I have this greater attachment than with Dolly." Their preplacement visits were conducted over one month's time and then, suddenly, both daughters were placed with John and his wife, Hong. The couple thought that before their new daughters came to them the youngsters had spent much time indoors in a tiny bare room with hardly any stimulation. "Dolly," according to John, "seemed very much in her own little fairyland, her world, daydreaming and things like that. Girly seemed to just read all the time; she has always been a reader. Dolly was in daydream land protecting her against what was happening in the house, etc., and Girly just sort of covered it up by reading. That was their way to cope with it." At the interview the attentive father believed their adjustment period was still in progress. He said that when daughter Dolly first sat in Hong's lap, "She just sat there like a piece of wood." On the other hand, Girly was much more verbal and active but became frustrated more easily. The father shared that initially the girls did not know how to wash themselves or how to use a knife and fork properly. Hong and John spent much energy teaching and monitoring the basics, their grooming and manners.

According to John his idea of rearing children is more relaxed than that of his spouse. "Hong is very strict Chinese; I'm an Irish Catholic. I do understand that you have to be firm and strict, but I would temper that with a little flexibility because children are children at times. Just little things that you let pass, but you jump on the important things and correct them, help guide them. But because we are of different cultures, it has at times, caused major differences of opinion in how we bring up children." The father shared that they were told by the agency workers to expect that their daughters' attitudes toward their birth mothers would make themselves known. They were warned that those behaviors would probably be leveled at the new mother. "Of course," John added, "the new mother feels horrible and the whole thing starts gathering momentum. Hong has found it extremely difficult to bond with Girly at all." Initially Girly's behaviors were very violent toward Dolly, something Hong found difficult to tolerate and which, no doubt, interfered with her feelings toward the older daughter. However, John believes he has bonded with their daughter in spite of the fact that they were warned by the psychologist that she would be difficult to parent.

The stress-filled couple discussed their daughters' futures, particularly that of their attachment affected daughter, Girly. John stated, "I would be extremely unhappy if they had to remove one. I would feel that it was morally wrong to split them anyway. I think that's wrong and I just couldn't send them back; the damage would be huge to them. Although, I have to bear in mind if it will stress our marriage, then it's not worth giving that up, surely. But I feel that we have to find the right answer to it how to best care for both daughters. I know it's difficult now but I think we will be okay in the end. Hong can't feel that hope because there's no bond there."

Reggie M. is the husband to Sunny and father of two adopted youngsters from San Luis Obispo. He openly shared his expectations about fatherhood and said he "always wanted children he could teach life to," as he put it. As a youngster, Reggie watched his father and could see his pride and the pleasure brought to him through his family. Reggie stated, "I could see it but I couldn't feel it," but wanted to. He said one of the biggest thrills he has in his life is to see some of the kids he'd coached in sports all grown up. It thrills him to learn about their lives and successes. He said his motive for fatherhood was to "bring somebody through the growing part of a life span—to mold them into something; to watch their happiness. The more I listen to myself talk maybe it's a selfish thing, but I thought that I had some good that I could share. It's always been with me; it was never an issue that we couldn't have children. I just wanted to be a parent."

Reggie and Sunny received Joshua when he was quite small and they felt he bonded to them immediately. Jennifer, on the other hand, came to them when she was three-and-a-half with a long, somewhat messy history with approximately twelve to fifteen moves in two years' time. Although it took him some time, eventually this father gained an understanding that Jennifer was a totally different child when he was not around. His experience taught him their daughter was cute and cuddly, nothing like the personality saved for Mom. While she verbally abused Sunny, she exuded charm for Reggie. The father said he was finally able to tell how things were the minute he returned from work. "I'll walk in the door and you can just see it on Sunny's face. It's like she's already been beat up by the army." And then their daughter greets her Daddy with big smiles and good cheer. "So I know that there was some type of emotional head butting situation that went on. I know these things happen, but I don't understand how they happen because they don't happen when I'm there." Reggie shared that the problems between his wife and daughter hurt him and that he'd like to do something to correct the situation, but can't. The sensitive father suspects that Jennifer is trying to pay her birth mother back through her behaviors toward Sunny. "And the only person that she knows how to pay back," stated the insightful father, "is to the one that she knows will never turn her back on her—no matter what she does." He has observed the push-pull between his wife and his daughter that characterizes their relationship. According to Reggie, Jennifer continuously gives her Mom come here/go away messages. As Dad puts it, "You can hug me, you can love me but it'll be on my terms."

"I don't know if it was the way I was brought up, but I don't get as emotionally attached as Sunny does. She's got the mother instincts and she would go to the ends of the earth. I will too, to a certain extent, but there's time that I've entertained the idea of if she doesn't work out, why should we lose the family we have?" Sunny believes that if or when Reggie got to the end of his tolerance of the problems, he would simply say so. "I would have no problem," the father confided, "making a call to the county and say, 'Come, come get her.' Sunny wouldn't do that; I know she wouldn't do that." But one thing the couple has consistently done had been to back each other up. "In some cases we didn't like what the other one says, but we've still backed it up because we knew we had to." Reggie shared that parenting a child like their Jennifer takes a greater toll on the couple than most people know because unless someone has been in a similar position, they cannot understand. He has suggested that their psychologist take Jennifer into her home for six months and "then she'll really know. She would be a better therapist. But until you've lived it, until you've walked the walk, you really don't know." The California father concluded with these thoughts: "I was just thinking life really shouldn't be this hard to live at our age. I mean, you're looking at two people who it was widely known twenty-three years ago when we got married it was only going to last a year. And I think even at that time we had this personal vendetta to prove the world wrong. I mean we've been through a lot, and I know we can go through a lot more. I just don't want to."

Tom T. is the father of six adopted children from the Kansas City, Missouri area, and married to Terry. Tom talked about his concerns while rearing several children with Reactive Attachment Disorder. He said that one of the things that he and Terry remained attentive to was their relationship. "And," Tom stated, "we were luckier than most of the parents of RAD kids in that our relationship has grown through this. Most of the time it goes the other way: relationships fall apart; marriages fall apart. Mom gets isolated and identified as the demon that's caused all this problem because she's crazy and she doesn't understand. And we were lucky in that we, instead of turning away from each other, we turned to each other." The busy father believes that if parents don't have someone to really talk to and share what is happening in their home, the individuals will have difficulty holding on to reality because this disorder is so crazy making. He was definite that relationships within a family get so confused that marriages can crumble without the necessary emotional support for the parents. Their primary goal, according to Tom, has been to establish and maintain communication between him and his spouse. Then with their children what he tries to do with each individual, "is to help him understand about himself, help him understand how he interacts and reacts with people in situations so that he can form some strategies that will allow him to function in life." Tom added, "That was a step for us that we didn't get to overnight. We got there as we kind of watched our kids get big, and we watched their problems get big with them. That's one of those things that we came to realize acceptance of who these people are, and to try, then, to start to think about looking at the world through their eyes instead of through our eyes and recognizing that they see the world differently than we do. Sometimes that has given us a little sanity."

Errol P. of Lee's Summit, Missouri, has a biological son and adopted twin girls who had been with he and his wife Anna for six years. He said that originally they were looking to adopt a single child, but weren't closed to ideas about other combinations. Errol said he and Anna "were best buddies; we had oodles and gobs of love to give." As a Respiratory

Therapist he was employed at a children's hospital, a position he dearly loved because of, among other things, increased contact with children. In retrospect he believed "we were looking for that magical, mystical, mythical completion of the family unit that all parents hope their children will be." Errol didn't think they were totally unrealistic but stated, "I don't think we expected the perfect little bundles of joy, but I don't think we quite expected what we got either."

Upon arrival their daughters were beautiful, active, charming six-year-olds. Errol thought that there may have been warning signs during their pre-placement visits, but they were lost in all the excitement. When looking back on the process, the communicative father stated, "I might have been a little more objective and been able to stand back and take an objective look, but because we'd been held in limbo for so long, we'd both lost our objectivity." They had not yet heard about the honeymoon phase but in retrospect Errol stated that both girls were definitely in it! "I mean, essentially they were just as wonderful as they could be." When they took the girls home and their charm began to fail, Errol felt somewhat duped by the adoption workers. Following a conversation with the adoption worker he stated, "I remember using every cuss word I could 'cause then I'm going, you know, 'What is she saying 'the honeymoon period?' I didn't know it existed; neither of us did."

Errol and Anna had been married for six years before the addition of their daughters. Suddenly, changes in their relationship were foisted upon them as the result of the new dynamics within their household. The attentive husband began to take note of the changes. He stated, "Well, first of all, I know Anna is no idiot that just flies off the handle for no good reason. So I knew beyond a shadow of a doubt when I came home and Anna was distraught and upset and hysterical about something, that something had occurred. Of course, when it happens day after day after day after day even the most believing person would say, 'maybe we need to see a therapist.'" Nonetheless, Errol tried to be supportive of Anna through changes he could not yet understand. During our interview he shared with much feeling, "I know in retrospect that a lot of times I offered advice when probably the best thing I could have done was just to shut up and listen to what Anna had to say."

Simultaneously Errol came to see that his daughters were manipulating him probably from the outset. They were, "running the old man a pretty good shot," as he put it. Today he believes their best efforts were designed to "divide and conquer." Both Judith and Ashley were accomplished at working him from early on, but the father believed that Judith "was six going on thirty-five" and wanted to be "in control of everything" since she'd joined them. According to Errol, "She would interrupt and interject her adult-sized opinion. She lied about everything; if she told you the sun was up, you'd better go check." Their girls' behaviors exacted a price. This is how Errol described it: "It was just all kind of a slow barrage, you'd just about get yourself situated and expect it from this flank and all of a sudden they'd hit you from another direction. I can't honestly say that there was a whole bunch of those horrible behaviors that were terrible, terrible, terrible. It was just that they were ongoing, constant little, the little jabs, the little button pushers. I think what I noticed most was that most of them liked to push Anna's buttons because they knew it really got me aggravated." Eventually Errol and Anna learned what was happening to their daughters and then met other couples who have had similar experiences. "Probably," stated Errol, "the thing that's made more difference to both of us is for us to know that we are not alone. And even though people can stand back and say, 'Oh, well, this is just childhood behavior.'" They now know that is not so. After much trial and error they finally learned it was called Reactive Attachment Disorder. He continued, "And yet for years and years and years we thought maybe we're just lousy parents. Maybe we're just too touchy; maybe we're just too sensitive. And yet we realize now this is not the case. And so I think one of the things that has really changed is that because we've gotten help, because we've gotten support, we're a little more prepared for things. When we see certain behavior, we can take a different approach. We're better prepared; we're more knowledgeable. They used to drive us crazy sitting for three hours over a five minute spelling assignment." Now, however, they can say, "It's not our responsibility; Child, it's yours."

Alan C. is the husband to Susan and the father of one particularly riotous adolescent girl from Kent in the United Kingdom. The father became breathless, and Susan tearful with powerful emotions, when he relayed experiences of the daughter they loved often beyond reason. Alan relayed that their daughter was adopted at eight weeks old but before long they had only an inkling of what was yet to come. By her teens Joanne was not taking any responsibility for her actions and, according to the father, was ever quick to blame others for her actions. The bewildered parent also believed that perhaps his child was incapable of thinking things through before she acted impulsively.

At about fourteen, with what may have been a spurt in hormonal activity, their daughter became even more unpredictable. Because they were unable to physically get her into a psychiatrist's office, "they actually did an assessment on her by proxy." According to the amazed father, any paperwork that had accumulated on Joanne was sent to a local specialist. Alan shared that she was pronounced normal through such means, by way of hearsay and telephone interviews. Then, later in adolescence, Joanne completely demolished her boyfriend's car by smashing it with a car jack during a fit of rage. She was ever so surprised when the local police showed up and took an interest in the situation. Alan stated, Joanne "does something and doesn't even think of the consequences. In fact, she's not even worried about the consequences; the consequences are irrelevant, you know." Around the same time the British schoolgirl threw fireworks into the front door of the Police Station without giving the outcome any forethought. Although the parents are often terrified of the possibility of their daughter's eventual incarceration, so far she's managed to skate out of serious situations.

Alan thinks her behaviors demonstrate the lack of cause-and-effect thinking common to victims of attachment difficulties. And in spite of their persistent efforts to get help with their out-of-control daughter, Alan stated, "We never got any help whatsoever."

Olaf R. is the married father of two from Manchester, England. He shared the experience he and his wife Daphne had with their adopted daughter. The thoughtful father said that the most difficult thing they'd been forced to cope with during their life with an adopted child was inability to understand what was going on. The couple felt they had been successfully conned by an adorable, eighteen-month, blue-eyed angel, baby girl. If anybody had wished for the perfect child, he claimed, it would have been their little Isabel. But, within six months the toddler "was controlling our lives, and we were losing it!" According to the attentive father with enormous energy, their child was able to "carry on and on and on" for seven or more years, and they ended up being "bested," as he put it, by their youngster. "There wasn't anything we could do," he continued. "We tried the physical way of doing it; we tried reason. We tried everything that you could possibly think of as you sort of like to think yourself as an educated adult." Whatever methods the worried couple used to help their child, however, were unsuccessful. He concluded, "the circle, the style that we were in was so viciously tight, it was unbelievable. And we didn't understand what was going on and that was the hardest thing. We were defeated by a two year old."

The fathers' stories broaden the readers' view of the astounding impact of one attachment disturbed child on the mettle of a family. These men represent those individuals who have come through their own hell and are on their way to a healing solution. You may have also noted that once the father wised up, so to speak, something significant began to happen within the family. Unfortunately, changes did not usually occur when the mother became exhausted or fearful of their child.

It was only when the father came out of denial that reconfiguration of the family constellation took place. And as you read in each story, often the attachment disturbed youngster was the one who needed to be moved to new surroundings in an effort to save the health, and perhaps the lives, of the remaining members. However, not all fathers had the internal strength to do what was ultimately in the best interest of their spouses and children. There were those represented in the interviews that remained resentful toward their wives for their lack of understanding, as they viewed the situation. You may have also noted, that the difference between these disturbed youngsters and the ones Dr. Welch described was the conspicuous absence of appropriate treatment for youngsters in such terrible need.

PART III—SOME SOLUTIONS

Unusual and bizarre behaviors displayed by attachment affected children develop out of an overwhelming sense of hurt, and fears of abandonment or loss. Even as little ones they are accomplished survivalists, willing to do *anything* to keep from being hurt again. Unconscious decisions can include not to love, not to allow themselves to be cared for, and a refusal to care for others. Because of their exceptional inner strength and the depth of such fears some youngsters will go to any length to prove themselves unlovable. Consequently, many become a threat to those around them, a sure way to scare off the very folks they need the most.

Consequently, the more we know about our children's histories—chemical, social, medical, and familial—the more capable we are of understanding their emotional make-up and their needs. It is possible that with more insight into their beginnings, the symptoms displayed by youngsters will begin to make sense to parents and the professionals who are attempting to provide help. Consequently, it is imperative that all available information be shared with the parents. Without a full picture, an extremely difficult job becomes a confounding and impossible one. Ultimately, the more we know about what makes damaged youngsters tick the better we can provide viable preventative and treatment measures.

CHAPTER EIGHT—
The Professionals and Their Therapies

For over twenty-five years the Attachment Center at Evergreen has been developing therapeutic methods which attempt to repair or undo the faulty neurological pathways in the brains of damaged children. Those same connections failed to develop properly due to inadequate environmental input or stimulation during the first thirty-three months of the youngsters' lives. The Colorado attachment specialists have believed for about the past decade, "that the therapeutic process utilized here actually helps to develop alternative neural pathways and changes the client's internal process" for all of the necessary brain functions. According to former ACE Director, Pickle, the tedious, difficult changes that develop slowly through specialized, intensive therapy combined into what is know as "attachment therapy." The changes come about "through clear expectations and loving structure in the therapeutic home and through cognitive restructuring, corrective emotional experiences, grief work, inner child work, and other appropriate treatment modalities. Through this particular work a child is able to develop a more positive working model, learns how to be respectful, responsible, and fun to be around. A child learns better ways to handle and express emotions. A child learns how to make good decisions. A child learns how to trust those who care for him/her, accepts their guidance, and allows them to meet his/her needs."

Over the past two decades some of the therapeutic approaches to this difficult problem have been considered somewhat controversial in nature. The severity and dangerousness of some of the behaviors of children with a RAD diagnosis combined with their failure to respond to usual therapeutic approaches has prompted professionals to consider extreme measures. Most parents living with attachment-disordered individuals eventually reach a state of sheer desperation, and out of their desire to save what appears to be an unsalvageable kid, they willingly agree to unconventional therapies. They already know that traditional approaches have shown themselves to be unsuccessful in changing their child's inappropriate or socially unacceptable behaviors.

The idea that a youngster is untreatable by age five or seven is as terrifying to a family as it is incorrect. It is generally believed by professionals offering attachment treatment that in order for the therapy to be effective, the child must have at least the smallest inkling of a desire to change. Without a drop of desire on the children's part there would be no point in trying to force change. As you may have guessed, RAD kids are some of the most determined individuals who ever pass through a family or show up in therapy. Many stubbornly continue to hold onto ideas long after their usefulness or the realities of their belief systems have been challenged. It seems their logic is on a collision course with the caretakers placed in their lives.

There are centers springing up across the United States, in Canada, and in the United Kingdom where children can receive a thorough assessment and appropriate treatment. Unfortunately, there are not yet enough professionals available to care for the actual number of children with attachment issues, but happily, the number has grown significantly during the writing of this book. A list of available therapeutic centers and professionals is found in the back of this volume in Appendix 1. The list is composed of individuals and treatment programs that have come into my awareness over the past four years, but the list is not complete. It is my prayer that no resource list ever be totally comprehensive, as more and more professionals are learning effective therapies and treatments, which then become available to families in need.

Initially it must be determined if all, some or just one of the children in the family demonstrates the symptoms. If all the children in the family manifest the same dysfunctional behaviors, it could be an indication of a family systems problem. When relatively successful children exist alongside a dysfunctional one, the problem may belong to one individual. It is not actually that simple, however. RAD kids are strong little characters and cause chaos in the lives of all the family members making it difficult to sort out just who is doing what. In addition, healthier children are often controlled or bullied into negative, sick behaviors by the stronger, more pathological sibling. Diagnosing a child with an attachment disorder is no easy feat and requires special training on the part of prepared professionals.

Even as a mental health professional Paula Pickle did not know what to do with or about the extraordinarily aggressive behaviors of her two foster children. Typical of most parents of emotionally and behaviorally disturbed youngsters, the couple went from professional to professional looking for answers. According to the astute mom, most of the professionals they consulted were her colleagues who also had no idea how to help. They even took the children to a nationally known psychiatrist who said he wished he could help them, but didn't.

Pickle and her husband were not told the full extent of their children's sad, complicated histories until about one year after her arrival when their daughter was five had already been admitted to a psychiatric hospital for care. The concerned couple was soon told that their daughter would never be able to live in a family so, essentially, they may as well give up on their efforts to help her. She stated, "I think five is a little young to write off a child, so we became obsessed with finding answers." About fifteen years into the field, Paula almost accidentally ran across some information about Attachment Disorder. She came to realize that at the time, the suggestion to abandon their efforts was standard fare for adoptive and fostering parents. Ingrained in institutional belief systems was the idea that burned out and over stressed parents *caused* the problem. Professionals just didn't believe that parents could overcome their physical or emotional exhaustion and pull the child through their problems. All of the blame, Paula Pickle shared, "was very demoralizing as a parent, because not only are you desperately trying to reach your children, but you have to fight the system, too." The amazing mother shared that not only did she feel blamed by professionals, but "you do a number on yourself, as well."

Aside from all the misconceptions and politics, the professionals were wrong about Pickle's daughter! No doubt due to the parents' level of commitment to their daughter, they found their way into challenging therapy at the Attachment Center at Evergreen. After several months the girl discovered that it was her own behaviors that diminished her life, and then she made some earth-shaking decisions about the quality of life she was willing to work for. The proud mama stated that by the time her daughter was fifteen, she was a "straight 'A' student in a regular classroom and has had friends for the past three or four years. She's a loving child; she has even helped a Special Education teacher with less fortunate children—so she's got empathy for other people. And considering her beginnings, I think she's a miracle!"

The sensitive woman talked about protecting her offspring and emphasized that along the way she has had to develop new ways to love and care for her children. As traditional therapy is ineffective with AD kids, so are traditional and usual approaches to loving them. Unfortunately, Pickle's son has not fared as well. In his childhood, love had been sexualized because of sexual abuse, so he has continuously struggled with love-and-sex issues, but during adolescence he received treatment for his problems. Ms. Pickle shared that one of the hardest things she'd ever had to do to help her youngster was to report him to the authorities for sexual abuse. The concerned mother shared that he remains at risk to re-offend, as he seems not to have that driving, internal desire necessary to prevent future aggressive behaviors. Paula and her husband learned that after they provided their son with therapeutic opportunities they then had to pray he'd use them. In addition, the couple has discovered that they must "love him from a distance," because their primary duty is to protect their daughter from harm. Although love-at-a-distance is more difficult on children and their parents, it is, ultimately, healthier for each family member.

Davis, from Atascadero, California, is what I describe as "a convert." In her early days as a psychologist to children and families, she utilized the usual therapeutic approaches learned as a mature graduate from the University of Southern California, and experienced many successes. However, eventually she stumbled on to a 'new breed of cat,' so to speak, children who responded differently to her ministrations than those before them. Her first negative gut reaction was toward their mothers who were extremely angry with their children, a level of rage in parents she'd rarely seen before. In her experiences, mothers of children with mental illness were worried or concerned or frightened, never furious as she was beginning to witness. Davis said she "remembers thinking, 'No wonder the child doesn't want to attach to this mother; I wouldn't either.'" The little ones would run to her with open-armed hugs and demonstrate endearing charm she'd never before seen. The youngsters' actions buffaloed Davis completely and that made their mothers even angrier. The Ph.D. developed a theory about the ineptitude of the parents in those situations and she talked to them, "I'd hear their level of frustration, but I couldn't connect with it because that wasn't the same child that I saw." In hindsight the professional admitted that now that she has been educated by several attachment disturbed children, it is "patently obvious what was going on, but I didn't see it then."

Eventually Davis began seeing more parents who presented striking similarities. When many sets of parents came into her office presenting "the same kind of anger, the same kind of frustration, the same pain, the same sense of hopelessness and failure," she was finally forced to examine her own personal attitudes. Once past her "professional ego," as she put it, she concluded that something was going on that she'd never seen before. Davis stated, "And I was just humbled because the kids do well in therapy. They'd come in, they'd talk about feelings, and they could identify feelings for me. They were wonderful! It felt like a really good connection, but nothing changed in their homes. They'd go home and life was awful for their families. They weren't fitting in with the families; they weren't developing appropriately in their social relationships. They weren't doing well other than during the hour they were in therapy."

With other emotional disabilities the families seemed to recover, no matter the outcome for the children with the problems. Not so with these families, Davis stated. "These children got into the family like some kind of vermin and they were tearing the fabric of the family apart, impacting on everybody in the family." Davis added: "My analogy is that they're corks; they will bob along. They may not do any better, but they may not do any worse until they get older, but the parents are devastated and the families are devastated." Her training and her beliefs taught her that you form a therapeutic alliance with the client and you try to see the world through the clients' eyes. But such an approach was not helpful in these new situations. The thoughtful professional stated candidly, "I really was brought to my knees. I felt like a total failure. I could see I was being an ineffectual therapist; I didn't know what I was doing." Finally, out of frustration and concern for the youngsters and their families, she was driven to reach out and explore new therapeutic alternatives. Eventually she made her way to the ACE by participating with a client during their "two-week intensive" program. That experience made a believer out of her. She returned from Colorado with a new understanding and the feeling that "I'd found the Holy Grail!" Her new belief included the ideas that there was hope for attachment-disordered kids which required a new way of working with them. Out of necessity the therapist became less gullible and more confrontive. She stopped working with just the child and started seeing them as part of the whole family unit. Davis also began holding them responsible for their part of the problem and they became an integral part in the healing process. Seeing the child alone adds to triangulation, she said—parent and child and therapist working *against* one another, instead of *with* each other. "I wanted the parent to work with the child, and I wanted to work with the child and the parent together to try to facilitate that bond." Hence, she converted to a new way of seeing and a new approach to caring. Davis added, that in spite of her increased sense of hope, "nothing is absolutely sure and not all of these kids can be fixed." She reported that one fact is the hardest for her to accept: the tools available to help such difficult children are still somewhat limited.

Lori Hunstad, MSW, LCSW, is a member of an aggressive adoption team from San Luis Obispo County, California. She stated, "We have taken a fairly progressive stance in learning and educating ourselves and our families" in many controversial topics, including Reactive Attachment Disorder, which affect many of their young clients. Although many believe RAD is the newest 'buzzword' in psychiatric illnesses affecting children, following ADHD and Bipolar Disorder, she still thinks some professionals remain shortsighted and aren't able to see the full picture. Hunstad told me her county organization is involved in every aspect of adoption and because of that she believes it is impossible to overlook any stages or outcomes of the potentially traumatic process. The professionals from the San Luis Obispo County Social Services do not yet specialize in particular areas of the adoption process so are able to grasp the breadth of the problems which both culminate in and are caused by the adoption process.

Because Hunstad's organization recognizes fostering and the adoption of children as so important, they want to prepare the parents for the demanding task. The SLO agency not only trains their staff, but they also offer a fifteen-hour pre-placement training program for prospective foster and adoptive parents. Classes cover the following topics: children, the court system, and reasons for removal; kinds of abuse and effects on kids; normal childhood development and the impact of trauma; how to agree to a placement, and to determine if a placement is appropriate; children's issues of self-esteem, separation, attachment, grief and loss; and planning for permanency.

The California county agency also has many comprehensive programs to support their families following the placement of a child as well. They have learned over the past years that it is fiscally smart to offer their clients programs that facilitate placement successes, rather than closing their eyes and hoping all will go well without needing any special services. According to Hunstad, the California laws are beginning to reflect concerns about the quality of the early lives of children. Approximately a dozen years ago the old laws allowed families in crisis twelve to eighteen months to get themselves together before their child was returned to their care. Now, Hunstad reports, the courts have decided the new laws require parental transformations to occur within only six months or the child would be removed. A significant difference in the laws also requires the social workers to have a "Permanency Plan" devised and ready for implementation should the biological parents fail to meet the goals necessary for reunification with their youngsters. The MSW shared that the shortened waiting periods can effectively diminish the number of moves experienced by children during the interim. The courts, according to the experienced professional, are "recognizing that children three and under are incredibly fragile."

Currently, California law recognizes that if the abuse or neglect was severe enough to warrant the removal of a child, the parents need immediately to "get their act together," as Hunstad put it, if they want to retain their parental rights. However, Hunstad reported, if the adults do not meet the goals set for them or solve their problems their parental rights will be terminated for any subsequent children born to them, as well. Apparently the old adage—If nothing changes, nothing changes—is known by lawmakers and they are serious about improving the quality of the lives of children in their state. The goal of legal planning is to reduce disruptions served on California youngsters through lengthy legal battles or indefinite periods in limbo. There is little room for inadequate, uninterested, or unmotivated parents to manipulate the system. Hunstad sadly added, even if "we don't touch prenatal and the drug exposure problems, at least maybe we can reduce the number of traumas or obstacles that these children have to overcome." She said youngsters coming into the legal system in the next two or three years will hopefully have fewer problems than those involved in their current system.

Because the State of California has put their focus on children, some funding is available to families who adopt children with emotional disturbances. The County adoption unit can provide assistance through the Adoption Assistance Program, federal funding for families who meet strict criteria for help in the care of their children. It is possible for families with identified 'special needs children' to receive funds for psychological or psychiatric, dental and medical cares until they are about eighteen years old. According to Lori Hunstad, the criteria includes children placed at three or older, minority children, sibling groups, and those with mental health or physical problems. She shared that youngsters with prenatal drug exposure could possibly fit into the category that deals with mental and physical health problems. Specially trained social workers work with the families and their service providers to meet the extreme needs of children with attachment problems. Hunstad and her colleagues also identify and provide local therapists with effective techniques for dealing with attachment disturbed youngsters rather than to continue to pour monies into traditional extended therapy, which has continually proved ineffective.

Author T. Levy earned a Ph.D. in clinical psychology in 1972 from the University of Miami. He shared that throughout his formal education he learned nothing about attachment problems and was never encouraged to read the work of Bowlby Mary Ainsworth and their cross-cultural literature on attachment patterns. He stated that he was forced to learn about attachment issues "out of frustration." Early in his professional career he discovered he was able to help some very disturbed children but still had no understanding that they had attachment disorders. "I knew" he said, "they had conduct disorders and Oppositional Defiant Disorder (ODD), all the diagnoses that kids get from psychologists and psychiatrists. But not knowing the core of their damage and of their emotional and social problems really rested in the area of attachment gone wrong." In the beginning he learned about children who were adopted by loving, middle-class, caring parents who had no idea how to handle them. Professionals didn't know how to handle then either, said Levy. Eventually, after being thwarted in his ability to effectively help such disturbed and disturbing youngsters, he began "feeling like a charlatan" because of his lack of expertise. Once open to new ideas, Levy began learning about attachment problems and how to help the children and their families. As a result, Levy has been diagnosing and treating attachment-disordered children for more than a dozen years.

When he discussed the societal problems which either cause or contribute to a lack of attachment, he stated: "You have the entire child welfare system, Social Services and mental health system that doesn't even diagnose Reactive Attachment Disorder a great deal of the time." The professionals in those particular systems don't, according to this seasoned professional, "even accurately see it, much less treat it. They miss the boat." Levy challenges that it is easy to diagnose youngsters with more common psychiatric maladies, such as ADHD and ODD. "Piece of cake!" he said. But informed and conscientious professionals must look beyond surface behaviors and determine the root of the problem. The psychologist believes therapists must look at the core of the problem and examine the first few years of the child's life. Mental health professionals must, according to Levy, look at the quality of their connections or the lack of them. He believes that many of those holding social service and mental health positions don't understand attachment, are not trained to identify or diagnose attachment disorders, and with no ability to diagnose it then "have no idea what to do about it."

When we discussed the ideal treatment approach, Levy said that even after many years of private practice he still thinks therapists should not provide therapy alone. Once a professional receives the special training needed to provide attachment therapy, including the holding process, a team of professionals is needed because of the demanding nature of the children and the difficulty of the job of helping them. The psychologist works in Evergreen, Colorado with two primary therapists for each child, including a male and a female, as role models and for extra energy, as he stated. A psychiatrist, a medical doctor who understands child trauma and attachment, also needs to be involved when there are biological and genetic issues or to provide medication and medical management. Levy said it is important to have someone oversee the therapeutic process from an administrative perspective as well. That person serves as the child's advocate and can monitor both therapeutic approaches and the individual's progress through treatment. Simply put, the administrator would make sure the correct therapeutic approach is used and to make sure the therapy is being done properly.

Another very important aspect is to have good solid, consistent follow-up therapy available for the child and the family. Levy believes that with such a team most children are ultimately treatable, especially if they are diagnosed and treated early in their lives. Ideally, treatment should begin before the teenage years, according to the specialist. Once the teen years set in, Levy shared, their hormones change, there are normal separations in preparation of leaving the nest, and peer groups and gangs gain importance. Consequently, the likelihood of children making the changes necessary for attachment while in the process of normal detachment from the family are diminished dramatically. In addition, he added, "the antisocial and psychopathic personality can become deeply entrenched by teenage years." He said catching the kids early and having good parents, including fostering and adoptive ones, provide the two best chances for positive treatment outcomes. The psychologist, although admittedly not the final word on what each child requires, believes a well-known approach to treatment, called a 'two week intensive,' is sufficient for most children. That is, providing the treatment includes the necessary follow-up care with attachment parenting techniques to be used afterward.

According to Pickle, there are several conditions that must be met before treatment for such disturbed youngsters can work. She stated clearly, "In order for treatment to be successful the child must demonstrate at least one iota of a desire to be different." Without that smidgen of desire or a spark of recognition that one's life could be different treatment will fail because AD children sabotage the efforts of even the most accomplished of therapists. Pickle said the goals of treatment include:

Resolution of early losses
Development of trust and reciprocal relationships
Modulation or variations of emotional affect (or responses)
Development of internal control and self respect
Correct distorted thinking patterns
Learn appropriate responses to external structure and social rules

During our interview Pickle discussed current therapeutic approaches with AD children. As you are learning, traditional therapies are unsuccessful because talk and play therapies are based on reciprocal efforts between client and therapist and must include the child's ability to trust and empathize. That lack of empathy, plus a basic lack of cause-and-effect thinking, prevents their success. "I'm a firm believer," the professional woman added, "that no therapy is better than the wrong kind of therapy for these children."

I asked her how she would advise new therapists about treatment issues and Paula Pickle had plenty to say. She replied that when one knows about normal child development, attachment therapy makes perfect sense. Pickle is convinced that we already know what infants and children need and those needs must be taken into consideration when helping kids who are stuck in the very first stages of their development. There is no way, the seasoned professional stated, that we can focus only on their behaviors when they do not have the basics, that primary connection that allows them to want to live in society or have the desire to share or reciprocate with others. Without an ability to trust, which develops out of a basic connection with another, they have no understanding of limits or how to handle their own emotionality. Therapy with such special needs children does not come naturally, nor is it part of the traditional training process. Therefore, therapists need extra and specially focused training in preparation of attachment work. "And if I'm not willing to face the depth of the emotions," stated Pickle emphatically, "that these children live with day in and day out, I better not do this work." According to the director, a therapist who cannot face the incredible depth of the youngsters' emotions cannot help them resolve their overwhelming issues.

According to Pickle, attachment therapy is a "synthesis of different methods that help to facilitate attachment." That initial connection forms the primary basis for the rest of the work. Attachment therapy includes inner child work, psychodrama, dealing with grief and loss issues, reciprocity training, as well as cognitive restructuring. In general, she told me, treatment of this sort requires a total reeducation process for the child. The successful child is one who is motivated to do the demanding work necessary to change how they think; to modify how they relate; to relearn how to behave; and to learn to regulate their own emotions.

Levy added that Attachment Therapy is not about *talking*, like traditional therapies, it's about *doing*. Therapists create "a human relationship experience that triggers in the child feelings of attachment for the first time. Remember, they're instinctual, pre-wired." The feelings of desire for intimate contact with another are buried deep within the child and have never been triggered or reinforced before. Attachment feelings in RAD children, according to Levy, have never been nurtured, much like untapped potential. The holding, nurturing process stimulates their attachment feelings and behaviors, those with biological, psychological, emotional and social origins. Such techniques are useful with individuals in every stage of their life, including adulthood, but most of the children he treats are from toddler age to adolescence. Levy said that the latency stage, seven through nine years of age, is an excellent time for success. He said they are old enough to have cognitive skills, ability to reason and to understand explanations. During that stage in their development therapists can—and should—explain what has happened to them, why they feel the way they do, and to contract with them. According to Levy, children "have a right to know why they are angry." The psychologist does not believe giving them information about their pasts will frighten them as he believes what really scares children is not knowing and being left in the dark. The therapist insists, however, that information should be given in such a way as to consider the child's age, mental abilities, and their developmental stage.

Levy warns—good and ethical therapists must always remain cognizant and respectful of the child's right to choose to participate in holding sessions; or not. Malicious and hurtful acts in their pasts left them feeling helpless and a victim; perpetrators did it to them. Attachment-disordered children were neglected or abused and they had no say, no choice in the matter. Now they do; now they *must* have a say if they are to get better. A child whose choices are removed would be retraumatized, even at the hands of the well meaning, and that would be unforgivable. During attachment therapy the control, the person in charge, is transferred from the child to the parent. In appropriate therapy specially trained therapists take control of the youngsters in a firm and loving manner, as the kids need that approach in order to feel safe. Changing the dynamics between the child and the adults, according to Levy, is necessary in the process of offering the child an opportunity to create an attachment.

Holding Therapy

Holding therapy is a part of attachment therapy utilized by several attachment centers across the country. Many readers may have heard of holding therapy, but few know what it is or its purpose. Pickle described it as follows: Holding therapy is "an across the lap cradling, nurturing hold that provides a safe posture for a child to express whatever feelings they may have. They're not all rage-filled children. Many of these children's emotions consist of primary fear," but frequently, she shared, youngsters cover their profound fears with rageful behaviors. During a holding session the therapist helps the children safely express their feelings in healthy manner, helping them to avoid acting their feelings out in a hurtful way. Pickle stated, "The holding posture itself allows for all the key components of bonding: the eye contact, the touch, the soothing, and the [rocking] movement." She added, "It's very easy, also, to track a child's emotional feelings in this position."

Because of the early bonding interruptions, most youngsters cannot cognitively remember the traumatic events that profoundly disturbed their lives. Pickle continued to explain that the holding posture itself helps the therapist access memories that are stored in the child's body or in a part of the brain that is inaccessible by talk or cognitive therapy alone. The social worker stated, "I don't know how you work through resolution with a child who hasn't learned to accept good touch or hasn't ever felt cared for or loved by not touching them." According to Pickle, children who have been sexually abused believe "that they are untouchable. And if, as a therapist, I refuse to touch them in a good way, I'm confirming for them that they're untouchable." In reality, the therapist stated, they need to learn that they are touchable and lovable "and there's good touch and there's bad touch and to be able to distinguish between the two." In holding therapy the holder, mom (adoptive/foster) or therapist, provides corrective emotional experiences. In the past infants were upset or frightened and had no one there to offer consolation or nurture them. During a holding, however, when old feelings are accessed and the child becomes upset, there is someone there who provides the good nurturing touch that they need so desperately. Ultimately, through the new experience the child is brought to a better resolution by getting their basic needs met. This process becomes only a part of a total a relearning experience.

Dr. Welch, stated that over the past two decades she has seen ever increasing attachment problems in addition to more hyperactivity, Attention Deficit Disorder (ADD), depression and conduct disorders among youngsters. One of the things most therapies have in common, according to Welch, is getting the kids to accept help. However, she does not believe that is enough. In Welch's experience it is only when true reciprocity, that ability to *give* and to *receive* love and caring, between mother and child is established can normal development be expected. During her extensive experience the eminent physician also discovered that the successful therapeutic attachment-increasing approaches were also amazingly helpful for youngsters with behavioral problems other than attachment difficulties. As the mother-child connection tightened the children became ever more loving and cooperative in their world. Welch stated, "Almost any adverse personality trait that you could think of went away once there was a good connection" between the child and its mother.

According to Welch, youngsters with disturbed attachments seem to be suspended in a state of conflict, much like many animal species in the wild. "If you can intervene and calm them down, they won't have conflict behavior, they'll have approach behavior instead." That state is a state known as 'calm arousal,' where little ones are alert, quiet, and survey their world with confidence. Dr. Welch added, "that kind of state is optimal for learning to handle emotions. The minute children are not in calm arousal they can't learn as well, and they don't handle various affects (expressions of emotions), their own or others." In her practice, Welch witnessed holdings between mother and child as a way for youngsters to reach that optimal state of arousal, which will eventually lead to attachment.

Jesse Hernandez, CSW, from the Casey Family Programs of Hilo, Hawai'i described the first RAD youngster he experienced from among children in his caseload. The girl of about eight would verbally and physically explode onto others during power struggles and "would get kind of like the movie 'The Exorcist;' she'd get profane. I mean her whole demeanor would just change, just like she was possessed." When Hernandez talked about the experience of observing holding sessions with his client while she participated in intensive therapy sessions at ACE in Colorado, his entire demeanor changed and he became more animated. Because he'd worked with the client prior to the intensive attachment work, he was there to encourage and support her through the difficult therapeutic process. He also felt he had a vested interest in her success. Jesse stated that the first time he saw the intensive attachment therapy "it was quite provoking. I wasn't prepared for the amount of emotion and rage that she let out. When it changed to the crying and the sobbing, it really impacted me. And I guess it kind of brought up some of my own stuff from my own childhood. It was both scary for me to see it and I felt really bad for her. I felt like I wanted to intervene and rescue her and at the same time I was totally thrilled by the changes I was seeing." The therapist said he was excited about the breakthroughs his young client made during holding therapy. Initially he believed most kids could benefit from such therapy, but time has tempered his attitude. Today Hernandez believes holding techniques can successfully be part of some children's therapy, but it is not for everyone. He concluded that there are many tools available to attachment affected youngsters and that the therapies utilized must be based on the individual needs of each child.

Rage Therapy

In the past decade or two, and before the development of Attachment Therapy, other techniques were used. One of the more widely known, and oftentimes controversial, approaches was called 'Rage therapy' or 'Rage Reduction Therapy.' Paula Pickle stated that approach was more cathartic in nature than the current choice in therapies and occasionally utilized physical stimulation to elicit responses from the children. Pickle stated that ACE does not employ "Rage Therapy" at all. When the topic is broached with other professionals, they voice important concerns about the techniques. She warned, however, about "throwing the baby out with the bath water," so to speak. Paula stated clearly, "We have to strive for quality; we have to strive for excellence. We have to strive to find better ways to reach these children and all our efforts should go in that direction."

Levy added that the cycle utilized in rage work has been useful—tension and discharge, rage, sobbing, relaxation, and attachment. However, the whole concept, he said, has been focused on the reduction of rage and was somewhat naïve and limited. Levy said the real issues of their grief, pain, fear, losses, and their need to connect with others were not recognized or dealt with through the use of "Rage Therapy." Basically, he said, all attachment-disordered children are profoundly lonely and frightened little ones who cover their vulnerability with angry, aggressive behaviors. Once their inner issues are identified then dealt with, their anger subsides and intimate relationships become possible. "We want to get into that fear and deal with the truth of that fear and help them to feel secure," Levy shared, which is not possible through "Rage Reduction Therapy."

Trauma Bonds

It is necessary to briefly discuss a phenomenon known as a "trauma bond." An example, according to Levy, is when a child is being abused—physically, emotionally, or sexually—they develop a bond with the abuser that is not based on love. The abused will do whatever they are told because they are frightened of being hurt, abused further, or killed. Such bonds have been observed between prisoners and prison guards, in prisoner-of-war camps, and in the relationships of domestic violence victims. Levy stated, "In psychoanalytic terms it used to be called 'identification with the aggressor.'" Such bonding is part of the survival tactics utilized by attachment affected youngsters. Somewhere they think that if they form a bond with the perpetrator they will have some control over the victimizer, or perhaps they won't be hurt as badly if they have a connection of some sort. Trauma bonds have nothing to do with good holding therapy, Levy emphatically stated. "Unfortunately, it does have something to do with bad holding therapy." He added, "Untrained therapists who don't really know how to utilize the holding, nurturing process could very well re-traumatize a child." In his Colorado practice the professional stated that he and his team of specialized therapists do not re-traumatize children. They remain ever alert to the ethics that guide them, the choices given the youngsters, and their practice of contracting with their clients. Approaches used by the Attachment Center at Evergreen seem to be the model for much of the current attachment therapy. Levy stated, "We're not holding these children against their will; we are containing these children as a loving parent contains an infant or toddler in their arms creating safety and protection and allowing love and caring and empathy to be communicated."

Consistent with an all-consuming desire that their attachment disturbed children fare well, the interviewed parents had become nearly militant in their search for effective therapy. As can be imagined, the parents of the youngsters who participated in the international research had serious concerns about appropriate approaches and ethical therapy for their young ones. Some had pleasant experiences, but, unfortunately, many did not. The anecdotes below give the reader an idea of how satisfying or frustrating the process of obtaining care for their beloved offspring had become:

Sarah D. of Shawnee, Kansas talked about the therapeutic experience arranged for her son David: "Rex and I were very much believers that if you pray for this, there will be an answer. So we just started praying. Well, I mean a miracle happened because we got this flyer in the mail. We'd never gotten a flyer before from the Foster Parent Association. We'd always gotten stuff from the state, but this was a private organization. But somehow we got this flyer and it said Dr. Nancy Spoolstra would be talking about Reactive Attachment Disorder. Now it didn't really give the criteria but the descriptions that it gave—'Oh, my God, that's our boy!' We go to the meeting. Nancy throws up this slide with the seventeen key points of diagnosis and we're just going, 'Oh my God! Look, David has fifteen of those!' At the time it was just a relief to know—there he is! That's the problem! Then it was very frustrating because it was unnerving to me.

"We went back to our counselor a week later and said we went to this foster parent's support group where they had talked about Reactive Attachment Disorder. We gave her the little packet that had the seventeen symptoms and she just pooh-poohed it." At about that same time, Sarah and took David to a therapy session without her husband because his work schedule had changed. As they were walking into the door, something happened and David balked. Sarah noticed her son's reaction but was determined to stay for the session. She observed David stomp into the office, throw himself on the couch, fold his arms across his chest, and stuck out his bottom lip out. The youngster stated immediately, "I'm not talking; you can't make me!" The therapist and Mom talked but David didn't like being ignored, so the little boy went and sat next to Sarah on the couch. Sarah explained, "And before she even had time to respond [he threw] the cushion that was on the couch across the room. All of a sudden it just became crystal clear to me this is not where my child belongs because her office is just immaculately decorated. She's got beautiful paintings, breakable things, and very valuable things.

And I'm thinking, "Oh my God! The bull in the china closet has been let loose.' So while he's grabbing for the second [couch] cushion I've got his arm and he's screaming at me, 'Don't you hurt me!' She's over there just very genteelly with her little legs crossed and the little skirt and perfectly coifed hair saying, 'Now we don't need to be getting upset.' Okay, we're beyond getting upset, Lady. David has a hold of the cushion; I have a hold of his arm. He's got "the look." The other arm is coming; I can see he's going to start swinging. So I just spun him around, pinned him to the floor. He is just getting loose with the, 'I hate you!' 'You're so mean!' 'I can't believe you're doing this to me!' 'You're hurting me, you're hurting me!' Just screaming and screaming and screaming. I'm pinning the hands down. I had my ankle over the lower part of his leg because he's kicking and flying and I can just see all the little crystal figurines on her end table somewhere in pieces. I have the trunk of my body on his pelvic region cause he's bucking and trying to swing and kick. This therapist, you know, here she's just in a roller chair just sitting there and she kind of wheels over to me and said, 'Oh, now how did you learn this restraint?' I must have given her the dirtiest look in the world, like 'Get down here and help me!' You're up there in your pretty little outfit and I am down here. Even though I have a hold of him, I am doing damage control.

"Well, somehow, he got loose. He gets very, very sweaty, so I don't know if he slipped or I let go to wipe and reposition, or what, but a hand got loose and, Oh my God, he just, bbbooonnnggg and blood went everywhere." David hit his mother in the face. She continued, "His knuckles just made direct contact. I never have experienced that. My teeth went through my lip because my lip went backward into my mouth and there was nowhere for my teeth to go. And like I said, the blood just went everywhere. Well, of course, it spurt on him, he starts screaming, thinking it's his blood." The therapist offered the tissue box then, and Sarah shared, "I just grabbed about fifty, stick it in my mouth. And the therapist is over there in her chair going...And again, you just have to picture she's very contained, legs crossed, arms folded across her knees. And if she could stroke us, 'Let's just calm ourselves, let's just calm ourselves.' And like doing this mantra over there. I scoop him up in the couch next to me and I'm rocking him. And she's just over, 'Let's calm ourselves.' I just went, 'Shut up, just shut up!' I've become a screaming maniac. I'm now yelling at this professional woman to shut up in her office. Blood is everywhere; I'm just rocking David. I'm bawling by now. When he gets angry, it scares me and I'm not going to let him destroy things. I'm not going to let him hurt himself. I'm not going to let him hurt me or I'm going to try not to" She reassured her son that it was her blood and that her lip was split, not his. "You're okay," the mother told the distraught son. "Here I am. I'm rocking and patting him and trying to stroke him, he's bawling and I'm bawling. The therapist, by this point, has kind of backed off, eyes as wide as they can be, with a look that said 'Oh, my goodness, she just told me to shut up.' I think she was truly more upset about that than the fact that we just had this huge take down in her office." As they left the office, David was calm and discussed supper possibilities, asked what was for supper, and told Sarah he was really hungry. As the result of that incident Sarah and Rex were even more worried about what was wrong with their child. After they sent literature on RAD to the therapist they decided they wouldn't return to her. "This isn't going to help anybody," stated the frustrated mother.

Mattie W., of Kearney, Nebraska, said she'd known couples whose first child was adopted and that fact alone was a terrible disadvantage to them as parents. Those couples had no way of knowing which behaviors were normal or not. She and her husband experienced five other kids and all five of them were different in just about every way possible. Mattie shared, "so right from the get-go I knew there was something wrong with this little guy. We didn't know until he was ten years old about the abuse that went on in his life before we got him. I think we should have known that the children's home was not truthful with us. I think the adoption laws should be changed so that adoptive parents know exactly what they're up against. We would have been so dumb we would have said, 'Hey, that's okay. We can handle that. Give us some time; we've got lots of love. We can fix this kid.' So it wouldn't have made any difference if they'd told us or not, except in the way that we went about getting help. We wouldn't have gone the educational, academic route." Had they known it was a psychological problem, the couple felt they could have gotten Scot help much earlier in his life, which might have made his life more productive.

At about eleven and twelve Scot had been sent to Omaha for hospitalization and psychiatric care. According to the treatment plan they were going to work with him for three months. Mattie stated, "In the end the psychiatrist said, 'I don't know what you're going to do with him. We can't help him—just take him home and good luck. The only thing I can suggest that you do is just put him in an empty room, give him a catalogue and let him tear it up.' We didn't have an empty room, for one thing. And I didn't think that was going to solve any problem, for another. That didn't turn out to be helpful at all. The psychiatrist tried some rage therapy, and was supposed to be the only one in Nebraska that had worked with it." Because of lack of experience with the methods, the approach was not effective. Next, they took their son to a clinical psychologist in a larger city nearby for an evaluation. They were in session "for twelve minutes" before the Ph.D. offered a diagnosis. "He was absolutely no help. What else could we do? You name it, we did it, until we just absolutely ran out of money. There was no more money, but we wanted very much to get him into Colorado (to the Youth Behavior Program, the forerunner of ACE), but the insurance wouldn't pay for it." By this time they'd looked into Boy's Town in Omaha, Nebraska and they were refused services because Scot came from a good home with parents who were doing the right thing. A friend and Boy's Town employee advised the couple to "just pack a bag and drop him off there, just drop him off at the gate. He said they would take him if you did that." Mattie and Dan were unable to summon the courage to take that drastic step.

Eventually, they worked with the Nebraska Children's Home and Scot was placed at the Omaha Home for Boys but was discharged before too long because of his unacceptable delinquent behaviors. Feeling completely at the end of her rope and terrified of her homicidal son, Mattie asked what would happen if she didn't come to pick him up at the Boy's Home. The official stated, 'I'm sorry, Lady, but we would have the State Patrol just drop him at your door.' Mattie and Dan thought, "What choice do you have then? After living with him and seeing his behaviors, I understood their decision." Sadly the mother concluded, "He is never, ever going to be a productive citizen. He's never going to be able to live in the real world, and that's a waste." When asked if she thought her son was a psychopath with no conscious or no guilt she replied, "There's absolutely no doubt in our minds that he is just that."

Laura R., of Scunthorpe, England, talked about working with the adoption agency and the experienced social worker that placed her child. "She didn't use the word disturbed, but she sure gave me the picture that Ann had a lot of problems." When they told the professional woman they wanted to adopt Ann when she became available, she advised them not to do so. Laura was afraid that when the girl became a teenager the couple wouldn't have the support necessary to raise her. But the couple did what they thought was right. They didn't actually adopt Ann until she was nine so in all that time the social worker was involved with the family. Their daughter was known to be a difficult child. "The social worker called her "Madam" which really sums her up—'How's Madam today?'" Ann had many issues and fears around her relationship with her birth mother. The British mum continued, "There never was a time when we thought we should not adopt her. That was what we wanted for us and we felt that would give her that ultimate security of knowing that she did belong to a family. So we actually fought quite hard to adopt her."

After Ann terrified an elderly couple by making 19 threatening phone calls, the parents knew it was time to get her help for mental problems. The incredulous mother stated that after three sessions and "one or two games she played with her and decided that Ann was quite a nervous child but basically, she was okay. She would benefit from some group sessions with some other girls and things like assertiveness, speaking up for what you want, but otherwise, 'She's normal.' We said we didn't think so." The sessions for Ann were terminated at that point but upon request the counselor agreed to see the parents again. Laura clearly told the therapist, "One of us has to go out and it is my home. I didn't see why I should be pushed out. In fact, what we're doing is to put her outside the door because we can't contain her in the house on occasion. We were advised, 'Well, just ignore her.' But you can't ignore her. 'Well, just let her go upstairs.' She'll go upstairs and then start throwing things off the banister. She'll start spitting or she'll start tearing the wallpaper off on the landing. You can't just ignore; she'll get worse and worse." At the suggestion of the therapist they tried a reward system. "So we did all the things we were advised to do but it actually just made it worse because then we had a daughter who wouldn't do anything at all unless she was getting a reward for it. So, I think that was the last actual outside help we got. (Ann was about thirteen and a half at that time.)"

Through a complicated process and a circuitous path Ann received a variety of therapies at the hand of several therapists. Some of the professionals proved to be creative but were ultimately unsupported by the adoption agency. Various talk and play therapies were used but remained ineffectual in bringing about the behavioral changes needed to help the adolescent get along within her family. "Eventually," Laura shared, "they gave us another worker from his team who was a female who decided that she could work with Ann, but she wouldn't work with me. She would only work on a confidential basis with her; we had no idea what was going on and she saw her for something like eighteen months. We don't think she did any good at all; she probably did more harm than good because Ann just told her what she wanted to tell her. There was no feedback; she felt like she was doing fine and telling her she was." Laura stated that the social worker would go months without contacting her then call and ask how Ann was doing. "I'd say, 'She's doing awfully. Her behavior is awful. And she said, 'Oh, I thought because Ann hadn't contacted me that things were okay.' She expected Ann to contact her. Useless." Laura concluded that one of the hardest things about living with RAD children "is not being understood by professionals and not having any support. We've been fortunate. We've got quite a good support network, [adoptive] families who have children in similar situations. I think Social Services tends to feel that whatever problems the child has stops with the adoption certificate. They can't recognize that it is ongoing and that it is difficult."

Tara and Bob W. from Edmonton, Canada: The frustrated mom shared when you begin fostering children, it was assumed you are told about your child's full history. The reality is, she said, you don't get very much information at all unless you've been around the system for a while and learn the right questions to ask. "We were pretty green," Tara stated, "and you know, you just go with what your social worker is telling you and did we think to ask if there was any drug related problems with Cassi? No, didn't even really dawn on us." They'd had previous experiences with children with fetal alcohol syndrome and learned what that was. They were told Cassi was placed with an aunt following her birth because the mother was in jail. The little girl remained with that aunt for three months. The couple found the information out after the fact through a private source then they pieced everything together by asking lots of questions. At approximately four months of age Cassi was placed with her biological mother, but after the mother suffered a drug overdose, was placed in Roseprest, an institution for mentally handicapped children.

Tara and Bob talked about the process that led them to look for answers to what is wrong with Cassi. Bob stated, simply, "Frustration with the system." Tara continued, "Tish, our social worker that placed Cassi in our home, is the best social worker in the whole wide world. We have total respect for Tish." When Cassi was placed in their home, she'd visit often; she went over and above her job as the couple reported. Apparently visits were only required every three months, but the vigorous social worker came when the pair had significant concerns about their daughter. She was the one who told Tara and Bob about attachment issues and RAD. The adoption worker didn't know a great deal about the disorder, but was able to direct them to the attachment disorder parents' group. Tara stated first they attended but began avoiding the group, "because I refused to believe that this could be Cassi. Denial. And then as time went on she'd just act out more and more. You couldn't just play; there was never any fun. Everything had to be a struggle. It was her way or there was no other way—but yet she's a little baby." What's wrong with this little baby? The couple began asking themselves. Their questions led them back to the group where they learned there was hope and there was something you could do. Bob stated attachment disorder is something that's not recognized by the professionals from Social Services. "They are finally starting, from what we understand, to get their heads out of the sand a little bit and recognize that maybe there is something going on here and maybe everything isn't solved by play therapy." They did not believe that Social Services, as an organization, was especially helpful but credit their social worker with setting them on the right path.

Martha G., from Kansas City, Missouri, is married to an attorney so has some idea about the legal systems in her area. The concerned mother stated that judges in their area, especially those in family court, have inadequate training in child or family development, nor did they know the importance of bonding and attachment. Martha went on to say the judges make rulings based on a law and how they interpret the law, which seems to supersede what's really in the best interest of the child. "Meaning," the worried mom of many stated, "they'll move kids or threaten to move children when they have a good attachment going on just because the adopted parents or foster parents aren't doing what they need to be doing." The couple has had experiences with a variety of courts when dealing with two children who came out of homes where the biological parents died of AIDS. One child was ill and died of AIDS in their home. Martha believes having the threat of the removal of a child hanging over one's head is not in the best interest of the child. When the child has started bonding, the authorities have no idea at all what they are doing to the child and the family. She went on, "The judges don't care whether these kids are moved or not. They're not taking care of them, and they don't understand what it's like to live day-in and day-out with the kids. And so I think the legal system is just horribly backward" due to a background that is inadequate to handle the job of placing youngsters. Martha thinks it is comparable to emotional blackmail. In her observation some judges' decisions are inconsistent—some children are removed when they need to stay and some stay when they should be removed for their safety. Martha reported that in Missouri, "The biological family is supposed to be having visits every week; they're supposed to be making the phone calls, coming to the doctor's appointments. Even if they miss the every week stuff, even if they miss the doctor's appointments, if they come to one thing right before the court hearing, the judge will put it off for another six months saying we'll go for unification. Kansas is better. If the parents haven't shown anything in six months, they will terminate."

The outspoken mom discussed subsidized adoptions and her observations of how their state systems worked. She said the only people who negotiate placements are the Division of Family Services and the adoptive parents, with no attorneys or the like involved. In her opinion the State of Missouri gets stingy with their funds so when an adoptive family asks for a subsidy to help rear a difficult, expensive child, they are labeled as "money hungry." Some authorities apparently believe that some folks adopt or foster children just for the subsidy. Martha said they don't realize that what many adopted and foster children need is long-term therapy which Medicaid doesn't cover. So the State won't write in benefits for long-term therapy and continues to believe "we're just there for the money," stated the disheartened woman.

Troy and Leslie W. of San Luis Obispo discussed Sam during his elementary days shortly after joining their family. Almost immediately Sam became too much for the teachers to handle so they called the parents to come and get him. The frequency increased dramatically so in kindergarten—where he landed rather than in first grade due to his behavior problems. The child spent more time at home than in school. Both parents found that very disturbing, both emotionally and professionally. Leslie, the mother, stated, "We looked at this as good. He's going to school, or however much time he's putting in at school and then he's home with us and what a perfect time for attaching." But eventually Troy felt resentful and angry about the disruptions and being pulled away from his professional work. He'd go pick Sam up and he'd appear totally innocent. The parents reported that they eventually tried other parenting approaches, every parenting approach including the "*Love and Logic*" methods, but nothing worked. They used natural consequences as best they could. Don't want to get dressed? Go to school in your pajamas, no big deal to him. Forget your glasses? Go to school without your glasses. No shoes on? Sorry, go to school. Troy stated, "I'm trying to do this and the school is looking at me like I'm frigging crazy. And I had given them all the literature on love and logic and this is what I'm trying to do. You know, it's not hurting him to go to school in pajamas. I did have shoes in the car because I knew that you have to have shoes in school. It was crazy making! It was crazy making where he'd go and say he didn't eat breakfast. He probably didn't eat breakfast because he sat there at the table refusing to eat what was in front of him. 'Well, okay, if you're not going to eat, it's time to go to school; we don't have all morning. So then it looks like we are depriving him.'"

The sensitive father continued: "RAD is a striking thing. As a professional I saw a lot of failure to thrive babies. I've studied Bowlby and all this in graduate school. I was in a very psychodynamic oriented graduate program, and I didn't get it. I saw all these kids for ADHD and other related things, and I didn't get it. I would evaluate them using the standard techniques and I could see there was some attachment difficulty. I'd also see that there were some little tendrils of attachment there. But I had no idea of the magnitude, the pervasiveness, and the extent to which it affected other things until I lived with Sam myself. And now I see it all the time. I do a lot of disability evaluations with little ADHD kids. I get a lot of evaluations from the regional center for cognitive things. What it turns out to be is Reactive Attachment Disorder. It's difficult to make a diagnosis in DSM terms because we're so medical model-ish, if that's even a word. But that's what it is." Troy changed his intake procedure and was amazed how much attachment, or lack of it, is there once one knows what they're observing. Other professionals diagnose ADHD or bipolar, or "they're this, they're that. But they won't look at what it is; it's a very difficult thing," the seasoned psychologist said with a shrug.

Leslie K. of Kent, England—shared her experiences in the following letter dated 3 June 1997:

"We had James as a baby of 18 days old. He was always a very lively toddler and small boy but what was fun (if tiring) for several years suddenly when James was 8 years old took on a whole new meaning.

"The first real indication we had that something was wrong was when we were summoned to his Primary school to discuss his lack of achievement and behaviour. Nobody, least of all us, had the slightest idea what was wrong and that started a round of interviews with different Practitioners over several years to try and find an answer. The question of AD never arose.

"We had a very damning report from the Educational Psychologist who said that James was paranoid and an extremely disturbed boy. He confirmed that he was a very bright child (he has an IQ of 125) but he was extremely disruptive in class, would not concentrate and would "go blank." At one time they thought he had petit mal.

"We attended the Child Guidance Clinic in Dover for some time with James seeing a Psychiatrist and me seeing a Social Worker. None of this achieved anything. We were then sent to Guys Hospital where James had a brain scan and EEG. Both were normal. We tell James that he has medical notes confirming that his brain is normal and intact! Which is more than the rest of us can boast.

"James' behaviour became increasingly difficult and bizarre and Primary school felt that they could no longer keep him. He was, therefore, Statemented and sent to residential school in a village near Dover—15 miles from home. This is one of the things on looking back that was such a mistake. Not knowing James' problem, this was just another rejection. We knew he did not like going—by this time he was 10 years old—and we did not like his going, but we felt we must take the advice of all the experts, Doctors, Social Workers, Psychologists, Psychiatrists, Teachers. I had had James at home with me, with a home tutor for 3 hours a week for 10 months. Can you imagine what that was like? Anyway, he attended two of the special schools until 16 years of age and although the Staff at both schools were very good and very kind, neither place made any impression at all on James' problems.

"There we were with James at 16 years old, no school, no psychologists (we were only referred all the time James was under 16 years old) no help of any sort and James' behaviour deteriorating all the time. During this time was when he became very violent towards me and his father, who had to work, left the house each morning worried and wondering what he would find when he returned home. Again, James was in the house with me all day, as he was not working.

"We became so desperate that we appealed to Social Services for help and we were assigned the most wonderful Social Worker without whom, I wonder what would have happened to us.

"One constant theme running through James' life was his need to meet his birth mother. So, when our Social Worker visited us and tried to help he started the ball rolling for James to meet his mother although he was still only 17 years. The Social Worker also found James' digs with a family where he then went to live, relieving the pressure on us all.

"James met his birth mother in January 1996 and this made a remarkable difference to him. All the aggression is gone and the violence. He is still completely unreliable and is still not holding onto a job and is still hopeless with money and still drives us round the bend! But at least we are not frightened of him anymore.

"We first heard of PPIAS on a radio programme about 4 years ago. My husband came home one night, he had been listening to the radio and told me of two families who had talked about their children and he said, they were describing James. A number was given out and I rang it. We then learned about AD and realised at long last what was wrong. Like many other adoptive parents, we thought that all that was needed was love, how we wished that was so. Since we learned about AD we have obtained the Resource Pack for Parents on understanding AD and have copied it several times. We have sent one copy to our local Social Services, the Special School James attendance [sic] and also the Department of Educational Psychologists at Maidstone, who replied very positively."

Nancy R. from Overland Park, Kansas shared, "For a long time we excused her behavior and we were certain that she'd change. You know, let's give her the benefit of the doubt, think of what she's been through.

We took her from therapist to therapist, psychiatrist to psychiatrist, to everyone in the world that we could find. We went hundreds of miles and spent hundreds of dollars. And at the therapists she would put on the best act. They saw nothing. She could be telling me in the back seat that she hated my guts and she was going to run away and I couldn't make her be my little girl and on and on. And then we would walk into the doctor's office and she would turn into this little angel. And then on the way home, if I didn't do what she wanted me to do, she would get her coke and throw it at the back of my head. But none of her therapists saw that. We put her in the hospital once for a week and she just thought it was like going to church camp. They tried medicine after medicine after medicine for depression or anxiety or for ADHD. Nothing ever did any good. Ever!

"We must have tried one hundred therapists during a five-year period. She was five and a half when she came to us. For four years we tried traditional therapy, you know, they would read her a therapeutic story while she was coloring. Or they would do play therapy." The therapists repeatedly told Nancy that if she treated her like she treated her other kids the little girl would do fine. "But," she added, "they did not know, and they did not see. They don't live with us. I would leave there so frustrated and cried all the way home. One day I was in the last appointment I had with a traditional psychologist and I began to cry. She said, 'Well, yes, I know she might be a pain in the neck sometimes, but she's a needy child.' Baloney! She doesn't know because Heather put on a very good act in front of her and we had been seeing her weekly for three years. And I realized there is nothing changing. Why am I paying all this money? There is no change at all. If anything, as Heather grew older her behavior was worse. The sad mother reported the most beneficial thing that therapist did was to tell Nancy about a nontraditional therapy called, "Holding therapy" and about The Attachment Center at Evergreen. The therapist also gave Nancy a brochure for the Center, which contained a list of the symptoms of Reactive Attachment

Disorder. "And as I read, with the exception of a few, every symptom down the list was Heather. And I thought this is it. This is it! And through networking and phone calls and visits we have found a therapist familiar with attachment therapy. He's been coming to our home now every other Tuesday evening to work with our family. And we are getting ready at the end of this month to go to New York to meet with Dr. Martha Welch. This is a scary thing to say, but we're hanging our hats on that. I love Heather and I want her and I want her to live with us, but I will not destroy the other kids. The six of us are going to Chattaqua July 1st to see Dr. Welch and our therapist is going too. If some big things do not happen…I am just tired; I'm worn out. The other kids have done wonderfully, they're good kids, but there has to be some changes made on Heather's part or we're going to have to look at some other options."

Anna and Errol P. of Lee's Summit, Missouri are the parents of twin daughters who joined their family at six-years-old. Before they had been introduced to the topic of Attachment Disorder their daughter Nicky had been in therapy since early in her life. The couple believed the therapy was vital to their daughter's health so continued it almost into the girls second year with them. Because Nicky was so controlling they believed she had the most difficult problems. However, once they understood their girls' connection and relationship—that Nicky was the parent and the protector—it was then possible to see the bizarre behaviors demonstrated by her twin, Liza, as well. Before the adoption was finalized, a process that was intentionally slowed because of their behavioral problems, the family saw a child psychologist. According to the mother, "He had his socks charmed off" by Nicky. Their little daughter "interviewed him, analyzed him," and was able to present the professionals credentials to her amazed parents when they got home. After his evaluation the psychologist assured Anna that the children were fine, but that she (the mother) was actually the problem. The doctor told Anna that she needed therapy because it was her unresolved issues that were causing the difficulties. He assured the worried mother that Nicky was a wonderful, perfectly charming child with a fully developed conscience. "Not to worry," was his final suggestion.

Anna had been feeling so anxious and depressed that for a time she believed the professional. Her own physician had prescribed Zoloft for depression and Xanax for the anxiety she'd been experiencing. For approximately two years Anna worked with her doctor trying to get the dosages regulated so she would feel better and be able to function as well. Gradually, she stated, "I went on to further higher doses of the Zoloft and Xanax and turned into a walking, talking zombie, which was, I think, the worst thing. Luckily I didn't choose to consume alcohol because I would have been a rip-roaring drunk on top of it. And so, instead I gained fifty pounds because I was stuffing it. I knew it was me because all the experts told me it was me."

In the meantime, their daughter's behaviors "were more manipulative, more search-and-destroy, more divide-and-conquer." The parents shared that the girls had a passive-aggressive, mutual pact going on at the same time. They seemed to revel in getting each other in trouble then sitting back and enjoying the show. After much pain on everyone's part and research by the couple their social worker connected them with a Kansas City attachment support group. Anna spoke with other mothers who had similar experiences, the beginning of her trip back to self-esteem. The couple was also led to professionals with backgrounds in attachment therapy that were able to help them. As a result, their daughters are making progress because now the educated parents are able to help them, something they wanted to do from the start. And as a footnote, Anna firmly stated, "I won't let anyone ever convince me, again, that I'm crazy!"

Kate and Dick H., an English couple from the Finedon area are the parents of two adopted children, but J.D., the older of the pair, was the most troubled. Kate shared that she had been given an article that explained attachment disorders and clearly described her son. With the help of the adoption worker the couple was able to obtain an appointment for J.D. at the Child and Family Guidance office. During the first time with the therapist, one which none of them liked at all, J.D. put on his "out in public" act; he sat on his father's knee and buried his head in Daddy's neck. After their first hour together the therapist dismissed Kate and Dick because he believed the parents were impeding their son's communication with him. After approximately ten minutes alone with the child, Kate said, "The man came out in a bit of a huff and said, 'There's no point in me working with him 'because be doesn't want to talk to me.' Then this gentleman went on to fresh fields and pastures anew; and we were given a new therapist." The replacement was a young man who spent two sessions with J.D. before making any recommendations. The worried couple was assured that there was nothing wrong with their son apart from the fact that they needed to "tighten up on your discipline." The way Kate and Dick heard the message was that they were totally inadequate parents that it wasn't the child's fault, but it was theirs because they were not giving the child enough direction. Kate stated, "And my husband and I came out feeling totally and utterly deflated."

Through a personal friend the concerned mother was introduced to an agency in England called "P.P.I.A.S," which is now "Adoption UK." They told her about American therapists who were treating children with AD and the mum spoke with the health authority about arranging a trip to America so J.D. could be evaluated and perhaps treated. But before that could happen the authorities insisted that an English specialist see their son. The couple complied and then Kate reported, "After a couple of sessions I found out he did specialize in attachment, but he didn't have a bloody clue about attachment disorder." Several sessions later the professional outlined his plan for treatment to the frustrated couple. Finally the former teacher "blew" as she put it and said, "I've had enough! A child that has been sitting here that you've been talking to for the last half-hour bears no resemblance whatsoever to the child I live with. That child has spent the last half-hour winding you 'round his little finger, and every word out of his mouth has been a lie and you have swallowed it hook, line, and sinker. I said, 'You may have written papers on attachment. You may have given talks about attachment, but you know sweet Fanny Adams about attachment disorder.'" But before she left the psychologists office she had provided him with a reading list about attachment disorders, including works by Dr. Greg Keck and Nancy Verrier, then referred him to P.P.I.A.S. for more literature. The assertive mum stated she would be back after he had read up on the topic. Kate told him that she refused to waste their time on avenues that would not work. "And while you're wasting time," she continued, "that child's life is being ruined." She asserted that by the time they waited for uninformed professionals to find the answer they'd be seeing J.D. sent to prison. Before leaving the office Dick and Kate discussed the possibility of obtaining a referral to the only treatment center in England, Keys Attachment Center. A final note regarding J.D.: the family has located and is working with a social worker who was trained and practiced attachment therapy in the United States. The couple shared it was an extremely slow process but they felt they were going in the right direction.

Joyce K. of Nipomo, California stated, "Obviously, the thing that makes me the maddest is the lack of help and the lack of support for these kids. It scares me to think what the end of their road is. That just scares me because they should be getting the help now when they need it and they're not." The concerned mom of several children talked to me about her experiences with therapy for her little boy. None of it, according to this highly educated woman, was effective. "It's been play therapy," Joyce went on to say, "I mean goofy stuff. I mean, for him it's just one more person to rope in and I just sit there and it's really disgusting.

Nobody wants to attack or to confront the kid. Everybody, you know, they see a little, cute five-year-old boy. They don't see what's inside him until they really know him, and then it's so scary that most people don't want to touch that. That's what's sad because that's the part that needs touching and it needs touching every day of his life, not just for six weeks of therapy somewhere. It needs to be touched every day of his life and I need to be given permission to touch that every day of his life. His social workers need to touch that part too, and his teachers, his brothers and sisters. Everybody around him needs to be given permission to say this is how we can help this kid. But I haven't heard that."

Bernadine Janzen, the mother of two attachment affected adolescents, is also a political and adoption activist from Alaska. The author gave her permission to share her November 3, 1998 "SOMETHING TO THINK ABOUT" position statement: President Clinton is hot to get foster children who have no possibility of returning to their biological parents adopted into homes. In our state, foster homes make approximately $23 a day for the care of a foster child. If the child has "issues," special needs that require more care the foster parent may be given additional money. If the child has severe emotional or behavioral issues the daily care rate can be increased to $65 a day for placement in a foster home. That amounts to approximately $1,950 a month for the care of a severely disabled child. There is no question in my mind that foster parents do not do this for the money. (Based on my own experiences of living with severely emotional/behaviorally disabled children, this is a tough job.) Foster parents earn every bit of that money. Many of the children who are or will be "up for adoption" in the next year are coming from neglectful or abusive homes. Many of the children may or may not come with severe emotional/behavioral disabilities. An adoptive subsidy in the State of Alaska is currently $492 per month. This may or may not cover additional hospital care or respite for the family. I wonder what will happen to President Clinton's hope for adoptive homes for children who have no possibility of returning to biological parents or when foster parents decline adopting because there is not substantial money to support a special needs child. With a difference of almost $1,500 a month there is reason to believe foster parents asked to adopt a severely emotionally/behaviorally disabled child would be hesitant."

Pickle stated she's concerned about a society that always believes the child. "Because those who parent children with attachment disorder know the children are very capable of lying with a straight face. They are very good actors and actresses. I know too many parents who've been falsely accused of abuse and then that placement had been disrupted because we tend to always believe the child." She thinks every situation needs to be thoroughly investigated before a final decision and judgement is made. "I've seen too many families who could provide loving homes totally destroyed" by such an experience, the concerned therapist shared.

Although this may appear as an afterthought, I'm pleased to add a note to this chapter on therapies. In the past few years some creative professionals have been laboring over new ideas and new approaches to such stubborn children. In the hands of learned therapists advances are being made with the use of new movement and light therapies, sensory integration techniques, cranial-sacral therapies and EMDR. EMDR—Eye Movement Desensitization and Retraining—has been around for several years now and has demonstrated exciting ways of changing a persons thought patterns and perceptions. In addition, Neurofeedback, an advanced form of biofeedback, is being used to identify then "rewire" the brain patterns of affected youngsters. All of the new techniques need to be provided at the hands of thoroughly trained professional and offer exciting possibilities for children with such severe difficulties.

In spite of frequent frustrations and some successes with professionals and their therapies, the parents of attachment affected children continued to demonstrate their indomitable spirit. Their sense of hope could not be explained by pure logic alone. Long after one could reasonably predict their next move, tearfully, each told their story fortified them to carry on. The pledge to care for their youngsters at all cost remained amazingly intact. These are stories of adults who are as stubborn a lot as their broken spirited children, ever determined to never give up on the youngsters they adore.

CHAPTER NINE— Meeting the Families' Needs

Martha Welch, M.D., has extensive experience with parents and their young, has many strong ideas about what is needed to help today's families. First she stated she believes attachment problems among children are increasing dramatically. When asked why she said, "All forces are in favor of disruption because the mothers are not home. They are not home when they're home! Once the mother is not meeting the child's needs, the child becomes resistant to having his or her needs met. Nobody can meet the child's needs as well as the mother—no day care, no anything." Welch added that since families continue to use day care providers, we must be prepared to remedy the deficits caused by such care. Mothers must find ways to meet their own needs, to solve their own problems of fatigue and of being overextended. They must also learn, the expert emphasized, *to be there and present* with their children when they are physically together. Welch thinks many mothers don't know how to intervene in their youngsters' destructive cycles, so don't. When children's needs are not met "they become disregulated, stressed, crying, totally out of sync." As children grow older and continue to harbor overwhelming feelings of anger and helplessness, then they become more selfish "which creates meanness, which then creates sadism in the worst form," according to the psychiatrist.

To successfully interrupt disruptive cycles, appropriate action must be taken as soon as problems appear. The physician's approach of utilizing "holding time" between mothers and their young was developed to interrupt negative cycles which seem to have a surreptitious beginning. The analyst stated, "So the real difference between holding time as you use it and holding therapy as some therapists use it, is who's doing the work." Welch is firm in her belief that the mothers should do the holding because that is where the bond must be first created. She also believes that her form of mother-child holding can compensate for many of the deficits caused by living in today's harried world. Sadly, Welch thinks there is practically no way that working mothers will be able to meet the needs of emotionally or behaviorally disturbed adopted or foster children. The doctor believes that mothers with multiple out-of-home responsibilities won't have the emotional or physical strength demanded by a developing attachment process. Most adoptive and fostering parents, she observed, are unprepared for what will be required of them. In her opinion most adopting parents are very caring and have good intentions but stated, "they are just not used to dealing with such primal emotion." Consequently, they would then have difficulty bearing the intensity of feelings demonstrated by youngsters with attachment problems. The psychiatrist described the best-to-worst living situations for kids: the best is material deprivation, high limits, high attention, and high love; next best: material well being, high limits, high attention, and low love; "And the worst is material well being, low limits, low attention. Love doesn't matter once you've got this."

By the time you arrive at this point in this book, you may feel overwhelmed and thoroughly discouraged about the prognosis for attachment-disordered children. Participating parents generally believed that this problem may never go away and that nothing can be done to overcome it. At this moment many readers may simply wring their hands, experience incredible feelings of apathy or grief, and wish to return to the head-in-the-sand position assumed by too many of today's professionals. The choice is yours, but not the one I would wish for you. There are solutions, and most are far less costly than continuing to let our families go unaided or letting our babies eventually end up in institutions. Prevention, discussed in Chapter Ten, in conjunction with early detection and diagnosis, are the answers. Education, however, is definitely our first line of defense! The eyes and ears of parents, families, and their support systems must be opened. I'm hoping this volume will initiate that process and tweak the consciousness of the reader. Learning about real families and their heartaches and triumphs may be the beginning of one's individual educational process.

As you've already come to learn, because of a rough start in life attachment-disordered kids come into this world with a skewed version, a crooked idea of what parents are supposed to be or do. Their view of the internalized parent tells them that parents, as a group and as individuals, are unloving, or frankly unreliable. They believe to the very depths of their being that they are on their own and cannot trust adults. And because the rudiments of those strongly held opinions were formed early in their lives simple logic will not change their minds. The need to have control over every person and situation is the source of their unrelenting drive. To be under the power of another feels dangerous to them and is ultimately too terrifying to be acceptable.

There is one concept upon which those dealing with terror-ridden and rage-filled children agree: AD kids *will not* internalize a parent they can control. Even power over them gained through manipulation or trickery will not alter their internal beliefs. Instead, such ploys will reinforce their notion that adults are not trustworthy, weak, or stupid, which ultimately continues to interfere with any bonding efforts. When my children were teenagers, a friend reminded me of some basic parenting principles. She told me that every time I did something *for* my children that they should be doing *for themselves,* I was robbing them of feelings of accomplishment. It made me sad to think that my interference in their experiences of success or learning to care for themselves was an unloving act and not the loving message I'd hoped for. By her definition that included every time I said "yes" when I really did not want them to do a particular thing, but just didn't have the guts to say "no." As you may have already experienced, it is difficult to refuse adolescents' requests. That is especially true for AD children of all ages.

Over the past several years some professionals have specialized in teaching parenting skills to those adults who are attempting to rear RAD children. Nancy Thomas of "Families by Design" in Glenwood Springs, Colorado, parenting expert and author of *When Love is Not Enough*, is one of the experts in the field. Thomas has both developed and taught loving, creative, and successful approaches to parents of those with attachment difficulties. Additional books that would be helpful are the *Love and Logic* Series by Foster Cline, M.D. and Jim Fay, and another called *Therapeutic Parenting, It's a Matter of Attitude!* by Deb Hage. Please refer to the "Bibliography" in the back of this volume for more specific information about these and other excellent resources.

As you know, teaching appropriate daily living and behavioral skills to your children is essential to helping them into adulthood. Just as love alone won't unravel the harm done; behavioral methods in isolation are not adequate to fill the void either. Most families also need some level of therapeutic intervention to gain or maintain any balance and serenity within their family life. I encourage you to locate appropriate workshops or contact any of the suggested authors for assistance in reaching your child through behavioral means. Many of the treatment programs identified on the "Resource List" in Appendix 1 offer programs to parents and would be pleased to be contacted for such important information.

Parenting Tough Kids

In addition to referring you to respected professionals, I would like to offer some guidance to an approach to child and teen care I call *Purposeful Parenting.* I espouse a policy of preparedness and gentleness because there is a fine line that oftentimes gets missed in the heat of conflict. Feelings easily evoked between parent and child are magnified in a family with tough kids. Consequently, it is in your best interest to plan ahead and have formulated some ideas about behavioral options that are available to you. Thus, I've so entitled my parenting approach to distinguish planned, purposeful skills from what I consider accidental parenting. That's the "Oops, I did that right! Now let's see if I can remember how I did that since it worked so well..." approach. Most parents I've met have had the basic skills required by attached, secure children; but few, if any, were available to aid in rearing children who would not respond to usual parenting methods. Overwhelmingly, the interviewees agreed that they were unable to find approaches that were effective with their RAD children. Either their kids would not pay attention, follow directions given to them, or they just didn't care enough about anything that could be used to reward positive behaviors. The skills presented are especially effective with youngsters with attachment problems but can easily be used for "normal" children and teens who are displaying acting out behaviors.

It's imperative to tell the reader that the following suggestions are tried and true and have been effective with tough youngsters displaying attachment issues and with those who have what is commonly termed "bad attitudes." In fact, I've seen such children dramatically change their stinky attitudes and become downright pleasant, and in record time, once their needs are identified and then met. I am talking needs here, not wants. (In my experience young ones who have all their wants met are spoiled and demanding, but more about this later.) However, to think my suggestions will be the final solution to what to do with a severely attachment-disordered child is unreasonable. I consider *Purposeful Parenting* a basic set of tools aimed at adding to your current kit of parenting skills and empowering you to engage your own natural creativity.

An important aspect of this particular parenting style for hard-to-rear youngsters requires the involved adults to be emotionally honest as well as "cash register honest." Sometimes this is difficult to accomplish because it may require new behaviors, ones that must be nurtured, as they may not have developed spontaneously. Most adults of today reported they grew up in families "where we didn't talk about things."

Especially about "things" that *really* mattered to them or that involved strong emotion content. Some cultures are purported to be more closed mouthed than others, as among the English and the Irish, for example. Others, like Italians, are perhaps unfairly known for their outwardly demonstrative behaviors, yet I found no evidence that beyond outward appearances there was not any one group known for rearing their children with the skills needed to discuss or to peacefully experience one's emotions engaged by highly charged issues. American and British societies continue to reinforce the idea of "not airing your dirty laundry in public."

Words to an old song implore us to "smile even though your heart is breaking." When was the last time you honestly shared with another about deep feelings of fear, shame, or hurt? It is more seductive and comfortable to just be angry. It is now known that the purpose of addictive substances is to minimize the impact of difficult, and what are considered to be negative, feelings. Interestingly enough, the primary goal of chemical dependency recovery programs is to help alcoholics and addicts identify and experience their feelings of fear, shame, and hurt in socially acceptable ways without needing to ingest mood altering chemicals to handle them. Those who have the courage to become emotionally honest then have a chance of getting and staying free of addictive substances. On the other hand, those who are constitutionally incapable of being brutally honest with themselves are in danger of serious relapses into their chemical use. Similarly, parents who become open and honest about their feelings are more capable of healthy emotional connections and to share with someone and thus, have an easier time weathering the storms initiated by their children's issues.

Parents who do not believe that they have a strong influence on their children or their behaviors are sadly mistaken. Adults who think their gene pool and then the youngster's peer groups, as I've read recently, are all that is necessary to meet the needs of their children are deluded. Those are fancy, modern justifications for abdicating parental responsibilities.

Let me say this strong and clear—*children need parents.* Under healthy circumstances there seems to be an underlying drive to be with one's parents, which I believe can last a lifetime. Recently a friend of mine lost her 80-year-old mother, her last remaining parent. She felt like an orphan and said so. That drive to connect with caretakers is especially strong in infancy and childhood. Serious abnormalities among the child and parental bond can cause that basic drive to be absent.

Purposeful Parenting focuses both on the messages we give our children and those that our progeny emit (or in the case of RAD kids—spew) back to us. Not all of the messages we give to others are those we speak with our mouths; nonverbal signals are generally telegraphed very clearly to the receiver, as well. Unfortunately, many of us remain deaf to our own behavioral messages so they can remain a mystery to us well into advanced age unless we make it our business to slow down and learn about them. It is only when we bring them into our conscious awareness are we able to reinforce the useful ones or modify those which may interfere with the clear messages we hope to communicate to our loved ones.

Messages: Parent to Child

I have long been concerned about the messages parents and caretakers send their children. The basis of any relationship is communication—the words, style, and rhythm–between individuals. Due to early neglect and/or abuse attachment-disordered children have been primed to expect rejection and failure within a family setting. Unfortunately, sometimes parents do not possess the necessary verbal skills so their behaviors out-shout their internal beliefs. Under some circumstances the actual messages remain unconscious and therefore get lost in the physical process of communicating them. The parents I met, those with very complicated parenting experiences, became increasingly sensitive to their own internal motives and to the messages they wanted to send their progeny.

A list of typical parental messages follows that may be helpful to you. It is important for you and your spouse, if applicable, to sit down and, together, clearly decide which messages apply to your own personal situation. If you are actually at the end of your rope and honestly do not want to be with the child, don't pretend differently. Our children know the truth of our attitudes long before we do; their survival has depended upon "reading" those around them. You did the same thing as a youngster; you knew which parent to ask for what and the optimal time for your approach. Throughout my career and personal life I have found that when I was kind *and* truthful with a child (no matter the age of the child or whose child it was) I eventually gained their respect, even when they did not want to hear reality. I may have not been *liked* but, as you already know, parenting is not a popularity contest. In their purist form the messages below were those all parents prayed their children would hear. We or I (for single parents):

- ❑ love you
- ❑ want you
- ❑ will protect you
- ❑ want to care for you
- ❑ choose to raise you
- ❑ do not expect perfection from you
- ❑ want to be with you
- ❑ will not harm you
- ❑ You belong to our family
- ❑ You are a person of value

Without exception each parent stated the same desire, dream, or wish to nurture and care for their children. Their common bond, no matter their race, ethnicity, or accent was their palpable desire to actively parent their child, no matter how that individual had come to be a part of their family. When parents have the ability to temporarily separate themselves from their feelings, or their perceived failings, their job as parent becomes much simpler. I've learned that mothers who are rested, supported, loved, and emotionally balanced are able to function in their multiple roles without as much difficulty. Fathers who are loved, satisfied, challenged, and respected are happy and supportive members of their family. I believe Mother Nature provides the instincts and natures required of both males and females within the family constellation. All one has to do to develop such an idea is to spend some quality time watching "Nova" or "Wild Kingdom." Nurturing is nurturing no matter which mammal is providing the care.

As an adult I've grown to believe that the hardest thing about being alive is being *human* with all its implications. When feelings and human frailties are added to intellect, the picture changes dramatically and tends to get messy. In all my years I have never met a mother fresh out of the delivery room that was not affected by a potentially overwhelming hormonal process. I have never witnessed an adult in the midst of change who did not exhibit some sort of response to it. And never have I observed a parent unmoved or uninvolved when their offspring was having difficulty growing up. All the situations mentioned call forth strong visceral emotions; at least one of the basic feelings of mad, sad, glad, hurt, fear, or shame is experienced.

When people *react* out of hurt or shame instead of coming from an internal place of love, security, and confidence, their external behaviors change and reflect the powerful internal belief. What is necessary is to match one's internal beliefs and intent with purposeful, thought out, external parenting behaviors; hence, the title of my approach. If the message we want to convey to our child is "Come here, I want you to be with me," then logically, we devise a plan to bring the child physically closer, so they can actually be with us. The act of sending a child to his/her room as a consequence is just what it implies—sending a child away. "Come here/go away" is what is known as a commonly used mixed message, and crazy-making for the child, at that. The only thing a broken spirited child is capable of hearing is the "go away" part. Remember that attachment disturbed children come to us with an already fully developed, overly sensitive rejection trigger. What they feel and demonstrate is rage born of an overwhelming primal sense of rejection and hurt, experienced again and again, then acted out in any number of hateful ways. Without direction, frustrations, anger, fear, and/or sadness for both the children and the parents result in touchy situations that will no doubt get worse.

Messages: Child to Parent

After many trials in which I was not listening attentively, my teenage sons finally taught me that acting ugly *around* or *toward* me actually meant they needed more of what I called, "Mama time." Because they were macho adolescents, they could not say—nor could they have lived it down among their peers—"I need more time with my mother." However, more time with me was exactly what was needed, and providing it worked like a charm. After a weekend full of mother-son bonding time they felt and acted better, kinder and gentler, toward themselves and me. Not one punishment was issued, just consequences: we talked; we cooked, ate, and cleaned up; played cards; watched one movie and played adapted games of in-the-living-room (usually a no-no!) volleyball. *Together*. The key for the success was increased interactions and shared time—child and parent. As with other *Purposeful Parenting* skills I had determined which messages I wanted to give them then made sure my communication of those was consistent and congruent, where my outsides matched my internal feelings and goals. By giving up some of my free time to *fully be with them* and remain attentive to what they communicated to me, increased my chances of truly *hearing* them. Each time I made one-to-one time with me the consequence of yucky, snotty behavior, they were eventually able to experience the truth that I really did want to be with them. In turn, they relaxed, felt more secure, and became more pleasurable to be around.

Just as there were only a few variations of basic messages from parents to kids, the list below includes important messages shouted at parents in a variety of forms from their offspring:

- ❑ I do not trust you
- ❑ I am not comfortable in my skin
- ❑ I am terrified of people
- ❑ I want to be close to you but do not know how
- ❑ Let's see if you are strong enough to handle me
- ❑ I do need you
- ❑ I have holes in me that need to be filled
- ❑ I do not deserve love
- ❑ I want all of you to myself
- ❑ Come here, go away

Our ultimate challenge as parents is to understand our kids' "lingo," and to decipher just what it is they want us to know about them. Actually, that is not correct; they *need* us to know certain things about them! Most, however, do not hand us the key to their insides on a platter; instead, the clues come woven into the mosaic of their personality. Healthy parenting means that we focus our attention on the needs of our progeny and either meet those needs or help them learn to meet their own as they mature. How helpful we are to them must depend upon providing appropriate and adequate responsibilities with consideration of each youngster's maturity level and their stage of development.

As many of you have already experienced, the messages given by attachment compromised kids are especially graphic and challenging. It is extremely difficult to be thoughtful and creative in one's responses during an onslaught when one's basic belief systems or sense of safety are under attacked. It is also hard to believe, without forewarning or forethought, that a broken spirited child of rage is demonstrating some—or probably all—of the above messages simultaneously. I know from experience that it is easier to believe the child is simply demonic or diabolical, with no internal thoughts or feelings except to follow their own path of destruction. In actuality, their thinking patterns do differ from those of bonded, secure youngsters. Their communication styles and messages match their unique internal confusion and (mis)understanding of the world around them.

Consequently, it is absolutely necessary to think about and plan appropriate responses ahead of the next emotional outburst. This is better accomplished in pairs or as a team, which could include spouses, grandparents, teachers, therapists, or respite givers. I have been known as a dreamer and understand a team approach is an ideal, which is rarely available to support these particular parents. Realistically, and a scenario more recognizable to the average parent of a RAD child (even though I doubt that such a person—an average parent—actually exists. Most parents in this situation prove themselves to be extraordinary) is that outbursts are usually handled by the mother. More times than not the mother is the target of the children's acting out as it takes the father a while to see past the youngsters angelic manipulation. Fortunately for all, I met wonderful parents and strong couples working in unison for the good of their family. Even two adults truly working together can send clear messages to the child. Such a team announces that a new day has begun; no longer is the child free to storm the walls of their home, to continue their campaign of disruption/destruction without serious consequences. The duo, armed with knowledge and a plan, can facilitate an end to their offspring's reign of terror. Then youngsters learn exactly who is in charge that you are *The Parents,* and strong enough handle him/her. Now the conditions are ripe for change. Once you begin supporting each other and working together, I promise you, the situation and their behaviors will not remain the same. I have seen one of two things happen: children's behavior either gets better or they completely blow their way out of the family. Unfortunately, not all AD children are able to successfully remain in a home with their family. But be reassured they have uncanny ways of greasing their way into the very living situation that they need the most.

Needs vs. Wants

It would be worthwhile listing the needs of children as have been identified by loving parents I've worked with over the past few years. Sometimes, it seems that our society has become so complex that we confuse a child's basic needs with their wants. The combined work of Abraham Maslow, father of the "Hierarchy of Needs," and John Bowlby, M.D. form the foundation for the following list: food; shelter; safety and protection; clothing; love and/or caring in the form of touch, eye contact, snuggles, smiles, verbalizations; guidance, direction, and limits. Many times I've been told by frustrated parents of troubled children, "He/she just wants attention!" That is correct; children *do need* attention. Attention is a need that involves many of the basics spelled out above. If kids don't get it in a positive way, they'll figure out how to get it some other way, as clearly demonstrated in the stories shared in this volume. The list of "wants" is endless but might include such items as: Nikes or Adidas; designer clothing; Nintendos; computers; Cabbage Patch dolls or beanie babies; trips to Disneyland; toys advertised in movies; or movies based on the lives of toys; cartoons which introduce the latest weaponry; etc., etc., ad nauseum.

Child and family psychiatrist, Martha Welch, told me that the most damaged children or adolescents she'd ever encountered were those who were emotionally neglected while simultaneously being financially or materially overindulged. Among the published newspaper and magazine articles describing the backgrounds of recent young American killers I believe I found ready evidence of Welch's observations. From the outside it looks like the killers of the Columbine High School students seemed to have experienced both neglect and indulgence. By several accounts, Eric Harris and Dylan Klebold came from upwardly mobile families living in upper middle income neighborhoods in Littleton, Colorado. On the weekend before their shooting spree both adolescents spent the entire weekend in the Harris garage readying weapons and building explosive devices. The parents of neither boy seemed especially concerned about their activities, which gave them free rein to complete their mission and place over thirty bombs and explosive devices in Columbine High School. It appeared they had unlimited funds available to them, but inadequate attention of two sets of parents. Klebold's father contacted the Littleton police during the shooting spree to report he thought his son might be involved. His offer to help came too late.

I don't expect parents to be saintly in their approach to child rearing, but certainly they need to be aware and attentive. An important part of deciding to become parents must include a commitment to be responsible and a determination to provide a minimum level of basic cares to one's offspring. A self-evaluation would require an honest assessment of one's skill level or the acceptance of feedback from a trusted spouse or family member. If an adult is incapable of such skills, the tasks can be easily learned in basic parenting courses. The fact that you are reading this indicates you have what it takes to be a sensitive parent who remains alert to the needs of their offspring.

Consistency

A true RAD kid, due to the earliest of experiences, never believed that he/she was somebody worthy of anything. Parents who have attempted to gift their children with nice clothes and teddy bears they've never had before in their lives know of the disastrous results. The popular belief is that you can fill the deficits by providing things to the person's outsides. In reality, self-esteem comes from the inside and develops by kids (and adults) doing loving, esteem-building acts. Even if one does not feel loving or generous while doing kind things feeling better about oneself is still the final prize. If a person does dirty, nasty things to others, they aren't supposed to feel good about themselves, and don't.

Attachment-disordered children are the victims of early malignant inconsistency. The adults in their early lives were unable or unwilling to provide love and caring to their offspring on a consistent basis. As newborns they learned in the early moments in their life that they could not depend on adults, especially on mothers. All children need to experience, first hand, the consistency of their parents love and positive attitudes toward them. That does not mean there is no room in parenting for human-ness or for your humanity. What needs to remain constant is a caring and loving attitude toward the child. However, consequences to infractions should be changed frequently. When children can predict what will happen when they fail to follow parents' directions those consequences eventually become meaningless.

Setting Limits

I am convinced that children need to hear the word "Yes." They also need to hear "No," to experience the frustration of hating that particular answer and of thinking they hate the "no" say-er. Then, the hardest thing of all, they need to learn to live with it. Saying "Yes" then "No," or saying "No" and changing your response to "Yes" when they whine or pout does not help youngsters learn to accept limits. If your response is not the perfect one, that is okay. Giving "mixed messages" ("Yes" but "No," "No" but "Yes," or "Yes" and "No") is confusing and crazy making for even the hardiest of kids. Ultimately the child grows to learn that you do not mean what you say and they cannot depend on you to take a stand. Children need to know that you have the moral, ethical, and emotional strength to take a stand for what you believe to be right and in their best interest. Caving in against their considerable emotional onslaught begs the loss of their respect. This is a concept worth repeating: attachment-disordered children will not internalize a parent they can control, nor are they likely to bond with them either. Kids, all of them, need to be able to symbolically bump up against their parents and know that they are strong enough to gently and lovingly handle them and their overwhelming needs.

I am a Nebraskan by birth so use a western concept to make a point. On the way to many pastures there is a fence configuration known as a 'fence row.' Simply stated it is usually two rows of barbed wire fencing several feet apart, which sets pasture boundaries and provides guidance to the horses and cattle as they make their way to graze. I think good parents construct symbolic fence rows for their progeny. Within the boundaries the young ones have room to maneuver and perhaps even to roam. Barbed wire is unforgiving and provides clear limits to relatively dumb farm animals. Like the farm example, parents need to provide clear limits with obvious consequences when those boundaries are crossed. That process requires thinking and planning out loving parental responses in preparation for when children cross the line. You noticed I said *when*, not *if*. Of course they will eventually cross the lines you have drawn in the sand; that is the nature of the beast. One might even say that's a kid's job!

Even if you consistently say "no" about the same issue later in their life, they can complain about you with some pride about how you would not let them do such-and-such. Have you ever listened to adults recounting childhood stories about how Mama or Daddy clearly set limits for them and how they eventually learned that was their parents' way of loving them? When my son, Todd, was seventeen, he lived with the delusion that he could live in my home without following any of my rules. Eventually I told him that he would be moving out on his own, by a particular date, so he could practice living his life as he saw fit. He courageously told me he thought I "wasn't doing a very good job of parenting right now." With good eye contact, and what I wanted to be a gentle smile, I thanked him for sharing. On moving day I remained loving and helped in ways that would make his transition easier. Several years later Todd wrote a college paper entitled, "My Mother, My Friend."

The theme was about that day several years earlier when I helped him out of the family home and into the world. My son was very clear about the importance of that incident in helping him become the responsible adult that he remains today.

Hold them accountable

In the early days of Attachment Disorders Foster Cline, M.D., in my opinion, the grandfather of attachment therapy, taught me about what he called the "Good Neighbor Policy." I grew to understand, and use the approach, because it finally made sense to me. I think I instinctively knew what *other* children in the neighborhood should do to be responsible individuals. But a distinct brand of myopia developed in my relationships with my own children, driven by love, sensitivity and a touch of insanity, perhaps. Because I prided myself on understanding my offspring, I was also especially good at rationalizing and justifying their yucky behaviors and attitudes. When they were little, missing a nap or having a poor appetite for the day, or week, initially became their reason to misbehave and my battle cry for them. Then it became theirs.

Eventually Cline's "Good Neighbor Policy" became useful. Since it dawned on me that I didn't care if Natasha or Billy down the street had a good nap or regular bowel movements, I didn't use that logic to accept nasty behaviors from those little stinkers. It was necessary that I learn to treat my own children as if they belonged to the neighbors. There were distinct advantages because in our society we tend to treat neighbors with more respect, and more sweetly, than we might our own family members. We don't let those who are unrelated to us to get away with the same junk we do with our own darlings. If the neighbor kid stole my car and took it for a joy ride, I'd press charges. With the intent of holding my children responsible for their behaviors and choices, it became necessary to report illegal behaviors to the police—no matter whose illegal behaviors they were. I don't believe you have fully experienced parenthood until you've called the cops on your kid! For me that was one of the most difficult things I ever had to do. And according to my recent interviews, most parents still believe that's the most heart-wrenching thing they have had to do, but it is absolutely necessary at times when children are not acting in safe or legal ways.

Involving law enforcement may be more extreme than most of you may ever have to experience. However, holding our children responsible in smaller, less dramatic, ways can be equally as onerous. It requires you, as the parent, to say what you mean, and then mean what you say. Examples of "responsibilities" can be setting the table, going to a concert, or getting to bed on time. Helping children become responsible involves a kind, thoughtful approach and a 6-step process:

1) Discuss responsibilities, limits, and ultimate consequences for noncompliance with your "team;"
2) Give clear instructions to the child including the limits and consequences—this is the "fence row." Make sure you use good eye contact during this step. Leave room within the instructions for their personality to shine, for them to "roam;"
3) Give them adequate time to do the deed and to have the fun in the process;
4) Pay attention to child's reactions and responses to the responsibilities and the limits;
5) Enforce the consequences if the child failed to follow the guidelines—without fail;
6) Let the incident go and don't hang on to resentments or hold grudges over what happened. You can then move on to the next situation that requires your attention and energy.

Sometimes it helps to reduce choices given to youngsters and the expected behaviors down to a formula for simplification. It also helps remove those messy feelings that spring from our own parental responses. As long as adults continue to *react* to children and their behaviors, it will be impossible to use thoughtful *responses* which will eventually help our children learn new, useful responses of their own. Sadly, one reaction feeds another. Like the reaction of quickly pulling your hand away from the heat of a flame, knee jerk reactions do not pass through the brain, so any value as a learning process is diminished or lost entirely. A simple, but burdensome suggestion: love your children enough to let them make mistakes or fail in their efforts to meet their goals. That's how children learn; that is how you learned. There is a commonly held notion that it is quite possible to avoid making mistakes, that humans can be perfect. Perfectionism, an illusion, or the quest for it can provide goals or the motivation to accomplish new personal growth. Making mistakes, however, is an invaluable learning tool.

Contracting

As with all the other parenting skills I've suggested, I've come by practically all of them the hard way. I suspect that is because I'm either blatantly or secretly stubborn and perhaps that is why I can understand strong willed children as well as I do. Nonetheless, eventually the advantages of negotiating for our needs came to me. As with most parents I've met I usually want full cooperation or some particular behaviors from my children. And they had expectations of me as well. As long as the list of our needs remained unspoken, we remained at loggerheads. The problems remained in silence; the solution required us to actually identify and talk about our needs and wants with each other. I've often wondered if the art of negotiation is inborn. But whether or not that is true, my adolescent youngsters took to it easily. The first requirement is for you to list, specifically, what it is you want from your child. And your child must list his/her needs as well, but not in the presence of the other. This is the preparation phase, which can ultimately lead to success for both of you. Besides, it is important that all that participate in the process be able to identify their own needs and those activities that are important. It is also important to commit them to paper as that reduces the chances of forgetting or missing necessary items or activities up for negotiation.

There was an important principle that I learned quickly (but didn't much like, I must admit): I had to give up some of my own expectations or demands. My child had to give up of some of his, too, as a satisfactory solution to *our* conflict lay somewhere in the middle between my perfectionism and his fantasy wish list. I say "our" because it takes two people on two sides of an issue to create conflict. Some of his behaviors were a problem for me and some of mine caused him difficulty. Together, we had a problem, but, fortunately, a solvable one. Later in this chapter I have suggested a practice task for you to gain strength in this area.

Consequences

When a child is young, many parents spend an inordinate amount of time attempting to gain control over them. This is especially true of the parents of RAD kids. And what an impossible task that can turn out to be! I offer you a mantra to be repeated to yourself, daily: *I am the parent. I am in charge of myself, first, then my child. All I do for my child must be out of my love for him/her.* I know that sounds pretty silly, right? However, parents with attachment disturbed children know what I am talking about. Those dealing with healthier individuals can also be helped by the simple task. Parents who are collected and have found some internal balance do a better job of consequencing their offspring; they don't take the children's misbehaviors personally and maintain a sense of humor. They may also remember the fits they dealt their parents as youngsters!

For a moment I would like to discuss the use of *ignoring* as a means of getting the upper hand over children. It is necessary to determine if they are out-of-control or already in-charge of the family; both are a problem. You must also determine just what needs to be ignored—the child or his/her behaviors. There are times when a parent's failure to notice a particularly bothersome behavior will diminish its frequency or repetition. On the other hand, ignoring the child, in my opinion, is a form of neglect and may actually increase the offensive behaviors. Many AD children have already been neglected, and claim to be "used to it," so ignoring them is what they repeatedly attempt to recreate within their current family. Their innate difficulty to form a trust bond continues to be compromised, the very reason they are unable to become full members of a family in the first place. Healthier children can also easily get into a negative cycle of acting out behaviors. The basic fact is that all children need attention. Our challenge is to give the proper amount and kind, and any repetition in this area is well worth it. I offer some guidelines for consequences, which should:

- ❑ be appropriate to the age and capabilities of the child
- ❑ be used as learning tools
- ❑ be given out of love, *not* out of anger
- ❑ fit the offense
- ❑ be possible for the child to comply
- ❑ be logical to you, but don't have to make sense to your child

Recently I've met adolescents who had been 'grounded for life' because they sassed their parent or reportedly ran away from home for a few hours. Under similar circumstances the kids felt like they had nothing more to *lose or gain* by cooperating with their totally frustrated parents. Of course, a power struggle ensued, which most kids win because they have more energy and persistence and are more invested in attempting to drive their parents mad. That is especially true of attachment-disordered youngsters.

Let me share some ideas I have about consequences in general. Have the child present to you a list of "rewards," those things they're willing to work for. If they "forget" (and I figure they wouldn't forget a hot date!) to do a chore or task, add another one to it next time. If they're late, double the time they missed and have them come in that much earlier the next time. For future use, you also need to compile a list of consequences, the kinds that require more time spent together. Remember that you want to give them clear "come here" messages.

Here's an example of a useful consequence used by parents for their stubborn son: Troy and Leslie, parents of Sam from the central region in California, talked about consequences they found that worked. "The most effective thing we found, behaviorally, I bought a cord of firewood. It was split so it wasn't giant pieces of wood. We had him move firewood from this place to that place; it was not very far. He could take hours to move one piece of firewood. That was okay, we didn't beat him, we weren't screaming at him, and he wasn't engaging us in a battle. He had to move a certain amount of firewood, a half a dozen pieces; it could take him three hours. Now at other times he could move it in five minutes. Sometimes he thought he was punishing us by taking a long time to move the firewood. Personally, whether the firewood was on the left side of this paved parking area or on the right, who cares? That was effective for a long period of time, and it gave us time to calm down, unplug the toilet. It was like psychological warfare, he didn't become physically aggressive until much later." Troy, a psychologist, continued: "It's structured and there are consequences, external consequences. He doesn't have to apply cause and effect; you supply it for him." Leslie talked about an important issue for her. "We always made it important that Sam be safe. One day he got on his bike and plowed into a cement wall. It was like trying to teach him to be safe, and now I look back and think why was I so worried about him being safe?"

Learning tasks for parents

It is imperative for parents to avoid taking the child's reactions personally. This is a repeat, but a worthy one: although it feels like the child is doing something *to* you, they are really doing it *for* themselves. As is true with adults as well, it is each child's internal goal to make itself comfortable. Their reaction to the world or whatever is happening is their attempt to do just that. Here is an exercise for you and your partner to do together. Take a blank piece of paper and draw lines down the center so you have two side-by-side columns; on one side write "Messages," the other "Consequences." If you want to be with the child, for example, write that under "Messages." Across the page write ideas that you have that will clearly convey your desires and appropriate to their age and development. Some examples: 1) have child sit on a chair near you for three minutes; 2) have child wash or dry the dishes with you; 3) have child participate in an activity (spelled out) of *your* choosing for a half hour. 4) ground your child with you for a weekend of communicating and bonding activities. Please recognize that these are consequences, *not* punishments. Consequences provide growth opportunities; punishments cause anger and can contribute to increased meanness.

Negotiation Practice:

First the child needs to make a list of the privileges he/she wants. Parents, on the other hand, list the responsibilities/chores they want done by the youngster. The initial part of this task is completed while separate from each other. When you sit together, at a planned and peaceful time, each individual list consists of the points to be negotiated. The bartering goes something like this: If you do the dishes each night, *without* fail and whining, I'll let you have a privilege you've put on your list. Or, if your homework is completed by suppertime (and I know that because you consistently show it to me), then I'll eventually trust you more. When my trust for you is improved, we could try letting you go out with your friends (and of course, you'll be where you say you will be!) until 9 p.m. on school nights. After each one of the points you offer your child is given the opportunity to voice his/her needs or choice of privilege. Remember that these are examples, and all privileges and responsibilities should be appropriate for each child. I cannot stress that enough. Hint: many children are more accomplished or capable than most parents know. If you have difficulty judging what is appropriate talk to your parenting mentor, your family physician, or the school counselor. In most negotiations both the child and the parents have to give in on different points. Neither can have everything that they want, and shouldn't. This is a perfect opportunity for adults to model reasonable and kind compromise!

The Needs of the Families

Moody, angry parents whose own needs have not been met cannot accomplish maintaining a watchful eye on the child's best interests. As many of you who live with RAD kids already know, those are the very feelings they evoke in the individuals around them. It is so important that you, too, get your needs met, but not from a child with attachment problems. They cannot fill you; they have nothing yet to give. Until they gain some emotional stability, they can only take from you. The answer for you, of course, is to get your needs met in other arenas of your life or within your own supportive relationships.

It is my observation that modern parents are unable to rear their children in the isolation of the nuclear family as our grandparents did. Although that may be the ideal for contemporary parents, due to increased mobility and decreased interactions with nuclear families, that is no longer the prevalent parenting style. Perhaps only thirty to forty years separate the three generations, but the changes which have occurred in the mores and lifestyles during that same period were inconceivable not long ago. As a child my family shared a phone using a party line with several other families in a small Nebraska town. Our first television came into our home when I was ten. Today my seven-year-old grandson plays computer games, can send e-mail messages, and has the capabilities of having a phone conference with his grandparents as they travel around the world. The make-up and norms of today's family are dramatically different from "the old days" of my youth.

During my research-gathering trip in the Spring of 1998 I asked the parents what it was they needed to make their job of parenting a RAD or attachment compromised child (more) possible. They provided me with the following information:

The Truth

It seems that the usual choice of social workers and adoption agencies is to withhold pertinent information about children being placed in new homes. I think they fear that if the children's backgrounds were fully disclosed, the child would be considered unadoptable. After meeting many, many adopters I do believe that would *not* be the case at all. Adopters and fostering parents maintain their dream that "love is enough" far beyond what is sometimes reasonable. Even so, they are nearly militant out of their desire to be told the details of the child's medical, psychiatric, and behavioral histories. Then, fully armed, they believe they could obtain appropriate and expeditious care for their progeny.

Sarah and Rex D. are professionals who live in rural Kansas. Prior to the adoption of David, their only child, Sarah requested, cajoled, insisted, and sometimes demanded that David's full medical and psychiatric history be revealed to them. The couple was frightened of the unknown but also believed earlier or more appropriate care, if necessary, would be available for the child if they knew his history. The caseworkers were just as stubborn and refused to divulge details of his disrupted past. By the age of seven, David had been treated unsuccessfully by a string of professionals and in local institutions. It was only after Sarah had been granted permission to review David's records was the boy referred to professionals who were familiar with attachment problems. After many frustrating months of searching, the midwestern family was finally able to bond with each other and experience exhilarating successes.

To Be Believed

Prior to adding the RAD child to their family many adoptive parents had exemplary reputations as loving caretakers, teachers of children, role models for younger parents, and upstanding citizens. In most cases the addition of a disturbed child changed all that. Then, after a series of events experienced by nearly all parents of attachment compromised kids, they were considered suspect by family and friends alike. Parents talked to me and cried about the hurt feelings that were the result of such experiences. Adopters and foster parents need the trust and faith of their own parents, siblings, and friends more than ever before. It is important to know that the adoption and foster process does not cause a total personality change in the parents. If a personality change is noted *after* the addition of a child to the family, it is likely to be caused by the added stress of a new member, and their antics, within their new family.

Ann N., an experienced mom from Indianapolis, talked about her experiences with her severely troubled teen. Because of her husband's professional commitments Ann was the primary parent and disciplinarian. When Allen returned home from work, their youngest son would become Daddy's "buddy." Especially troubling for Ann was the way her spouse would excuse all the behaviors that she was having difficulty dealing with. She was the one at home seeing the behaviors for what they really were. She remembered that Allen frequently commented that Anthony, their youngest child, was "a good boy." Before long the mother of four began questioning her own perceptions and would think, "What would that make me? If he's such a good boy, why am I seeing all these awful behaviors?" Ann harbored enormous resentments that began to effect her marriage. Ann added sadly, "I was beginning to feel more and more like a terrible person. I know I'm handling this terribly, but I'm doing the best I can, and here you are, telling me he's a good boy. I think there was more conflict than Allen cares to admit. Anthony—that's what we fought and argued about all the time."

Martha and Joe L. of Grande Prairie, Alberta, Canada are the parents of two children. Kurt, the second child and only boy, was seven when placed with the couple. Martha stated that before Kurt came to them, she was the person called on at community events to organize games to amuse large groups of forty children or more. Once a short "honeymoon" period was completed, Kurt's true nature began to show. Martha said because of those behaviors, "I'm certain everyone thought I was a big mean bag by this time. All of a sudden I was no longer asked to do any of these community things." The parents said that in public Kurt presented with an angelic facade, but he'd surreptitiously call his sister "a bitch" or pinch or rub her buttocks with his hands, "Something" his mother said, "that put me in a position of having to discipline him in public. He'd done it so very slyly that no one else noticed." When she disciplined the child the townsfolk felt sorry for the little boy. As a consequence for inappropriate behaviors at a town party she gave him a few minutes of "time out" during the community event. "I took him to the truck and other people were collecting candy for him. They put it on our table saying, 'This is for Kurt.' It just made me feel like a sack of shit." Martha believes she has lost her good and solid reputation at the hands of her young son.

A Support System

In order to meet the emotional needs of the family the necessary support can come from many arenas. It can include spouses, families of origin, family physicians, social workers, therapists, psychiatrists and psychologists, members of law enforcement including judges and police, teachers, and other parents. Interestingly, the list mentioned is made up of the members of society that untreated RAD victims and their parents will probably have dealings with, perhaps, throughout the child's life. Not all interactions between the AD individual and the professionals will be pleasant. In fact, all of the parents told me about the stressful adversarial relationships which had developed and which always interfered with finding a solution to the problem of "What to do with this kid?" Parents' support groups were reported as extremely helpful to the family living in their own brand of hell as the result of attachment problems.

Tara W. from rural Alberta, Canada, said with a voice filled with emotion: "I didn't realize how stressed out I really was. You're just walking on pins and needles all the time and you're trying to do everything right, everything is such a struggle." Eventually she discovered the value of attending a support group with parents of AD children. Tara shared that being with others that understood helped her handle and rid herself of the frustration and guilt, which consumed her. The following thoughts riveted through her brain: "This is just a tiny, little girl and I'm so angry. Why am I feeling this way? And why can't I reach this baby? I'm such a horrible rotten parent because I can't reach this little girl. This girl is going to get worse if I don't reach her." "And you just have this overwhelming guilt," sighed the mother.

Martha L., Kurt's mom, also from Canada, stated emotionally that she experienced what felt like a complete lack of understanding from those around her. She grew to expect ignorance among her community, but was hurt most by the negative attitudes they had developed. The way Martha explained it, she thought the people in her town "knew me better than anyone else in the world." She discovered that her husband didn't know her well enough, either, to recognize significant changes in her caused by the stress of being with Kurt. She learned that Joe didn't truly understand what rearing Kurt was like for her, and she felt totally abandoned by "my mother, my family, people that had trusted me with their children for years." Martha added, "I resent my community and my family for not knowing me better, for assuming that I could be a rotten miserable parent who would just be mean for the fun of it. I just wanted to just get in my car and drive and just go. I was worried that I would end up in Toronto and not quite know how I got there. I remember one day sitting at the kitchen table and I looked at the clock and two hours had gone by and I had not moved. I thought I was going crazy." Soon after those experiences her psychiatrist diagnosed her with Post-Traumatic Stress Disorder (PTSD), a common condition for parents of attachment-disordered children. "I tell you, it has been a rocky, rocky road."

Financial Support

Foster families receive financial aid to help the child through childhood and adolescent problems. In some cases adoption is out of the question because of the extraordinary financial needs of a RAD individual. One year of institutional care for my own son cost $300,000 and initially the insurance company refused to pay for the services provided him. As disturbing as that experience was, it was not so terribly unusual. Many interviewees told me stories of lost homes and of retirement funds depleted long before their career was completed because of the enormous financial demands of their disturbed children. I believe subsidized adoption is a necessity for families trying to cope with any long-term illness or a disorder such as this. There also need to be emergency funds available to assist families with early diagnosis, treatment, and the follow-up phases of care.

When considering subsidized adoptions, Pickle, mother and attachment professional stated, "There is no parity with mental health issues and insurance." Insurance companies often don't recognize RAD, or they consider it to be a "preexisting" condition so won't cover the costs for required long-term psychiatric or psychological care. Pickle recommends that parents be provided resources and alternatives to the kind of help they obtain for their offspring. "They should not," she continued, "be forced into a particular system just because that's what the state pays for when the child needs something else." Pickle shared that the most appalling situation she'd ever encountered was with parents who'd asked their state for financial help with their troubled adopted child. The parents were told there were no funds available once the adoption was finalized. "But," she reported, "if they relinquished their child back to the foster care system, there may be funds in that system to provide for the child's needs. How much sense does that make if you have a committed family who's willing to go the limit with this child and they're told to relinquish the child back to the foster care system? Parents shouldn't have to wait 2 or 3 years fighting the system to get help for their children," the social worker concluded, as time and the available window of opportunity for treatment is of the essence.

Fred, today, is an adorable thirteen-year-old living with his therapeutic foster parents in a Denver, Colorado suburb. Initially the child was completely unbonded and unsocialized and demonstrated somewhat animalistic behaviors. Fortunately for Fred, his parents had already parented thirty-five boys before him, so were fully experienced with the problems of Attachment Disorder. After dramatic changes in his daily regime and a behavioral approach appropriate for RAD victims, he began to come around and showed dramatic improvements. At the time of my visit the trio—mom, dad, and son—were apparently thrilled with each other and tightly bonded together. Sadly, the couple said they wanted to adopt Fred but was unable to because of the financial demands inherent in their situation. Although the youngster had made gigantic emotional strides, he will continue to require specialized therapy throughout his adolescence. Such costs are prohibitive without assistance provided as the result of their foster parent status.

Joyce K. of Nipomo, California, mother of a five-year-old AD son, stated very clearly: "It's not cost-effective to wait until he's screwed up, and he's going to be in prison the rest of his life. Spend that money now and help this child when, maybe, we can do something about it and he won't be a burden on society for the rest of his life, and mine." But that wasn't all she had to say. Joyce continued: "You've put the burden on a family and expected that…I mean, the Vietnam vets got more help than these little kids get. When they came back with Post-Traumatic Stress Disorder, all these things, they were given more help than these three, four and five year old kids get. Because these are little kids and they're placed in loving families, they're supposed to get better. There's nothing to get better. That's not going to make them better; it's not going to make a family better. It makes a kid sicker and it makes a family sicker. And when you ask for help, you can't have it because it costs too much. That's the bottom line—it's a dollar thing. It's got nothing to do with efficiency; it's got nothing to do with anything else. It's a dollar thing. You find a good therapist and, guess what, it's a dollar thing again. You can't afford to do it and your department won't sponsor you; you can't get it. That's it! So we wait until they turn sixteen and we put them in juvenile instead; or whatever age they are when they get there."

Mentors

The parents verbalized a need to be assisted by others who have already experienced the difficulties of rearing such disturbed youngsters. In *Motherhood at the Crossroads* I identified the need for "mommy mentors," someone with both experience and the wisdom to help moms find solutions to the day-to-day issues with their youngsters. During the interviews the fathers also identified a need for "daddy mentors." I believe the need for parenting mentors is quadrupled in situations involving attachment problems. RAD children are experts at pitting parents against one another. Parental roles and responses to those children are so distinct that both partners require maximum support and guidance from other parents who are wise to the tricks and in the ways of caring for themselves.

Now that son Scot is no longer at home, his parents, *Mattie and Dan W.*, continue to devote time to other members of their extensive support network. Because of their own terrifying experiences with their homicidal adolescent son, they are especially empathetic toward parents still living with dangerous children. The Nebraska couple have received phone calls from parents across the United States in need of their special kind of support and understanding. Dan, having been delivered from a common state of denial which tends to plague fathers, now assists other men. Typically, fathers of RAD children are manipulated by the youngsters and do not fall prey to the dangerous behaviors that befall the mothers. Dan's awareness and increased sensitivity to Marsha's difficulties at their son's hands has made him valuable in assisting others with situations that could easily cause serious marital problems.

Respite Care

An effective respite care system would require a cooperative system between parents, therapists, caregivers, and educational systems. Parents of AD children continuously run out of energy and drive long before the child runs out of symptoms or bonds with parents. If a village is needed to raise a normal child, then an attachment-disordered individual requires an armored fortress. I have interviewed families from towns and cities that would easily lend itself to a well-developed respite system. In such a place there are many families living with and who have educated themselves about this disorder. Support groups, which include enlightened therapists, are already in place and a local university is aware of attachment issues are interested in helping out. Counseling and social work students are sensitive, enlightened, and enthusiastic to learn more and lend their assistance. RAD kids do very well in front of and in the care of strangers. Imagine the relief parents would experience if their acting-out youngster had a safe, structured environment—one that was not continually understaffed—to go to for a few days or a few weeks. In such an environment the child's physical, emotional, and educational needs could be met. The parents then could have a break, time to care for themselves and regroup before redoubling their parenting efforts. I believe such a system would help sustain families to remain intact longer and more efficiently.

Bob W., father of three adopted teens from Kearney, Nebraska stated, "Something else Paula did when she was in the midst of this trauma—she walked around our area with headphones on—she needed to find a haven. Every night she'd go out and walk, four miles or so a night. And that was her one little time that she had by herself, away from anybody else. I think people need to realize that they have to have a break of some sort. It's important for the spouse to step in and give them that too."

Troy W. shared that their marriage was in trouble within a year of Sam's inclusion in their family. Sadly, he added, Sam was, "was destroying our marriage, and our family life was nonexistent. His behavior was so disruptive that it threatened my ability to make a living." Plus that, Sam's behavioral problems were affecting his wife Leslie's work performance as well. According to the sensitive husband, his wife had no escape, night or day, from attachment issues demonstrated by the younger of their two boys. By then Troy had left his position as a psychologist at a local state hospital and had started a private practice. The couple found they were unable to leave the youngster with sitters or in day care because of his frank antisocial, aggressive behaviors. Both were on alert, so to speak, and prepared to leave their jobs instantly when necessary to remove Sam from distressful situations and care for him. Consequently, eventually they were forced to consider alternative living options and placed Sam in a residential treatment program. Even when securely ensconced in the program Troy and Leslie continued to receive reports about Sam's unacceptable and aggressive behaviors. According to the concerned parents, there were repeated incidences of injuring staff members and escaping from the secure, locked environment.

Education

Because AD youngsters do not respond to living problems in a usual way, specialized educational programs are needed. It is imperative to expose professionals, paraprofessionals, and students of medicine, psychology, sociology, counseling, and social work to a new way of looking a parenting and treating attachment disabled kids. Biological, adoptive, fostering parents, grandparents, teachers, ministers, and police needed to be included. It is inevitable that the professionals above will eventually come in contact with AD children.

It will be helpful to all involved if they are informed so they can help or intervene in the destructive process before them, or at least, to protect themselves. This can be accomplished for parents and professionals through workshops, educational materials, and books on the topic. An increased informed dialogue between families and professionals improves the outcome for the children and their families. Because Reactive Attachment Disorder is an emotionally charged disorder, it impacts us at our most basic level, at our families. It is possible to grasp attachment problems intellectually but to entirely miss the emotional impact of these disturbed individuals on our society. Getting to know a family struggling with the problem, fully listening to their fears and heartaches, will get you closer to an understanding of the total essence of attachment disorders. Newsletters are useful tools used to announce available resources, offer therapeutic updates and successful approaches. They also promote communication and understanding between the involved parties. Specialized parenting classes, as have already been discussed, can help improve skills for those dealing with daily behaviors that chip away at the parent's strength and resolve to go on.

Mattie W., from the Great Plains region shared that before she learned of Scot's attachment disorder, she began reading everything she could find on similar behavioral problems. It seemed to her and her husband, a university professor, that there must be connection of some kind missing in his brain. They thought it was a learning disorder so took him to a regional medical center for testing. The parents were told he had some retrieval problems as Scot could absorb the information but couldn't play it back. Somehow, he excelled at math but had difficulty with reading. Out of necessity, Mattie took an active role in Scot's education and continuously worked with the teachers in an attempt to get the help he needed. In spite of his reading problem the teachers were passing Scot on to the next grade for the sole purpose of getting him out of their classroom. The couple persisted but the mother stated that the teachers and the school system fought her all the way. Every time they'd see her coming to school, they'd avoid her with a "here-she-comes-again" attitude. But Mattie found if she wasn't persistent, then nothing happened. No changes were actually accomplished until Scot was in the fifth grade. It was then that the teachers finally relented and reluctantly agreed to provide the youth with some extra help. An aide was hired to sit next to the boy throughout the day to help him organize and complete his schoolwork. Unfortunately, the child still did not do his work. When reminded to complete his work, he said to the aide, "You're getting paid for it, you do it." So all their efforts to help their son failed miserably. They wanted the changes for their boy worse than he did, a common problem with AD youngsters.

Therapy

The needs of attachment-disordered persons and their family members are so unique that resources need to be developed to meet those highly specialized needs, to facilitate early diagnosis, and to offer the intense treatment programs required. The only chance of resolving attachment issues is to introduce appropriate therapeutic interventions very early in life. Educational programs train therapists in traditional therapies but do not prepare them for this degree of disturbance. RAD children do not respond to traditional therapies because such approaches depend on an ability to trust and to be intimate with another; skills that are not available to attachment-disordered children. In addition, the family members of an AD child require a unique approach and perhaps more attention than do members of traditional families. It is imperative for therapists to receive specialized training so they can understand the unique history, behaviors, and recovery path needed by an attachment disturbed member. Then they need to be able to deliver those services in a kind, non-judgmental manner.

Jeannette N. of rural Hawai'i, tearfully discussed her feelings about her RAD daughter. The exhausted mother said she was "angry, upset, wondering how much more of this I can take. It finally got to the point where I realized that I could not give her what she needed. She didn't need just a home, family, love, structure and consistency, which I was giving her. She really needed help!" The tender foster mother of many shared that the only way she could live with her daughter was to detach with love. She worked hard at not getting caught up in her girl's emotional reactions and frequent physical outbursts. After agonizing, Jeannette finally decided the teen needed to be in a facility that provided increased security and the skills necessary to usher her into adulthood. Once her daughter was gone from the home, Jeannette experienced a "lot of relief and a whole lot of anger. I know I did the right thing because she really needed help. She was seeing a psychologist every week, but it wasn't penetrating. She needed some kind of facility where she could be under control 24 hours a day, seven days a week."

Grief assistance

I would like to speak for a moment about the grief process which must be experienced by parents *and* siblings of attachment-disordered children. Even when the family remains intact, parents must eventually grieve the loss of their "ideal" family. A family containing members with severe attachment difficulties is not the one envisioned prior to the child's birth or adoption. The difference between the hoped-for version and the reality can cause enormous emotional pain. I am told losing a child to death causes pain that never goes away. I do know that loving a child who is capable of initiating havoc in the lives of others but who must be launched into the world anyway is another potential source of overwhelming grief. Parents of dangerous AD children, or those with ineffective or no treatment, carry a yoke of sorrow and shame that is unmatched by any other parenting experience. Every parent I met harbored the idea that they were powerful enough to love the child out of their disturbance. When that did not happen, the parents shouldered the responsibility and decided it was because there was something intrinsically wrong or weak about their own character. There is enormous fear involved, both for and of the child or for the potential of harm that could be inflicted upon the world. All those feelings can overwhelm and paralyze healthier family members.

The predictable five-stage grief process, as identified by Elizabeth Kubler-Ross, has been recognized for many years. Recently Monica Acord published "The Nine Stages of Grief in Parents of RAD kids" in the KC Attachment Network newsletter. Ms. Acord believes that families living with attachment-disordered youngsters have special needs which are not solved using tried-and-true, i.e. traditional, approaches. She identified the stages of this unique process as follows: shock; denial; anger; depression; physical symptoms of distress; inability to renew normal activities; guilt feelings; gradually overcoming grief; readjustment to new realities. As with the usual process, all stages must be resolved before one can move on and experience relief or regain any balance or perspective in daily living.

D.E.H., the mother of an adopted daughter from western Nebraska, has been fortunate in working with a therapist whose had specialized training in working with RAD children and their families. She recently wrote these words during her own healing process: "I have this hard chunk of ANGER in my heart! I'm angry that some person, some supposed mother, could do this to her child, and then that child could turn on others who love and treat them so badly. The nastiness that drips from her causes my love to grow cold, my compassion to fly away, and my dreams to shatter. All the dreams of a mother-daughter relationship, all the sharing, all the hopes of someday having grandchildren are crushed under the weight of the here/now behaviors. My tears pour endlessly as I consider how much I loved, how much I still love, and how little it has mattered to her. She was a victim; she is now a victimizer. She was abused; she now abuses. She was abandoned; she now abandons."

Susan R., the mother from Overland Park, Kansas suggested: "I almost think that, potentially, adoptive families need to go and live with families that have adopted and just see the day-to-day stuff. I think there needs to be times when they could spend a couple days here, a couple days there with different adoptive families. I'm sure that at the start of privatization, people will set all these rules and regulations up aren't going to go for it. But I think some time needs to be spent. I don't think you'd see it in a weekend; I don't think you'd see it in a month. I think you need to experience this family who has adopted this kid and not just for the first two weeks. You need to really take a look and listen to them hard. I know a lot of professionals mean well, but unless you live it, I don't think you really understand. We have a thing here in Kansas called MAP training (restraining techniques used with aggressive individuals). To be an adoptive or a foster parent, you go to these MAP training sessions. I think here is one little segment there about unattached kids and about all kinds of difficulties that you may encounter. But you know, David and I didn't believe it; we thought we come from strong stock. We can do this we thought, not having any idea how hard it was going to be.

Looking back and saying, "Thank you, God, that we're still married and we're still an intact family. You need one family or two, I don't know how many it would take to just be really straightforward with people and tell some of the things you really need to think about. Everybody needs as much awareness as they can possibly get but especially if you're going to bring kids and try to blend a family. It's even gone into our marriage because I think we all would like to go around having everybody think that we have these wonderful relationships, there's no problems, and we've got everything all figured out and our sex life is great. You know, all those silly things that you read in magazines. It's not the way people live, I'm convinced of it, but I think they're lying because I think everybody struggles and they just don't want to let you know. It's made us a little bit different." Susan continued to share openly: "I take care of myself by just having time with a couple of dear friends. David is my dearest friend. We have our struggles, no doubt, but we can really get to the point where we have to sit down and talk through things. We might be a little distant or he might be a little bit busy, but bottom line is when I just can't go forward any more, I know I can come to David. It's not nearly as intense as it was because our daughter is not here, and James, virtually, isn't here. So I count on David a lot. I have two dear friends that I feel like I can tell them anything that's going on with me and they're not going to walk away from me shaking their heads, and I could do that any time of the day or night."

Parenting children who are considered "normal" is a difficult enough long-term task. Rearing an attachment-disordered youngster is so extraordinary and fraught with emotional traps that you will absolutely need the support and council of others. I encourage and support you to throw in the towel, so to speak, and give up the idea of raising your child in the isolation of your nuclear family. Do what it takes to overcome any shame or sense of failure you may be experiencing. Those strong feelings have the power to keep you away from the very support you require if you are to meet your needs or the demands of such a youngster. Members of your family of origin may not be able to comprehend what is happening to your family, even when they have the desire to do so, because of the bizarre and covert behaviors of RAD children. No doubt there have been times when even you have had difficulty believing they were real and you have been living with them! Denial is a wondrous and protective concept. No one I've ever met has wanted their child to have such severe problems. For a while it is easier, and possible, to pretend to oneself that everything is okay and the child will outgrow the extraordinary problems. Your own personal child rearing "village" may require a great deal of creativity, acceptance, and be of your own imaginative design.

CHAPTER TEN—
Faith, Hope, and Conclusions

One of the most amazing observations made during my trip across North America and England was repeatedly experiencing the tangible love the parents demonstrated toward their children. You could feel it in their words, you could see it in their faces, and then in their tears. Typical logic would make one believe that these parents might be disheartened, discouraged, and fearful both of and for their children. On the face of ample evidence one would expect they might welcome or wish the expedient removal of such a child from their home or an exit from their life completely. Those children, as you have read, left immeasurable heartache in their wake and brought unbelievable pain to naïve, unsuspecting, and unprepared families. Most parents had never dealt with such profound emotional issues or seen the seamier side of life before. Time and time again they wept over deeply felt emotions when they talked about the disturbing and sometimes unbelievable moments they'd lived through with their children.

Three British families, incomparable support for one another, come immediately to mind. They continued a daily struggle with their children in spite of the fact that they were all adults, nineteen to twenty-one years of age. The youngsters were all old enough to be out on their own, even in traditional, perhaps old-fashioned environments. The parents displayed frank grief and shared their sadness through profuse tears. As an observer I was forced to ask them "Why? What makes you continue to fight for your child? What makes you spend all your energy trying to contain this child who has played havoc and at least threatened to kill you? What keeps you from washing your hands of the problem, abandoning him or her to the authorities, hospitals, or institutions? What keeps you from running away from your children to just save yourself?" Across the hamlets and counties their answers were identical and would appear somewhat nonsensical in the minds of those less informed: We love them. No one else loves or understands them as we do. No one else can care about how this turns out like we do. No one understands their needs as clearly as we can. They do not deserve a bad life; they did not bring this on themselves. They are disturbed or sick because of what happened to them when they were young. They did not have a choice; they were the victims of unloving, uneducated, or neglectful parents. We know it does not make a bit of sense, but in spite of all that has happened, in spite of all they have done and continue to do, they are our children and we love them!

Some of the parents I met were forced, because of terrible circumstances or lack of adequate resources, to sadly relinquish their children back into the system from whence they came. Even under those extreme circumstances the parents experienced overwhelming, protracted periods of grief. On the heels of their life with their disturbed and disturbing children many were diagnosed with a condition common to those returning from active combat called PTSD. Even under such dire circumstances most experienced a rage of their own toward the social workers, the adoption agencies, or the systems that had closed their eyes to their plight. Few, if any, leveled their frustration toward the child themselves. They knew, from a source deep within, that blaming the true victim of neglect—their child—was unacceptable. All knew, to the depth of their souls, that crippling sense of loss that accompanies the removal of an untreated disturbed child who's been unable to bond and whose placement has failed. Both the children and their families will bear the scars of unsuccessful placements for the rest of their lives. Families are left with grief, resentment, and the loss of trust in their basic social systems. Tragically, the young ones become more damaged and potentially more lethal than ever before.

However, when the combining of strangers into family units works, when placements go well, it is the most incredible miracle that exists in modern times! Attachment disturbed kids are born into a world where the deck is stacked against them, so they develop into complicated individuals. By some stroke of luck (or perhaps another silent miracle) they found themselves placed in families with adults who would not give up on them. I believe the parents I met were perfect matches for children with attachment difficulties. The young ones become champion rejecters; the selected parents were militant lovers in action! One common trait among the American, Canadian, and British families was their dogged tenacity. Theirs was a dance of incredible power that possessed a beauty all its own. The intricacies of the unique relationships between injured youngsters and tough, determined parents was lost on all those but a few sensitive individuals who could grasp and understand the delicate, complicated interactions between them.

Fred was a wild animal-like 8-year-old when he was placed with a loving, experienced therapeutic foster couple in Colorado. A psychiatrist, in his ignorance and desperation to treat Fred, had placed him on a daily dose of 800mg of Mellaril, a major antipsychotic medication. Such a dose might be enough to immobilize a large animal. When the child arrived at the Colorado home he wore a diaper, drooled, was lethargic, and could not go to school or function on any intellectual level. His behaviors remained animalistic but were executed almost in slow motion. Fortunately for Fred, his foster parents were experienced with attachment disorder, knew exactly what the problem was, and immediately began taking charge of Fred's life. Under the guidance of a knowledgeable psychiatrist, the Mellaril was the first to go. Today, four years later, Fred is a magnificent kid! He has bonded tightly to his parents, attends regular school, and is in full control of all his faculties. His skin is no longer sallow or his eyes dull and lackluster. He is medication free and he shines! He smiles a deep smile that starts in his soul and sends flashes of light to his eyes. Fred's dimples seem to wink as he talks. You can tell he has come miles and is no longer attachment-disordered by his incredible response to both parents. Fred's sincerity is profound. He hugs his parents, openly and unabashedly professes his love for them, and at 12 he is able to follow directions, tell the truth, think through and talk about his problems as he calmly takes appropriate action. However, young Fred must constantly practice his hard-won skills, including risking the temptation to be a guppy for the childish and sinister pranksters around him, and can now utilize successful skills that were not available to him while he was emotionally unbonded. His successes have become possibilities because he was blessed with new parents and some professionals who knew about attachment difficulties. Behold the power of knowledge!

Clare and Blair are parents of two boys from western Canada. Their second son, an adopted child, showed severe signs of attachment difficulties from early in his placement with them. During the personal interviews they shared about the trials they had hurdled with him. Both were pleased, but remain cautious, about the progress "D" had made in their home. Both parents demonstrated a wild, kind, but unconventional sense of humor and believed that trait had been extremely helpful in meeting the challenge of rearing a special needs child such as "D." In a recent letter the proud woman wrote: ""D" turned 13 this year. We've given him the motto 'It sucks to be you.' He has brought more insight into our lives and I'm always amazed by how much I learn about myself through "D." He is a tremendous teacher. He has never let us down, always providing new learning opportunities for us. We have made it through the first 6 months of his teens. Only 78 more to go. "D" has grown more than anyone in the family. He works hard to fight his daily challenges and is doing a remarkable job. School is getting easier for him to manage and socially he has begun to realize the value of good friends. He continues to need support, but the support is not nearly as intense and "D" is able to manage life more responsibly. These days he spends every free moment snowboarding; he loves it. I can't watch."

Sarah and Rex D. took son David to New York to receive the specialized therapy offered by Dr. Welch. Sarah stated: "To be honest, the weekends are a lot lighter because now he will redirect or he will stop. He may still get mad but there's been no more destruction. We had his whole room redone, in a sense to reward him, but mostly to say this is a fresh start. Every wall had to be re-plastered and fixed and painted. The windows got fixed; we'd just boarded them up. We said, hell, if you're going to break more windows, there's no point in fixing them. We did say to him, we cannot afford to be replacing things daily or weekly." They instituted a behavior-mod type of a program although they did not believe it would be beneficial.

As his behavior improved, they gradually replaced the items missing from his room. "He started with a mattress and a pillow and pretty quickly he got the headboard and foot board, the springs. I mean, we went in little spurts." They decided they did not want to return items too rapidly and have to restart the entire process over again. "So now," she continued, "he's got everything back in his room plus a couple of new things. He got a little clock radio. Oh, my gosh, now when he gets mad, that's the first thing he protects! He doesn't grab the clock radio and throw it like he would have before. Before he would have just destroyed anything, and especially because we gave it to him. He's just so angry, but teeny-tiny things are changing. Sometimes I get very frustrated because I think we should be further along," but that's when she's forgotten his background. When the mother returns to herself, she sees that he was able to attend school an entire day occasionally. He was able to play with the kids down the street and not be a bully and not come home crying or send one of them home mad. "The other kids don't usually cry. They're just like, 'Well, we're done; we don't put up with that behavior. Bye.' I have to remind myself to slow down." The couple believes the biggest changes their son has made are with those behaviors that stem back to when he was eighteen to twenty-four months old. The noted changes seem to be coming in the area of bathroom, hygiene, and social skills. The mother excitedly continued, "I mean he doesn't poop his pants any more he uses the bathroom appropriately. I haven't had to scrub the carpet every other minute like I was doing. Now he brushes his teeth!"

Toward the end of her interview ***Kristin C.*** of rural Indiana, stated emphatically: "I'm crazy about Ryan. The last hospitalization and the psychiatrist and the medication and the methods have turned this kid into a neat kid. He hasn't gotten angry since late December. He and I write in a journal several times a week. I love hugging him. I love teasing him. I love trusting him and I'm enjoying him! Michaela is still distant, her heart is still somewhere else and she stiffens when I try to hug her. She can emotionally shut down on you just as quickly as she did when she first came to live with us. She goes deep, deep inside of herself where nothing can hurt her. Both of them are Honor Roll students; both of them are healthy and physically active. They're intelligent; they contribute to the community. They are good with animals and that's a big thing at our house. I've read and I believe that if a child feels loved, if a child gives himself permission to believe he is home, that he will physically change. Ryan has grown three inches in about three months."

David and Susan from the Kansas City area have been so encouraged by the growth experiences they gained through the lives with their first two attachment affected children that they have adopted a third child. Micah, 2 at the time of our interview, already kept Susan busy and extremely fulfilled. The pleased mom shared, "I get to stay home with Micah and that's what we decided when he was born and that was our plan. It's almost like I get to have too much fun; it's almost too lopsided.

Why should I get to do all this and have all this fun and David has to go and work hard all day?"

These pages are filled with suggestions, ideas of how to care for oneself on a personal level while still living in the midst of child-driven turmoil. These pearls of wisdom came from the wonderful parents I had the pleasure of meeting. They are practical, loving ideas, which came out of their pain and similar daily struggles. The second half includes recommendations that could be applied in a preventative manner on both continents. Prevention programs are of the utmost importance to diminish the ever-growing numbers of families living in chaos and turmoil, not a problems that is limited to our country alone.

Personal Care

When loving and living with attachment-disordered individuals it is imperative to take care of self. When parents continue to fall for the manipulation of their child, or do not recognize their tricks in the first place, they sacrifice themselves and their love for the child. If a decision to ignore oneself helped the child, any child, I would support and encourage more sacrifice. But it doesn't. This book is about children with out-of-control behaviors. The more out-of-control they feel internally the more pressure they exert on those around them. As you have learned, the desire to be "in charge" leads to enormous control battles within the family. A challenge to the parents of such a child is to learn to care for self–*first*–then model those behaviors for their children. I can already hear, "But you don't understand! This kid takes everything I have then, venomously, spits it back at me." That is, after all, the nature of this particular beast. The good news: parents of these kids are so frazzled and worn-out, their capacity to become good students increases dramatically. Willingness to share and change is borne of one's emotional and psychological desperation.

Here's a dreaded generalization for you: I believe that the British, Canadian, and American parents I met were more readily equipped to tend to the needs of others than they were to care for themselves. There was a fear, especially among the women, that they might grow up to be selfish. It was under that banner that mothers, as well as most of the fathers I interviewed, had difficulty identifying their own needs or then getting them met. Out of boundless love for their families many adults seemed to have gotten lost in the shuffle. In spite of that, or perhaps because of it, the interviewees were willing to provide me with ideas or suggestions of how to care for self that could be passed on to other parents of difficult children. They believed that sharing with others was one of the gifts they had to give to the world. They are shared ideas the parents had tried and considered useful in making their own situation more livable. Remember that these are *real* parents who are still in the process of doing the fieldwork with young, tough customers. Their experiences are invaluable and I would be remiss if I did not pass them on to the reader. Here are their suggestions:

First, pray…

…for the children, their parents, and for the professionals. I've grown to believe the problem of Attachment Disorder is the sign of a spiritual problem. If that is really true then the basic solution to it must also be spiritual in nature. I also have come to understand that attachment compromised children, like their healthier siblings, are gifts from God, a Higher Source, or from whomever you believe rules the universe. AD children are the toughest individuals in the world with one exception: their parents. The more I learn on the topic it still seems to me in His mercy He handpicked parents and children to go together; a matched set. The parents I encountered were either frankly religious or quietly spiritual and their decisions to give a home to a tough child came out of their core beliefs about their role in this world. It appears to me that the tougher the kid, their life-assisting adults also became more stubborn and tenacious. Although the parents continually thought they might not outlive their children—they have, they do, and they are continuing to survive. Their most useful and powerful defensive position has been on their knees with their heads bowed and hands folded. That may actually be the only real option available to effect changes in the twisted thinking and bizarre behaviors of those children who are loved beyond their comprehension.

Prepare Yourself

Susan R. reported she grew through her experiences and now believes adoptive and foster families need more preparation than is required of biological families. Susan suggested it would be beneficial "to go and live with families that have adopted and just see the day-to-day stuff." That's not a process the Kansas mother thinks should be rushed. Under the best of circumstances parents-to-be should spend several days with a variety of adoptive families in order to get the full flavor of what could lie ahead. She doesn't feel a weekend would be long enough to learn the needed lessons. The intelligent mom felt that although she and her husband had prepared themselves thoroughly for the addition of new children to their family, in reality they had no clue what a difficult task lay before them. Out of concern for new families she recommended they understand that it is possible for anyone to receive a transplanted child with problems similar to the ones Susan and David experienced.

Eat, sleep—don't forget the basics

If I believed giving yourself away, emotionally and a piece at a time, to save your disturbed child would work—even for a second—I'd strongly recommend such a saintly approach. Unfortunately, it doesn't work and then the family is in danger of losing more than just one member. I often compare having no limits or no boundaries with the basis of all life, the cell. Individual boundaries, in my mind, are comparable to the protective outer wall of a cell: the layer gives character and sets limits. A cell without boundaries is considered cancerous. It is aggressive with the goal of invading healthy tissues of nearby organs. A healthy individual must develop the ability to say "no" to those activities and people who would drain them of energy or strength needed to get through the day. Over the years I've known several boundary-less individuals: initially they appear to be limitless in their generosity, but under a thin façade of perfection they are exhausted, scattered, and unable to focus on any one thing for long. On the other hand, those who were clear about their roles and responsibilities, who were focused and had ample energy to step out of the way of another's necessary growth experiences, in the long view, fared the adventures of adulthood and parenthood best.

Take time for yourself daily to read, rest, daydream, and play

An individual who is all-give eventually dries up without a means of supplying their own energy or needs. It seems that in our American culture "doing nothing" is not valued as a worthwhile pastime. Many creative folks, the dreamers among us, have been considered lazy or good-for-nothing. But the truth is that we are renewed when we take the time to rest or play or just do nothing. RAD children, by their very nature, are incredibly needy and can suck parents dry. I believe parenting to be the most creative and demanding activity in existence—and totally impossible if attempted by dry, lifeless adults. Among the continuous chaos it is difficult for parents to remember that they, too, have needs which *must* also be met.

Stay in contact with others, in person or by phone

Many of the mothers, out of frustration, shame, or fear of being misunderstood, became isolated and isolative. In their solitude two things happened: they became even more of a victim of their children's rage and they slowly began to lose touch with reality. In the recesses of their own minds they began to believe they had caused their children's problems or that they alone were the solution to their overwhelming difficulties. What an unbelievable dilemma! Such ideas are eventually "crazy-making" for the woman or man who has already found themselves alone, unsupported, and overly responsible. It is imperative to make oneself lift the seemingly thousand-pound telephone receiver and to reach out to others who have had similar experiences. For your sanity you must take the risks necessary to establish that all-important supportive link with others.

Tell your truth and share your deepest feelings

After enough professionals tell parents they are "the crazy one," most parents work very hard to develop a façade of normalcy. That usually involves stoicism, phoniness, and a "smile though your heart is breaking" approach to daily life. The problem with that, aside from the fact that it's a lie, is that it deepens the level of denial and adds to the feelings of craziness within the family. The obvious antidote is to tell the truth. Everyone you know will not be able to hear you or to support you. It would be terrific if even most of those who listened to you turned out to be believers, but that's not probable. Your job is to find the one(s) who can hear you and then spill your guts, so to speak. The very act of speaking your truth, while it is frightening is also powerfully healing. Your search is not over until you find someone with whom you can be emotionally honest and share your tears.

Commit to dating your spouse

Many adults I met during the interview process told me about the price exacted from their marriages. Children with severe attachment issues are champs at "splitting" parents, families, etc., a tactic used to keep the heat off them. Such behaviors have caused enormous strife between couples, families, and outside sources of assistance. Many couples told me about divorces that occurred in the wake of the incredible stress placed on their marital union. But the healthy couples, and I met many wonderful ones, were finally able to establish their relationship as their first priority and then act accordingly. They told me that if they weren't able to save their marriage from the onslaught of attachment related behaviors, they would not be able to salvage their family or its' individual members. Once the partners re-committed to each other the destructive, divisive behaviors of their disturbed children lost their power to destroy peace and joy within the family. It did not necessarily signal increased happiness of the AD children, but the family members began enjoying life again. Thus, the tone and tenor of the family changed significantly, led by happy, satisfied parents. The disturbed members then had the choice to change, to join in or not.

Develop respite cares

Hand picking your own "relatives" can be fun and will bring many unforeseen advantages into your life. I suggest that you do it up BIG—choose those who are ultra loveable and accepting of you, then have a ceremony and a full-on celebration! Often, during the rough times there is so little to celebrate with attachment disturbed children that such a party can be fun and provide the encouragement and pizzazz that might be missing from your day-to-day life. Sometimes those unrelated to you can offer more empathy than can relatives-by-birth and can gift you with the love, caring, peace, and respite you have sorely missed, and the personal attention you require to go on.

Spend time with your other children

I'm sure by now you have discovered that it is the very nature of AD children to attempt to rule the roost. They want to be "the Director" or "the Boss" to the detriment of all the members of the family, including themselves. My greatest sense of regret, which was echoed by the international cast of parents of similar kids, was related to the difficulty I had in giving *all* my children the attention they needed. Thus, my suggestion is for you to make and take frequent opportunities to spend quiet, happy times with your other children. After all, guarding the mental health of your brood has become your driving goal. Fulfilling that aim may require colossal expenditure of energy on your part, but one that has life long value.

Get counseling, grieve with assistance

I understand that one of your goals is to get your disturbed child into therapy. But if you're a usual family (if there is such a thing) with a RAD child there may be periods when professional assistance is either impossible or unavailable. Even so, there should be nothing stopping you from getting the emotional help and support you need. It is not my intention to be insulting and indicate that you are unbalanced. However, I do know the devastating toll life with AD children exacts and about the bone deep loneliness that goes with the forced isolation. Fortunately, your therapeutic needs are not as specialized as your child's, so locating a loving, nurturing counselor who can help you cope with stress and to strengthen your already significant survival skills should not be at all burdensome.

Take up a hobby; do something beside kids

Do whatever is necessary to regain your sense of wholeness and value and to become part of a healthy, vibrant world. Finding a class that feeds you should be a snap. Years ago I remember thinking that macramé for mama might be a valuable thing. Although I didn't do much of it the thought of working with rope and beads appealed to me as a welcome break from screaming, demanding babies. What did not get past me, however, was the importance of doing something—*in addition to*—child rearing. At one time I raised fifty houseplants, which blossomed to my touch. Gardening can be an enormously therapeutic for parents of AD kids. To classify this particular group of parenting adults as "simply nurturing" does them a gross disservice. Their native ability to care for others goes far beyond the norm. They give not to get back, but because they were, perhaps, born to give; it's an integral part of their nature. It would be lovely for them to get something in return, but unreasonable to expect any such return will come from AD children. Therefore, gardening is a natural solution. Flowers and vegetables bloom and grow under the loving eyes and gentle hands of the gardener. They provide beauty, nourishment, and peace to the world. And, like houseplants, they do not talk back, a trait most parents thoroughly appreciate.

Join a support group, or start one

I suppose misery really does love company. However, there is *no one* who will understand your feelings and fears and concerns like another parent who has tried to love an attachment disturbed child. Most parents, because of the covert nature of AD kids, feel crazy and are isolated from their usual support systems. I recall the very first time I found myself in a group of parents who were also becoming aware of their children's difficulties. It was a feeling I am still unable to describe but it was a miraculous gift to me on the heels of eight years of social and familial isolation. It might have been a bit like going to another country, one who's language I had not learned; or like going to Mars. Folks I'd never met were consoling me and assuring me that there indeed was a problem, first, and that now, too, there might be a solution. My experiences were suddenly validated, something that had never before happened during my life as a mother. Every time I am with parents who have had similar experiences I get an enormous sense of relief. I observe it among newer parents as well; you can see their pain flow from them mixed with their tears. There was nothing in my life with my child that was as healing as being with others who truly understand. No more pretending, no more hiding.

Recruit help to get your needs met

AD children do so well with strangers that it pays to hire a few to give you an occasional break. You might recall times when you described the devil you lived with only to have the saintly version appear in person. Part of the illness is to make you look and feel crazy as it takes the heat off them. So whenever you let it slip that your child is not what he/she appears to be, the challenge (to them) is on! They are driven to present the very opposite of how you have painted them. The hiring of a babysitter (preferably one who is a stranger to the child) is the perfect time to depend on a state of phony angel-hood adopted by most attachment disturbed kids. I suggest that you instruct the childcare attendant in front of the child, making sure to tell them that your child will be absolutely *unable* to follow their instructions. It is okay to tell them the truth about his/her real personality traits, but you may not want to tell them about *all* of them. Then say they can't follow directions because they are too young or too weak or too small (which pulls them onto your playing field!). Of course, it may scare the liver out of the sitter, but it will present a challenge to your child they may not be able to pass up—to be good as gold and to prove you a liar! Then you can take a break knowing the sitter is ready for mayhem and that the child will be as sweet as pie. Of course, if your child remains phony and angel-like around extended family members, use them while they are available to you. There are two points not to be missed: you need a break and the child needs active supervision, sometimes even into their adolescence.

Develop and use a "parenting mentor"

Another idea with merit is the use of parenting mentors. For example, a "mommy mentor" is a woman who is experienced and has successfully reared her family. She now has the personal resources to be of emotional, and perhaps physical, support to younger, less experienced mothers. Parents of attachment-disordered youngsters are in dire need of the guidance of veteran parents whose AD children are already grown. During the interviews the calmest and most satisfied parents were those who had the benefit of guidance from parents whose families were similar to their own. Having survived their own battlefields left some fortunate individuals with the status of a sage. Out of their own pain mothers and fathers alike gladly gave support and assistance to the newer generation of parents. At times their wisdom was shared in support group meetings, over the telephone, or in person during times of family crises.

Seek out appropriate professionals

A good place to start in finding the right therapist for your child is in the back of this book. Appendix 1 offers a "Resource List" with names and addresses of many of the professionals in the U.S. and abroad who possess the skills your child may require. In addition, don't hesitate to call or write any of the resources to request credentials, references, or names of former or current clients who you can interview. Organizations relating to the education about Attachment Disorders, such as ATTACh or Adoption UK, maintain a list of current professionals in the field. I am certain that a phone call to the identified agencies will lead you in a direction that will be therapeutic for your child and your family.

Don't waste time in useless therapy

Throughout the stories presented in this book are the heartbreaks of wasting valuable resources, energy, time, or money, on therapies that cannot work with professionals who do not have the skills necessary to help attachment disturbed youngsters. I suppose some form of desperation or loyalty leads parents to believe if they hang in there long enough, a miracle will occur. When parents of attachment compromised children find empathetic therapists, their personal traits of willingness and kindness are seductive, especially following experiences with the unkind, judgmental variety. One needs to remember, however, that the window of opportunity for successful treatment of kids with RAD is narrow. Since time is of the essence, thoroughly research potential therapists and treatment centers for their appropriateness to your situation. Fortunately, today those resources are becoming more plentiful. There are a couple of generalities you need to consider; traditional therapies—talk, play, or group—tend to be ineffective. If your child remains phony throughout the sessions or seems to be calling the shots, it's time to consider a change. First, however, discuss your concerns with the therapist as such an opportunity could be an effective tool for either improving the therapeutic approach or for judging the overall therapeutic value to the child. Invite therapists who seem unaware of newer, more effective approaches to call some of the resources at the back of this book for additional training.

Laugh, develop an appreciation for wacky behaviors

As long as parents believe they are the cause of their child's bizarre behaviors, evidence of those traits will increase parental fears or their feelings of guilt or shame. It will be helpful to nurture the belief that your child does whatever he or she does because it makes him/her feel better or because it makes sense *to them*. That is a far cry from he/she does it "*to me*" or "*because of me*." After many years of feeling sorry for myself because of how he treated *me* I realized he always treated himself poorly, as well. It is impossible to enjoy what is happening around you while you sit on a "pity pot." When you are able to separate yourself from your child's pathology, it becomes possible to watch and appreciate the creativity required by someone attempting to raise themselves without one iota of knowledge of how to accomplish that feat. You know you don't know how to rear them; and there is no way possible that they have it figured out either! A common trait among the interviewees was a wacky, off-kilter sense of humor. So develop a laugh however you can; silly movies or fanciful play are good starts. The kind that bubbles up from way down deep inside you, the kind that reassures you that although all looks crazy around you, you are really all right.

Know your limits

Central California is the home to concerned parents of four youngsters. *Sam and Samantha* made the following suggestions: "Learn about yourself, if you have the potential to be abusive do not adopt as these kids who are begging to be abused. Know your limits." That included being aware of one's financial limitations following many very expensive lessons with their disturbed child. They heartily recommended that parents need to have adequate financial resources if they are to be able to handle the expensive financial requirements of children with attachment problems. Most of all, they said, "Be honest about your motivation to adopt. Know how much you're willing to give up."

Get other parenting experiences

Bob, husband to Tara from Alberta, added to the conversation, "I think you have to be a parent first to even begin. I don't think you could do this a first time, this being your only child. I don't think you would be able to cope. Kids always, from the time they're born, are always trying to push buttons, and these kids try and push them more." He believed that the frustration level of raising a RAD child first might be crippling without having some additional, healthy, parenting experiences beforehand. He said, "I think that you'd end up banging your head against the wall because you wouldn't be able to separate AD behaviors from normal behaviors."

Educate yourself

Martha G. of Kansas City, Missouri suggested that before an adoption occurs that every adoptive parent spend time with parents of RAD kids. It would be her hopes that some of the disillusionment inherent in facing the reality of this disorder could be diminished with an introduction to reality on a personal, one-to-one level. "There's nothing wrong with anyone else for doing this, for believing that we can make a difference and that we will made a difference in a child's life. I think we need to have that belief." Martha's beliefs were so deeply embedded that the reality of her situation was unable to get through her "love-will-cure-all" thinking. She believes some intimate personal experience with a family living with attachment difficulties would be very helpful in the long run. One suggestion was to have therapeutic sessions with a family currently in the throes of the illness; visit a therapeutic foster family; assign a book to read or a video on the topic. Martha thought educating the potential parents and providing them with an understanding of attachment problems would be a start in the right direction. Also, attend every workshop or seminar on the topic that you can locate.

Become fully informed

The Nebraska couple, *Dan and Mattie*, think their own awakening process has changed them significantly. "We're more cautious; we're more knowledgeable," Mattie shared. They wholeheartedly believe the prospective parents need to be fully informed of their child's history and potential. They struggle with the idea that the news might frighten off prospective parents. Often, however, their denial systems of the inexperienced families remain intact. One new mother told the couple that attachment difficulties would never happen in her home because she and her husband wouldn't allow it. So while the mature couple exercises caution when advising new parents, they are also "a lot more truthful with them." Many "just have to find out for themselves," Mattie stated wistfully.

Make thoughtful decisions

When I asked *Nancy R.* of rural Kansas what she needed to make such a difficult job more manageable she stated: "Respite care. An understanding family, not my kids and my husband, but my extended family." Her birth family was not able to understand or offer their support. Consequently, she had a great need for a designed support system including people "who know about this kind of child." When asked what she would say to prospective parents, "I would want them to be very, very careful. Don't be rushed. Do not be rushed into making a quick decision before you are really, truly convinced that that child is the child for you." In hindsight, Nancy said she was concerned right away that the adoption workers were pushing the couple to make a quick decision. She added that she was so afraid that if we did not immediately take the child being offered that they might not get another child. And, she said sadly, her notion that the love could overcome all obstacles was untrue.

Make a commitment

One of the experienced couples, Sarah D. and her husband Rex, spoke at length with a woman from their support group. The knowledgeable mother explained that she was going to New York City with her family for treatment with Dr. Welch. Sarah had just read Welch's *Holding Time* the week before but needed to read it again and give it more thought. If the couple decided they wanted to do holdings with their son they were sure Welch would help. Sarah added, but first "We needed to see about getting ourselves to New York and we needed to decide if we were committed enough to David to stick it out. If we were, well then, by God, we'd better get his butt out of Call Valley, a long-term institution, because all they were doing is reinforcing the non-attachment."

Be persistent

Kristin C. of rural Rome, Indiana; the now experienced mother shared, "Something that would have helped me from the beginning is if someone would have said these kids have attachment issues. These are the things you're going to go through because we already know Ryan kicks and Michaela steals. You need to locate this psychiatrist within a month and start sessions. I was messing around with our local counseling center, and they, in their well-meaning egos, make things worse. I needed someone who could get in my kid's face and say, 'I'm not like anyone you've ever met. I know how to help you and this is the way it's going to be. Because if you can't handle it, you're going to the psychiatric hospital.' I needed someone to point the finger at the kid first and set limits on the kid with skill and expertise before they even get around to pointing a finger at me. There were things that I needed to do differently, also. I'm as tenacious as a bulldog! I understand what it means to advocate for my kids and, by God, that is what I was going to do."

Become an activist

Paula W. shared that when you're in the midst of undiagnosed attachment disorders, it is nearly impossible to comprehend or to see the big picture. "There are times that you just go berserk. You're not perfect; you just don't know how to hold it together because there's no support." Having survived their daughter, they now want to start a support group and to actively help others in similar situations. "If I ever get a word that someone might have an attachment-disordered child, I send them a brochure and I don't care if they look at it and throw it away," stated the midwestern mother. Paula's husband, Bob added: "We've met some counselors-in-training at the university. They ask our group to come in so we could reach out to the professionals and reach out to other parents which is a source of strength for us, too."

Establish realistic expectations

Martha G. stated that potential parents need to look at their motives for adopting and their expectations of their new child. The adoptive mother was most emphatic about establishing realistic expectations of each child, "because that's when we've gotten into the most trouble along the way." In response to questions about those expectations, Martha shared that she was so shocked to witness or be victim to her children's violent reactions that she found it difficult to discipline in a way that did not engage her anger. She found herself shaming them for the way they were and became mortified about her own reactions to them. She also wants guidance with her own parental responses that would be helpful and loving for the child. Martha added, "We need to see and hear hopeful stories along the way. If we can't find hopeful stories we need to find ways that, day-by-day, we can live with it so that we're not afraid and we're not disheartened every single day."

Share experiences with others

Mattie W., said, "If your family can survive a kid like this, you're certainly stronger than you were before, and if a marriage can survive, that's even better. Our marriage is strong; it's great." When they finally decided they needed to remove their son Scot from the home, they "believed we were doing a good thing for us. So I think it's made us more understanding in a lot of ways." On the heels of their painful experiences the midwestern couple have supported and shared themselves with other parents both in their area and across the United States. "And I think," Mattie stated emphatically, "maybe that's what it was all about. We were supposed to go through this so that we could maybe help somebody else, some other time. You know, all they need to know is that somebody's listening to them." For years they did not know what was wrong with their son, but they learned about RAD by persistently researching the topic themselves. They believed they were the only family in the world with a kid like Scot and wondered what they'd done to deserve him, but they experienced significant relief once they found an organization made up of other parents like themselves. Finally, there were others with whom they could share their common concerns. "Then," the mother stated, "you don't feel like such a complete failure."

Reality test

Bob W., "I think one of the keys for us was finally finding out what we were dealing with because before that it's like walking around in a fog.

You know you're in trouble, but you don't know which side it comes from, what it is, how to solve it. The support we had from people in the church, some friends and my mother was another key. That was really important because otherwise you tend to second-guess yourself. Well, maybe I'm really the problem. Even after Susie was diagnosed, Paula kept saying 'Am I the problem? Am I the problem?' I wasn't very good support to Paula early on. If hugs have been denied, the wife is almost doomed and we've seen some other marriages that have crashed. Just a little handout we received with the different symptoms of attachment disorder was probably the most helpful thing. Susie was a very classic case of attachment disorder, but wasn't as severe a case as we've seen since. She's got a much better chance than most people have in her situation. She was 17 years old before we found out what she had. If we'd known when she was ten, maybe we could have done something."

Don't pretend another life

The Midwestern *Susan R.* said, like many others, there were times when she tried to be too independent and to pretend that all is well, even in the middle of chaos. She admitted there were many times in her home "when we weren't doing fine, we absolutely weren't. And I suppose there were times when I was too proud to say to people 'It's just awful.' Finally, I think I have come to a place where I can say that to some people, not everybody. I can just have a big old cry with somebody and not feel bad and that's a good thing." Yet, Susan stated, "I think I make people uncomfortable sometimes when I really share with them some of the tough things that still go on. I don't want to embarrass James; that's not my point, but I'm okay with where he is because it's a reality of his life. I'm sad that Ann is making the choices that she's making, but I'm not going to make up stories and pretend that she has this wonderful life. She doesn't and I don't want to sugar coat any of that." It is Susan's hope that by talking about the realities of her life, maybe one person will hear something that is helpful to them. Susan gives herself permission to share even if someone less experienced is slightly uncomfortable by her openness and honesty. "I won't send anybody screaming from the room if I admit that I've got a kid a little bit off center." She believes that frank sharing gives others encouragement to express their own feelings and frustrations "even when we don't have any answers. At least they can unload a bit and maybe not have such a heavy burden on their shoulders."

Protect yourself

Leslie W. shared her thoughts about living with Sam: "I cannot go back to living like that. I don't like it. I have to work through the grieving and the guilt and every once in a while it hits me. And then I think maybe he does need to come home and we need to try it again and if it fails, it's okay. Well, you know it's not going to work. The thought of even going through a few months of it is not appealing to me at all. We have agreed that we will be his family; we're not going to have the adoption set aside. We will be his family, no matter what. But it may mean that he's not living with us and it took a lot for me to get to that. That's okay. I really have to protect myself."

Hang in there, Don't give up—yet

Sarah D., of Kansas talked about her involvement in the ATTACh support group. After reading the extensive old records for their son she and her husband knew they needed to take some action but were unclear just what that might be. She and her husband thought they had abandoned their child by taking him for treatment to an institution that used isolation and food as consequences for unacceptable behaviors. They were afraid that particular behavior modification program would deepen the wounds and further disturb any developing attachments. "I mean, we put him in Call Valley. He's out there, I'm thinking that was best for him. Then the thought that went through my head is 'I cannot give up on this boy. We cannot give up on this boy!' I don't know if he can live with us, but I cannot give up yet!"

Just do the best you can

Tara W., is the parent of a young girl who received treatment for RAD. Tara suggested: "It's okay to get time away. You can talk for hours and hours and hours. You become so wrapped up in their problems so it's almost like your life is controlled without even realizing what's happening. I didn't even realize how stressed out I was really. You're just walking on pins and needles all the time and you're trying to do everything right and everything's just a struggle. And you don't want to have to deal with the struggle but just going to the support group and being able to say that and letting your frustration and your guilt go. Because you're thinking, 'This is just a tiny little girl and I'm so angry. Why am I feeling this way? Why can't I reach this baby? I'm such a horrible rotten parent because I can't reach this little girl. This little girl is just going to get worse if I don't reach her.' You just have this overwhelming guilt about it. And to be able to say that and not feel like you're going to be judged because you're saying that really helps to know that taking time for yourself is okay." According to the young mother it's not possible to control or be responsible for everything, but she found herself trying to do just that. Tara reported that she thought that if she and her spouse controlled everything then nothing bad would happen to their daughter. Her goal was to never leave her daughter alone, but, she said wistfully, "You can't live your life like that. And don't feel guilty! Don't feel that it's your fault that you haven't reached this child. It's not your fault and just do the best you can."

Above all, count on God (Buddha, Allah, Yahweh…)

Susan R. talked about how different she is now that she has parented two attachment disturbed children. "It's made me realize how there are so many different families and situations out there and I wouldn't have had a clue; I had this little Ozzie and Harriet view of life." While driving through the city the ironies of life were not lost on her. "There are a lot of 'My kid's on the honor roll' bumper stickers on cars around here. I was never driving James to soccer practice; I was always driving him to the probation office." Her son was 10 at the time and that was not a pleasant task. "But you work it through. You just do it!" Susan is quite certain one doesn't necessarily *have* to cope with the situation and could, instead, just feel miserable. But, she made a conscious decision that she didn't want to sit around feeling miserable, "so I guess it's made me stretch." She's learned to depend on her husband more and to reach out to others for the support that she's needed, but mostly, the young mother stated clearly, "It's made me count on God more, to ask for help and to say I can't do this alone."

Prevention, Nationally and Internationally!

At the beginning there is the bonding process. Most professionals who work with attachment compromised children now believe that the process actually begins before birth. I share that belief, which drives many of my recommendations for prevention programs. Nurturing can be taught; it can be made up or replaced when there has been a deficiency. It is imperative that we nurture each other and then teach parents and potential parents to do the same. That is the basis of almost all of the proposed programs that follow. Some of the following ideas may currently be in practice, but other may be underdeveloped or not yet in use:

Pre-and Post-natal Parenting Classes

Like many other states, Hawai'i discovered that it was fiscally responsible to be proactive in their dealings with families with special needs. The Casey Family Programs, leaders in family and childcare, are already teaching at-risk mothers. "High Risk" mothers and children are those who grew up in dysfunction, abuse and poverty, or those who have already demonstrated difficulties with emotional or mental health issues. The Honolulu program began with mothers who were receiving welfare support and parents who had been reported to Hawai'i's Child Protective Services (CPS) due to parenting deficiencies or irregularities. Unfortunately, mothers known to be drug or alcohol abusers were not included in the program. The plan required parents from both social agencies to receive extensive therapy and parenting classes in an effort to fill their knowledge and experience gaps. The parents receiving welfare were already receiving "Med Quest," a state medical plan, so the monies were already available for therapists and counselors who would assist them in this program. When using such a bold plan both private and public therapists and medical personnel were utilized to teach mother and baby care classes. Parents were grouped by the child's age and then provided varied skills in dealing with their youngsters from before birth through their adolescence.

Keith Kuboyama, a social worker starts at the beginning. He said the pre-and post-natal classes emphasized the use of nurturing skills using reading, playing music and singing to the child, as well as techniques for soothing the unborn baby *and* the mother. Parents are taught the basics, everything from bonding techniques to feeding, safety, potty training, and the like. Many parents participate in the program from early pregnancy throughout their child's adolescence. Pre-and post-natal classes have been offered long enough by Casey Family Programs that they are now helping the second generation of clients. Kuboyama reported that they are very encouraged by the dramatic behavioral improvements they are seeing in the second-generation children—the mothers were calmer, had more confidence, and consequently, were more loving with their own youngsters.

Early Diagnosis

For those little ones who do not come into this world under prime conditions, there is still hope. The sooner our children are identified, the greater the chances of undoing any harm that may have occurred since the nature of these particular children is so tough. The rule of thumb is the sooner the symptoms appear, the more severe the illness. I recall observing a three-month old girl, the foster child of a couple in the San Luis Obispo area, who was already demonstrating recognizable symptoms of attachment problems. Now, however, the chances for that particular little girl are fantastic for several reasons. Fortunately, the foster parents were told the truth about her early traumatic experiences. They were well educated in the RAD symptoms and prognosis with and without treatment and had already established a therapeutic relationship with a knowledgeable professional. Thanks to early intervention a therapeutic alliance was established and through intensive work with the parents the infant was able to get her needs met immediately. It is easy to imagine that by the time she is a year old her attachment issues could be resolved. Thanks to early, appropriate action she may not have to suffer severe emotional pain or cause her family the extreme difficulties as is typical of these children. Had her symptoms been overlooked, the prognosis would have been completely different. It would be beneficial to be watchful of children born to known psychiatric patients, those with histories of child neglect or abuse, and those with chemical abuse problems.

Parenting Classes in Schools

Years ago when unmarried girls became pregnant; they were spirited away to a secret out-of-town location where they remained until after the baby's birth. Under such circumstances the newborns were usually given up for adoption and the mother had little say in the process. Today that scenario seems archaic. Motherhood during the teen years, in one culture or another, has been a forever thing. Now the only real difference is that pregnancies are no longer kept secret and many mothers keep their babies. Not so long ago young mothers began returning to school rather that abandoning their junior or senior high school careers.

Over the years progressive teachers and schools systems have included parenting classes in the curriculum. It would be in our best interest to add a class in nurturing to the basics of reading, writing, and arithmetic. Since the purpose of getting an education is, after all, to prepare one for life, adding classes that would teach child care to young parents would be a wise use of time. In addition, lessons in problem solving, communication skills, identifying and meeting one's needs, and the identification and sharing of feelings would also be invaluable. While in my late twenties I was invited to spend two weeks with graduating senior girls. I was directed by the regular (male) instructor to teach them whatever they needed to get along after graduation. They were most interested in learning about birth control and about love, in that order. So, I taught them what I knew about safe sex, love and how to live within a limited budget. We all thoroughly enjoyed the class and I still believe it was helpful to them because it was practical, what they wanted, and met them in their daily lives. Sensitive teachers could teach such classes under the "Health Education" umbrella after special preparation for presenting those particular classes without extra costs involved. Producing students with a modicum of emotional maturity who would make better parents is a worthy goal for any school system.

Parenting Mentors

During the 1977 and 1995 research interviews with mothers for *Motherhood at the Crossroads* the women came up with a wonderful suggestion. They requested the assistance of a person I termed a "mommy mentor." What they had in mind was to meet a mature mother or grandmother with whom they could maintain a close personal relationship while rearing their children, or, they could utilize a series of mentors who would "specialize" in certain ages. Such a woman would assist them by providing the needed emotional support and a calm perspective. An appropriate candidate would have, through experience and additional training, learned and practiced a variety of parenting approaches and would be full of useful tips and suggestions. In many ways the "mommy mentor" would be a mother substitute for those whose own mothers were not available to them. It would also create an extended family that might be missing from their lives. This concept would not be restricted to just mothers as "daddy mentors" would also be useful to fathers in need of additional parenting skills and practical support. Such a program could be run out of a local volunteer bureau or someone's kitchen. It would require little, other the attention and energy of an enthusiastic organizer and focused volunteers. This would be a wonderful program for those who believe in giving back something of what they have received.

Home Health Visits

Once I was the coordinator of a home health agency located in Western Nebraska. As part of the protocol, registered nurses made at least one home visit to check on the health of new mothers and their babies. Insurance companies, especially in the case of very young mothers, or with those experiencing difficulties, generally authorize two visits. It seems that long term use of the services of home health nurses would be medically and financially justifiable for identified mothers-in-need. Home health visits are ordered by physicians and are authorized and paid for by individual insurance carriers. Although the initial outlay for a woman considered "high risk" (those with medical, emotional, or chemical problems) might appear significant, in the long run it would pay for itself. If the mothers were adolescent, disenfranchised, or the infant had complications, the services of a trained nurse would actually save money. Without proper care, hospital charges and subsequent hospitalizations or institutional care could eat away any front-end profits.

The kinds of assistance needed would be evaluation by physicians and the insurance companies on a regular basis. Today hospitalizations for children with behavioral or emotional problems can run into thousands of dollars. Intensive support during the early months of a child's life would not be that costly and could avoid enormous expenditures later.

Ministerial Outreach

Years ago I volunteered at a Rhode Island church with the goal of supporting and guiding a young mother with limited mothering skills in the care of her newborn. In hindsight, I don't know today how successful my visits were, but in the short run they were valuable. However, I think the program and the approach were innovative and worth duplicating. Since churches generally maintain an interest in the body and soul of their parishioners, they have an advantage over governmental agencies. Offering such services through one's church affiliation could provide mature, parental types with an opportunity to broaden their religious and spiritual commitments. Many of the parents you met in Part Two of this book made their decisions to adopt or foster children as the result of their personal religious or spiritual beliefs. Then when many discovered their children had behavioral difficulties they first sought help through their ministers and priests. For those families this program would be a natural extension of that same process. Classes on basic parenting and nurturing skills would be required for the volunteer assistants.

Tax Breaks for Direct Parenting

For my first book I interviewed professional women who had reinvented themselves and become stay-at-home mothers. They talked about the joys and benefits of their decision to stay home and rear their children themselves. The moms had been employed outside the home before having children and their mothering experiences included the use of day cares or other hired caretakers. They were worried about the long-term effects of extensive other-care on their children's personalities and value systems that led to their decision to stay home. However, none of them remained at home without great emotional and financial costs to themselves and their spouses. Although they deliberately chose to remain with their children, not a popular approach at the time, they verbalized much frustration about the double-speak they experienced, that age-old debate about the high value of parenthood without any inherent benefits. Virtually all the mothers were willing to live on less, and risk the consequences of interrupted successful careers, the price paid for leaving their high level professional positions. They did not want to pay such an exorbitant price forever because of their enormous love and concern for their offspring.

An especially astute group of mothers from the Arlington, Texas area had developed a plan which included tax breaks to be given parents in their position. I, too, would like to see a system developed that would encourage and support those providing daily hands-on parenting to their own children. I still hear couples wishing they could stay home and rear their youngsters, but not being able to afford to do so with the current tax structure. In reality, not all parents would want to stay home, but I wish those who are interested and would be able to do so without suffering financially. I encourage tax experts to make the dramatic changes necessary in our current system to provide financial incentives for stay-at-home parents. When a parent chooses to remain at home, especially during the child's early years, the emotional benefits to the family, and ultimately, to society are immeasurable. Because of that, financial advantages should be available to them. The improved medical and mental health status of our young citizens would be a benefit that could not otherwise be purchased.

Stipends for Adoptive and Foster Parenting

Many children available for adoption were considered to be "special needs" or "hard to place" due to the presence of physical or emotional conditions. Two decades ago most 'handicaps' were thought to be physical in nature. However, today, that is not necessarily the case: emotional and behavioral disorders including attachment problems, according to M. Welch, M.D., ODD, ADHD, and ADD are rampant. In the past decade or so some enlightened adoption agencies realized the dilemma caused by such an increased financial burden and took steps to rectify the situation. Because of the changes in policy many adopters of children with Attachment Disorder receive adoption allowances or are provided medical and mental health benefits. Such plans aim to cover the exorbitant psychiatric and psychological services, which are required to get these individuals through childhood. Ultimately, financial assistance made more children available for adoption and helped them receive the quality of care they require and deserve.

Unfortunately, not all adoption agencies provide either an adoption allowance or the medical/mental health benefits. Parents who adopt through the "black" or "gray" markets, those who do not go through licensed adoption agencies, have no protection or assistance available to them for the child's current or potential health issues. Ultimately, it would be in the best interest of the children, their families, and adoption agencies to develop a means of financially aiding parents of those determined to have "special needs" children. Currently there is a glut of children available for adoption, and the numbers continue to rise dramatically. There might be adequate numbers of families available for foster/adoptive care if financial and emotional support were provided by every agency.

Professional Parents

There are some adults who could provide necessary services by just being the parents they already are. Over the years I have met parents who were sensitive, bright, loving, creative, humorous and were quite close to being perfect parents, if such individuals actually exist. It would have been wonderful for their children and for those of us who used them as role models if they could have been full-time parents with no other outside responsibilities. It would also be in the interest of families to raise parenthood to the level of a profession. To that end, a governing board would need to be formed to establish standards and to offer specialized training to the potential parents. Also, a wage would be required, vacation and sick leaves would have to be added, plus an ample benefit package thrown in. In other words, everything that other professions *demand* and *have!* Why not? Since most say that parenting children is the most important job in the world, let us do what is necessary to elevate it to a level that will demand the respect and comparable benefits of other professions!

Bernadine Janzen is a persistent political activist living in Wasilla, Alaska, who goes by the pen name of "Alaska Bernie." For a time she produced a column under the title of "SOMETHING TO THINK ABOUT!" On Wednesday, May 19, 1999, she wrote: "For the last two years our group, the Alaska Attachment & Bonding Associates (AAB A), has been talking about "Professional Parenting." We would like to train families to provide therapeutic foster and respite care for children who experience mild to severe attachment disorder. The family "in training" would work with a trained therapeutic mom, one who has lived with children who experience this devastating disorder.

"It is our belief that even the most severe child does not need to live in an institution. Yet, the State of Alaska is placing children with mental illnesses in juvenile halls at a much more rapid pace. As the State of Alaska brings more kids back from out-of-state care, we will hope that additional training is made available to foster families to care for these children. We will hope the idea of "Professional Parenting" becomes a reality for the many children in the State of Alaska who do not have a permanent placement."

I believe Janzen is on the right track. Her ideas could save Alaska, or any other state utilizing such a system, thousands of dollars on institutional care. Professional parents would require financial support, and respite care, but such a package would be significantly less costly than the care of one child in a long-term institution. Aside from the poignant emotional issues, it could simply be a solution of economics.

Develop Parenting Teams

Teams of parents could be developed with the help of mental health agencies, schools, churches, health departments, and/or hospitals. With this program, when parents are in crisis, a team would be sent out into their home to provide immediate support by helping the parent remain calm and to make appropriate decisions during the emergency. The parenting team could also help the parents with long term planning, problem solving, or new parenting skills that would ultimately benefit all the family members. Such team members could make referrals into the medical or mental health systems and parenting options, as needed. Team membership should consist of experienced and specially trained men and women who represent diverse ethnic and cultural groups, as well as multilingual individuals. Parenting teams could also be formed and function as part of currently existing governmental agencies, perhaps through Social Service, child welfare agencies, or public health departments. With such a team in place citizens would have an appropriate resource for complaints and concerns about children in trouble. They could also act as ombudsmen and monitor difficult situations.

Respite Care

I've heard it said that one of the difficulties with parenting, as with living, is that it is so daily. Most parents report that in retrospect the parenting years went by too quickly; but while in it each seemed an eternity. That is especially true of special families or for parents who don't feel confident or creative in their responses to their child's misdeeds. Many parents interviewed felt completely overwhelmed by the vigorous demands of rearing children with attachment problems. What was true of couples who were parenting teams was especially true for single parents:

they did not have enough hands (or minds!) to keep up. Most foster and adoption agencies and adoptive systems have a common trait—too many kids and not enough parents. It would be important to establish and nurture respite families. Families already fostering or adopting could act in this capacity as long as the addition of more children would not destroy any reserve they may have. Ideally, though, respite families would remain outside the fostering or adoption loop. Perhaps these are a crude comparison, but I think of respite caregivers as relief pitchers or like additional back-up stock used by the pony express. Both extra hurlers and horses were necessary to insure their success in meeting the established objectives.

I believe respite care for an acting out child can be effective in a way that remaining with their weary family cannot. Effective care could be an overnighter to give the parents a breather or as long as two weeks to help the child or family get over a big bump in their journey. Respite care is best used in tandem with therapy and should not be used as a punishment. When used correctly it can be very therapeutic, helpful as a learning tool, and can ease tough situations. Respite parents would need specialized parenting skills and work closely with the primary caretakers and their therapist to maintain the continuity of care for the child. Once refreshed, the parents could continue on in their daily lives with increased vigor. The Casey Family Programs has discovered an effective use of respite care. Rather than waiting until troubled youth to "blow" his/her way out of a home, they automatically schedule troubled children for respite care. Under ordinary circumstances the primary caretakers would be unable to go on and complete such a difficult task. But with this program they know they will have a sorely needed break every two to four weekends. Planned respite breaks give parents and kids the energy to go on. The child receives care consistent with his/her daily life and easily becomes accustomed to the scheduled changes. Folks who are fortunate to have a cooperative extended family available to them have been using such a system for years.

Develop New Parenting Approaches

Parents, teachers, and therapists who live or work with attachment conflicted youngsters agree on one thing: usual parenting approaches and consequences appear to work for a while, but in the long run are unsuccessful. Personal and therapeutic relationships are based on an intrinsic ability of both individuals to empathize and reciprocate. Those are descriptors of the parents, teachers, and therapists; but not of attachment disturbed children. Disruptions in their early lives leave them with lack of trust, incapable of empathy or reciprocity, the core of one's ability to relate to others.

There is another problem that gets in the way of the responses of those who are attachment-disordered to others. It is important to know that all children harbor some fears of abandonment; it is a usual part of childhood and the separation process. Often, however, those fears are carried into adulthood and then interfere with relationships with ones children and other adults. Perhaps put like this will make it more understandable: most children have abandonment issues, while still others have ***abandonment issues***. However, children with attachment disorders experience ***ABANDONMENT ISSUES!!*** I think you can readily grasp the difference. Successful parenting approaches must take all the children's issues into account. For example, most parents use time-outs, limited time away from the family, so their offspring can collect themselves and start their day again. Children with *ABANDONMENT ISSUES!!* experience the consequence of being sent away from the parents (to their room or another part of the home) as being abandoned, again. So instead of calming the child, as the parent hopes, it could further frighten those already terrified.

New approaches need to be developed, ones that keep the basic needs and psychology of special youngsters in mind. Chapter Nine offers an adapted parenting approach that has been successful with children with attachment issues and other tough kids. I'll give you an example of viable alternative consequences that would decrease children's natural fears. If your message to your child—"I want to be with you"—is not clear, it would be imperative to devise a consequence that is congruent with, or matches, that message. Instead of sending an acting-out child to a room away from you, bring the child toward you or physically closer to you. Depending on the child's age they could sit on a chair near you for three minutes or spend a weekend with you (although such a notion may make you feel like hurling!). Please refer back to the section entitled *Purposeful Parenting* to get some more practical ideas which can be adapted to your situation.

Train Professionals

I believe it is imperative to provide specially trained counselors, social workers, nurses, and teachers to effectively deal with youngsters with attachment issues. They are not like other children at home or in the classroom; they tend to be more stubborn and disruptive and do not regard others with an acceptable level of respect. Also, the techniques you used on Tuesday won't work for you on Wednesday. There is good news! Practically every parent, and virtually all professionals, who are aware of Attachment Disorders are willing and active teachers. I think their personal frustration and a desire to spread the news drive most. The sooner all parents and professionals learn about this malady, the better off our families will be. There is a bountiful list of resources for your assistance in Appendix 1. I invite you to call the agencies or individuals listed to obtain speakers for your organization or school PTA. It is also possible to arrange for therapy for your child or for individualized training programs for therapists or for therapeutic parents. Feel free to contact the specialists identified, as they are experts on attachment problems.

Identify Parents and Children-at-Risk

Recently Keith Kuboyama, of Honolulu, went to the Hawaiian Legislature in an effort to enlist the assistance of local obstetricians and pediatricians. He wanted the medical professionals to ask five simple questions of welfare recipients. The plan was this: parents identified as those with children having potential emotional or behavioral problems would then be required to participate in parenting classes and groups both during the pregnancy and post-natal period. The physicians were to be the first step in a line of highly trained professionals who would have the collective goal of improving the parenting and nurturing skills of parents. From the doctors' initial questionnaire the parents would be referred to yet another evaluator for the final determination of "high risk" status. The physicians balked and were not cooperative with the simple, preventative process. They stated that before they took action, they wanted it to be proven to them that those mothers would eventually have problem children. Collectively, they responded that they did not want to worry about prevention but to focus their resources on fixing the problems that already existed. Sadly, they did not have the mindset necessary to take valuable preventative action.

I think we need to take lessons from our teachers in Hawai'i, California, and Alaska. Any state that puts the welfare of their children and families first has its priorities straight. When we fail to put families first, we perpetuate the current dangerous trend. Although some of the suggested programs were not initially successful, I encourage a continuation of the valiant efforts of those ahead of their time. We need to analyze what happened in situations like Littleton, so we have viable alternatives in the future. The parents and professionals who brought their troubled children into emergency rooms across the United States for mental health assessments were on the right track. A good thing about the yucky behaviors of attachment-disordered children is that they usually get noticed. Perhaps their acting out doesn't *yet* get them where they need to go, but eventually that will happen. The more educated you become, and the more you learn about the disorder, the sooner our children and their families will get the assistance they so desperately need.

Conclusions

As you have read, problems that occur when infants or children experience early neglect or abuse oftentimes have overwhelming and long-reaching consequences. If those consequences were limited to the child or their immediate family, we might get away with continuing to ignore the situation. However, that is not the case as all of the relationships that involve attachment affected kids are profoundly and negatively affected. Like the ripples that are made by a pebble thrown in a pool, the far-reaching effects of one attachment-disordered individual go on forever. Initially the interactions between the child and their family are the only ones affected. Eventually, however, the members of the extended family are involved; the neighbors; the teachers and schoolmates; then the police and legal systems. As with all other mental illnesses, the prognosis without appropriate treatment is predictable. The eventual outcome causes personal, familial, and societal disaster.

Just how can a problem with such serious consequences be avoided? Exactly what can be done? Earlier in this chapter many preventative solutions have been proposed. Good solid parenting given lovingly by mature adults with the goal of protecting and meeting the needs of vulnerable children *is* the answer. Education in the form of a book such as *Broken Spirits ~ Lost Souls* is a start, but just that—a beginning. We need to inform and educate parents, mental health professionals, teachers, grandparents, childcare workers, police and judges. Any format that educates is acceptable: books, lectures, movies, interactive educational programs and discussions, to name a few. It is imperative for the mental health of our American citizens and beyond, that we disseminate accurate information about this mysterious and ever-growing phenomenon.

There is value in a work such as this. As well as adding to the current educational pool, I encourage and support further study of the topic. I hope that eventually funding will be provided for the training of professionals. This volume is part of my commitment to the children and their families. Another of the discouraging aspects of the problem of RAD and attachment issues is the considerable ignorance that stubbornly persists among mental health professionals. Not long ago I proposed an international symposium on Reactive Attachment Disorders be held at the University of Hawai'i. I thought it would be a wonderful opportunity to invite all the experts in the field in Hawai'i for the purpose of teaching medical and mental health professionals about the symptoms, the causes, and the treatment for Reactive Attachment Disorder. Many experts had already agreed to participate in such an endeavor, so they stood ready. It was heartening to learn that the Dean of the School of Medicine had a particular interest in attachment issues. The staff, it was reported, was very interested in the topic and enthusiastic about the proposed symposium. In the end, however, I was told that the plan was not accepted because the topic was "too controversial." I wonder how controversial those untreated RAD adolescents and adults (by then carrying a label of "Psychopath") will be a few years from now while sitting on death row.

I've presented some simple ideas, very simple concepts. The problem of course is that, in general, these ideas cannot be legislated and free will continues to exist. Mothers continue to believe whatever it is they do or that their mother did was best. I've grown to believe that one of the most difficult things to change is the mind or the ideas of another. If you want to pick a fight the easiest way is to indicate to a mother you think she made a mistake, or that she may have been misled. Such a challenge strikes feelings at the very soul of her existence and you will quickly learn about the strength of her defense mechanisms! It is likely that you will also find yourself being ostracized for being a know-it-all!

This is an area where the 'experts' must tread gently while recognizing and honoring the delicate balance and nature of the issues.

If there were only one concept that I would use to summarize a viable solution to this terrible problem it would be this: early diagnosis with early intervention. It is imperative that at-risk-mothers be identified early in their pregnancy or in the beginning of the life of their newborn. Among the women who might warrant additional resources are teenagers or emotionally immature mothers; mothers with few financial or social resources; women who are alcohol or drug involved; mentally challenged mothers; or those who come from families with identified mental, psychological, or legal problems. Also, women who have been the victims of rape, incest, or any physical abuse will need additional nurturing. As stated earlier in this book any time a mother feels conflicted about her pregnancy, or is not getting her own needs met, there is the possibility that the unborn fetus will be vulnerable to attachment difficulties.

If the answer is really all that simple, why isn't it already being done? I used to believe that parenting came naturally, perhaps, through our genetic inheritance or maybe by osmosis. Another idea I had was that it occurred by some magical process! But now that I have parented children of my own and worked with parents of troubled kids, I have changed my mind. I now know parenting skills are gained through hard work and through a continuous educational process. Most valuable skills come with a high price attached and that we need to take action to acquire them. Attending parenting classes, working with a successful parenting mentor or by picking the brain of a beloved, experienced auntie would form the groundwork for positive parenting styles. Being willing to go to any length is absolutely necessary to learn to effectively love our babies and to be able to both identify and meet their needs. We need to teach others that for the sake of their children mothers absolutely *must not* use alcohol or drugs during pregnancy. We need to pass on the concept of nurturing our mothers and their unborn child long before they join us in the world. And somehow, only babies who are wanted should be born to mothers who are emotionally mature enough to focus on someone other than self. Our children need to be raised by adults who can make a persistent and continual commitment to the child, a commitment that can be sustained until all the infants and toddlers basic needs have been met and throughout their formative years.

Our children are salvageable, but not by magic or by osmosis! A concerted effort on the part of individuals and professionals working in unison is required. We must challenge our old ideas about babies and bonding and the need for therapy early in life. The old idea that babies will outgrow, or forget, a neglectful start is bunk. Those experiences are stored in places not visible to the naked eye and interfere with their relationships for the rest of their lives. The professionals listed later in this book also play such an important role in educating the public and professionals, supporting families, and providing the invaluable therapy needed by children with attachment difficulties. It is encouraging to me to note that the list is several pages long. Not so long ago the list filled only a page or so. Slowly, ever so slowly, through careful planning and concerted effort, the educational process continues.

Some children survive seemingly whole, having come through the most tragic of circumstances. For the same unknown reasons, others are damaged but, hopefully not beyond repair. I do not know why that is, and doubt that anyone yet knows the actual cause but we can make educated guesses. The entire topic of Reactive Attachment Disorder needs generous funding and intense study and I think a good look at the contribution of human spirit and internal strength needs to be included. It does seem that some children are made of sterner stuff as someone once stated. Many, sadly, are unable to withstand rough beginnings, leaving their egos and mettle compromised. It is my personal hope that the information on these pages has enlightened and guided you into your journey into a fascinating twist of thinking, and ultimately, of behavior.

You are added to my prayer list, and I ask for continued blessings in your life as you love your children and meet their needs so, together, we can announce the end of this dreadful disorder. JER

Epilogue

Several years ago, while on a temporary assignment in New Orleans, I attended a Mardi Gras parade for the first time. Two friends and I made our way curbside to get a better view of the 70th anniversary of the Charlton Crue. There were thousands of people attending that day, sometimes up to six deep on the sidewalk. I was attempting to pay full attention to the activities at hand, a new promise to myself to remain present to the events in my life. However, I was having some difficulty paying attention, as my mind was full of thoughts of Quinn that day. My sleep had been disturbed and restless the two nights before, I'd had nightmares both nights. Perhaps, I thought, the dreams were psychic messages telling me that Quinn really was dying of AIDS and that he had returned to violent activities. My child's father had told me that he was somewhere in the New Orleans area, but no one knew where for sure. I found myself looking for him everywhere and searching the faces of every young man present. I had not seen my son for three years as he'd been in institutions, jails, and prison during the time since our last meeting. I attempted to force myself to enjoy the Mardi Gras activities and to catch the beads, while chiding myself for being so silly. "Typical Nebraska Mom," I thought. "Here I am in New Orleans thinking I'm going to find my baby boy among all these people!"

About half way through the festivities a young man asked if he and his friends could occupy the empty space on the curb in front of us. My friend and I reluctantly agreed but I secretly and childishly worried that they might catch some of the beads meant for me. A male and a female stooped over to pass between us; then we immediately closed the empty space. The man said there was a third person, so we begrudgingly let another young man pass to the edge of the street. The third, obviously a

Mardi Gras veteran, sat at my feet. Even though I wanted to ignore the trio, I was unable to because of the behavior of the third person. He stood up, danced and demonstrated some acceptable Mardi Gras sexual behaviors, those usually considered unacceptable any other time, and then sat down on the curb. He was so close that his buttocks touched my toes. He repeated his ritual while fully bedecked in beads and decoration. In fact, his appearance and his lewd behaviors were what led me to the conclusion that he'd been to Mardi Gras before.

My friend pointed out his behaviors, and I attempted not to look, out of my own embarrassment. But as hard as I tried not to, I was drawn to examine him. I actually could see very little of him as he was covered with a variety of Mardi Gras decorative items. His head was full of curly black hair that covered his face to his eyes and the rim of his dark glasses. The neck of his jacket was unzipped to his waist, with the bare space filled in with rows and rows of beads; long sleeves; long legged wind suit and sneakers. But the most disturbing thing of all was that he *felt* familiar. I remember looking at his fingers, which peeked out from inside his sleeve, and thinking, "Quinn's hands looked like that." And, once when he was sitting touching my toes I leaned forward to get a better view of his eyes behind the sunglasses. With an unexpected start I discovered that young man had eyes which matched my memory of my son's own.

My heart started pounding and I could feel the blood pulsating through my head and my chest. "God, I think this is my child." I said out loud, to no one in particular. I was overwhelmed with ambivalence! I experienced disbelief, embarrassment, and awe simultaneously. The exact thoughts that passed behind my eyes in a flash, were: "It can't be true." "This guy's behavior was so obnoxious I don't want this to be my child!" "God, You might have pulled off a reunion for us." I first planned not to say anything, to leave this an eternal mystery. My second thought, however, reminded me that were this truly my son I would never sleep again knowing I hadn't had the courage to discover the truth. After summoning all the strength I could, I reached out to the young man in front of me, called his name, and laid my left hand on his left shoulder. He remained seated but turned to get a better look at me.

"What?" He said angrily.

I almost backed off, sure I was making an incredible fool of myself. I said another quick, silent prayer, "Oh, God!"

"Quinn?"

The young man stood up, turned to face me, removed his sunglasses, then stretched out his arms and smiled sheepishly.

"Mom!" He replied with amazement and tears that matched my own.

Before this event I had not seen him since he was chubby, searching and sixteen. Since that time he'd been imprisoned for I don't-know-what and lost somewhere in Louisiana. But for about forty minutes on a sunny February New Orleans holiday I had the most wonderful moments becoming reacquainted with my child. He looked similar to the old Quinn with some incidental changes: his hair was free and longer; his complexion was fairer. Maybe it was I who was different, as I was finally able to set aside all the pain that had put a wedge between us. I was given the opportunity of a lifetime, a chance to see him as an individual in his own right. I was able to touch, hug and kiss him; to look at him; and to listen to his story and his dreams. I was able to appreciate his beauty, fully, perhaps for the first time since his early days with me. I was able to understand that his path was just that, *his* path. Whatever he did in the past or still does was *not* against me or to me, but *for* him. I also learned that he is a man and does not need my advice, my guidance, or my approval, nor do I need to like what he is doing with or in his life. It is, after all, *his life, to do with as he sees fit.* All I have to give him, that he may—or may not—need or want, are my acceptance and my love. For his sake, and mine, I need to remember that Quinn is *not* his behavior; he is *not* his disorder or his psychopathology. He is my son. On that magnificent afternoon in New Orleans I was able to feel, to experience, and to love his spirit, however broken.

I believe the experience was, simply, a miracle. I had been so stuck in the negative and fearful part of our relationship that I had been unable to separate the baby from the bath water, my son from his history. Today I believe our "chance" meeting was absolutely necessary for both of us. I don't know what Quinn got out of our last time together. However, for me, I don't believe I would have written this book without the healing and the insights that were bestowed upon me during those few, Blessed moments.

Appendix 1 — Professionals & Agencies

The following is a list of professionals and agencies who work directly with attachment disturbed children and their families or act as referring agencies. I'm glad to report this list is not totally comprehensive; fortunately new resources become available at an increasing rate. I encourage you to contact any of the resources below for their assistance.

CANADA

Adoption Council of Canada
P. O. Box 8443 St T, Ottawa, Ontario,
Canada, K1G 3H8, Fax: (613) 235-1728

Attachment Disorder Support and Resource
Karen Braid and Lynne Yanchuk, Adoption Council of Alberta,
8116 187St., Edmonton, Alberta, T5T 1K3, (980) 484-9179

Forest Cottage Center
Tanya Roberts, Executive Director, 10512—102 Avenue, Fort St. John,
BC, Canada V1J 2E6, Phone: (250)261-3750, Fax: (250) 785-0344,
E-mail: forest_cottage@hotmail.com

NuWay Consulting
Roxanne Whitford-Numan, M.S.W., R.S.W. #200, 4826—47 Street, Red Deer, Alberta, Canada T4N 1R2, Phone: (403) 341-3773

UNITED KINGDOM

Adoption UK (A Referral Agency)
Philippa Morrall, National Director, Lower Boddington, Daventry, Northamptonshire NN11 6YB, Phone: (011-44) 01327-260295,
Fax: (011-44) 01327-263565

Keys Attachment Centre
Sheila Fearnley, Executive Director, Mickledone, Haslingdon Old Road Rawtenstall, Rossendale, Leicestershire, England BB4 6hh,
Phone: 01706-227226, Fax: 01706-224500

Family Futures Consortium
Alan Burnett, Director, 86 Mildmay Park, Islington,
London N1 4PR, Phone: 0171-2410503

After Adoption, Yorkshire
Grove Villas, 80/82 Cardigan Road, Headlingly, Leeds LS6 3BJ,
Phone: 0113-2302100

UNITED STATES

ALASKA

RAD Contact and Newsletter
Bernadine Janzen, 3300 E. Palmdale Drive, Wasilla, AK 99654
Phone: (907) 376-0366; Fax: (907) 376-3840,
Web site: www.akattachment.org

CALIFORNIA

The Attachment Center
Beryl R. Davis, Ph.D., 5805 Capistrano Ave, Suite E.,
Atascadero, CA 93422, Phone: (805) 466-4892

Family Contact
Lori Hunstad, LSW, S.L.O. County D. S. S., 3433 So. Higuera, P. O. Box 8119, San Luis Obispo, CA. 93403, Phone: (805) 788-2597

Family Contact
Laurie and Thomas F. Wylie, Ph.D., R.N., P.O. Box 1515, 11573 Los Osos Valley Road, Suite C, San Luis Obispo, CA 93405,
Phone: (805) 545-8951

COLORADO

The Attachment Center at Evergreen, Inc
Paula Pickle, LCSW, Executive Director, 27618 Fireweed Drive, P. O. Box 2764 Evergreen, CO 80437. Ph: (303) 674-1910,
Website: http://www.attachmentcenter.org

Evergreen Consultants in Human Behavior
Terry M. Levy, Ph.D., 28000 Meadow Drive, Suite 206, Evergreen, CO 80439, Ph: (303) 674-5503; Fax: (303) 674-7665

A Children's Counseling Center
Carolyn L. Hall, MA and Melinda Hardage, MA, LPC, RPT/S
3055 Austin Bluffs Parkway, Colorado Springs, C0 80918,
Phone: (719) 570-7188

Foster Cline, M.D.
Website: HTTP://members.aol.com/drfcline/

DELAWARE

Tressler Center of Delaware
Victoria J. Kelly, LCSW, Psy. D.,5143-A W. Woodmill, Suite 24, Wilmington, DE 19808, Ph: (302) 995-2294, E-mail: vkelly@tressler.org

CONNECTICUT

Wellspring Foundation
Herbert L. Hall, Director, contact: Kevin Makarewicz, 21 Arch Bridge Road, P.O. Box 370, Bethlehem, CT 06751, Ph: (203) 266-7235,
E-mail: Herb@wellspring.org

GEORGIA

Peachtree Attachment Resources, L.L.C.
M. Lisa Riley, L.C.S.W., P.O.Box 49068, Athens, GA 30604
Phone: (706) 227-0044; Fax: (706) 543-4658,
E-mail: radriley@bellsouth.net, Website: www.attachment-ga.com

HAWAI'I

The Casey Family Program
Keith Kuboyama, LSW, ACSW, 1848 Nuuanu Avenue, Honolulu, HI 96817, Phone: (808) 521-9531, Fax: (808) 533-1018

IDAHO

The Advocacy & Learning Center
Stacey Hoem, BA, 850 E. Lander,
Pocatello, ID 83201, Phone: (208) 234-2094, Website: www.aol1.com

ILLINOIS

Post Institutionalized Network
Tais Teptler, Chicago, IL, Phone: (412) 222-1766

INDIANA

Family Bonding and Attachment Center
Lawrence B. Lennon, Ph.D., H.S.P.P., 2633 East 136th Street, P.O. Box 501, Carmel, IN 46032, Phone: (317) 575-9645

IOWA

IowaConnects
Debbie Hoyt, 149 35th Place, Runnels, IA, Valerie Owens, 2517 Carver Road, Winterset, IA 50273, Phone: 800-484-9617, code 4244, or (515) 462-2024, E-mail: IAConnects@aol.com

MAINE

Dan Hughes, Ph.D.
RR2, Box 1060, South China, Maine 04358,
Ph: (207) 445-3120, Fax: (207) 445-5624, E-mail: dhughes@pivot.net

MASSACHUSETTS

New England Institute for Attachment and Bonding
21 Cedar Street, Worcester, MA 01609

MINNESOTA

North American Council on Adoptable Children
Mary Ford, M.S.W., 970 Raymond Avenue, Suite 106, St. Paul, MN 55114, Phone: (612)644-3036, E-mail: NACAC@aol.com

MISSOURI

The Adoptive Family Treatment Center
Grey Endres, Director of Treatment Services, P. O. Box 25434, Kansas City, MO 64119,
Phone: (816) 453-9792, (913) 422-3607, E-mail: aftckc@crn.org

MONTANA

Intermountain Children's Home
C/O Tina Johnson, 500 Lamborn, Helena, MT 59601, Phone: (406) 442-7920

NEBRASKA

Attachment & Bonding Center of NE,
Debra Kelley, LCSW, 1307 1st Ave., Nebraska City, NE 68410,
Phone: (402) 873-3174, E-mail: pw41094@navix.net

Counseling Enrichment Center
Nancy Carlson, MS, P.O. Box 1073, 1515 E. Hwy. 6,
Holdrege, NE 68949, Phone: (800) 231-5034

The Counseling & Enrichment Center
Jacquelyn E. Meyer, CPC, LMHP and Koni Purdy Purscell, MA, NCC, QMPH Bonnie Hines, MS, 118 N. 5th Street, O'Neill, NE 68763,
Ph: (800) 689-0945, (402) 336-4841

Family Contacts
Don and Marcia Welch, 611 West 27th Street, Kearney, NE 68847,
Phone: (308) 237-3861

Therapy Resource Associates
Debra Wesselman, MS, SPC, 10824 Old Mill Road, #21, Omaha,
NE 68154, Ph: (402) 330-6060, E-mail: debwess@home.com

Support Group
Grand Island RAD Support Group, with Janie Watson, Wholeness Healing Center, Grand Island, NE (308) 382-5297

NEW MEXICO

Namaste Child & Development Center
P.O.Box 270, Peralta, NM, 87042, Phone: (505) 865-6176,
E-mail: manaste@nm.net

Villa Santa Maria
Joseph J. McGuill, CEO, and Barbara Wise, LPCC, LADAC, NCC, P.O. Box 156, Cedar Crest, NM 87008, Phone: (505) 281-3609

NEW YORK

Martha G. Welch, M.D.
7 East 85th Street, New York, New York 10028,
Phone: (212) 879-6505, Website: www.marthawelch.com

NORTH CAROLINA

The Piedmont Attachment Center
Melissa Kirkland, MA, **LPC407** Thurston Street, Winston Salem, NC 27103, Phone: (336) 774-9144, E-mail: cace@bellsouth.net

NORTH DAKOTA

AASK Adoption Specialist
Shirley Hoffarth, LSW,311 S. 4th Street,
Grand Forks, ND 58201, Phone: (701) 775-4196

OHIO

Attachment and Bonding Center of Ohio
Gregory C. Keck, Ph.D. and Regina Kupecky, MSW,
12608 State Road, Suite 1, Cleveland, OH, Ph: (440) 230-1960

SOUTH CAROLINA

Children Unlimited, Inc.
1825 Gadsen Street, P.O. Box 11463, Columbia, SC 29211,
Phone: (803) 799-8311, (800) 822-0877, E-mail: cuadop@scsn.net,
Web: www.midnet.sc.edu/children/child1.htm

UTAH

Cascade Center for Family Growth
Lawrence Van Bloem, L.C.S.W.,
P.O.Box 1144, American Fork, UT 84003 & 1145 East 800 North, Orem, UT 84097, Ph: (801) 229-2218, Fax: (801) 229-2213,
E-mail: cascade@attachment.org

VERMONT

United Counseling Service
Nancy Nystul, LICSW, Ledge Hill Drive, Bennington, VT 05201,
Ph: (802) 442-5491, E-mail: popel@sover.net

Vermont Achievement Center
Karin Bar-Zeev, Rutland, VT 05730,
Phone: (802) 273-4225, ex. 605, E-mail: KBZ50@excite.com

VIRGINIA

Adoption / Attachment Partners, P.C.
4300 Evergreen Lane #300, Annandale, VA 22003,
Phone: (703) 658-7103

Lifeworks
Janet deHoll, NCTMB
4300 Evergreen Lane, Suite 300, Annandale, VA 22003,
Ph: (703) 914-4545

Psychiatric and Neuropsychological Associates, P.C.
Ronald S. Federici, Psy.D.
620 Wolfe Street, Alexandria, VA 22314 and 400 South Washington Street, Alexandria, VA 22314, Ph: (703) 548-0721, Fax: (703) 836-8995

U.S. REFERRAL AGENCIES

ATTACh—Assoc. for Treatment & Training in the Attachment of Children
Linda Eisele, LISW, Executive Director, P. O. Box 11347, Columbia, SC 29211, Voice: (866) 453-8224, E-mail: info@attach.org,
Website: www.attach.org

Thomas J. Croke and Associates
816 Ligonier St., #205, Latrobe, PA 15650, Ph: (724) 532-0490,
Fax: (425) 576-8274; E-mail: attachnw@earthlink.net

Iowa ATTACh
Karen Combs, 66684 110th Street, McCallsberg, IA 50154,
Ph: (515)433-7836, E-mail: connects@netins.net

National Adoption Information Clearinghouse
330 C Street, SW, Washington, D.C. 20447
Phone: (703) 352-3488, (888) 251-0075,
E-mail: naic@calib.com; Website: http://www.calib.com/naic

The Attachment Network of Georgia, Inc

Laurie Anderson, Executive Director, 186 Hidden Hills Lane, Athens, GA 30605

Phone: (706) 546-5626, E-mail: Lauren.Anderson@worldnet.att.net

Appendix 2—Outtakes

Herein lie additional comments, outtakes of sorts, made by parents who have lived with children with attachment difficulties. These quotes are so significant that I did not want them to be forever lost in a drawer with unused portions of such important interviews.

Marcey D. of San Luis Obispo, said her daughter demonstrated animalistic behaviors. Alli, "went as far as going in the backyard and getting in the dog house and howling and barking. We thought that was her way of controlling us; if we reacted to her actions then she had control of the situation." Instead, "the less we reacted to her manipulation schemes, the more they would escalate; she would try harder and harder" to get our attention. Eventually, "she attacked one of our cats and was strangling it," which worked.

Dan D. of San Luis Obispo, stated: "I guess we were kind of blessed—everything has its' own blessing. I don't view adopting Alli as a mistake, but I think you should learn from every situation, not just mistakes. I have clearer goals in life now than I did before. I know what I can do and what I can't. And I know now how to set an attainable goal versus a dream."

Connie R. of Lompoc stated, "My girlfriend would come over because she was afraid to leave me alone with Alexis, because Alexis was chasing me around the house with knives, throwing chairs at me, and was hurting me. She'd already broken my face by second grade."

Pamela H. of San Luis Obispo was told that adopted son and daughter (9 ½ and 7 years old) had an extensive history of abuse: "Physical and sexual, drugs, abandonment, malnutrition, those types of things. We were also told they had been going to counseling and most of their childhood issues were pretty resolved." Pamela added, "I've lost a child but we're exhausted 'cause we're still trying to parent him and he doesn't live with us any more. His life is falling apart the last few months and that's hard to watch."

John and Hong B. of Bechenham, England believed adopting children from China was fraught with difficulties because of China's political and legal structure. John stated: "We couldn't be sure that any child they would give us would be okay. They (the officials) would say and sign anything just to say that a child is okay. I don't know if there are any facilities who will document a child's history correctly or honestly."

Sunny M. of San Luis Obispo shared that Jennifer's eyes were "kind of scary, shut-down eyes. First of all, she has two looks: one is 'I hate you eyes.' I'd never been looked at the way she looks at me with so much hatred in them. I didn't make her that angry but I have to take those eyes, I have to take that abuse. And her other eyes are the shutdown ones when I start getting a little bit too close to her. The wall just goes up, her eyes just change and she's turned off. There's nothing I can say to her, she's gone, she's in another room, on another planet. You might as well just stop right there 'cause you're going to get nowhere!"

Terry and Tom T. of Kansas City shared that "Forgiveness plays an awful big part in raising these kids." When asked what needed to be forgiven and let go Terry responded: "My lost dreams, my lost hopes of what should be. To be able to let go of being the mom I wanted to be and maybe my ideals, which I never saw as radical or way out there, just plain old ordinary ways. I just wanted to be a mom. It hurts me to let go of that and to not blame them—they weren't to blame, we weren't to blame. Not just saying I'm sorry, I mean really working at forgiveness and being able to let go of some of the things these kids did."

Anna P. of Lee's Summit, Missouri shared: "Ashley intentionally let my dog out and then after he was killed sat on the couch and started laughing. It wasn't like a nervous laugh—it was a kind of sadistic kind of a laugh. We live in a combat zone, no one should have to live in a combat zone. My door is locked. I lock it every night because I don't know what she's going to do." According to Anna and husband Errol, living with a RAD child "is biding our time, thinking, 'Okay, can we make it through the next six years without going insane or getting hurt?'"

Kate H. is a mother from Northants, England: shared that her son "has an explosive temper. You never know what will trigger it off, but it usually comes out as strings of obscenities. Some of them are quite amazing, you know. The number of adjectives he manages to incorporate into one short sentence will be worthy of—What can I say?—a professor of English at Oxford."

Lizzy V., mother of a girl from Bucks, England stated that the last foster mother reported, that her 3-year-old spent a lot of time alone in her bedroom and "that she was never naughty. She never had to worry about her because she knew she would never be doing anything naughty." Looking back, of course, "she was never doing anything naughty, 'cause she never did anything. She never does anything in our house." The frustrated mother reported her daughter sits in a state of suspended animation, just waiting…

Louie F. of Finedon, England, shared some hard-won insight: "When he began to know all the swear words, he would actually violate me with his language. Before Adrian I didn't swear." It wasn't until Louie and her husband met with psychologist Greg Keck that she, "realized what a tool I was giving him. How marvelous," the mother reported, "for Adrian to be able to do this, to upset me without any effort at all. He could turn his mother into a gibbering idiot who was raging furiously at him just by calling her a few names!"

Mary J. of Gravesend, England stated she began to worry. "What happens when they hit adolescents? Are they going to turn more violent towards us? Because if they're destructive now they may be more destructive later on." The mother had been told, "'Oh, they'll probably grow out of it by then. You know, give them time, it does take quite a few years for them to settle.' But in the back of my mind I carry this fear with me all the time. I keep thinking, 'Are you really going to turn out monsters?'"

Joyce K. of Nipomo, California reported her AD son killed some small chicks by taking fishing wire, wrapping it around their necks, and swung them around until they died. The frightened mom shared, "And he started laughing and had a cold look in his eye. This five-year-old kid started laughing like the devil himself was inside him." "I know one day there's a real good chance he'll end up in jail. If there's nothing we can do to change that direction, there's nothing that we can do. In the meantime, I'm going to try as hard as I can to help that kid and if at the end of all that, he stills screws up, that his problem." When asked what she would do to help children given unlimited resources, she heard only "If you had all the money in the world?" Joyce mused, "I'd be living on a yacht, I wouldn't have any children, and be I'd be surrounded by several large men named Sven!"

Lucy G. of Knebworth, England discussed her oldest child and stated, "He would taunt me and aggravate until the anger was there in my voice and then he felt justified in pushing me against a wall or throwing me around. Eventually he started attacking me—he rushed at me with a pair of hairdressing shears, which have a very long tips. That was the point which I decided that was enough and I called the police." The frustrated mum thought she should have done a better job because they had only two children. She tortured herself wondering, "'Why was Daniel so easy to manage, and Simon so difficult? Was it me? Did I love Daniel more?' And, of course, as the parent I believed I should be able to sort it all out and I couldn't. It was hell. It was just such a hell. I felt so alone. There was absolutely no support; nobody to understand."

Helen O-J., wife of David from Darby, England discussed the difficult relationship with her daughter. She found it hard "to live with the lying, the stealing, the fact that I had absolutely no control over this child, whatsoever. When I told her she mustn't do this—she did it. And all these things, all the time, and this very hostile look on her face made me feel 'I don't want to be in this situation anymore.'" Eventually Helen began making suicide plans. She hoped that by killing herself "I could actually escape this. I only ever thought about it but never planned it properly. But it occurred to me again and again when I was driving just how easy it would be."

Rozy, wife of Norm, from Hawai'i said daughter Martie "is a powerful person. Just powerful! In control and wanting to be in control of everything in her area." The family adopted Melanie when Martie was two. The mother stated one year later, "Melanie was cowering in the corner in the hall. I remember looking at her and thinking 'Who is Melanie? Where has she gone?' This was a scary thought. This kid who was flowering and beautiful, this baby that I loved, that was so wonderful. Her personality was growing beautifully. Then she had retreated like she was a flower that was smashed. I remember standing looking at her and thinking, 'God, this is horrible! Where has she gone? What's happening here?' It was one of those moments, a kind of recognition, of how awful things had gotten" for the baby who was the younger sister to Martie. Rozy talked about her feelings later in her girls' lives: "I remember kind of like spacing off. I was conscious of what I was doing. I was conscious that I was wandering off and I didn't care. I had visions all through the years of going off and jumping off a cliff or something. I mean, I had suicide visions."

Moira B. of Central England said that their daughter's arrival in their home was her sixth move in her short life. She shared, "Oh, she was very articulate, much more speech than we would have expected of a seventeen-month-old. She was a little girl rather than a baby. She pranced about in black patent shoes and a bow in her hair, very poised, very articulate, very grown up. We didn't actually see that as a problem, we thought, how fantastic, you know, she's that resilient, she's that together. The social worker described her to us as bright, alert, and responsive. She was certainly bright and alert, but it took a few weeks for there to be an actual response." But by age 7 they started looking for professional help for her due playground bullying and violence. "It was this Jekyll and Hyde bit that we were getting all the time so we never knew where we were. On-off, hot-cold, love-hate; everything was all jumbled up and nobody else saw that."

Marion W., a mother from Brighton, England discussed the behaviors of her 6 ½ year old adopted daughter toward her brother. She was "quite dominant, domineering, dominant and quite cruel, actually. She would get him into her bedroom, shut the door, and make sure he couldn't get out, and then I could hear him screaming and crying. What she was doing was playing a game of pretending to be dead. He was sobbing and sobbing and sobbing and saying, 'Please don't die, Tina! Please don't die, Tina, please don't die!' That was how she acted out with him. She couldn't see beyond her need." The mother thought within the first three days of bringing her home, "'Give it a couple of years, yes, and we'll see the light at the end of the tunnel.' I'm still waiting to see that light at the end of the tunnel."

May D., a nurse from Brighton in the U.K. Nicole was placed with May at two years and two months old. "She's very, very controlling, especially where I'm concerned. As soon as I sit down she wants something or she has to talk to me. She'll talk garbage, it's a lot of rubbish—it's not proper conversation. It's just literally to have my undivided attention." In addition, May added, "She also displayed very sexual behavior. We've had things inserted in every orifice she has. She actually put a shuttlecock into her vagina. I thought I was going to have to take her to the hospital and have it taken out, but I managed to do it. Which, of course, she absolutely reveled in." In addition, "she literally flew at us—she gouged our eyes, she pulled my earrings, she pulled clumps of my hair out. She gouged my face; she kicked me. I'm not an inexperienced parent. I've got two natural children and one of them autistic, so I was certainly used to behavior problems. Her rage was definitely geared at women. She's definitely very angry with women."

Janice B., the mother of several from Ashton-Under-Lyne, Lancashire, England stated, "My children were known to a psychiatrist before they were actually placed with us. The two older children had been referred by the birth mother because of severe problems she was experienced in the home. There was violence towards each other and their younger sibling, who was a new baby at the time. We were roped into sessions at the Children's Hospital with various psychiatrists. They were sure, like everybody else, that with love, patience and reassurance these children would be perfectly okay." They there told after many professionals and a court case that there was a significant amount of information withheld from them.

Pam W., the mother of two from Manchester, England shared that the most difficult part of living AD youngsters was, "losing contact with your friends and family because they can't cope with the child you've got. So you find yourself not invited out and people not understanding." The sad mother found that having no one to share her "feelings and wounds with" was extremely difficult for her. "Because," Pam added, "you know you're in a situation where if you tell people what's happening, it doesn't actually help. It just gives them a further bad impression of you, which drives them further away. So, you're really on your own. That was one of the worst things for me."

Helen S. from Manchester, England shared that the worst part of parenting such a child, "is the fear and the powerlessness. The fact that she could, anytime she wanted, go and take twelve Seconals, enough to kill her, and just say 'That's done.' I couldn't help her. I couldn't reach her! I couldn't do anything to prevent the distress that she was in." She concluded,

"What she was doing to herself or what she was doing to me, I couldn't do anything about it at all. I just feel I lived in faith."

Susan C. is the mother of a severely disturbed child from Kent, United Kingdom verbalized fears that she and her husband wouldn't be around as long as their daughter would need their help and guidance. She tearfully stated, "What's going to happen when we're not here any longer? She needs some help, a lot of help." Before her daughters' frequent violent outbursts Susan loved being at home. However, robbed of that happiness by the unpredictability of her daughter's actions, she stated, "I didn't feel secure at home anymore and I just had to get out of the house. I just couldn't stay in the house and that's how I feel now. When I have trouble I just want to get out. It's a horrible feeling."

Frances E., the mother of Marc from Essex, England stated she believes her son was a high risk for legal and social problems since his fourteenth year. "I think now we need help with social services; we need help with housing. Marc needs financial help and he cannot go and get it himself and we are not legally allowed to do it for him. So it's a catch-22. Unless he physically goes to these people and asks for help he's not going to get it. And he won't go. The problem is from the top to the bottom and includes education and employment. These children need help in society. Maybe they need an intermediary hostel of some sort between leaving home and work. I don't think that keeping them at home is really doing them any good because I don't think we are actually capable of sorting their problems out."

Jamie N., the mother of two adopted Russian children from Brookfield, Wisconsin shared, "I had expectations that were way too high; that my kids were going to get along so great because I was just going to be the coolest mom. I was going to be the greatest thing since sliced bread! But, you know, there are a lot of problems here. I knew life was going to change and that I was going to be incredibly busier than we were. I really had no idea that it was going to be the way it was or the way that it is now. I was not prepared for how incredibly challenging parent hood was going to be. I really wasn't!" At some moment she started realizing that maybe her kids weren't like other children. When everyone else was talking about how great motherhood was I thought, "something is wrong with me. I was thinking I can't do this because I'm exhausted all the time. I never get to just kick back for a second and relax with my kids. I always felt that I had to be two to five steps ahead of them."

Louise A., mother of two adopted bio-siblings from Richfield, Wisconsin stated, "At this year-and-a-half point it dawned on me that I didn't feel my kids were emotionally dependent on me. We were clothing them. We were going to the parks as a family. We were doing all this family stuff, but I didn't feel they had a real deep connection to me or need for me as a mom. That seemed remarkable to me." In pre-school her son, "would bully the teachers—he would break their jewelry, he'd punch them or kick them or throw his cot at nap time. And then it didn't seem to matter to him, he wouldn't show remorse, and that worried them."

Elizabeth K. is the adopted mother of one and grandmother of two Russian children from Franklin, Wisconsin. When discussing daughter Anastasia she stated, "I think the way she survived in the orphanage was learning to engage people and she's very good at it. If you put her in a room of adults she's in her glory! She works the room and she can have people in the palm of her hand faster than you know what's happened. We'll go out to eat and pretty soon she'll be at the table next to us talking to people that she doesn't know and charming them. People love her! She knows how to manipulate people." One day, after a trip to a farm with a friend of the family, "Anastasia came home and said, 'I want Nancy to be my mother.' She sometimes doesn't really understand. Of course it's upsetting to me, but I understand what's going on with her. I'm sometimes interchangeable."

Rena C. of Waverly, Ohio stated that a psychologist told her that her daughter would purposely start fights with family members so her husband would jump into the foray and side with their daughter. The mother reported, when successful, "she would go to her room and laugh. That had a profound effect on me. The more I thought about it the more I thought the psychologist was trying to warn us that she is trying to ruin our family. Up until that point I really did love her and I overlooked a lot of things. However, when I saw her as a threat to our family, a Damien, if you will, I started treating her differently." Rena believed that her daughter hated the mother who gave her away and hated the mother who abused her but acted out her feelings on the adoptive mother. "She always told me she hated me," the mother shared. "She would scream how much she hated me and she would accuse us of knowing who her natural mother was and not telling her. I believed that some day, when she grew up, she'd realize that it wasn't really me she hated, that it was these other people. But by the time she was seventeen, I realized that that was never going to take place 'cause she really did hate me. I finally accepted it."

Samantha M. from Santa Margarita, California said, "I'm angry because I couldn't figure it out, because there's no answer, because it isn't something you can fix, and because my self-esteem is destroyed. Our life is destroyed. My marriage will never be the same. My image to my family or in my community will never be the same. My whole 'who I am and what I stand for' is gone now. I erased Samantha by setting the adoption aside. I have to find myself again; I'm not the same person. I had my own preschool for twelve years working with kids and never saw anything like this. Then having a child with attachment problems come into my life and destroy it…I'm angry!" The frustrated mother concluded, "Kids need to stay with their birth mother, if at all possible. I think if we could change the rules I know we give the birth parents a lot of help, but we don't give it the intensity it needs. Everybody has too many rights—except the children!"

Kristin C., mother of two adopted youngsters from Indiana reported, "The kids were so good when they first came to live with us," but then eventually made "all the parents who had failed them in the past. I tried to be patient, to be the therapeutic psychiatric nurse that I am, and to love the children that we worked so hard to bring into our home. I eventually became the screaming, angry, unreasonable, demanding, controlling, bitch-mother from their past." Kristin lamented, "I could not go find these women and men and scream at them for what I was now living through because of their failures. A lot of times I would look at the kids and say, 'Do you even know who I am? I'm Kristin. I'm the good guy. I didn't do these things to you. You're here and you're going to stay here. You are part of our family—I've adopted you. I've taken care of your physical needs that hadn't been addressed when you lived in a previous placement. Just go look in the mirror and you can see your teeth are straight. What does this mean to you?' I know that meant something, even though they had blank looks on their face. Even though they didn't say thank you they had to test this some more; they had to punish us some more. They were testing to see if they were really going to live with us. And, they were punishing us to punish the other six sets of parents. It took a big chunk of my self-esteem."

Nancy R. mother of several Overland Park, Kansas talked about her relationship with her five-year-old adopted daughter. "I really felt sorry for her at the first. Not only was she lifted out of one life and plunked down in a new life with a new family, a new name, and within a month, she stated kindergarten. It was so tough on her. It was as though she were airlifted out of one whole life and just plunked down with a new mom, new dad, new siblings."

Paula W. of Kearney, Nebraska stated that having her adolescent daughter in her home became "like an oppression, it was just a heaviness all the time with her around. Every time I turned my van to come home after work I'd have such a heavy heart. She'd always be there opening the door to hug me and I knew that she had some other ulterior motive. I knew she was out to destroy me. I have never before been around a person who wanted to destroy everything I stand for and everything I am. It seemed like she was saying, 'I'm going to conquer you. You will no longer get to say that that is something of value because I'll destroy it for you.' I always used to think I was a pretty soft-spoken person but she would have me a screaming idiot. I couldn't control my thought processes any more. It just seemed like everything that I ever thought I wanted to be or wanted to strive for was just stripped away by her."

Ann C., a graduate student from Olathe, Kansas talked about her understanding of the beginnings of attachment difficulties with her child: "The world wasn't safe because no one met his needs. He didn't understand or was never given the opportunity to test the world or to say 'I hurt' and have someone say it's okay and then meet his needs." When asked if her son could have no conscience and yet be attached to her, stated: "I think these are contradictory kids who have a struggle going on inside them. When the qualities we would like to see develop are dominant, he still isn't normally attached, but I think he can exhibit certain behaviors that show a potential to love. But then when the selfish, narcissistic, me-oriented side is dominant I don't see any conscious or any love. It sounds contradictory except I think they are dual-natured kids. "Tanner has what I call "Good heart/Bad heart." His good heart dominates for maybe a couple of months, followed by a time where his behaviors get consistently more violent, more selfish, more defiant."

Susan R., mother of an adopted son from Overland Park: "When he actually got taken from us and was put in the state hospital it was real sad and it was real emotional. But life was so simple all of a sudden. It was like, WOW! We forgot how simple everything could be."

Martha G. of Kansas City asked, "Can we go back and make that trust bond? I don't know. If we can't get it, then how do we make the next step, promising they are going to be safe enough to live with and in society and not stuck behind bars making other people's lives miserable? I guess that's one of my biggest fears—that they will grow up and hurt other people."

Pat F., of rural Elkton, Maryland shared that when her son with severe Attachment Disorder was in his twenties he acknowledged that he had surreptitiously done many harmful things to her, including spiking her tea with cocaine. Thereafter, he referred to Pat's reactions to his antics as "Mom's hallucinations."

Peter and Helen, of England adopted Simon (10) at 4 years old. After four years of being the unwitting victims of the boys' intentional aggression and mean behaviors he was placed in a special care facility to provide safety to the youngster and his family members. The frustrated mother stated, "He has destroyed or stole anything of mine, especially if it was important to me. I was frightened of him. I think he is evil and could do anything dangerous later on."

Ruth W. of Cheshire, England discussed some difficulties with her twenty-two-year-old son who was placed with her at 4. During discussions, Peter always had to have the last word. Ruth reported that she had argued with him, a behavior that she described as "stupid" for her part in the exchanges. As she expected, the disagreements got worse and in the end Peter would frighten his mother with threats of physical harm. "Then he would be in control again," she said.

Connie R. of Lompoc, California shared that her daughter Alexis began self-mutilating behaviors and would "pick at herself and make herself bloody." By fourth grade, when she was instructed to write sentences using their current spelling words, her deep rage would be revealed. She would write, "I am going to kill doctors. You don't know it yet, but you're going to die."

Sarah D. from Kansas talked about experiences with son, David. "He got himself kicked out of daycare for the violence. We don't want to set him up for failure at another day care or have another non-parent taking care of him. So what we've tried to do is a tag team." She works days while husband Rex works evenings. "Rex is with him during the day," she continued, "and I'm with him during the evening. Then we all go to bed and we get up and start over. To some degree I think that's helping, but he other day I was feeling very frustrated. I think I was getting ahead of myself. Then we watched the videotape that we made with Martha Welch (M.D.) in New York. It was just astounding! It's amazing to see the differences in his behavior, in his face, and in his body language. Even in his "holdings," there are things he used to do all the time and now even when he's mad he doesn't revert to those. So we're still hanging in there—sometimes it's by our fingernails with me at the end of the rope praying, 'Please give me enough to make a knot.' Well, actually, I guess the knot is made. I mean, the knot is holding and we cling to that very dearly."

Dear Reader,

Thank you so much for getting all the way to this moment. I am talking about both living this long and reading this much! I'm leaving you space on this page so you can add your own quotes or you own notes from your life with your children. If you would like to share them please e-mail your comments to me at jane.ryan@prodigy.net. If you do not have access to the Internet please feel free to call me at 402-742-3663. I would love hearing from you and to be given the opportunity to support and listen to you.

Blessings to you during whatever process you need to take good care of you and to then help your children.

With Aloha, Jane Ryan

NOTES

BIBLIOGRAPHY

BOOKS

1. Ackerman, Robert J., *Silent Sons: A Book For and About Men*, Simon and Schuster, New York, 1993.
2. Berger, Gilda, *Violence and the Family*, Franklin Watts, New York, 1990.
3. Bowlby, John, *Attachment and Loss: Vol. 2, Separation Anxiety and Anger*, Basic Books, Inc., New York, 1969.
4. Bowlby, John, *Separation, Anxiety and Anger*, Basic Books, Inc., New York, 1973.
5. Cline, Foster W., M. D., *Understanding and Treating the Severely Disturbed Child*, Evergreen Consultants in Human Behavior, Evergreen, Colorado, 1979.
6. Cline, Foster W., M.D. and Cathy Helding, *Cline/Helding Adopted & Foster Child Assessment* (*CHAFCA*), World Enterprises, City Desktop Productions Inc., Franksville, Wisconsin,1998.
7. Cline, Foster, M.D., *Hope for High Risk and Rage Filled Children: Reactive Attachment Disorder*, Evergreen Consultants, Evergreen, Colorado, 1994.
8. Cline, Foster, M.D., *Parenting Teens with Love & Logic*, NavPress, Colorado Springs, Colorado, 1993.
9. Delaney, Richard J., Ph.D., *Fostering Changes: Treating Attachment Disordered Foster Children*, Walter J. Corbett Publishing, Fort Collins, Colorado, 1991.
10. Delaney, Richard J., Ph.D. and Frank R. Kunstal, Ed.D, *Troubled Transplants: Unconventional Strategies for Helping Disturbed Foster and Adopted Children*, National Child Welfare Resource

Center for Management and Administration, Edmund S. Muskie Institute of Public Affairs, University of Southern Maine, 1993.

11. Dutton, Donald G. and Susan K. Golant, *The Batterer: A Psychological Profile*, Basic Books, New York, 1995.
12. Fearnley, Sheila, *The Extra Dimension*, Printoff Graphics Arts Ltd., England, 1996.
13. Hage, Deborah, *Therapeutic Parenting: It's a Matter of Attitude*!, Frisco, Colorado, 1985.
14. Hare, Robert D., Ph.D., *Without Conscience: The Disturbing World of the Psychopaths Among Us*, Pocket Books, New York, 1993.
15. Jarratt, Claudia Jewett, *Helping Children Cope with Separation and Loss*, The Harvard Common Press, Boston, MA, 1994.
16. Johnson, Anthony Godby, *A Rock and a Hard Place: One Boy's Triumphant Story*, Crown Publishers, Inc., New York, 1993.
17. Karr-Morse, Robin, and Meredith S. Wiley, *Ghosts from the Nursery: Tracing the Roots of Violence*, The Atlantic Monthly Press, New York, 1997.
18. Kranowitz, Carol Stock, *The Out-Of-Sync Child: Recognizing and Coping with Sensory Integration Dysfunction*, A Skylight Press Book, New York, 1998.
19. Levy, Terry M., Ph.D., and Michael Orlans, MA, *Attachment, Trauma, and Healing: Understanding and Treating Attachment Disorder in Children and Families*, Child Welfare League of America, 1998.
20. Liptak, Karen, *Adoption Controversies*, Franklin Watts, New York, 1993.
21. Magid, Ken and Carole A. McKelvey, *High Risk: Children Without a Conscience*, Bantam Books, Toronto, 1987.
22. Mansfield, Lynda Gianforte and Christopher H. Waldmann, MA, LPC, *Don't Touch My Heart: Healing the Pain of an*

Unattached Child, Pinon Press, Colorado Springs, Colorado, 1994.

23. McKelvey, Carole A., MA, Editor, *Give Them Roots, Then Let Them Fly: Understanding Attachment Therapy*, The Attachment Center Press, Evergreen, Co., 1995.
24. McKelvey, C.A. & Stevens, J.E., *Adoption Crisis: The Truth Behind Adoption and Foster Care*, Fulcrum Press, Golden, Colorado, 1994.
25. Meloy, J. Reid, *The Psychopathic Mind: Origins, Dynamics, and Treatment*, Jason Aronson Inc., Northvale, New Jersey, 1988.
26. Peck, Gregory & Kupecky, R., *Adopting the Hurt Child*, Pinon Press, Colorado Springs, Colorado, 1995.
27. Pelzer, Dave, *A Child Called "It": One Child's Courage to Survive*, Health Communications, Inc., Deerfield Beach, Florida, 1993.
28. Pickle, Paula, *Life in the Trenches*, Attachment Center Press, Evergreen, Colorado, 1997.
29. Pienciak, Richard T., *Mama's Boy: The True Story of a Serial Killer and His Mother*, A Dutton Book, New York, 1996.
30. Randolph, Elizabeth, RN, Ph.D.. *Children Who Shock And Surprise*, RFR Publications, Evergreen, Colorado, 1994.
31. Robbins, Jim, *A Symphony in the Brain*, Grove Press, New York, 2000.
32. Sears, Donald J., *To Kill Again: The Motivation and Development of Serial Murder*, A Scholarly Resources Imprint, Wilmington, Delaware, 1991.
33. Sears, William and Martha Sears, *Parenting the Fussy Baby and High Need Child*, Little, Brown and Company, Boston, 1996.
34. Sereny, Gitta, *Cries Unheard—Why Children Kill: The Story of Mary Bell*, Metropolitan Books, Henry Holt and Company; New York, 1998.
35. Spungen, Deborah, *And I Don't Want to Live This Life*, Villard Books, New York, 1983.

36. Terr, Lenore, *Too Scared to Cry*, Basic Books, New York, 1990.
37. Thomas, Nancy, *When Love is Not Enough*, Glenwood Springs, Colorado, 1997.
38. Verny, Thomas, M. D., with John Kelly, *The Secret Life of the Unborn Child*, Dell Publishing, New York 1981.
39. Verrier, Nancy Newton, *The Primal Wound: Understanding the Adopted Child*, Gateway Press, Inc, Baltimore, MD, 1996.
40. Villani, Sue with Jane E Ryan, *Motherhood at the Crossroads: Meeting the Needs of a Changing Role*, Insight Books, Plenum Publishing Corporation, New York, 1997.
41. Welch, Martha G., M. D., *Holding Time*, Simon & Schuster, New York, 1988.

ARTICLES

1. Associated Press, "Child Slaying Suspects Sent Home," *The Honolulu Advertiser*, Nation and World (August 14, 1998): A3.
2. Begley, Sharon with Adam Rogers, "You're OK, I'm Terrific: 'Self-Esteem' Backfires", *Newsweek* (July 13, 1998): 69.
3. Drummond, Tammerlin, "Touch Early and Often", *Time* (July 27, 1998): Vol. 152, No. 4, 54.

Index

0-595-29717-X